Negotiating Culture and Hun

Negotiating Culture and Human Rights

Lynda S. Bell, Andrew J. Nathan,
and Ilan Peleg, Editors

COLUMBIA   UNIVERSITY   PRESS   NEW   YORK

COLUMBIA UNIVERSITY PRESS
Publishers Since 1893
New York Chichester, West Sussex
Copyright © 2001 Columbia University Press
All rights reserved

Library of Congress Cataloging-in-Publication Data

Negotiating culture and human rights / Lynda S. Bell,
    Andrew J. Nathan, and Ilan Peleg, editors.
        p. cm.
    Includes bibliographical references and index.
    ISBN 0–231-12080-X (cloth : alk. paper) — ISBN 0–231-12081-8
(pbk. : alk. paper)
    1. Human rights—Cross-cultural studies. I. Bell, Lynda Schaefer. II.
Nathan, Andrew J. (Andrew James) III. Peleg, Ilan, 1944–

    JC571 .N37 2001
    323—dc21

                                                            00–060256

Casebound editions of Columbia University Press books
are printed on permanent and durable acid-free paper.
Printed in the United States of America

c 10 9 8 7 6 5 4 3 2 1
p 10 9 8 7 6 5 4 3 2

Contents

Part 3. Human Rights Law and Its Limits

Part 4. Rights Discourse and Power Relations

Part 5. Beyond Universalism and Relativism

Acknowledgments

The editors and contributors wish to thank the many institutions and individuals who have supported this work. Primary among these is the National Endowment for the Humanities, which funded Andrew J. Nathan's NEH Summer Seminar at Columbia University in the summer of 1997 (grant no. FS-23037–96). We also thank Columbia's Office of Summer Session and the East Asian Institute for hosting the seminar. In addition to the contributors, the following individuals were seminar participants: Andrew Kipnis, Orrayb Najjar, and Cortland Smith. We gratefully acknowledge their intellectual collaboration during the seminar proceedings.

An NEH focus grant (ED-21028–98) was awarded to Lynda S. Bell for a curriculum project workshop and follow up activities at the University of California, Riverside. The workshop, at which the contributors presented the essays that make up this volume, was held in January, 1998, at the Center for Ideas and Society and the Mission Inn in Riverside, California. We wish to thank Professor Emory Elliott, Director of the Center for Ideas and Society, for the opportunity to use the Center's facilities; the College of Humanities, Arts, and Social Sciences at U.C.-Riverside for administrative and financial support; and several U.C.-Riverside faculty who attended the workshop and gave us much needed criticism and feedback—Professors Stephen Cullenberg, Robert Hanneman, Vivian-Lee Nyitray, June O'Connor, and Deborah Willis.

At Columbia University Press, Senior Executive Editor Kate Wittenberg and manuscript editor Leslie Bialler lent the project invaluable support. Each of the editors also wishes to thank her/his research assistant(s): Kate Fawver and Dawn Marsh at UC-Riverside; Shefali Trivedi at Columbia University; and Chantal Pasquarello at Lafayette College. In addition, we thank Sharon K. Hom and *The Buffalo Journal of International Law* for permission to reprint as chapter 7 an abridged version of an article with the same title. Need we also say that our family members tolerated our activities and gave us their undying loyalty? To all of them, we also are grateful.

Contributors

Michael G. Barnhart is associate professor in the History, Philosophy, and Political Science Department at Kingsborough Community College of the City University of New York. His area of current interest is ethics from a cross-cultural perspective. His published papers principally concern Buddhist Philosophy under comparative analysis. At present, his edited work, *Varieties of Ethical Reflection* is under consideration for publication.

Lynda S. Bell is associate professor of history at the University of California, Riverside. Her most recent publication is *One Industry, Two Chinas: Silk Filatures and Peasant-Family Production in Wuxi County, 1865–1937* (Stanford: Stanford University Press, 1999). She is currently serving as Director of the University of California Education Abroad Program in Beijing, where she is also pursuing research on women, politics, and the law in twentieth-century China.

Michael William Dowdle is a senior research fellow at the Center for Chinese Legal Studies of Columbia Law School and visiting associate professor at the City University of Hong Kong School of Law. He is author of many studies of institutional and legal evolution in China, especially of the constitutional system.

Jennifer R. Goodman is a professor of English at Texas A&M University. Her most recent book is *Chivalry and Exploration, 1298–1630* (Boydell and Brewer, 1998). Her areas of research interest include the role of chivalry in diverse cultures from the Middle Ages up to the present, late medieval fiction and its publication history, and questions of translation and cultural geography.

Farhat Haq is a professor and chair of the Department of Political Science at Monmouth College in Illinois. Her research interests are political Islam, politics of ethnicity, and gender and politics. She is currently working on a research project on globalization and formation of Muslim-American identities.

Sharon K. Hom is a professor of law at the City University of New York School of Law at Queens and a supervising attorney in the Immigrant and Refugee Rights Clinic. From 1986 to 1988 she was a Fulbright scholar in the People's Republic of China and continues to be active in U.S.-China legal training exchanges and Chinese women's studies work. She sits on the boards of Human Rights Watch/Asia, and Human Rights in China, and has also served as a judge for the Global Tribunal on Violence Against Women, convened for the fourth World Conference on Women and the NGO Forum 95.

Steven J. Hood is professor and chair of the Department of Politics and International Relations at Ursinus College, Collegeville, Pennsylvania. He has written extensively on the politics of East Asia, including two books, *Dragons Entangled: Indochina and the China-Vietnam War*, and *The Kuomintang and the Democratization of Taiwan*. He has just completed a book on democratization theory and a manuscript on political education in China.

Kenneth E. Morris teaches sociology at Georgia Perimeter College in metropolitan Atlanta. His publications include *Jimmy Carter, American Moralist* and *Bonhoeffer's Ethic of Discipleship*, along with several articles. His interests center on the social criticism of Western societies, especially the critique of liberalism and the alternatives to it.

Andrew J. Nathan is professor of political science and former Director of the East Asian Institute at Columbia University, and chair of the Advisory Committee of Human Rights Watch, Asia. He directed NEH Summer Seminars in 1986, 1988, 1997, and 1999. He wrote *Chinese Democracy* (New York: Knopf, 1985) and co-authored *Human Rights in Contemporary China* (New York: Columbia University Press, 1986). His most recent books are *China's Transition* (New York: Columbia University Press, 1997) and (with Robert S. Ross) *The Great Wall and the Empty Fortress: China's Search for Security* (New York: Norton, 1997).

Lucinda Joy Peach is an assistant professor in the Department of Philosophy and Religion at American University (Ph.D. Department of Religious Studies, Indiana University; J.D. New York University School of Law). She has published widely in the areas of applied ethics (including bioethics, feminist ethics, and legal ethics), religion and politics, gender and religion, gender and military combat, and women's human rights (most recently on the trafficking of women for the sex trade in Buddhist countries).

Ilan Peleg is the author of *Human Rights in the West Bank and Gaza* (1995), selected by *Choice* magazine for its Scholarly Excellence Award (1996), *Censorhip and Freedom of Expression Around the World* (1993), *Begin's Foreign Policy* (1987), several other volumes, and numerous essays. He is the editor of *Israel Studies Bulletin* and a frequent commentator on Middle Eastern affairs. In 1995–1997 he served as the President of the Association for Israel Studies. Dr. Peleg is the Charles A. Dana Professor of Government and Law at Lafayette College.

Tomas N. Santos is professor of English at the University of Northern Colorado, where he served as Director of Life of the Mind Program between 1988 and 1998. His publications include contributions to *Standing with the Public: The Humanities and Democratic Practice* (1997), and fiction in *The Ohio Journal, The North American Review, The Grenfield Reivew,* and *The Amerasia Journal.*

Dmitry Shlapentokh is associate professor of Russian/world history at Indiana University, South Bend. He was born and educated in the former Soviet Union. He received his Ph.D. from the University of Chicago. Among his recent works are *The French Revolution and Russian Anti-Democratic Tradition, The French Revolution in Russian Intellectual Life,* and *The Counter-Revolution in Revolution* released by Mac-Millan in 1999. He is also the author of nearly 100 articles and book chapters.

Xiaoqun Xu holds a Ph.D. in modern Chinese history from Columbia University and teaches at Francis Marion University. Engaging in research on institutional, social, and cultural history of twentieth-century China, Xu is the author of *Chinese Professionals and the Republican State: The Rise of Professional Associations in Shanghai, 1912–1937* (Cambridge University Press, 2000).

Part 1

Human Rights
and the Asian Values Debate

Introduction

Culture and Human Rights

Lynda S. Bell, Andrew J. Nathan, and Ilan Peleg

The devastating human atrocities of World War II produced a major international commitment to the concept and practice of "universal human rights." This commitment was demonstrated in 1948, with the United Nations' adoption of the "Universal Declaration on Human Rights" and the "Convention on the Prevention and Punishment of the Crime of Genocide." Although these documents were negotiated among most of the then-existing states, from all regions of the world, the following decades were characterized by conflictual approaches to rights, with Western states supporting civic, political, and individual rights, and Socialist states championing socioeconomic and collective rights. Since the end of the Cold War, there has been a sharpening international conflict among governments over human rights. While many formerly communist Eastern European nations have adopted a position sympathetic to civic and political rights of individuals, many governments in the developing world remain uneasy with, and on occasion even resentful of, what they perceive as Western triumphalism, interventionism, and cultural imperialism in the area of rights.

While the question of universal human rights is embroiled in power politics, it has also given rise to renewed intellectual debate over long-standing issues of cultural relativism and universalism. Because the relativist side of the argument has been articulated most forcefully in this latest round of debate by some Asian governments, the discussion has been labeled the "Asian values debate." The debate has been at its best intense, multicultural, and intellectually substantial, developing arguments of significance within the areas of ethics, international law, and comparative politics.

In 1997, as part of its series of Summer Seminars for College Teachers, the National Endowment for the Humanities sponsored an eight-week seminar at Columbia University, led by Andrew J. Nathan, on "The Asian Values Debate: Human Rights and the Study of Culture as Problems for Area Studies." Fifteen college and university teachers gathered to discuss a series of issues related to the Asian values debate. Our members included two historians of modern China; five experts in comparative politics, with specialities in Chinese, Israeli, and Islamic (especially Pakistani) affairs; a moral philosopher, with interest and expertise in both Western and Buddhist thought; two lawyers, one of whom has a strong background in Chinese legal affairs and the other also having an advanced degree in ethics (and a strong interest in Buddhism); a communications specialist, with a focus on the Palestinian and Israeli presses; an anthropologist with a China focus, interested in issues of language and culture; a sociologist with a strong interest in communitarian thought; a historian of modern Russia; and two literature specialists. We also had visiting participants who were experts of one kind or another on human rights issues. Three among the core group of fifteen had a very strong interest in feminist issues related to the Asian values debate, and encouraged the group as a whole to integrate feminist thinking and approaches into our discussions.

From the start, we were uncomfortable with the rigid dichotomy embedded in the Asian values debate, between an arrogant universalism that seemed to force its values on others, and a morally vacuous relativism that seemed to flee from hard judgments and to justify nondemocratic practices. Through group debate and personal struggle we found common ground by the end of the summer in a chastened universalism which would seek to reconstitute the debate as a respectful, yet still assertive dialogue across cultures, in search not so much for preexisting common values, but for ways to create them. This book articulates this position and its complexities, from a variety of disciplinary points of view. In so doing, it offers a new synthesis between uncritical (and even imperialistic) universalism and unquestioning (and sometimes aggressive) relativism.

Universalism vs. Relativism in Thought and Politics

In the world of international affairs among governments and citizenries attempting to define and live within a framework of mutually-agreed-upon rights, those taking the universalist position usually have maintained that human rights are derived from the essence of humanity itself. Every person has (or should have) comprehensive and equal rights, as an individual living within human society.[1] Although under international law some rights are derogable (that is, they can be restricted), derogation is permitted only for specific purposes of the highest urgency, and certain rights are not derogable under any circumstances. To the extent that individual rights might sometimes be curtailed by the state, this could be done only under severe stress (war, for example) or to protect other rights, and for limited duration. Moreover, rights are absolute in the sense that they cannot be taken away or given away, and they are seen by universalists as constituting the highest purpose of the political order. Rights are either "sacred" in origin (that is, God-given), or "inalienable" and "self-evident" (to use Thomas Jefferson's more secular language). While universalists do not deny that "cultures" are different, they argue (in effect) that individual sameness, or similarity, among human beings should prevail over cultural difference when it comes to human rights.

Those taking a relativist position on the question of human rights reject the above notions of universal human rights as naive, lacking empirical validity, ahistorical, and (worst of all) culturally imperialistic. The relativists begin by asserting the empirical fact that historically, different societies have had different (or no) notions of rights. They also claim that individual rights are not God-given or self-evident; rather, they are a historical construct. They began in Europe, and were given particularly clear and forceful articulation in the writings of the eighteenth-century British thinker John Locke. They then spread to the American colonies (reflected especially in the Virginia and Massachusetts constitutions), and were eventually enshrined in two documents—the American Declaration of Independence (1776) and the French Declaration on the Rights of Man (1791). Thus, argue the relativists, individual human rights are not universal, but rather, particularistic Western values masquerading as universal concepts. Today's relativists in Asia, the Middle East, and elsewhere, see the universalists as imperialistic—dictating Anglo-American values to everyone else. In the parlance of modern political science, this is a form of coercion by intellectual means, the use of "soft power" *par excellence* (see, for example, Nye 1990).

These conflicting political positions on human rights developed side-by-side with an expanding intellectual debate on universalism and relativism, as well as institutional substructures through which the debate was advanced. In the post World War II period, American universities carved out new territories for intellectual inquiry into the nature of other societies, or "cultures." Supported by a governmental desire to better understand both our potential friends and enemies, huge sums of government funding were poured into the creation of "area studies" centers, dedicated to studying "areas" of the world about which Americans knew little, and located at some of the most prestigious institutions of higher learning in the nation. Subsequently, the foreign policy approaches of several U.S. presidents—Jimmy Carter's emphasis on human rights, Ronald Reagan's anti-Soviet thrust, and Bill Clinton's return to a human-rights-centered approach, with a critique of Asian governments that do not seem to share U.S. goals—have kept citizens and academics alike pondering the "correct" cross-cultural approach to human rights. As Richard Haass points out, U.S. foreign policy often has been argued from a moral perspective, emphasizing democracy, civil society, and human rights, a line of argument that has characterized both the left and the right in American politics (Haass 1997: 60–63). And yet, many "cultural experts," trained to a large extent in government-supported area studies centers, were not always sure that they shared the universalistic position on human rights. They countered with their own, and varied, brands of cultural relativism, often arguing for the uniqueness of "cultures" around the globe.

In various ways, by the 1990s, the strains long inherent in debates over universalism and relativism had reached a newly heightened point of tension. The fall of the Soviet Union and the Western victory in the Persian Gulf War brought a note of triumphalism to Western public discourse and foreign policy. Francis Fukuyama, former Deputy Director the U.S. State Department's policy planning staff, argued that we had reached "the end of history" with the victory of democracy, free markets, and Western ideals (Fukuyama 1989 and 1992). Playing on another potential outcome of the collapse of the Soviet Union as the main "counterpoint" to the democratic West, the influential Harvard-based scholar, Samuel Huntington, argued that the world was facing an impending "clash of civilizations," which in effect described the contemporary world as an arena for continuous conflict between a West claiming to possess universalistic values and a series of rival civilizations each proud of its uniqueness (Huntington 1993 and 1996). Whether the previous era's struggles between "communism and democracy" meant the end of global struggles altogether (à la Fukuyama), or their shifting to new axes of conflict (à la Huntington), it was clear that the traditional forms and expectations of area studies, as we had once known them, were now over. Funding for area studies centers as they had existed in the Cold War era began to evaporate, and defining the study of global "cultures" was now up for grabs. It is in this context that some intellectuals and several governments in East Asia, Russia, and the Middle East began to subscribe to cultural relativism.

The "Asian Values Debate"

In the American frame of reference, one of the most graphic demonstrations of what could go wrong when Western values were ignored is the Tiananmen Square incident in the People's Republic of China in the spring of 1989. Although accounts of what happened in the early morning hours of June 4 in Tiananmen vary widely, one thing is clear—there was a brutal government crackdown on demonstrators, most of whom were young students advocating democratic reforms. Many died that night, although exactly where, when, and how is a matter of dispute. Nonetheless, for our purposes, these events are critical because of the degree to which they captured the American imagination about the nature of the Chinese government, and its apparent total disregard for Western notions of universal human rights.

In response to Western sanctions placed on China in the aftermath of this incident, many Third World countries began to counter what they saw as an American-led Western trend toward intervention in the affairs of weaker countries and to assert the validity of different national approaches to political questions. The Foreign Ministry of Singapore played an especially active role in this process, concerned lest the force of American cultural self-confidence collide with Chinese defensiveness and lead to dangerous polarization in Asia and a threat to the security of smaller countries there. In many ways, Singapore's UN Ambassador Bilahari Kausikan, a former official of the Singaporean Foreign Ministry trained in the U.S. at Columbia University, has become a bellwether for this debate, articulating the Singaporean government's particular "take" on Asian values along with several of his colleagues. As a seminar group, we had a chance to meet with Ambassador Kausikan, to hear his rationales for Asian governments to define and defend Asian values in opposition to Western notions of universal human rights, and to implement them in their own countries. As a result, several chapters in this book discuss Ambassador Kausikan's statements, as well as some of his many influential writings on Asian values.

The position Ambassador Kausikan ascribes to in terms of Asian values is a strongly cultural relativist one, adhered to not only by the government of Singapore, but also by the Chinese, Indonesian, and Malaysian governments, and also democratic India. The view expressed by these governments is that human rights have a different meaning in group-oriented Asian cultures from their meaning in the individualistic West. They argue that Asian cultures value family over the individual, harmony over conflict, discipline and deference to authority over self-assertion, and welfare over freedom. A set of related arguments cites state sovereignty, economic development, and political stability as current Third-World goals to which Western-style human rights policies are inimical.

Within the West, human rights diplomacy has attracted criticism from those who argue that rights conceptions vary across cultures or by levels of economic development; from specialists who stress the importance of strategic considerations in foreign policy; and from constituencies who believe that business ties and economic growth will solve human rights problems more effectively than political pressure. Lively debates over most-favored-nation trading privileges for China have mobilized both the human rights constituency and business and other groups. Human rights issues have also entered into domestic discussion of American policy in Haiti, Rwanda, Bosnia, and elsewhere, and into American dialogue with allies like Japan and France over foreign policy cooperation.

Such claims have prompted counter moves against the Asian values position. To cite some of the most prominent examples, the UN's 1993 Vienna Conference on Human Rights affirmed the universality of concepts embodied in the original 1948 UN Universal Declaration on Human Rights and subsequent conventions. At the same time, the political declaration of the 1993 Tokyo Summit of the G-7 countries emphasized the industrialized nations' commitment to the principles of human rights. The American administration, backed by Canada, Australia, and New Zealand, argued for the universality and indivisibility of human rights, and gave the issue prominence in its foreign policy declarations. The American position found support from the growing movement of dissident Asian human rights nongovernmental organizations (NGOs).

Within Asia, governments taking the Asian values position face challenges by increasingly vocal human rights activists and movements. Debates have occurred in China, Korea, Taiwan, and Singapore, among other countries, over the relationships among human rights, economic development, and political stability. Voices for the rule of law and political liberalization in China are persistent and seem to be growing stronger. In Thailand and China, population planning and the AIDS crisis have forced issues of women's rights onto the domestic and foreign policy agendas. Democratization in the Republic of Korea led to a new foreign policy that included the appointment of a special Ambassador for Human Rights Affairs. Japan asserted the universality of human rights at the 1993 Bangkok preparatory conference on human rights (see Dowdle's chapter in this volume for more on the Bangkok meetings), but Japanese human rights politics remain cautious in light of Japan's wartime history, its concern with Asian regional stability, and its commitment to economic growth as the key to improvement in the conditions of life.

Outside the political sphere, the Asian values debate has revived and sharpened a series of classic questions regarding universal human rights and cultural differences. These issues reach in many disciplinary directions, involving the humanities, social sciences, and law, and they are being discussed in a growing scholarly literature. The debate involves two broad issues that involve several disciplines. The first is how to justify human rights, which is usually discussed as part of political philosophy; the second is the nature of culture and how cultures differ, which is studied in the context of area studies, but also as part of anthropology, sociology, political science, and the growing interdisciplinary field of "cultural studies." Triangulating these issues raises the central question of whether justifications for human rights are, or should be, culturally specific or universalistic. It is a question dealt with uneasily by several disciplines and successfully by none alone.

Recrafting the Study of Culture

It was with these realizations about the centrality of assessing cultural differences in the context of the Asian values debate that our seminar group began its discussions. We were all aware, to varying degrees, of the large role played by area studies in major U.S. universities in the study of cultures in the non-Western world, including Asia. There were certain strengths that we recognized in the past history of area studies (indeed, several of us were trained as area studies specialists). Area studies scholars learned to confront problems of culture central to the modern humanities and social sciences, but which usually had been overlooked by those who investigate the same culture they occupy. A twentieth-century American student of nineteenth-century American literature may have to translate from one cultural context to another, but does not have to notice that she is doing so (although some do). By contrast, scholars in area studies, by definition, have been trained to operate from within one cultural context in seeking to understand another.

Thus, some of the central concerns of area studies scholars are exactly what we as a seminar group were interested in confronting: What do we mean by culture when we compare cultures? How can a culture's distinctiveness be conceptualized? What is required to demonstrate that such distinctiveness exists, what it consists of, and what influence it has on the performance of societies? And how does, or should, the difference of cultures matter to the value judgments we make, and to the political actions that flow from these judgments? At this intersection between knowledge and values the issues are both epistemological and ethical. Area studies scholars have traditionally responded to these issues by acknowledging—or asserting—a fundamental difference in the value commitments of cultures and then by disclaiming any right to make value judgments in the face of such differences. This position has been criticized on several grounds: that it essentializes cultures and ignores differences within cultures; that the value differences across cultures are more often assumed than demonstrated; and that it creates a moral equivalence between good and bad values. On the other hand, the universalist alternative is counter-criticized for its impatient attack on others' values without an understanding of the contexts in which they have become the preferences of large groups of people around the world. But area studies' dilemmas have been only a special, and perhaps in some respects especially clear, case of problems that underlie all studies of culture. Understanding people across the world is not categorically different from understanding people across the street.

These considerations pushed us to explore more deeply new ways of studying culture. At this point, insights from current developments in the realm of "cultural studies" came into play, and we discussed and debated these for several days in the seminar setting, and for the next several months as we prepared this volume. We do not claim that as a group we have arrived at a unified definition of "culture"; what we do have is a shared realization of the importance of debating the meaning of culture, including the practical and political ways in which the exploration of cultural difference should inform our position on the question of human rights.

Scholars who have been active in the field commonly called "cultural studies" in American and European academia see their enterprise as both ethical and political. Like many of the contributors to this volume, they are self-consciously opposed to rigid disciplinary boundaries as they are currently constituted in Western academic life. Accordingly, practitioners of cultural studies eclectically borrow analytical and critical methods, and the propensity to theorize findings, from across many disciplinary perspectives. Feminism, race consciousness, and the study of sexual identity have all played a role in crafting recent trends in cultural studies. One of the central commitments among many practitioners of cultural studies is that "difference" should not be obliterated in the study of culture; rather, it should be understood as an ongoing tension in all human interaction, something to be recognized, understood, and lived with. Sometimes, people with different perspectives, arising from their culture, their gender, or some other aspect of their identity, if they are to coexist and work together productively, must simply "agree to disagree."

The development of cultural studies has, among many things, generated new understandings of the meaning of culture itself. An earlier notion of culture was that it constituted a core set of values, psychological dispositions, and behaviors (both individual and social) that gave a group of people a common identity and way of life. Thus, to give an example, in the earlier way of thinking, often developed within the context of area studies, most people believed that the Chinese had a core "culture" the characteristics of which could be discovered, itemized, analyzed, and understood, as a way to predict individual and social behavior and outcomes of that behavior. Within the context of cultural studies, however, this "positivistic" view of culture has waned considerably; culture is now more likely to be viewed as unstable, "processual," or "discursive," as a repertoire of ways of thinking and acting that are constantly in the process of becoming. Moreover, culture is usually viewed by the new cultural theorists as contested—a social context in which power struggles are constantly waged over the meaning and control of what Pierre Bourdieu has called "symbolic capital" as well as over more overtly material forms of wealth and power. In short, culture is not a given, but rather a congeries of ways of thinking, believing, and acting that are constantly in the state of being produced; it is contingent and always unstable, especially as the forces of "modernity" have barreled down upon most people throughout the world over the course of the twentieth century. Explaining the ways in which these cultural battles are played out, therefore, has become one of the primary goals of cultural studies, with the more theoretically-minded inclined to be seeking comparative insights across newly evolving cultural formations.

The recognition that culture is not a unitary, stable formation, but rather something constantly contested and in flux gave the contributors to this volume the opportunity to analyze and critique the Asian values debate in new and, we believe, profitable ways. It allowed us to see that even within a single culture, values and their meaning are subject to different interpretations. In this book we work toward varied strategies, developed through different disciplinary approaches, to determine when and how human rights claims might be agreed upon across treacherous philosophical, ethical, political, and sexual divides. Cultural difference is not erased in the process; rather, it is negotiated, as part of an effort to create a world in which all people should be free to deliberate, develop, and choose values to help them live more equitable and fulfilling lives.

Looking Ahead

As individuals, we have oscillated over the course of working together between "more universalist" versus "more relativist" positions. In the final versions of our individual chapters, we have ended up with variations on what we believe is a thoughtful, informed universalism that is tenable both intellectually and ethically. The chapters can be read independently, or in sequence, as a progressive dialogue. They are synthetic, approaching and discussing a wide variety of pertinent previous literature, and written in a way that, we hope, makes them accessible not only to specialists, but also to college and university students and other interested readers with no prior background or specialized knowledge of Asia. Each chapter is oriented to contemporary issues, yet places them in a perspective of long-standing intellectual concerns. Following this introduction, the first chapter, by Lynda S. Bell, introduces and critiques the Asian values debate in light of discursive notions of culture, demonstrating that arguments on both sides of the debate are designed by states to enhance their dominance in world affairs. As an ethnographically minded historian of modern China, Bell also uses interview data to ferret out diverse understandings of "rights" and "identities" (as opposed to a single set of Asian values or a single Asian "identity"). She discovers a high degree of consensus on the issue of equality for women among those she interviewed in one Chinese village, and thus argues that the primary difficulty in attaining the goal of "equal pay for equal work" is not one of cultural difference, but rather of gender difference. In this matter, Bell worries that human rights legal instruments may not help since gender discrimination laws in all cultures have had a checkered past in actual implementation. Thus, Bell observes a high degree of universal moral consciousness about women's rights, but remains cautious about the prospects of using international legal strategies and western-derived human rights' instruments to better Third World women's lives.

The remaining chapters are arranged in a "yes to universalism" grouping (part II), followed by parts III and IV, which raise, from varied perspectives, the qualifying "but. . . . " Michael Barnhart's opening essay in part II cuts to the heart of the issue of cultural difference and values: we know that cultures differ in some of their central value commitments, but what does it matter for the universality of rights? It is common to make the leap from cultural difference to value relativism, but Barnhart questions this. He presents a surprising, counterintuitive, yet in the end eloquently convincing argument that cultural difference does not matter for moral reasoning. His reason is apparently simple, yet full of complexities: it is that moral reasoning is autonomous. But Barnhart does not conclude with a doctrinaire absolutism. He argues for intercultural dialogue toward a value consensus, converging on this point with Charles Taylor in a paper that influenced many of the seminar participants (Taylor 1999).

Kenneth Morris tacitly accepts Barnhart's premise that moral reasoning is autonomous, but he reminds us that this does not settle the question of the universality of human rights. The human rights idea has been subjected to devastating critiques not just from Asia, but from within the Western philosophical tradition as well, so even on the pure ground of moral reasoning it may not be all that easy to defend. The strongest criticisms were voiced by the classic conservative authors and have been revived in recent years especially by feminists and communitarians. Taking all these criticisms into consideration, the strongest case that can be made for rights is a fairly weak one, says Morris; indeed, he thinks this is why rights proponents often modulate or qualify their claims for universality in such a way that the gap between them and the Asian values proponents narrows to a matter of rhetorical style. But like Barnhart, Morris ends with a final twist that modifies his argument. He critiques the critics (both Western and Asian) and shows that the human rights idea survives much of their fire. He believes that this idea holds promise of universal appeal if it can be reconstructed on the basis of communitarian ideology.

The next contribution, by Steven Hood, rotates the perspective on these issues yet another few degrees. For him, as for Barnhart and Morris, the human rights idea is universally valid, but he disagrees with those who might argue that it is a Rome that can be reached by many roads. For Hood, human rights is a concept of Western origin that can only be grounded in Western ideas. Among these, he stresses the Western conception of nature (as differentiated from the human realm of morality and religion) and the Western belief in the equal status of each person. The search for alternative roots, he believes, is fated to fail. Yet cultures may converge, he suggests, on another set of related values, which he labels virtues. He illustrates his arguments with sympathetic yet critical interpretations of classical Confucianism and Islam. Although all great traditions are equally deserving of respect, he concludes, this does not mean that they converge on common values. If the rights idea is to spread, it will have to do so through the acceptance of the distinctively Western values that underlie it, by civilizations where these values are not indigenous.

The three philosophically informed perspectives share a commitment to universalism of values as well as a chastened awareness of the reality of value diversity. Yet on the details of this common position they differ more than they agree. Many in the West, including the most influential NGOs in the human rights field, respond to this problem by shifting the debate to the ground of international law. According to this viewpoint, whatever their origins and philosophical basis, fundamental rights have now become legal obligations under the law of nations, as embodied in such declarations, treaties, and conventions as the Universal Declaration of Human Rights, the International Covenant on Civil and Political Rights, the International Covenant on Social, Economic, and Cultural Rights, and the Convention on the Elimination of All Forms of Discrimination against Women (CEDAW). States are obligated by these instruments regardless of the degree to which, or the ways in which, their cultures support the human rights idea. The essays in part II contribute some original and surprising perspectives to this part of the debate. All three of the authors in this section are lawyers, and they provide expert knowledge of, and analytical insights into, the legal dimension of the Asian values debate.

Michael W. Dowdle argues that rights cannot be merely a matter of law, because they are commands to justice which involve an intrinsic appeal to an overarching standard of morality. It is precisely because they are moral rules that rights prescriptions are neither universal nor absolute, since moral prescriptions always involve tradeoffs along various other dimensions of moral concern. To construe human rights law as nothing but positive law is to deprive it both of the moral force that makes it special, and of the room to grow. Dowdle makes these points through an analysis of the 1993 Bangkok Declaration, a statement of the Asian values viewpoint which was widely dismissed in the West as a propaganda statement by authoritarian Asian regimes. To accept the Declaration's views of the cultural conditionality of rights, Dowdle suggests, is actually to acknowledge rather than threaten rights' moral standing.

Lucinda Joy Peach exposes the limits of a legal approach to redressing one of the most pervasive categories of rights violations, those against women. This issue is crucial for understanding the relationship between culture and values precisely because the status of women is so central to the self-definition of every culture. Peach grounds her analysis in a review of the status of women's rights in international law and of the criticisms that have been offered from several perspectives of a rights-based approach to the rights of women. If in the West women are "human" in the sense of being rights-bearers equivalent to men, in some other cultures women, however highly valued, are considered to be too different from men to be treated as legally equivalent. To illustrate this problem, Peach presents the case of Buddhist Thailand and its attitudes toward women engaged in sex work. In such a culture, women themselves are among the people least sympathetic to a rights-based approach to their problems, and international and even domestic law offer few resources of practical benefit to improving women's lot. To grapple with this issue Peach suggests what she calls a feminist pragmatist approach to women's rights which aims to achieve the universalistic ends of improvement of the status of women by particularistic means, designed to function effectively within—and even by taking advantage of—the constraints of particular cultural situations. Such a fine-grained analysis suggests ways in which the universalism-particularism opposition dissolves when one moves from the realm of human rights theory to that of praxis.

Sharon Hom, although not a member of the seminar, visited with us as a guest speaker for a lively session on human rights issues in the People's Republic of China, with special emphasis on her own experiences at the UN's 1995 International Forum on Women, which met in Beijing, and also on NGO activities, in China and elsewhere, concerning the status of women. The paper we include here is reprinted from an American law school's legal journal. In this piece, Hom eloquently argues the position that states have intervened far too much in human rights issues on both sides of the Asian values debate. She notes the difficulties inherent in practical human rights work that involve translation—not only of words (from English to Chinese and vice versa), but also of ideas. As a result, she advocates an activist role for women such as herself, who are not just bilingual but bicultural, in the processes of "cultural translation" that must take place in order to cooperate across cultures to advance human rights. This is especially important in the treacherous territory in which a variety of NGOs seek legal redress for human rights violations, when expectations are so different across cultural divides as to what law might be capable of achieving.

Peach and Hom thus have suggested how different the human rights idea looks when seen from the trenches of struggle. Human rights are not just a matter of philosophy and law. From the beginning the human rights idea has been a political tool, used by various governments and social forces to increase their influence. And in the current period, they have also become part of international politics. Chapters in part IV, on rights discourse and power relations, further explore some of these dilemmas as the human rights idea has come down to earth historically, in particular locales and in specific political struggles. But, given the context of the earlier essays in the volume, we do not present these case studies to reach the familiar, facile conclusion that because human rights are political, they are also meaningless and not worth striving for. Just the opposite is true: the contextualizing of the human rights idea in time and space reveals its persistence and importance.

Xiaoqun Xu sets forth the general position that the "discourse on universality"—the claim to be in possession of a universally valid concept—is always put forward by historical actors pursuing particular purposes. Rhetorically and politically, universalism is a form of seizing the discursive high ground that is repeated over and over in historically situated struggles. Xu illustrates this point with three such power struggles among contending groups in modern Chinese history—Christian missionaries and their opponents, proponents of Western-style versus native-style medicine, and proponents of judicial independence and those who resisted their policies. But to say that universalism is a power claim is not to say that it is wrong: in fact, it is often both right and successful. Applying his insight to the contemporary debate over human rights, Xu suggests that the idea has become widely accepted in principle and that the struggle has shifted from legitimizing human rights to identifying the balance among different kinds of rights.

Farhat Haq takes us into the important realm of Islamic fundamentalism in the context of the Asian values debate. Some Islamicists have seen the Western human rights movement as a kind of cultural jihad against Islam, and many Westerners see Muslim resistance to the human rights idea as part of a jihad against the West. Yet, Haq points out, the Islamic concept of jihad, or holy war, is itself subject to varied interpretations from within and outside the Islamic tradition. Her opening discussion of jihad functions as a metaphor for her central point—that within the apparently conservative, authoritarian traditions of Islam, there has been room for several modernist intellectuals to construct new rights-seeking strategies. Islam cannot be seen as a unitary, closed cultural system inimical to all forms of rights-seeking, as many believe, but rather as a fluid, evolving bundle of ideas, beliefs, and social practices within which some of its members might construct strategies for improving personal and group rights. On the important question of women's rights, however, Haq is pessimistic, arguing that the issue of women's nonequality with men in Islam is so politically charged that to evoke human rights law in the name of Muslim women is a highly problematic strategy at present.

The human rights idea is not the only one in world history that has made a claim to universal validity. Some other examples that come easily to mind are Islam, Confucianism, Buddhism, and Catholicism, which all claim to be universally valid systems of belief. But most commentators view these traditions as more or less compatible in theory or practice with much if not all of the human rights agenda. Less commonly noted are competing universalisms that are entirely antagonistic to the human rights idea. Dmitry Shlapentokh explores in detail one such stream of thought: nineteenth-century Slavicist nationalism, which posited as a universal value the active rejection of the human rights idea. Indeed, what was universal for the late-nineteenth-century Slavicists in Russia, he shows, was not the sameness but rather the uniqueness of each nation and the superiority of the Russian soul above those of other nations. Although the position sounds paradoxical, it only seems so when we view it from the perspective of Western rights-based individualism. Shlapentokh's vivid account of an entirely different cast of mind reminds us that messianic, all-encompassing value systems are not limited to those which purport to apply equally to everybody. Seen in Shlapentokh's historical retrospective, the Slavophiles were almost endearingly eccentric, but their ideas carried forward to exert great influence in the Soviet regime and still have strong echoes not only in Russia but in the various nationalisms of other parts of the post-Soviet empire as well. His analysis underscores the fragility and, in a sense, the parochialism inherent in the very universalism of the human rights idea, and the way in which both the Western liberal value system and that of various messianic nationalisms grow out of power relations specifically located in time and place.

Ilan Peleg explores the intense conflict between the "communal agenda" and the "rights agenda" that often explodes in countries where several ethnic or religious communities coexist, as indeed they do in most parts of the world. It is precisely when such a country becomes democratic that the dilemma of communal versus individual rights is likely to become most challenging. If the equal political rights of individuals are juridically guaranteed, the largest ethnic group is likely to use these rights to dominate the minority group or groups. In that sense, a rights-based system may, through democracy, be used for oppressive purposes. Peleg cites several such cases, focusing his analysis on the example of Israel. But he sees an internal evolution in the Israeli system away from the ethnically oppressive uses of democracy to a more liberal view that protects the rights of the minority as effectively as those of the majority. This process, too, is political, Peleg argues: it is primarily the struggle of the Israeli Arabs themselves, as well as international pressure, that have moved elements of the Israeli political system and public opinion toward more protection for the civil rights of Arab citizens.

Tomas Santos shifts the locus of discussion from the power struggle of groups to the striving of individuals for integrity and insight. He offers a writer's appreciation for three Chinese short stories read in translation. His reading illuminates both the authors' struggle for freedom of expression within political constraints, and the fictional protagonists' struggles for personal integrity under conditions of powerlessness and turmoil. Santos implies that the actual struggle for human rights is carried on in millions of specific venues, and that it matters little whether or not the language of rights is used since the values at stake are intensely personal at the same time that they are universally human.

The final section of the book offers two sets of concluding thoughts. The first, by Andrew J. Nathan, interrogates the concept of the universal which underlies so much of the discussion in the book. Nathan asks what there is about the contemporary version of this concept that creates so much difficulty over cross-cultural values. He suggests that contemporary intellectual life is strongly shaped by the opposition and symbiosis between area studies and the disciplines. This structure of knowledge depends on a conceptual division between universal forms of rationality and culturally particular values which makes it difficult to ascribe universality to whatever is conceived of as culturally situated. In short, our present notions set the universal against culture, creating the fallacy that whatever is culturally valued cannot be conceived of as universal. The recognition that all social facts and all values are culturally situated would dissolve this dilemma and might open new prospects not only for the human rights debate but for the study of culture more generally.

Finally, Jennifer Goodman takes a long historical and comparative view of the Asian values debate, reminding us that the dualisms underlying it have been rejected by sages East and West in centuries past. Universal and relative, self and other, freedom and constraint, man and nature, and for that matter East and West themselves, are oppositions that may mislead us. Arguing for the value of harmony rather than conflict in human affairs, she suggests we may find our rights best guaranteed not in opposition to others but in cooperation with them. Hers is not intended as a practical program, but as a reminder that our cultural resources, and those of others, offer alternative ways to conceive of the problems which bother us today. The Asian values debate, we believe, is a constructive one, but it need not be resolved entirely within its current terms of reference.

Endnote

1. The most commonly agreed upon rights may be found in the Universal Declaration on Human Rights, substantial portions of which are included as Appendix A of this book.

Bibliography

Fukuyama, Francis. 1989. "The End of History?" *The National Interest* 16 (Summer):3–18.

———. 1992. *The End of History and the Last Man.* New York: The Free Press.

Haass, Richard. 1997. *The Reluctant Sheriff.* New York: Council on Foreign Relations.

Huntington, Samuel P. 1993. "The Clash of Civilizations?" *Foreign Affairs* 72 (3) (Summer):22–49.

————. 1996. *The Clash of Civilizations and the Remaking of the World Order.* New York: Simon and Schuster.

Nye, Joseph S., Jr. 1990. "Soft Power." *Foreign Policy* 80 (Fall):153–171.

Taylor, Charles. 1999. "Conditions of an Unforced Consensus on Human Rights." In Joanne R. Bauer and Daniel A. Bell, eds., *The East Asian Challenge for Human Rights.* Cambridge, England: Cambridge University Press.

1 Who Produces Asian Identity? Discourse, Discrimination, and Chinese Peasant Women in the Quest for Human Rights

Lynda S. Bell

As a social historian of modern China, professionally trained in the study of another culture, I have viewed skeptically the efforts of Westerners to promote human rights in the non-Western world. My purpose in this chapter is to unravel my skepticism, and in the process to suggest new ways to think about promoting rights that stem from ethnographic and historical study. To realize greater social justice on an international scale, activists and intellectuals must take culture seriously, but not in the totalizing, undifferentiated way in which some leaders of non-Western nations have used it as a trump card in the Asian values debate. To counter arguments about nonnegotiable formulations of unitary cultural difference between East and West, or a single "Asian identity," we must find ways to discover multiply layered differences concerning rights within Asian societies, and the ways that people articulate these differences in language, thought, and the practice of daily life.

The first part of this chapter explores the bitter contention generated in the international political arena over human rights and Asian values. As a means to get behind the scenes of the debate, the discussion turns to concepts of culture that permeate it. These sections lay groundwork for a more detailed and concrete discussion of notions of discrimination against women; of Western legal tools designed to tackle such discrimination; and the possible application of such tools in another cultural context—rural China in the late 1980s. Here I use an interview with a group of peasants and local cadres that took place during fieldwork in the Chinese countryside concerning issues of workplace discrimination against local peasant women. Analysis of multiple forms of difference embodied in that interview—not only of culture, but also of gender and class—mirrors the bigger struggle many of us face in finding common ground on issues of human rights.

Human Rights Discourse and the Asian Values Debate

In the international political arena, a series of declarations on human rights, coupled with a plethora of institutions, both governmental and non-governmental, enable human rights advocates to mount a carefully planned and well-articulated campaign against authoritarian political regimes. This trajectory began in 1948, with the United Nations Universal Declaration on Human Rights, and has proceeded unabated since that time. Recent decades have seen rapid proliferation of human rights instruments, with various declarations and conventions designed to govern the perceived needs of special interest groups suffering the most extreme forms of human rights abuses and, more generally, the most blatant forms of discrimination in terms of employment, education, and access to resources.

The source of my discomfort with the efforts of Western human rights activists arises from within this international context. Although I know that Western human rights activists act from sincerely held, morally upright convictions and beliefs, I do have some hesitancy regarding their efforts. It is not the rights in and of themselves to which I object—things like freedom from torture and from detention without trial, freedom to express one's political opinion, freedom from discrimination, and so on—but rather *universal human rights as discourse* that makes me uncomfortable.

I use the term discourse here in a Foucauldian sense to refer not merely to language or texts, but rather to a historically and socially specific combination of words, categories of meaning, beliefs, and institutions used to assert power and legitimating truth (cf. Scott 1994:359). Social critic Stuart Hall explains how the functioning of a discourse produces its own subjects who speak a language developed through the internal logic of the discourse itself (Hall 1996).[1] Building upon these ideas, we can view human rights advocates not just as well-meaning individuals who believe in better lives for the world's peoples, but also as spokespersons for the Western Enlightenment project from which the human rights discourse ultimately emanates (cf. discussion on this point found in this volume's introduction). Thus, human rights proponents' activities, speech, and writing carry with them—inadvertently or not—the weightiness of the entire Western liberal democratic tradition. This becomes a heavy burden to bear, especially when facing critics who claim a sympathy for conflicting values and traditions produced by other cultures.

As modern nation-states in East Asia have risen to international economic and political prominence in the last two decades, leaders and individuals within them have reacted to Western human rights discourse with their own brand of outraged cultural relativism. The principal agents of this counter trend have been state agencies and political figures from Singapore, the People's Republic of China, and Malaysia. Among the most prominent proponents of the counter position is Lee Kuan Yew, former Prime Minister, and now retired "Senior Minister," of Singapore. In 1994, Fareed Zakaria, managing editor of the journal *Foreign Affairs*, published the transcript of a personal interview with Lee entitled, "Culture is Destiny." Quoting Lee at length, Zakaria noted the extreme degree to which discussion of (superior) East Asian values and culture, in distinction to (inferior) Western values, permeated Lee's responses:

> Asian societies are unlike Western ones. The fundamental difference between Western concepts of society and government and East Asian concepts . . . is that Eastern societies believe that the individual exists in the context of his family. He is not pristine and separate. The family is part of the extended family, and then friends and the wider society. The ruler or the government does not try to provide for a person what the family best provides. . . .
>
> We have focused on basics in Singapore. We used the family to push economic growth, factoring the ambitions of a person and his family into our planning. . . . The government can create a setting in which people can live happily and succeed and express themselves, but finally it is what people do with their lives that determines economic success or failure. Again, we were fortunate we had this cultural backdrop, the belief in thrift, hard work, filial piety and loyalty in the extended family, and most of all, the respect for scholarship and learning (Zakaria 1994:113–114).

One need not look very far within the Asian tradition to understand the implications of Lee Kuan Yew's statements. Clearly, for him, it is the East

Asian Confucian past upon which Singapore has drawn to assure its economic and political success. Family, filial piety, commitment to education, hard work, and thrift—all of these have their common roots in the East Asian Confucian tradition.

Although Lee Kuan Yew has been one of the most prominent spokespersons for Asian values, he has hardly been alone in his analysis of Singapore's and other East Asian nations' successes. As China historian Arif Dirlik has pointed out, a vast array of conferences and workshops has been organized in recent years, both in East Asia and in the U.S., dedicated to outlining a "Chinese" and/or "Confucian" model of cultural behavior (Dirlik 1997). According to Dirlik, we should view the proliferation of this intellectual activity not only as explanation but also as justification for the paths taken by many countries in East and Southeast Asia within the emerging contexts of global capitalism. For as their economic growth rates have soared, Western expectations of political liberalization, especially in the area of human rights, have failed to materialize. The reason, if one ascribes to the Asian values position, is that "most" Asians would prefer to retain their own "cultural identity" in the face of "Western cultural imperialism." For the sake of the well-being of the group as a whole—the East Asian "family-state"—they are willing to forego the luxuries of Western-inspired, individually oriented human rights.

It is important to recognize that Lee Kuan Yew's views, and those of his counterparts in China and Malaysia, have not been simply a spontaneous outburst of ethnically inspired, nationalistic fervor. They have arisen in direct opposition to the human rights discourse emanating from the West. Another Singaporean, United Nations Ambassador Bilahari Kausikan, has been among those most actively engaged in developing the Asian values position in this larger contentious field. Kausikan has appeared widely at international meetings and conferences on human rights, and was one of those instrumental in drafting the 1993 Bangkok Declaration, in which representatives of Asian nations came together to produce their own statement on human rights (for more on the Bangkok Declaration, see Michael Dowdle's essay, chapter 5 in this volume). Through the lens of Ambassador Kausikan's published papers and his most recent personal statements, we can begin to understand the Asian values position in its fullest, most clearly etched political form—what I believe we might call a "counter-hegemonic" discourse against the already-powerful and prominent Western discourse on universal human rights.

Ambassador Kausikan's views are neatly summarized in the following statements drawn from some of his most important writings on Asian values and human rights:

> Universality is not uniformity. The extent and exercise of rights and freedoms is a product of the historical experiences of particular peoples and therefore, vary from one culture or political community to another, and over time. Many Asian societies are more group-oriented and more accepting of a wider sphere of governmental responsibility and intervention than is common in the West (Kausikan 1995–96, 265).

While this statement directly parallels Lee Kuan Yew on Confucianism's legacy in the East, the following is even more dramatic in its adversarial position against the West:

> The Western media, NGOs, and human rights activists, especially in the United States, tend to press the human rights dialogue beyond the legitimate insistence on humane standards of behavior by calling for the summary implementation of abstract concepts without regard for a country's unique cultural, social, economic, and political circumstances.
>
> . . . many East and southeast Asians tend to look askance at the starkly individualistic ethos of the West in which authority tends to be seen as oppressive and rights are an individual's "trump" over the state. Most people of the region prefer a situation in which distinctions between the individual, society, and state are less clear-cut, or at least less adversarial. It will be far more difficult to deepen and expand the international consensus on human rights if East and Southeast Asian countries believe that the Western promotion of human rights is aimed at what they regard as the foundation of their economic success. In fact, many Asians perceive the values and practices insisted upon by Western human rights purists as exacerbating the thorny problems faced by the West (Kausikan 1993:33 and 36).

In a meeting in June of 1997, Ambassador Kausikan made his political positioning with respect to the West even clearer. The Ambassador claimed that Singaporean officials entered into the debate in the first place because they perceived Western human rights activists to be taking an adversarial position against them. Moreover, he made the point that it is only people who want to challenge prevailing governmental power in the East Asian region who adhere to the Western position on universal human rights. The implication was that such people were looking for ways to seize state power themselves rather than seeking higher forms of social justice in its own right (Kausikan 1997).

Hence we see one hegemonic discourse giving rise to yet another, on Asian culture and Asian values. Ambassador Kausikan's phrasing is important here—he claims to be speaking for "most people of the region"—not just of Singapore—but for most Asians generally on the topic of human rights. This is a bold move to replace a discursive universalist strategy with a discursive relativistic one, albeit with equally far-reaching implications for all Asian peoples. This point has not been lost on human rights activists. In an impassioned reply to Ambassador Kausikan, Aryeh Neier, former director of Human Rights Watch, argued that the Ambassador was not really interested in "consensus-seeking," but rather in an attempt to cover up Asian governments' authoritarian, repressive rules (Neier 1993).

While we may critique the Asian values debate along the above lines, the issue of what to do about it still remains. From what I have said thus far, it should be clear that I do not agree fully with either side in the debate. But if critique of the political dynamics of the debate is not all one is seeking— if one truly believes that new strategies in the rights arena are necessary to secure social justice—then what should one do next? The best strategy, I would argue, is to formulate new understandings of Asian cultures and new political tactics accordingly. But on what grounds can we construct such understandings, starting from what vantage points?

What Is Culture?

Participants in the NEH summer seminar from which this volume emanates spent a great deal of time arguing over the concept of culture, a seemingly necessary next step in our efforts to move through and beyond the Asian values debate. Ultimately, how we decided to think about culture—its meaning, its formation, its effects—conditioned what each of us came to think and feel about Asian values and the way they are invoked in the current struggle over human rights. As discussed in this volume's introduction, to varying degrees, we each were prepared to accept changing understandings of culture, a trend that has emerged most recently from the interdisciplinary realm of cultural studies.

If one ascribes to a positivist view, culture is a set of common characteristics of a social group, including ways of thinking and behaving. The "culture" of a people, therefore, can be discovered, analyzed, and compared with other cultures, to see how they differ both in content and outcomes. Once a culture has been subjected to this sort of scrutiny, its characteristics are "known" and tend to be thought of as fixed for the purposes of cross-cultural comparison. Thus, in modern times, Americans have become rugged individualists, who ascribe to notions of freedom for the individual and the right to choose one's own destiny; Chinese, by contrast, are group and family-oriented, concerned with common welfare rather than individual rights. These are the sorts of assumptions about culture that thus far have informed the Asian values debate (for a more finely nuanced discussion of positivist notions of culture, see Andrew J. Nathan's essay, chapter 13 in this volume).

On the other hand, the proponents of cultural studies see culture as process. They stress the fluidity of culture, as a series of actions and behaviors that are constantly becoming. Seen in this light, cultural values can be, and often are, contested from within. Social, economic, and political modes of domination (including the right to determine widely accepted cultural values), are met with various forms of individual and group resistance, and it is often the least powerful members of society—workers, peasants, or women, for example—who have the potential to create the most dramatic forms of cultural struggle. Patterns and practices of everyday life of the ordinary people in society, therefore, are of great interest to cultural studies scholars, including how new subject positions—often called "identities"—are formed from within a culture. How new senses of the self emerge, and how cultural "norms" are disrupted and challenged in the process, are among the central concerns of cultural studies (cf. Poster 1997, ch. 4).

If we apply these alternative thoughts about what constitutes culture to our evolving critique of the Asian values debate, it is impossible to assume that there could be only one fixed way of understanding, or living, the East Asian Confucian tradition. While certain Confucian values, such as the importance of obedience to authority and social hierarchy, may have been important to the shapers of that tradition—male social and political elites in various historical settings—other less prominent members of Confucian societies may have found other interpretations of Confucianism more meaningful. For example, Confucianism also has a lot to say about reciprocity in human affairs, and the importance of virtues, aspects of the tradition that those with little political, social, or economic power might find compelling.

With this different notion of culture in mind, we can envision both state actors and ordinary people in various Asian locales struggling to define and redefine various notions of cultural identity. "Asian identity," as currently constituted through the Asian values debate, may be one possible cultural construct, but clearly the possibility of other, multiple identities rising from within social groups also becomes imminent. These ideas resonate with those of cultural theorist Arjun Appadurai, who says, "I suggest that we regard as cultural only those differences that either express, or set the groundwork for, the mobilization of group identities" (Appadurai 1996:13). For the outsider attempting to analyze and understand such situations, historical and ethnographic study must come into play if one is to understand how cultural practice might evolve, or be disrupted, through not just one but many mobilizations of group identities.

Culture and Discrimination

When I applied to be part of the NEH summer seminar on the Asian values debate, I was interested in thinking through the issues of human rights and cultural difference based on my own past work as an ethnographically minded historian of modern China, paying particular attention to the special needs and problems of Chinese peasant women. I had studied Chinese peasant women's work in relationship to economic development over the course of the twentieth century, but I had never given much sustained thought to their potential political agendas — their subject positions and identities — with respect to rights. Moreover, I felt that human rights issues for China had been explored almost exclusively in the previous literature based on the aspirations of young, well-educated, urban-based democracy advocates (such as the students who demonstrated in Tiananmen square in the spring of 1989), and that little attention had been given to other, less visible social groups.

As I learned more about the Asian values debate, it seemed natural for me to consider Chinese peasant women in relationship to the human rights instrument called CEDAW, the Convention on All Forms of Discrimination against Women (for the text of this document, see Appendix 4). Other feminists who are also human rights activists have suggested that to use such instruments is one among many tactics needed to refocus the Asian values debate (see, for example, Sharon Hom 1996, and her essay, chapter 7 in this volume). This suggestion precipitated exploration into the issues facing not just Chinese peasant women, but ALL women in relationship to international human rights law.

A key foundational concept embedded in CEDAW is that of discrimination, defined according to Western notions of historical patterns of inequality for women and the need to right past wrongs through special efforts of courts and other formally constituted institutions, such as workplaces and schools. A huge body of critical feminist literature exists on the perils and pitfalls of the use of comparable laws on discrimination in the U.S. Some of the discussion embedded in this literature helps us to focus on exactly what is required if discrimination law is to be used effectively, which many argue has proven very difficult to do, even in the "cultural location" of the West, where it arose.

Much of the writing on the equality "debate" or "crisis" as it is often called (see, for example, Williams 1997), has occurred in American legal journals over the past decade or so. Fortunately, much of this literature is now being anthologized, with helpful introductions and explanatory notes for those less familiar with the intricacies of case reports and legal decision-making in the courts (see, for example, Weisberg 1993; and Danielsen and Engle 1995). An excellent recent summary of the issues discussed in this literature has been written by Judith G. Greenberg (1992).[2] Greenberg succinctly describes the problems for feminist lawyers who have approached the courts with the position that women should have the same rights as men—in other words, that women are "equal." Calling this position "sameness feminism," Greenberg notes that, "The problem with sameness feminism lies in the very claim to equality that provided the basis for its success. A determination of equality requires a comparison of the subject with a model. When the subject is women and the model is men, the points of comparison are infinite. Which ones one chooses, and thus whether one sees equality or not, will depend on the chooser's point of view" (xi).

Greenberg bases her assessment of the "equality" position, or sameness feminism, on a now infamous legal case from the early 1970s, when women attempted to claim that a state disability insurance program ought to provide benefits to pregnant women because all conditions that disable men were covered, including those that uniquely or primarily affected men. The U.S. Supreme Court ruled against the women on the following grounds:

> the challenged programs simply "divided potential recipients into two groups—pregnant women and non-pregnant persons." Since women were in both groups, there was no discrimination based on sex! Unlike the plaintiffs, the Court did not see pregnancy as a characteristic that distinguished women from men. Instead, pregnancy simply distinguished some women from other women who were not pregnant (and from all men). According to the Court, all people who were not pregnant were treated the same; only pregnant women were treated differently. *Geduldig* demonstrates the manipulability of equality as a standard. The Court could affirm women's equality with men while rejecting the plaintiff's position; to do so it simply needed to redefine the point of comparison (Greenberg 1992:xii).

Equally depressing for legal feminists was that if women could not use the law very effectively to gain equal treatment in all instances before the courts, aggressive manipulation of women's "difference," a position celebrated by another emerging group of feminist lawyers and theorists in the 1970s and 1980s, also began to work against them. The well-known "Sears case" best exemplifies the dilemma for the "difference" position. In this case,

> the EEOC sued Sears for failing to employ women as commission sales representatives. The EEOC based its case on the statistically low percentage of women who obtained positions in commission sales. In its defense, Sears argued that women chose not to seek commission sales positions. Its claim was that these positions required aggressive, highly informed, self-motivated, risk-takers, whereas women were nurturant, relation-centered and not competitive. Ultimately, Sears won. The emphasis on women as caretakers reintroduced all the negative, subordinating aspects of difference. In *Sears*, difference feminism was subverted from a source of gender pride and power to a conservative force in opposition to change (Greenberg 1992:xiv).

Most distressing, perhaps, for a generation of feminist scholars contemplating this turn of events was that two women's historians testified on opposing sides of the case, Alice Kessler-Harris for the EEOC and Rosalind Rosenberg for Sears. In the minds of some, the fact that both historians based their arguments on essentialist notions of female "difference" (from men) rather than on the specific actions of Sears as an nonemployer of women, demonstrated the flawed nature of difference feminism as a political tool in the struggle for women's rights. As Joan Scott argued, even Kessler-Harris, who used historical statistics to argue for past discrimination against women, fell into an essentialist trap, failing to recognize that any quest for women's equality must rest on the recognition of multiple differences—"differences that confound, disrupt, and render ambiguous the meaning of any fixed binary opposition [between men and women]" (Scott 1988:177).

In reaction to the multiple crises extending from the manipulation of anti-discrimination law in the U.S. courts in ways that did not necessarily work well for women, another wave of feminist critique appeared. Famous for her contributions in this next round of discussion and debate has been Catherine MacKinnon, who has posited a view of social relations generally, and of the law in particular, as defined by the sexual domination of women by men. MacKinnon advocates the jettisoning altogether of reliance on, or belief in the efficacy of anti-discrimination law in favor of a more radical approach, in which the "law should support freedom from systematic subordination because of sex rather than freedom to be treated without regard to sex" (Charlesworth 1994, 67). In her writings and practice, this has meant targeting pornography and sexual harassment as issues that the law should take more seriously because they speak directly to women's social subordination to men. An approach akin to MacKinnon's but viewed as less extreme and more practical has been that of Christine Littleton, who has argued for redefining "equality as acceptance," and advocating new laws that would require institutions to restructure themselves to fit women's different life patterns (Charlesworth 1994).

This discussion of the perils and critiques of anti-discrimination law in the U.S. lays the groundwork for considering Chinese peasant women in relationship to human rights law. As international human rights law expert Hilary Charlesworth (1994) has put the issue, in describing the hazardous course of anti-discrimination law and its application to the international human rights arena:

The comparatively broad definition of discrimination contained in the UN Convention on the Elimination of All Forms of Discrimination Against Women, which covers both equality of opportunity (formal equality) and equality of outcome (de facto equality), is nevertheless based on the same limited approach [placing women in the same position as men in the public sphere]. The measure of equality in Article 1 is still a male one. And the discrimination it prohibits is confined to accepted human rights and fundamental freedoms. If these rights and freedoms can be shown to be defined in a gendered way, access to them will be unlikely to promote any real form of equality (64).

Charlesworth goes on to make an impassioned plea for a restructuring of human rights legal instruments in the international arena to account for the problems women encounter in the "private sphere" of domestic life as opposed to the male-dominated "public sphere."

While Charlesworth makes an important point—that women's lives in non-Western societies are still much more limited to, and constrained by, family roles in the "private sphere"—I would suggest that she is still missing an important component of what a new feminist political strategy in the human rights arena needs to encompass—recognition of not just the sexual differences that divide men and women's tasks and roles, but also the cultural and class differences that render meaningless essentialist notions of "woman."

Sex, Class, and Culture

Ethnographic encounters with Chinese peasant women during China's reform era of the 1980s force us to struggle with overlapping patterns of sex, class, and cultural difference as they intersect and influence each other. In 1987, I visited the central China village of Maocun, in Wuxi county, finishing a project on the history of Wuxi's modern silk industry. My interviews at that time were not aimed directly at rights issues, or even political issues more generally. Rather, I was interested in knowing, through the language and interpretation of peasants themselves, what peasant women's former roles in silk production had been like, and how peasant family strategies with regard to "supplemental household-based economic activity" (fuye, in Chinese idiom) had changed in recent decades. However, in retrospect, the rich material contained in the transcripts of those interviews provides an opportunity to think about questions of difference, the potential perils of cultural misinterpretation, and how new strategies with respect to Chinese peasant women's rights might begin to take shape through such experiences and re-readings of ethnographic encounters.

Historically in Maocun, *fuye* had been almost exclusively women's work in silkworm raising. Women had raised silkworms twice, sometimes three times yearly, producing cocoons for sale to local, modern silk filatures, where the cocoons' silken threads were mechanically spun into silk yarn for export. When I asked why peasant women no longer did this work in Maocun, after a moment of quiet reflection, the answer given by an elderly peasant woman was that it was simply too much work. In recent decades, the proliferation of locally based factories for the production of other consumer products, both for home consumption and for export, provided "easier" and more lucrative wage work for young peasant women. In her words, "We didn't want to 'eat bitterness' (*chiku*) anymore."

The discussion then rotated to the entire spectrum of change in village incomes and living standards since the onset of the "reform period," an era dating to Deng Xiaoping's ascendancy to leadership in 1978. Toward the end of the session, in a lively exchange in which many joined in at will—several local cadres, including one village woman, the elderly peasants, and myself—a claim was made that the highest yearly household incomes in the village approached fifteen thousand *yuan*, at that time, approximately US $500. A lot of discussion ensued about how this was achieved, with one of the local cadres using the term *laoli*, a nongendered term meaning something like "unit of labor power," to assert that it depended on how many such units a household had as the basis for its ability to accumulate income.

Searching for an inroad into this discussion, I then asked how many "units of labor," *laoli*, the wealthiest households had, receiving the prompt answer, "four or five"—a typical size for village households in both the past and present. In an effort to get more specific, I then said: "At present, how do you evaluate labor power (*suan laoli*)? Women and men are not the same, right?" There was tension inherent in the phrasing of this question because I was implying that Chinese men and women were unequal rather than equal based on my knowledge of a wide array of Western studies that claimed women had never achieved equality with men in terms of remuneration to labor under the older collectively-based work points system. It was surprising to me, therefore, that the immediate, unqualified response coming from one of the male cadres was simply, "They are the same (*yiyang*)." The cadre and I had now staked out our positions based on what we believed to be true about men and women in socialist Chinese "culture." I implied men and women were not equal; he said, unequivocally, that they were.

The way the conversation moved next revealed the degree to which the question of equality could be mutually understood across cultures, yet not easily agreed upon as a course of action. The cadre's initial response had been so strong both in tone and certainty that many other voices, including my own, also chimed in, "*yiyang?*" It was a knee-jerk reaction, and no one in the room, save the man who had made the statement to begin with, seemed comfortable with leaving it at that. In an effort to get more information, I then said, "Wages are the same?" Again, the adamant response by the male cadre was, "*Yiyang*" — the same. But then other villagers and cadres began to qualify his answer. Another male cadre began, "Factories are not the same . . . "; and then a female cadre's voice chimed in, "Here, occupations are not the same, so wages are not the same" (*hangye butong, gongzi butong*). And then, finally, a general cacophony of voices, discussing among themselves, the correct phrasing of the issue, of which there were at least three additional variants: "Skills are not the same, so wages are not the same" (*zhiye butong, gongzi butong*); "When the type of work is different, then wages are not the same" (*gongzhong butong, gongzi buyiyang*); and finally, a more refined rendering of the problem, this time phrased in the affirmative, "When men and women do the same work they receive the same remuneration: it all hinges on how well the enterprise is doing" (*nannü tonggong tongchou: guanjian zaiyu chiye shouyi*).

As the more detailed answers poured forth, the locus of discussion of male-female difference shifted away from the cultural insider/outsider problem (the Chinese male cadre vs. the female Westerner questioner) to consideration among cultural insiders on the best way to describe the problems of equality and discrimination. Everyone present understood that, in the reform era, new village-based industries simultaneously provided many people, men and women alike, with new employment opportunities. But jobs were different, skills were different, and they were all new. In past agricultural life in Maocun, the sexual division of labor had been clear, even during the collectivization process that swept through all Chinese villages in the 1950s — men had remained responsible for the tasks requiring the most strength and stamina — plowing and harvesting crops, and building what was needed in terms of physical structures, like irrigation works, village government structures, shops, and dwellings. Women, on the other hand, continued to do "supplementary work," raising silkworms, tending vegetable plots, and raising household animals such as pigs and chickens. Undoubtedly, as elsewhere in rural China, men had also monopolized political life, although under the revolutionary rubric, "Women hold up half the sky," a few women had entered the political arena in a limited way, assuming responsibility for "women's political work," orchestrated through the state's official political agency, the Women's Federation.

The reform era, by contrast, opened up the possibility of reshaping this picture, not only from the perspective of the sexual division of labor, but also from the side of politics. One rarely hears the revolutionary dictum in China anymore, that "Women hold up half the sky." But what are the expectations for women in this new and rapidly changing village environment? And how are these expectations to be realized? Although peasant women now work more and differently, often when they are very young, as unskilled labor in small-scale, locally based factories, what forces are at work to shape their participation, and make it understandable in terms of local family and village life? How do sex roles within families, as well as within the workplace, for example, condition the possibilities? Cultural process among insiders, I would argue, not the interjection of an outsider's complaints about inequality, or new knowledge about an abstract and culturally distant body of international human rights law, will occupy center stage in this projected transformation, just as it replaced the momentary exchange between the male cadre and myself on the question of male-female equality.

Moments of discussion about gendering of new work roles, like the one recounted above, provide insight into certain dimensions of that cultural process. They do not reveal all there is to know, by any means, but they are indicative of at least some aspects of what is going on today in Chinese village settings in terms of men and women in relationship to work. There is no longer one way to understand how men and women are supposed to become equal in socialist China. The goal of equality must be reconstituted in relationship to a constant reshaping of material life. In the minds of those present at the above discussion, it was the development of new factories at the village level through which the goal of male-female equality had to be reconstituted. When men and women did the same work, then their wages would be the same, a "modern" ideal of both liberal democracy and of socialism. Thus, all of those participating in the interview—myself and Chinese participants included—had a common view that male-female equality was an important end goal. There was no insurmountable cultural barrier to common understanding, and even agreement, on the key issue of male-female equality. But under what concrete circumstances could such equality be realized?

Let us imagine for a moment, a situation in which CEDAW might be invoked by human rights activists in village settings in China to try to guarantee equal pay for equal work. Would Chinese peasant women be well served using the language and reasoning of Western anti-discrimination law? Would a tool like CEDAW assist them in their daily efforts to get more skills and earn higher wages, or would it introduce the same dilemmas Western women have faced with "sameness/difference" arguments? Or, perhaps even worse, would such a tool, imbued with characteristics of Western human rights discourse, simply do more harm than good? Might it not in fact, suggest Western intellectuals' construction of sexual "sameness and difference" in ways entirely foreign, and perhaps even "culturally imperialistic," to at least some Chinese ears? In her essay (chapter 6 below), Lucinda Peach argues quite convincingly for new style of "feminist pragmatism," in which a tool like CEDAW might become useful, but only after careful assessment of the precise local situation and the potential for reception of an outside presence in local affairs. In short, questions about whether or not to use an international human rights tool like CEDAW cannot be answered in any hypothetical, abstract way. Only by collecting detailed ethnographic evidence can we begin to map out new understandings of multiple differences of culture, sex, and class that affect the interests and aspirations of Chinese peasant women.

Some such ethnographic projects have been underway in China in recent years. One in particular stands out for its contributions to understanding more about the constraints facing Chinese peasant women in the era of economic reform, a study conducted by anthropologist Ellen Judd in rural north China (Judd 1994). Judd's study covers a wide range of economic structural change in three north China villages since the onset of the reform period, and the relationship of both women and men to those changes and to each other as a result of those changes.

In one chapter entitled "Women's Agency," Judd reviews the work of the official political "mass organization" in China, the Women's Federation, that acts as intermediary between state and Party policy and all Chinese women. She finds that in each of the three villages she studied, one woman was responsible for all "women's work" (funü gongzuo), that is, any political objective or policy related to women, that might be passed down to the village. In the late 1980s when Judd did her fieldwork, the primary task of these representatives was to make sure that all women of childbearing age were aware of the state's goals in relationship to population policy (the one-child policy), and that they adhered to it. Judd's major conclusion was that in terms of affecting real, substantive change at the village level in women's lives, the structural components of the economic reform itself were likely to be much more important than the overtly political activities of the Women's Federation.

Surprisingly, and quite contrary to prior speculation and reasoning on such issues by other scholars who study Chinese peasant women, Judd found that the return to a household-based economy under the reform period was creating spaces for the emergence of new forms of peasant women's agency, especially in terms of their ability to carve out special income-earning niches which only they could formulate and control. In the collective economy of the past, there had been special, collective-based women's work, but peasant women participated in those activities only grudgingly, as a way to augment the total income of the village as a whole, or of the collective group. But since the onset of the reform period, with its reinstatement of the household as the primary economic unit in the countryside, women were now encouraged to exercise more "freedom" (*ziyou*) to develop their special abilities as household-based producers of "socialist commodities," an activity they had engaged in previously (such as the growing of vegetables for limited, locally-based peasant markets), but had never been praised for before. Likewise, since the 1980s, the Women's Federation has also been actively advocating improving the "quality" (*suzhi*) of women. In this regard, there are "four selfs" to pay attention to: self-esteem, self-respect, self-possession, and self-strengthening. In Judd's words, "The aim here is to suggest that women are as able as men, and to provide at least moral encouragement to the rural women whose sense of agency is critical to prospects for change in the countryside." Importantly for our discussion, Judd goes on to say,

> This policy of improving the "quality" of women does not directly confront the problem of gender discrimination; rather, it implicitly accepts the proposition that in some respects, such as formal education and economically useful knowledge, women are at a disadvantage compared with men. The emphasis of the policy is less on combating discrimination than on placing women in a stronger position to improve their lives. This is a realistic approach under conditions of entrenched patriarchy and women's organizational weakness in the pub-

lic realm in the countryside. "Quality" is an issue because so much
depends on relatively isolated women and their effective agency (238).

Judd's ultimate conclusion is that conditions for women in the villages she
studied are not conducive under the reforms to any widespread groundswell
among peasant women to demand "equality" in relationship to men. Nonetheless, through her patient probing and careful listening, she found a way
to begin to understand peasant women's heightened consciousness about
their prospects of quietly and covertly subverting patriarchal structures (239).

Of course, there might also be other strategies for understanding and
negotiating cultural difference beyond the careful listening of the historically
minded ethnographer. Sharon Hom, for example, has worked on a very
ambitious project in creating a lexicon of terminology used to discuss
women's issues in both China and the West. Her collaborator on this volume
is a highly educated Chinese woman, Xin Chunying, a professor in the
Institute of Law of the Chinese Academy of Social Sciences. In their Introduction to the volume, they say:

> As scholars, teachers, and activists, we encounter in numerous inter-
> national meetings, conferences, and exchanges many key terms in
> discussions such as feminism, gender, and sexuality, that do not trans-
> late easily or clearly across languages and cultures. How can we un-
> derstand struggles and envision dreams woven from different lan-
> guages and cultural contexts? Perhaps one small place to begin is to
> pay attention to our speaking and the silences of missed meanings that
> often go unnoticed when common languages are assumed. . . . This
> first edition is intended to provide a beginning tool for facilitating this
> "noticing" of the terms and concepts we use in communication across
> English-Chinese cultural contexts. We hope that this volume will have
> significance for projects that explore other languages and cross-cultural
> exchanges (Hom and Xin 1995:18).

The lexicon explores a fascinating array of terms, ranging from "discrimination" and "essentialism" from the Western side, to Chinese idioms, like
"Husband sings and wife accompanies." As another intellectual woman, I
find this volume of extraordinary interest and value. And yet, I still find
myself wondering what Chinese peasant women might think of it. I make
these observations only to underscore the complexities of multiple differ-

ences—of culture and sex, but also of class—that must be considered if we are to achieve new cultural understandings and political strategies in the struggle for human rights.

Cultural Study and the Struggle for Human Rights

This chapter has reviewed the promotion of universal human rights and of Asian values as competing discourses, infused with power politics by those on both sides of the Asian values debate. I also have queried the concept of culture, arguing that it is not static and fixed, but rather fluid and subject to contestation, thus making the notion of a unitary set of Asian values impossible. The ideas of some Chinese peasants and local cadres concerning women's equality in terms of work and wages have been considered as well, as a way to illustrate the importance of multiple differences of culture, sex, and class in coping with basic concepts in the human rights debate, such as male-female equality. All of this is aimed at helping us move beyond the simplistic East/West cultural divide proposed by the Asian values debate.

At the forefront of our future agenda in the struggle for human rights must be further inquiries into the real meanings of multiple difference among human beings and close scrutiny of real-life experiences of the marginalized. At the same time, I believe we can cautiously pursue varied strategies to promote awareness of past failures and present abuses within particular cultural formations, convinced that there are some core moral values in the human experience in which we can all believe and work toward achieving, as Michael Barnhart forcefully argues in his chapter in this volume. We can also seek ways to facilitate human rights strategies with an attitude of respect for other cultures and the multiple differences within them, as the authors of several other chapters suggest. More specifically, on the question of women's rights, I have come to accept the possibility of a "feminist pragmatist" strategy outlined by Lucinda Peach in her chapter, in which activists might look carefully for concrete times, places, and circumstances in which human rights instruments such as CEDAW *can* become useful tools.

At the same time, as I have tried to argue here, we must be constantly aware that we Westerners cannot singlehandedly, from our outsiders' position, create new forms of cultural contestation and self-identification for others' future betterment. Identities formation "from below" must be engaged in by those who are also "within." In the final analysis, while I have developed a new degree of optimism for the prospects of a more culturally sensitive form of international human rights work, I continue to believe that studying and supporting local struggles of the politically and socially marginalized will be our best weapon in international efforts to promote social justice for all.

Acknowledgments

I gratefully acknowledge Andy Nathan's input into making this a better essay through his seemingly endless capacity to discuss and debate many of the difficult issues raised here, and his generosity in providing comments on more than one previous draft. Lucinda Peach and Farhat Haq also provided much stimulating discussion along the way, helping me to hone my own perspective on women's issues in the context of the Asian values debate.

Endnotes

1. Hall's discussion of Foucault is much more complex that I have indicated here. Hall provides a historical reading of Foucault's changing notions of subjectivity in the course of his writings, and argues that Foucault does not go far enough in resolving the unanswered question he creates in his earlier writings of "why it is that certain individuals occupy some subject positions rather than others" (Hall 1996, 10). Hall's point is that subjects have too little agency in Foucault's early renderings, thus making it impossible to theorize the possibility of resistance within his theory of power. Hall's proposed resolution of this problem is to suggest the need for a "suturing of the psychic and the discursive" in the construction of subjective identities. Since it is not my purpose here to develop an entirely new reading of Foucault, but rather to borrow what I find to be a useful notion—that at least a *partial* constitution of the subject arises from her position within discursive practice, I simply reiterate Foucault's original notion.

2. Judith Greenberg's essay draws moving inspiration from the larger, book-length work of Mary Joe Frug, *Postmodern Legal Feminism*, New York and London: Routledge, 1992. Greenberg and Frug were colleagues and friends at the New England School of Law in Boston. Frug was murdered in an apparently random assault near her home on April 4, 1991. Along with Gerald E. Frug (Mary Joe's husband), Greenberg helped put together Mary Joe's unfinished manuscripts for publication—in this instance, by writing the superb introduction to the published book.

Bibliography

Appadurai, Arjun. 1996. *Modernity at Large: Cultural Dimensions of Globalization.* Minneapolis: University of Minnesota Press.

Charlesworth, Hilary. 1994. "What are 'Women's International Human Rights?' " In *Human Rights of Women: National and International Perspectives,* ed. Rebecca J. Cook. Philadelphia: University of Pennsylvania press.

Danielsen, Dan, and Karen Engle, eds. 1995. *After Identity: A Reader in Law and Culture.* New York and London: Routledge.

Dirlik, Arif. 1997. "Critical Reflections on 'Chinese Capitalism' as Paradigm." *Identities: Global Studies in Culture and Power* 3(3, January):303–330.

Greenberg, Judith G. 1992. "Introduction to Postmodern Legal Feminism." In *Postmodern Legal Feminism,* by Mary Joe Frug. New York and London: Routledge.

Hall, Stuart. 1996. "Introduction: Who Needs 'Identity?' " In *Questions of Cultural Identity,* ed. Stuart Hall and Paul du Gay. London: Sage Publications.

Hom, Sharon K. 1996. "Commentary: Re-Positioning Human Rights Discourse on 'Asian' Perspectives." *The Buffalo Journal of International Law* 3(1, Summer): 209–234.

———, and Chunying Xin. 1995. *English-Chinese Lexicon of Women and Law* (Chinese title: *Ying-Han funü yu falü cihui shiyi*). Paris and Beijing: United Nations Education, Scientific and Cultural Organization (UNESCO) and China Translation and Publishing Corporation (CTPC).

Judd, Ellen R. 1994. *Gender and Power in Rural North China.* Stanford: Stanford University Press.

Kausikan, Bilahari. 1993. "Asia's Different Standard." *Foreign Policy,* Fall, 24–41.

———. 1995–96. "An East Asian Approach to Human Rights." *The Buffalo Journal of International Law* 2 (2) (Winter):263–283.

———. 1997. The Asian Values Debate. New York, NEH Summer Seminar at Columbia University, June 17.

Maocun villagers and cadres interview. 1987. Compiler, Lynda S. Bell. Maocun, Wuxi county, People's Republic of China, December.

Neier, Aryeh. 1993. "Asia's Unacceptable Standard." *Foreign Policy,* Fall, 42–51.

Poster, Mark. 1997. *Cultural History and Postmodernity: Disciplinary Readings and Challenges.* New York: Columbia University Press.

Scott, Joan Wallach. 1988. *Gender and the Politics of History.* New York: Columbia University Press.

———. 1994. "Deconstructing Equality-Versus-Difference: or, the Uses of Poststructuralist Theory for Feminism." In *Theorizing Feminism: Parallel Trends in the Humanities and Social Sciences,* ed. Anne C. Herrmann and Abigail J. Stewart. Boulder: Westview Press.

Weisberg, D. Kelly, ed. 1993. *Feminist Legal Theory: Foundations.* Philadelphia: Temple University Press.

Williams, Wendy W. 1997. "The Equality Crisis: Some Reflections on Culture, Courts, and Feminism." In *The Second Wave: A Reader in Feminist Theory*, ed. Linda Nicholson. New York and London: Routledge.

Zakaria, Fareed. 1994. "Culture is Destiny: A Conversation with Lee Kuan Yew." *Foreign Affairs* 73 (2) (March/April):109–126.

Part 2

Culturally Informed Arguments for
Universal Human Rights

2 Getting Beyond Cross-Talk

Why Persisting Disagreements Are Philosophically Nonfatal

Michael G. Barnhart

It is an intellectual commonplace that cultures differ with regard to basic values. By "basic," I mean those values that establish our sense of identity and purpose in life and are expressed in fundamental choices, if they are choices, of religion, lifestyle, and political and social affiliation. Living an orthodox Muslim life, a secular Western-European life, or a Native American tribal life are considerably different — different enough that anthropologists, those who make it their business to study such differences, prefer the metaphors "world" and "world view" to dramatize the enormity of the gaps.

Philosophically, however, one is tempted to ask how different such values can be. Is there a common core that all humans share by virtue of their humanity? Is there a common human nature? Could we bring the variety of cultures together, perhaps evolving a set of core values? But if such consensus is impossible, what are humanity's prospects for constructively handling conflict?

The issue of consensus raises an additional set of moral questions. Should we seek consensus? Is it desirable or necessary? Is the predisposition to accommodation a virtue? And if we find that cultures seriously diverge with regard to basic values, are we under any obligation to respect such divergence? What does respect for cultural difference entail in the context of international politics and law? Or is any attempt to promote a core set of values a thinly disguised partisan bid for cultural, usually Western, hegemony? Does Western advocacy of universal moral values such as are found in the UN's Universal Declaration of Human Rights mean that those values are tainted in some sense, perhaps parochially Western?

Typically, culture is used as a foil for countering perceived attempts at moral hegemony. Proclamations made on the high ground of moral values are portrayed as culturally biased and therefore without commanding authority. For many Asian and developing nations, a charge of cultural imperialism represents one of the few effective rallying points for resisting pressure from international organizations such as the UN or the World Bank that are perceived as Western-dominated. A particularly good example is the use of "culture" and "tradition" to challenge the hegemony of universal human rights. In the words, of Bilihari Kausikan,

> The diversity of cultural traditions, political structures, and levels of development will make it difficult, if not impossible, to define a single distinctive and coherent human rights regime that can encompass the vast region from Japan to Burma, with its Confucianist, Buddhist, Islamic, and Hindu traditions. . . . What is clear is that there is a general discontent throughout the region with a purely Western interpretation of human rights (Kausikan 1993:26).

Which is not to say that there are no universal human rights according to Kausikan. But he argues that the core of truly universal rights is quite small and limited to, for example, the right to freedom from torture or the right to freedom from arbitrary detention. Beyond that, whether a *de facto* consensus exists or not, genuine commitment to a wide range of rights is neither possible nor desirable.[1]

The response to this sort of argument comes from a variety of fronts and follows a variety of strategies. On the one hand, human rights activists argue that this is simply self-serving reasoning on the part of elites who are trying to protect their power and privileges from internal challenge.[2] On the other hand, many academics argue that far from having a distinct set of values, Asian cultures, societies, and traditions harbor a large range of opinions and beliefs, some very supportive of those rights found in international rights regimes.[3] The first argument, even though I would agree with it, is less than satisfying largely because it does not deal with the substance of Kausikan's claims. The second argument does, and so it is the one I wish to focus on.

The typical response to academic exercises in finding congenial settings for universal human rights in the world's non-Western traditions is to argue that these erudite games . . . can be played endlessly without uncovering anything with practical relevance to current concerns. Most Asian societies have such long histories and rich cultures that it is possible to "prove" nearly anything about them if the context of the recovered references is ignored. . . . A variety of views and beliefs are present in every society. The real question is whether—notwithstanding this change and diversity—different kinds of societies exhibit *general* differences in the realm of values (Kausikan 1993:30).

Actually, the argument Kausikan pushes here could just as well be turned on his own claim of distinctive Asian values that militate against the idea of universal human rights. If Asian societies are so rich, varied, and diverse, then how can he claim to discern a distinctively different set of Asian values? What criteria can he offer to justify his competing evaluation of the moral consensus of Asian societies? I imagine he might argue that "the context of the recovered references" has to do with their antiquity, and his present status as a contemporary spokesman for an Asian government gives him some knowledge of the historical direction of social consensus regarding these sources.

However, I do think there is some merit to Kausikan's view. If one closely examines scholarly attempts to embed human rights in Confucian, Buddhist, or Islamic sources, the effort sometimes seems strained and interpreters are often forced to admit that they are basing their effort on an unconventional reading, a minority interpretation, or at best an intraculturally contested reading of traditional texts.[4] So, what value does attach to finding a Buddhist or Islamic understanding of human rights, especially when some other interpreter can come along and offer a compelling counterinterpretation? In the end, must we settle for a fundamental diversity of views either within or across cultures with regard to human rights and other moral issues? Conversely, how much normative significance ought we attach to whatever worldwide consensus seems to have developed around various internationally recognized human rights? These are the questions which need to be answered if we are to find any value or larger purpose in the enterprise of cultural interpretation whether it be through the lens of anthropology, comparative politics, religion, or philosophy.

i

Taking the human rights debate as a test case, we need to examine the philosophical content of relativistic claims which find an in-principle difficulty with the very idea of intercultural moral consensus. To begin with, the idea of consensus must be distinguished from the fact of consensus. Since the 1948 Universal Declaration of Human rights there has been a de facto consensus regarding human rights which has been subsequently expanded on to the point where various generations of rights, running from the civil and political to the socioeconomic and even to the rights of peoples and nations, are now internationally recognized. One might assume, and indeed Ambassador Kausikan admits, that there is no debate regarding the universality of some human rights.[5]

As UN members and signatories to various conventions, many nations are on record as supporting a wide variety of human rights. What such agreement signifies, however, is another matter. Two points can be made. The first, already alluded to, is that the core of truly universal rights may be quite small, and particular nations may not even in principle, let alone in practice, support the whole list of rights covered in various international covenants. Secondly, the fact of consensus is one thing. The desirability of consensus is another. Part of the resentment that nations such as China and Singapore may feel over human rights activism may stem from the feeling of being pressured or coerced into accepting a foreign concept, even if it is only on paper. And of course, things on paper adopt a life of their own. In other words, if this is a forced consensus, it is no consensus at all.[6] Just because a country accepts certain regimes and conventions, it doesn't follow that its people approve of them. If human rights agreements represent a triumph of Western economic and diplomatic power, then the relativist charge that human rights are a Western notion, unsuited to Eastern or Asian societies, remains unanswered. Consequently, the merit of relativistic claims that "Asian values" are unique because they are Asian needs testing.

In assessing any such argument invoking cultural relativism, the first problem is to clarify exactly what the underlying claim is. Sometimes, it is expressed as the view that values and norms are relative to culture; other times, that they are relative to traditions, religions, civilizations, philosophical perspectives, and even geopolitical interests.[7] The Bangkok Declaration of 1993 mentions several such relativities affecting the universality of human rights, namely "national and regional particularities and various historical, cultural and religious backgrounds." However, a suitably broad definition of culture may be able to subsume most of these under its rubric. Therefore, for purposes of argument, I am initially assuming the "interpretive" understanding of culture as "an historically transmitted pattern of meanings embodied in symbols, a system of inherited conceptions expressed in symbolic forms by means of which men communicate, perpetuate, and develop their knowledge about and attitudes toward life" (Geertz 1973:89). As such, culture includes those values by which we determine the overall meaningfulness of our lives. Though there are other more positivistically oriented versions of culture in terms of distributions of representative attitudes and opinions as measured by surveys or perhaps focus groups, the interpretive approach gives culture its strongest normative or philosophical weight.[8]

Our definition of culture as a "web of meaning," when coupled with the view that meaning itself is entirely determined by context and usage, logically implies that distinct patterns of culture are, perforce, systematically different and embed different sets of basic values. If they are systematically different and share no basic concepts, then there can be no neutral basis of comparison because we cannot say in what way different cultures either agree or disagree with regard to human experience. Therefore, strong contextualism with regard to meaning and usage ultimately commits us to the view that cultures are fundamentally incommensurable and that there are no overarching and universally accepted basic values binding on all cultures. Hence, the doctrine known as cultural relativism. Universalists, on the other hand, tend to argue that cultures are not systematically different, which is to say that they are fully commensurable, even though a good deal of interpretation may be necessary to bring out their similarities and assess their differences. On the basis of such claims, various recommendations are made regarding the ethics of dealing with other cultures. On the one hand, if cultures are strongly incommensurable, then we are to refrain from criticism and interference in a context where our values have no relevance. On the other hand, if cultures are fully commensurable, at least regarding basic matters, then consistency of some moral values points to the universality of at least some moral principles and a certain "moral realism" that sees objective truth value in our shared commitments.[9]

Examples of both tendencies are plentiful, especially in philosophy. Moral universalists are often impressed with the confluence of opinion cross-culturally regarding the unacceptability of murder, theft, deceit, and so on.

This is viewed as at least *prima facie* evidence that moral universals exist.[10] Moral relativists are more impressed by the evident differences that history and culture teach, for example, the endorsement of human sacrifice in one society and not another. Furthermore, relativists will argue that while different societies may indeed frown on murder or deception, each of them understands such conduct quite differently. That is, there is no neutral, culturally noninfected understanding of the very terms in which consensus is stated.[11]

For purposes of argument, first let us analyze what follows if we assume that the universalists are right, and that cultures are broadly commensurable or even largely the same. Then, let us explore the consequences of the opposite assumption, that the relativists are right, and cultures are incommensurable. What conclusions can we draw from either assumption in favor of either moral universalism or relativism? Very little, I will argue. That is, the normative implications of cultural difference turn out to be genuinely uncertain. However, such uncertainty, I will contend, supports the value of intercultural study and suggests a profound linkage between culture and morality.

Cultures Are Strongly Commensurable

Suppose that we can make a coherent case that all cultures share certain core values, moral principles, or concepts, and that the range of interpretive disagreement is insignificant. Does moral universalism follow? At the outset we are confronted with an ambiguity. As Samuel Fleischacker (1994:6–7) notes in his book *The Ethics of Culture,* "Saying that an ethical claim "holds universally" may mean that it applies to every human being or it may mean that every human being ought to believe it, and the two are by no means the same." Roughly, is moral universalism universal in the descriptive or the prescriptive sense? Our question here concerns prescriptive universalism. If we assume that descriptively all cultures do subscribe to certain core values, does moral universalism in the prescriptive sense follow?

I think not. Without undue reliance of the fact/value distinction, a critic could urge that agreement regarding certain core values merely records a fact. Some special argument is needed to ground the inference that these core values are therefore morally obligatory. Just because all societies or perhaps the overwhelming majority of human societies have adopted one or another judgment, it doesn't follow that any one judgment is correct or universally binding. For example, the majority of human societies have held that slavery is acceptable and that women constitute a naturally inferior kind to men. Should anything follow from this? The overwhelming majority of human cultures are carnivorous. Does this confer any moral inferiority on vegetarianism?

Few moral universalists would take seriously the view that what is moral is strictly a matter of converging opinions. Take, for example, justice. As Will Kymlicka notes,

> justice cannot be equated with or defined in terms of, "congruence" with a community's deepest understandings or deepest self-image. Since acts which are congruent . . . can none the less be unjust, we must test our deepest self-image against other possible standards of justice. . . . The fact that something is congruent with a community's deepest self-image does not foreclose the argument about its justice.[12]

Substituting "culture" for "self-image," the point is that moral criticism of our view of justice cannot be foreclosed by appeal to cultural consensus.

Indeed, what drives moral universalism is just this sense that moral criticism cannot be foreclosed by appeals to consensus. One must appeal to "other possible standards," as Kymlicka puts it, if one is to vindicate a particular vision of justice. Moral discourse is autonomous, independent from sociocultural considerations. Moral universalism then, becomes the search for those standards of acceptability that govern moral discourse and allow for, say, the relevant comparison of various standards of justice.

Does this make moral criticism a purely rational enterprise in the Kantian mold? I think not; Hume's emphasis on the sentiments might furnish us equally well with a universal basis for moral reflection. In fact, it's hard to imagine a "purely rational" *and* fully compelling moral theory. Human emotion must underlie our commitment to whatever norms or rules we accept, very much Hume's point. But whether based on reason or sentiment, the logic of moral discourse must appeal to standards of acceptability that are independent of preferences embedded in particular cultures. Hence, consensus can never be more than *prima facie* evidence for prescriptively universal norms.

Of course, there remains the question whether moral universalism so defined is possible or true. However, this is a separate issue. My point is simply that the search for moral universals cannot stop at the existence of moral consensus. This poses a problem for moral universalisms such as Jack Donnelly's that ground universal human rights, for example, in the existence of intercultural consensus regarding some core set as found in such documents as the Universal Declaration of Human Rights. I mentioned before that an individual country's or culture's participation in such conventions may be merely strategic, perhaps having little to do with its basic values. The further point I am now urging is that such assent of itself is not prescriptively binding. Even if based on widely accepted values or ways of thinking about moral issues, intercultural consensus cannot foreclose moral criticism unless the moral basis for such consensus can claim some kind of objective correctness.

Cultures Are Strongly Incommensurable

Suppose that relativists are right to the extent that cultures do vary in ways that make all comparisons suspect and no norms or values the common property of all human beings. Suppose all cultures contribute unique patterns of symbolic meaning in the manner Geertz suggests. What follows regarding prescriptive universality? Again, I think very little. Just because we all disagree, it does not follow that we are all right, each of us in our separate ways. Some of us, perhaps those who support slavery, the subjugation of women, or the commitment to animal experimentation may be wrong.

Of course, the rejoinder might be that we have not taken seriously enough the incommensurability of cultures. If the associational context of a cultural element is what confers its significance, there are no culturally approved practices, especially of reflection and argument, by which we could establish moral universals. Short of a "space" of autonomous reflection uninfected by circumstances of history and culture, we lack the necessary resources to make such supracultural moral judgments. To assess is always to do so in subscription to some set of culturally freighted norms.

Despite its formidable appearance, there are, I believe a number of significant gaps in the cultural relativist's argument. The biggest gap is exposed when we realize that we can accept the criticism while pointing out that it in no way constrains our criticizing others, even others outside our cultural context, if that is an accepted or even ethically mandated activity *within* our culture. Arguably, Richard Rorty has taken this position.[13] In other words, there is the gap between what I would call a descriptive cultural relativism and a prescriptive or "ethical" cultural relativism. A descriptive relativism insists that all descriptions are relative to some cultural context or other. That is, the terms in which we make sense of the world and register our experience are culturally relative. The prescriptive cultural relativist insists on equal respect for all cultures, the right of each culture to its uniqueness or entitlement to be different from other cultures. That is, we are to refrain from "dictating to another society." The two are different doctrines, however. To be sure, the imperative of ethical relativism enjoys a great deal of support amongst those who subscribe to one variety of relativism or another. As Abdullahi Ahmed An-Na'im writes, "The appreciation of our own ethnocentricity should lead us to respect the ethnocentricity of others. Enlightened ethnocentricity would therefore concede the right of others to be 'different,' whether as members of another society or as individuals within the same society" (An-Na'im 1992:24). Yet, just as descriptive universalism does not imply prescriptive universalism, so too moral or ethical relativism is a distinct doctrine not entailed by descriptive, cultural relativism.

The proponents of an ethical relativism, as I am calling it, have tended to blur this distinction. An-Na'im goes on to claim "the merits of a reasonable degree of *cultural relativism* [my emphasis] are obvious, especially when compared to claims of universalism that are in fact based on the claimant's rigid and exclusive ethnocentricity" (An-Na'im 1992:24).

Even Donnelly, otherwise a universalist regarding human rights, endorses a form of "weak cultural relativism" that allows "occasional and strictly limited local variations and exceptions" (Donnelly 1989:110). That is, cultural relativism means respect for the variability of human practices. However, it is exactly this linkage between the descriptive claim that cultures vary and the prescriptive claim that we ought to respect and allow such variations that I want to call into question. It remains unargued in An-Na'im's and Donnelly's versions of relativism why the observation that cultures vary should mandate respect for that variety.

Indeed, ethical relativism is arguably self-contradictory on the grounds that it lacks the conceptual resources to articulate its requirement of intercultural respect. Is such tolerance a universal moral norm that we must all follow? On culture-independent grounds?[14] To what standard beyond culture do we appeal in justifying a requirement of universal tolerance? In fact, similar questions arise for the legitimacy even of the descriptive basis for cultural relativism. If culture determines meaning and therefore intercultural universals are suspect, how can one ascertain that cultures differ? If there are no culture-independent grounds for meaning and truth, then there is no neutral standpoint from which to characterize the objective nature of any particular culture or its differences from all other cultures.

In other words, we might question the intelligibility of such radical differences as the advocates of descriptive cultural relativism maintain. Can cultures really diverge so much that they share absolutely no beliefs or, more importantly, no legitimating strategies whatsoever? If, indeed, others are so completely different from us, then how can we or they make such difference intelligible?[15] Understanding the difference between ourselves and some putatively remote and incomprehensible culture is going to require some degree of translation. In whose terms is this translation to be made, theirs or ours? Of course, if some neutral and objective metalanguage is available, we can make use of its terms in stating deep cultural differences. However, on the hypothesis of cultural relativism, to understand and value one must be able to take up a standpoint within a cultural perspective, because values and norms acquire their force within such a context. Therefore, adopting the metalanguage of anthropology, for example, could jeopardize our ability to understand the other's moral point of view. How can we make their moral norms seem compelling? And without such an appreciation of the moral force of another's position, the sense that it is a moral alternative to our own disappears.[16]

If we cannot make sense of deep cultural differences, would we ever have occasion to impute radically different beliefs to members of another group? Wouldn't we tend to treat culturally divergent others more or less like ourselves? In effect, the predicament radical relativism presents is analogous to the philosophical perplexities of individual solipsism. One can never fully know the mind of the other. In fact, one cannot really be certain that the other is a functional rational mind at all. A version of the incommensurability thesis is as applicable to individuals as to cultures. Yet, despite the inability to intimately know the mind of the other, we *treat* the other as a sentient, rational creature rather than as an automaton. In the face of possible cultural incommensurability, perhaps our temptation is analogously to treat other cultures as though they are at some basic level similar to our own. In which case, incommensurability makes no practical difference, whatever its truth.

Another difficulty with descriptive relativism and the incommensurability thesis consists in its tendency to essentialize particular cultures. One can

only insist on a variety of a priori radical divergence between cultures if they
are relatively determinate entities. That is, there must be enough internal
homogeneity and coherence that we can say exactly what is a product or
feature of an Islamic culture or Indonesian culture or Chinese civilization,
to name just a few such examples. However, once one gains some first-hand
knowledge of the human realities such abstractions identify, two related
points become apparent. The first is that such categories distort as much as
they illumine; their utility is solely relative to some purpose or other. And
secondly, they mask a great deal of internal diversity and controversy. Especially when the categories by which scholars organize human societies
into neat bundles have a meaning internal to those societies themselves,
such as in the case of Islam, one finds that the meaning and implications
of the categories themselves are a point of deep internal debate. All of which
suggests that cultures are not monolithic structures deterministically constructing the minds and values of their adherents. If anything, they are more
shared languages of controversy and disagreement. Looked at in this way,
culture seems more a matter of how far or in what ways one's conception of
the world can be stretched than it does a matter of necessary limits to one's
understanding.

In short, the complaint is that by offering a picture of mutually incompatible worlds, like so many self-enclosed bubbles, cultural relativism potentially oversimplifies and perhaps derogates the very cultures and peoples it
seeks to respect in its prescriptive guise. Philosophically, relativism valorizes
culture by way of the perspectivist argument that you cannot make sense of
the world without reference to supporting categories, and these can systematically differ. However, are not such categories, insofar as they are also part
of one's world, also subject to the same demand? Are not they also dependent
on the individual's scheme of reference? The particulars of his or her personality and life experiences?

Consistent relativism seems more suited to a skeptical, deconstructive
purpose than to a descriptive or normative one. On the prescriptive level,
ethical relativism cannot legitimate its insistence that we show tolerance
toward those who are profoundly different. At the descriptive level, cultural
relativism cannot defend the objective status of its underlying accounts of
cultural difference. In fact, thorough relativism suggests that our character-
izations of another culture say more about what we think valuable and less
about what it values.[17] The demand to respect another culture for its specifically different practices can, therefore, be portrayed as patronizing, smug,

and inherently parochial. Consistent relativism may even prompt one to look for ulterior motives in the advocacy of "cultural respect" and the right to be different. The imperative of noninterference when demanded by a culture that supposedly celebrates authoritarianism can seem a convenient tactic on the part elites to ward off international scrutiny.

If profound cultural differences rob us of a God's-eye view, they do so in terms of our ability to establish moral equivalence as well as moral hierarchy. And they leave untouched and in-place whatever practices a society engages in, even the practice of moral criticism. However, the entire frame of reference that sees culture in such monolithic terms, as so completely hegemonic, ought to be discarded if it can contribute so little to an understanding of cultural difference or intercultural moral criticism. If cultural differences exist, as surely they must, then perhaps they cannot be conceptualized as incommensurable differences. Rather, the problem may lie in our definition of culture and require moving from a semiotic to a more empiricist view, in which culture cannot claim hegemony over all facets of our mental life. An empiricistic approach sees culture as a collection of attitudes differentially subscribed to by different people, rather than a systematic perspective determining one's lived experience. Such a collection of attitudes or set of subjective beliefs, as a mere set, does not necessarily predetermine future beliefs or attitudes. If so, one's culture does not fully account for moral commitment, becoming even less a full justification for the beliefs one holds. Consequently, one cannot claim that disagreement *per se* across cultures has normative significance superior to what moral reflection can tell us, and in dealing with differences, we can move from regarding them as incommensurable to seeing them as dialogical. Differences are there to be articulated and understood, defended and criticized, but in no way as a trump against intercultural dialogue.

In short, once we detach normative significance from our understanding of culture, there is nothing to stop us from both comparing and comparatively evaluating the beliefs of different cultural groups. We may find on reflection, for example in the case of abortion where their seems to be widespread disagreement,[18] that one culture seems to have a more justifiable position or that the range of disagreement is correlated to nonmoral issues pertaining to abortion such as whether birth control is widely available or not. In this view, moral reflection is one thing, culture is another. Indeed, moral reflection itself could be seen as the province of only one or, more realistically, no culture—as beyond culture.

The gap between premise and conclusion in our initial relativist argument not only points to a need to loosen our account of culture but also offers the hope of moral convergence between cultures. Under an empiricist account of culture, present beliefs do not necessarily predict future beliefs so that the context-dependence of moral reflection does not foreclose encouraging a particular tradition in the direction of some widely accepted moral norms such as exist regarding human rights. Such norms can even make a meaningful contribution to the internal debates which are distinctive of a given culture, perhaps highlighting and supporting possibilities that were traditionally unrecognized. Thus, even if every culture were to embed different, even distinctive norms, values, or styles of reflection, we couldn't say those resources might not, each in its own way, establish moral universals. This is part of the point Charles Taylor makes when he speaks of an "unforced consensus" regarding human rights.[19]

If cultural divergence is the case, however, I think it probable that specifically moral norms, what we might call "emergent universals," will be what Joseph Margolis has called "second-best" moral principles (Margolis 1996:207ff). What he has in mind recalls Plato's distinction between knowledge and true belief. In the absence of an understanding of the forms, we are thrown back on the resources of true belief, opinions which reliably guide intuition but lack the certainty of knowledge.[20] For Margolis, who believes that all attempts at legitimation are contingent and historied, persuasive only when time and place are taken into account, our moral principles will invariably fall short of Plato's gold standard of certainty. Our second-best principles, then, will be those we think are most "projectible" in Nelson Goodman's sense or most worth "betting on" for their durability.[21] Needless to say, such principles will hardly be absolute or immune from modification or reinterpretation as circumstances change. No moral principle will be more than *prima facie* valid.[22]

However, the secondary status of such projectible norms need not compromise their universality. As increasingly more inclusive conversations between world cultures (or their representatives) take place, there is no a priori reason to think that some incipient universals which represent our collective bet wouldn't emerge. If these conversations are carried out at the appropriate level of principle there is every reason to think that such emergent norms might anchor deeply in the moral resources of the separate traditions. If human rights are such emergent norms, then we can see them as humanity's (with some exceptions duly noted) collective bet regarding what is projectible at the level of moral principle. That is, "universal" need not mean defensible by an absolutely correct form of rational reflection ("best principles") but defensible by all current standards or versions of moral reflection ("second-best"). Universal in the sense still means that moral principles are judged by their performance under moral criticism and not by the mere fact of consensus. However, this is not to prejudge what standards now govern moral criticism or will in the future.[23]

Cultures Are Neither Fully Commensurable Nor Fully Incommensurable

Let us consider what follows from a third assumption: Cultures may share significant customs, mores, or values, similar patterns of development, family life, political structures, and so on. However, one cannot say that there is a uniform pattern of cultural particulars or a convergence of attitudes or beliefs. In many ways this seems the most realistic option for conceptualizing intercultural relations. The normative question becomes: to what degree does a possible overlap of cultural beliefs or values suggest a degree of consensus which ought to be given moral legitimacy? If all cultures seem to value some version of at least some individual rights, does this lend moral weight to the cause of universality?

Of course, there are interpretive questions to begin with regarding the nature of such overlaps. For example, though at first glance rights may seem to be a concept embedded in a wide variety of cultural contexts, one can question the univocity of the term. Apart from problems of linguistic translation, are rights as understood from extrapolation in a Chinese Confucian context in any way *significantly* similar to rights understood in the context of the French or American Revolutions? When is an overlap really a "fusion of horizons" rather than the overlaying of one horizon on another or the eclipse of one horizon in another?[24] But assuming such hermeneutic difficulties can be overcome or set aside, there remains the question of relevance. As we noticed in the case of complete or radical commensurability or translatability, the fact of consensus is not necessarily of normative significance. Contesting the results of consensus is hardly out of the question, and it is hard to discern a moral imperative that confers the moral legitimacy that consensus builders seek.

Nor again, do the failures of overlap assume any particular normative significance. Just because there are aspects of U.S. culture or Malaysian culture which other cultures resist doesn't of itself delegitimize such characteristics (or legitimize them either). In short, whatever difficulties attach to the previous two positions, that cultures are fully comparable and that cultures are completely incomparable also attach to the middle ground that cultures are both commensurable and incommensurable.

ii

The main lesson of our discussion so far is that culture is one thing and distinctively *moral* values another. That is, those prescriptive values that can command our adherence no matter our particular circumstances are in principle inoculated from the vicissitudes of culture. However, one must concede the present lack of any agreed upon and descriptively universal norms. If the Asian values debate exposes anything, it is disagreement over what the "universal" in documents such as the Universal Declaration of Human Rights means. Some evidently do not view universal human rights as universally accepted by all peoples; universal simply means internationally recognized or recognized in international forums. If there are descriptive universal norms, we evidently haven't found them yet. I have argued that this proves little regarding the possibility of prescriptively universal principles, though they will in all probability be "second-best" in the sense discussed previously. Nonetheless, the range of philosophical thinking over the world's traditions is rich and complex enough that, given the state of comparative philosophy, relativism jumps the gun on this issue.

At the same time that I have maintained the conceptual independence of morality and culture, I have paradoxically argued that comparative cultural study, "the erudite games of scholars" as Kausikan calls them, are important to the development of universal moral norms. It is paradoxical because the independence of moral discourse seems to diminish the importance of studying the actual norms of existing cultures or societies. What moral importance can these norms have?

To insist on the principled independence of moral norms seems to suggest that they hail from the "view from nowhere" which requires transcendence beyond the specific assumptions of one's home culture.[25] However, even if moral value hails from nowhere, the role of cultural interpretation remains undiminished. To say that values hail from nowhere cannot mean that they are God-given absolutes. It simply means that they are accessible to reflection and buttressed by rational justification where reflection and justification necessarily entail some intersubjective process of interpersonal deliberation at the widest practicable level. The fact that no moral principles or intuitions have ever been wholly immune to challenge and critical reflection whether within or across cultural contexts supports this sort of consensus model. The fact that we aim for inclusive dialogue and open mindedness regarding the range of eligible justifications, styles of reflection, and so on suggests an unwillingness to close off the process or accept a particular set of circumstances such as history, culture, position, or power as definitive with regard to these issues. That is, the Rawlsian picture of a dynamic "reflective equilibrium" sustained by a fully open process of deliberation or perhaps a Habermasian ideal conversation represents the most defensible "view from nowhere" conception of moral universalism, and both attempt to define a just procedure for handling differences rather than dictating what sorts of solutions should result.

Such a vision of moral consensus makes no claim that the actual process of moral reflection and the operative concepts in which one articulates moral issues conform to some single, substantive model. Presumably, it allows for a wide, although not infinite, variety of styles of ethical reflection perhaps corresponding to the world's intellectual or religious traditions. Universalist aspirations, in this case, mainly have to do with the expectation of convergence as a result of dialogical interchange. Reflective equilibrium is consensus model, but as such it depends heavily on the possibility of genuine dialogue, with cross-talk being the ever-present danger. In fact, real-life exchanges of this sort more often than not do degenerate into such mutual misunderstanding. Therefore, a strong role for cultural interpretation is suggested in the need and desire to avoid this problem. Only through "erudite" interpretation is any clarity possible, and only through this process is genuine consensus possible. I suppose the model might be that of simultaneous interpretation in a manner analogous to simultaneous translation, although the former is certainly infinitely more complicated and subject to controversy than the latter.

There is another role for cultural interpretation with the nowhere view of morality. Since all moral codes and justificatory strategies arise in some cultural context or other, none of them can claim exclusively to represent moral universals. In regard to Western moral codes, whatever is universal is not exclusively Western. However, that is not to say that Westerners will understand other cultural instantiations of such universal values. In fact, clarity about what is really or genuinely universal may require such alternative exposure. Furthermore, the way in which Westerners have instantiated moral universals need not provide a guide to other cultures. Erudite interpretation may be needed in order to understand and participate in the process of moral universalization.

As an example, one need only consider the claim that Buddhist moral principles ground a strong commitment to universal human rights without invoking atomistic views of the self commonly attributed to Western secular humanism.[26] Generally, Buddhism is unique in world religions in its understanding of the self. In contrast to Hinduism's *atman* or Christianity's soul, Buddhism understands individual identity as built upon no foundation. Instead of a unifying element that becomes the bearer of eternal life, Buddhism understands the individual as a composite of five elements: the body, sense perception, thought, character, and consciousness.[27] As long as these elements remain associated in a specific context, there exists an individual or "person." Their dissociation represents the dissolution of the individual with no remainder. A more radical break with traditions that emphasize the divinity of human nature is difficult to imagine. However, Buddhism also emphasizes the radically individual nature of enlightenment. Only the individual can accomplish the breakthrough to nirvana. Therefore, even though traditional Buddhist religious life centers around following monkish rules and precepts and undergoing various ritual actions, it also involves one of the most individualized of teacher-novice relationships. The effective teacher can reach into the student's very perception of things and prompt the radical shifts of perspective that Buddhism demands. Not surprisingly, therefore, Buddhism stresses a form of religiously based compassion for the individual just as unique as its view of the self. This ideal culminates in the figure of the *Bodhisattva* who puts off his own Buddhahood to work for the enlightenment of all suffering and sentient being. In terms of human rights, many Buddhists, particularly "engaged" Buddhists, see this element of the tradition as translating into strong support for social justice and respect for the inviolability of individual conscience. In this regard, it's worth noting that much advocacy on behalf of the rights of man in the eighteenth century was based on a similar interest in protecting the freedom to worship in accord with one's conscience.[28] The version of freedom of conscience many Buddhists hold is also linked to the traditional rights of freedom of speech and association required for the practice and spread of enlightenment.

One should realize that such a picture of a Buddhist understanding of universal human rights is controversial even within Buddhism itself. And it is not altogether clear that Buddhism would support the whole range of rights that are ratified in the various international conventions governing human rights. Nor would Buddhism ground all the rights associated with liberal societies such as the United States. For example, many Buddhists consider abortion to be inconsistent with Buddhist values.[29] But if my *prima facie* case for a Buddhist defense of universal human rights is at all plausible, then one cannot say that Western instantiations of moral universals, especially rights, are the only or best way to ground and articulate a defensible moral universalism.

So far, I've been considering the issue of moral consensus under the assumption that moral codes do and will continue to vary from culture to culture. However, there is evidence of some degree of convergence with regard to values and norms, across the world's peoples.[30] Indeed, I have argued that some form of normative convergence is certainly possible. Should the process of dialogue and intercultural exchange actually foster such convergence? Must such consensus be entitled to moral approval? Is there still an important place for comparative cultural analysis? Does it have anything significant to add to this sort of emerging moral agreement?

In regard to these questions, our reflections on the normative implications of culture have a direct bearing. Though there may be a discernible and statistically significant trend the world over toward increasing interest in "postmodern" quality of life issues and an increasing tolerance of individually assertive behavior, for example rising divorce rates, it doesn't follow that such a trend is the right way to go. As we saw with the commensurability of cultures argument, such facts of consensus do not disable moral criticism. Furthermore, critical evaluation of such trends will inevitably be a very erudite process indeed, involving sustained consideration of the basic norms of developing societies. As Ronald Inglehart points out in his study of postmodernizing societies (Inglehart 1997), culture counts for more not less in determining attitudes and individual choices. Since economic conditions of scarcity no longer apply in these societies, the need for a purely instrumental rationality bent on material acquisition has diminished. His findings are that it is replaced by an interest in making life meaningful, expanding the range of individual choice, or what he calls "value rationality" (Inglehart 1997:65).

Criticism and dialogue over the standards governing such value rationality will engage issues of culture and interpretation more and not less as post-modernization unfolds.

Endnotes

1. See Kausikan 1993. This view is widespread among Asian leaders, particularly Singapore's Lee Kuan Yew or Malaysia's Mahathir and is sometimes linked to a political doctrine known as "soft authoritarianism." See Fareed Zakaria 1994. While the evidence for the cultural embeddedness of Kausikan's views seems equivocal, David Hitchcock, in his interviews with Asian elites, did detect a general tendency to downplay issues of human rights and to view some rights as more universal than others. See David Hitchcock 1994.
2. See Aryeh Neier 1993 or for a more temperate argument see Yash Ghai 1994.
3. Yash Ghai 1994, also makes this point. But a particularly strong set of arguments to this effect can be found in the collection edited by Irene Bloom, J. Paul Martin, and Wayne L. Proudfoot (Bloom et al. 1996).
4. See Norani Othman, "Grounding Human Rights Arguments in Non-Western Culture: Shari'a and the Citizenship rights of Women in a Modern Islamic Nation-State," in Bauer and Bell, eds. (1999). Othman sets out to combat the literalism of Islamic fundamentalism by showing how a "civilization of modernity" can be "based on [the] cultural and ethical foundations of Islam" (41). While I agree with her views and am sympathetic to the project, I don't think every Muslim would share the goal of cultural modernization. Does such a goal itself spring from specifically Islamic fundamentals?
5. Bilihari Kausikan has made this point more emphatically in informal discussion than in published remarks. But see Bilihari Kausikan 1995, 1997.
6. See Charles Taylor, "Conditions of an Unforced Consensus on Human Rights," in Bauer and Bell (1999). Taylor argues that an unforced consensus requires that individual parties to consensus find deep-level reasons for agreement, although they need not be the same reasons.
7. See, for example, Kishore Mahbubani 1993 and 1995. For the case that values are relative to civilization see Samuel P. Huntington 1993.
8. For some examples of the "positivist" approach to culture in the literature of political science see Ronald Inglehart (Inglehart 1997:15); Alex Inkeles 1997; also following Almond and Verba's survey approach to political culture, Andrew J. Nathan and Tianjian Shi 1993.
9. See Margolis's account of moral realism, particularly his discussion of the work of Mark Platts and Sabina Lovibond (Margolis 1996:158–171) where he argues, as I will, against conflating cultural consensus with prescriptively valid moral universalism.

10. See Fleischacker 1994:11. He cites the natural law theories of John Finnis and Terry Nardin.

11. This doctrine is variously labeled textualism or historicism by Margolis (1996). See also Robert D'Amico 1988.

12. See Will Kymlicka 1993, entitled "Some Questions about Justice and Community."?

13. See Richard Rorty 1983. Also, more recently "Justice as a Larger Loyalty," in Bontekoe and Stepaniants 1997.

14. See Bernard Williams's discussion of relativism in the chapter "Relativism and Reflection" in Williams 1985.

15. This a widely endorsed criticism that ultimately derives from Plato's *Protagoras* but most recently from Donald Davidson. See his "On the Very Idea of Conceptual Scheme" in Davidson 1984. For a criticism of the realist implications of Davidson's thesis see Margolis 1996:160–161. Margolis's complaint is essentially that even if one accepts Davidson's general claim that our sentences are representative *en bloc* of the way the world is, this confers no privileged status on any particular sentence or belief. Thus, correspondence with reality can never provide specific truth conditions for specific truth claims. Rather, truth conditions are a function of conceptual or interpretive particulars of history and context.

16. Williams makes a somewhat similar point in his distinction between "notional" as opposed to "real" divergence in moral outlook. "An outlook is a real option for a group either if it already is their outlook or they could go over to it; and they could go over to it if they could live inside it in their actual historical circumstances and retain their hold on reality, not engage in extensive self-deception, and so on" (Williams 1985:160–161). I am arguing that for the moral force of another's point of view to be clear *to us*, it must reflect such a "real" or "live" option for us. We must be able to connect with its moral language.

17. I take these to be the central features of what Edward Said calls "orientalism" in his book of the same title (Said 1978).

18. There is a large literature on this subject which reveals dissensus within and across societies. For a wide-ranging survey of this issue see Lucinda Joy Peach, "Reproductive Rights as Human Rights: the Influence of Religion on Women's Rights in Cross-Cultural Perspective." For a thorough and fascinating look at Japan in particular see William R. LaFleur 1992. For a general argument against abortion from the perspective of Buddhism, see Damien Keown 1995, especially chapter 2.

19. Charles Taylor in Bauer and Bell (see note 4). Hints of this vision of consensus, inspired by Gadamer's notion of a "fusion of horizons" can also be found in "Comparison, History, Truth" in Taylor 1995, chapter 8.

20. See Plato's discussion of true belief at the conclusion of the *Meno*.

21. See Nelson Goodman 1978:125ff for an application of projectibility with regard to predicates to the "rightness of a categorial system." Categorial systems, in Goodman's view, cannot be justified by appeals to truth or reality but to "its efficacy in worldmaking and understanding." Such criteria are also applied to moral systems, see especially Fleischacker 1994:34–46.

22. Where I differ with Margolis in his advocacy of a second-best morality is in his view that no universalism can be compatible with a commitment to historicism. See Margolis 1985:chapter 2. My argument is that historicism, in the sense that all standards of truth and rationality are ultimately historical in origin, does not of itself predetermine or limit their projectibility.

23. However, as Gadamer (1975) has pointed out, moral principles and standards of criticism will tend to reflect the weight of tradition because criticism and innovation will always have a background reference point, will always be in dialogue with the past and the other.

24. This is a specific criticism of applying Gadamer's notion to the problem of establishing consensus. Charles Taylor, as noted above (note 19), utilizes this idea but so does Richard Bernstein (1985), see especially Part Four, "From Hermeneutics to Practice."

25. I owe this conception to Thomas Nagel's book *The View From Nowhere* (1986) in which he describes this point of view in terms of the "objective self" which is centerless. Though an adequate explanation is beyond the scope of this essay, I believe I share the same approach to moral language and practical rationality.

26. This a position often associated with "engaged Buddhism" and its various advocates, such as the Thai intellectual Sulak Sivaraksa. See Queen and King 1996.

27. This is the well-known *skandha* theory of human compositeness. I am incorporating Damien Keown's interpretation of each of the five *skandhas*. See Keown 1995:23–26.

28. See David Little, Abdulaziz Sachedina, and John Kelsay's article "Human rights and the World's Religions: Christianity, Islam, and Religious Liberty" in Bloom et al 1996:213–239.

29. See Keown 1995, Chapters 2 and 3.

30. This is the general conclusion of Ronald Inglehart's studies of world values (Inglehart 1997). Inglehart argues that the transformation in values and attitudes that is taking place and which he labels "postmodernization" is making the world increasingly hospitable to democracy. See especially chapter 1, "Value Systems: the Subjective Aspect of Politics and Economics."

Bibliography

An-Na'im, Abdullahi A. 1992. "Towards a Cross-Cultural Approach to Defining International Standards of Human Rights." In *Human Rights in Cross Cultural*

66 MICHAEL G. BARNHART

Perspectives: A Quest for Consensus, ed. An Na'im, Abdullahi. Philadelphia: University of Pennsylvania Press.

Bauer, Joanne R. and Daniel A. Bell, eds. 1999. *The East Asian Challenge for Human Rights*. Cambridge: Cambridge University Press.

Bernstein, Richard J. 1985. *Beyond Objectivism and Relativism: Science, Hermeneutics, and Praxis*. Philadelphia: University of Pennsylvania Press.

Bloom, Irene, J. Paul Martin, and Wayne L. Proudfoot, eds. 1996. *Religious Diversity and Human Rights*. New York: Columbia University Press.

D'Amico, Robert. 1988. "Relativism and Conceptual Schemes." *Philosophy of the Social Sciences* 18 (2) (June):201–212.

Davidson, Donald. 1984. "On the Very Idea of a Conceptual Scheme." In Davidson, *Inquiries into Truth and Interpretation*, 183–198. Oxford: Oxford University Press.

Donnelly, Jack. 1989. *Universal Human Rights in Theory and Practice*. Ithaca, New York: Cornell University Press.

Fleischacker, Samuel. 1994. *The Ethics of Culture*. Ithaca, New York: Cornell University Press.

Gadamer, Hans-Georg. 1975. *Truth and Method*. New York: Seabury Press.

Geertz, Clifford. 1973. *The Interpretation of Cultures: Selected Essays*. New York: Basic Books.

Ghai, Yash. 1994. "Human rights and Governance: The Asia Debate." Occasional Paper 4. The Asia Foundation's Center for Asian Pacific Affairs (November).

Goodman, Nelson. 1978. *Ways of Worldmaking*. Indianapolis: Hackett Publishing Co.

Hitchcock, David. 1994. *Asian Values and the United States: How Much Conflict?* The Center for Strategic and International Studies.

Huntington, Samuel P. 1993. "'The Clash of Civilizations'" *Foreign Affairs* 72 (3) (Summer):22–49.

Inglehart, Ronald. 1997. *Modernization and Postmodernization: Cultural, Economic, and Political Change in 43 Societies*. Princeton: Princeton University Press.

Inkeles, Alex. 1997. *National Character: A Psycho-Social Perspective*. New Brunswick: Transaction Publishers.

Kausikan, Bilhari. 1997. "Governance That Works." *Journal of Democracy* 8 (2) (April):24–33.

———. 1995. "An East Asian Approach to Human Rights." *Buffalo Journal of International Law* 2 (2) (Winter):263–283.

———. 1993. "Asia's Different Standard." *Foreign Policy* (Fall):24–41.

Keown, Damien. 1995. *Buddhism and Bioethics*. New York: St. Martin's Press.

Kymlicka, Will. 1993. In *Communitarianism and its Critics*, ed. Daniel Bell. Oxford: Oxford University Press.

LaFleur, William R. 1992. *Liquid Life: Abortion and Buddhism in Japan*. Princeton: Princeton University Press.

Mahbubani, Kishore. 1995. "The Pacific Way." *Foreign Affairs* (January/February): 100–111.

———. 1993. "The Dangers of Decadence: What the Rest Can Teach the West." *Foreign Affairs* (September/October):10–14.

Margolis, Joseph. 1996. *Life Without Principles: Reconciling Theory and Practice.* Cambridge: Blackwell Publishers.

———. 1985. *Pragmatism Without Foundations: Reconciling Realism and Relativism.* Oxford: Basil Blackwell.

Nagel, Thomas. 1986. *The View From Nowhere.* Oxford: Oxford University Press.

Nathan, Andrew J. and Tianjian Shi. 1993. "Cultural Requisites for Democracy in China: Findings from a Survey." *Daedulus* 122 (2) (Spring):95–123.

Neier, Aryeh. 1993. "Asia's Unacceptable Standard." *Foreign Policy* (Fall):42–51.

Queen, Christopher S. and Sallie B. King, eds. 1996. *Engaged Buddhism: Buddhist Liberation Movements in Asia.* Albany: State University of New York Press.

Rorty, Richard. 1997. "Justice as a Larger Loyalty." In Ron Bontekoe and Marietta Stepaniants, eds., *Justice and Democracy: Cross-Cultural Perspectives,* 9–22. Honolulu: University of Hawaii Press.

———. 1983. "Postmodernist Bourgeois Liberalism." *The Journal of Philosophy* 80 (10) (October):583–589.

Said, Edward. 1978. *Orientalism.* New York: Vintage Books.

Taylor, Charles. 1995. *Philosophical Arguments.* Cambridge: Harvard University Press.

Williams, Bernard. 1985. *Ethics and the Limits of Philosophy.* Cambridge: Harvard University Press.

Zakaria, Fareed. 1994. "Culture is Destiny." *Foreign Affairs* (March/April):109–126.

3 Western Defensiveness and the Defense of Rights

A Communitarian Alternative

Kenneth E. Morris

If the response of the human rights community to the "Asian values" debate is a reliable indicator, human rights are in more trouble than is generally recognized. For striking about this response was its failure to make a positive case for rights. "Liberal critics . . . devoted their efforts to refuting Asian states' claims," notes Joseph Chan (1996), instead of "substantiating and determining the scope of international human rights law." So, for example, Sharon Hom's (1996) rebuttal to Singapore apologist Bilahari Kausikan (1993, 1995–96, 1997) fails to mention that a positive case for rights might also be made. Or Charles Taylor (1999) urges rights proponents to make their case by seeking values similar to their own in other cultural traditions because he concedes that a universal claim for rights cannot be made across cultures. Even Chan, although obviously sensitive to the problem of a human rights community cornered into a defensive position, adopts a similar stance in his work. Calling for a "search for a political morality" that can promote "human rights norms in Asia," he does not say why rights are good in the first place. That good is simply presupposed.

The mushrooming numbers of NGOs and human rights activists who have been quick to reassert their position in response to the Asian challenge suggest that Chan overstates the defensiveness of the human rights community. Yet, busy activism may not signal rational assurance. As one critic of rights charged more than a century ago, many rights proponents seem to hold their beliefs "as a religious faith" and "truths . . . to do battle for" rather than as rational convictions (Stephen 1967 [1873]). Nor does the activists' affirmative of rights under the guise of the "positive law" of international document signal rational certainty. Proponents of "Asian values" were not challenging the existence of international human rights law or even its binding character, but its moral and philosophical foundation. Responses in terms of "positive law" dodge this challenge.

Recent philosophical justifications of rights also typically fail to support the absolute positions many activists promote. Ronald Dworkin's (1978) work may come the closest, but even it is replete with qualifications. John Rawls's work—at least since A *Theory of Justice* (1971)—is however less useful. Rawls now asks to avoid "claims to universal truth, or claims about the essential nature and identity of persons" (1985:223) in favor of a more modest "moral conception worked out for a specific subject, namely, the basic structure of a constitutional democratic regime" (1988:252). This conception of justice obviously cannot be transposed to other "subjects" in Asia. Even Jack Donnelly (1989), who takes up the challenge of defending rights across cultures, abdicates at the outset. In the same introductory paragraph in which he declares that human rights are the "highest moral rights" and "hold 'universally' against all other persons and institutions," he concedes that this only applies "in ordinary circumstances." Since the gist of the "Asian values" challenge has been the claim that rights are relative to cultural circumstances, it is difficult to understand how this kind of immediately qualified case for rights answers the challenge.

The reticence of rights proponents when confronted by the "Asian values" challenge, coupled with the weak contemporary philosophical defense of rights, suggests that something is seriously amiss in the rights agenda. This is the conjecture I want to explore in the initial portions of this chapter. Specifically, I want to remind rights advocates that long before the "Asian values" debate erupted Western intellectual traditions had themselves leveled similar criticisms of human rights. These criticisms have yet to be adequately answered by the proponents of rights and therefore continue to resurface, particularly in contemporary communitarianism. My thesis will then be that only by squarely confronting these criticisms can a confident— albeit more modest—rights agenda be affirmed. Later portions of the chapter are devoted to this confrontation.

The Western Critique of Rights

In an essay on "The Permanent Structure of Antiliberal Thought," Stephen Holmes (1989) identifies fully twenty major recurring Western objections to liberalism, and so to human rights. The objections, while often substantively similar, come from a wide array of philosophical traditions. Thus, while Jeremy Bentham's (1987 [1843]) notion of human rights as "nonsense upon stilts" is perhaps the most cited of all Western anti-rights aphorisms, objections to rights arise from within conservatism and Marxism as well as Bentham's utilitarianism, and were of course a cornerstone of fascist ideology too (see also Waldron 1987).

Despite this array of criticisms (and at some risk of oversimplification), the major criticisms can be grouped into two main categories, the ontological and the teleological. Further, while diverse thinkers have advanced ontological criticisms of rights, the conservative tradition can perhaps best serve as a template for the teleological criticism. This is so because conservative critics have generally been more articulate and forceful in their criticisms than others. Michael Freeman (1996) even concludes that "almost all of the values said to be 'Asian,' are similar to conservative Western values." Although this may be an overstatement, any summary of the teleological critique of rights should probably emphasize the conservative tradition—which of course also advances the ontological critique.

The Ontological Critique

The ontological critique states that rights do not actually exist except by social convention. Most serious critics of rights embrace this critique and assert that there is neither evidence of persons possessing these rights in nature nor any plausible reason for imagining them this way.

Consider what the champions of human rights believe them to be (Donnelly 1989:12–14). Human rights are a "special class of rights" that individuals possesses simply because they are "human." They are "extralegal" in that they exist prior to and even in defiance of the state and other social institutions. They are derived from the fundamental equality of persons. Indeed, society (including the state) is understood to be at least an implicit contract among rights-bearing persons legitimated primarily on the grounds that is the insurer of rights.

The case against this notion of rights was first and most famously made by David Hume (1997 [1748]). To the advocates of rights, Hume simply asked: Where is the evidence? For him John Locke's notion "that government in its earliest infancy arose from consent or rather the voluntary acquiescence of the people" is at most a plausible conjecture. But Locke's further insistence that "even at present" government "rests on no other foundation" is contradicted by all available evidence. "Almost all governments, which exist at present, or of which there remains any record in story," observed Hume, "have been founded originally, either on usurpation or conquest, or both, without any pretense of fair consent, or voluntary subjection of the people." Hume adds that "when a new government is established, by whatever means, the people are commonly dissatisfied with it, and pay obedience more from fear and necessity, than from any idea of allegiance or of moral obligation." Nevertheless, "everywhere" one finds "princes, who claim their subjects as their property," and "subjects, who acknowledge this right in their prince." To have thought otherwise in most societies would have been to run the risk of having "your friends . . . shut you up as delirious."

Hume's critique of rights thus rests upon empirical evidence. Since the record of human history reveals little or no evidence of natural human rights, the original equality from which they are thought to spring, or the contractual society and state, Hume dismisses these notions as pure fancy. "So refined and philosophical a system," he writes, "corresponds" to "nothing" in "the world."

From Hume there stretches an almost unbroken line of thought—generally regarded as conservative—which repeats his arguments. Edmund Burke (1986 [1790]) was perhaps the most famous of these challengers. His *Reflections on the Revolution in France*, often considered the classic work of the conservative tradition (Muller 1997; Nisbet 1978), was at base a strident attack on the notion of universal human rights founded in nature. Everywhere Burke looked he saw people not as possessors of abstract rights but as embedded in particular traditions, enmeshed in concrete attachments, obligated to others in reciprocal relationships. To conceive of persons as endowed with abstract rights of the sort that supersede their social attachments and obligations struck him as absurd and dangerous.

Complementing these conservative criticisms of rights ontology are the similar criticisms leveled by Jeremy Bentham and Karl Marx. For Bentham, rights as expressed in the French *Declaration of the Rights of Man* were literally nonsense. His point-for-point critique of that document was not so much a moral polemic as it was a logical and ontological critique of the rhetoric of rights (Bentham 1987 [1843]). The basis for Marx's criticism was similar. The "so-called rights of man," he writes, "are nothing but the rights of the member of civil society." This "egoistic man," or "man separated from other from other men and the community," derived not from any universal ontology but "from the relationship of the political state to civil society" in the bourgeois era (Marx 1987 [1844]).

Rights proponents have generally been willing to concede the empirical case against rights. But they consider the lack of evidence for rights to be beside the point. For them the truth of rights is ascertained not by appealing to the evidence of history but to the evidence of conscience. This conscience is—in good Kantian fashion—a priori, that is, it exists prior to experience and shapes experience. For many proponents of rights this moral logic is written into human hearts from the beginning. Ask rational human beings how they might ideally conceive of justice, the proponents say, and the answer given will correspond at least roughly to a notion of human rights. From this standpoint, the affirmation of rights is a normative posture that, by corresponding to a moral imperative embedded in the psyche, need not correspond to anything in the empirical world.

Of course, this defense of rights does not effectively counter the critics who deny it—since it amounts to simply positing an alternative epistemology and metaphysics. Perhaps for this reason, it is increasingly avoided even by many rights advocates who, like Rawls, advance it not as a universal moral position but merely as one consistent with the "intuitive ideas . . . latent in the public political culture of a democratic society" (1988:252). But such consistency is a far cry from the rationalist defense of rights, as Rawls acknowledges. It also opens the door to other, equally "intuitive" moral ideas, like those communitarians claim to discover by appealing to a "final position" (Bell 1993). In contrast to Rawls's "original position" in which autonomous individuals behind a "veil of ignorance" arrive at moral ideas, the "final position" asks that the reflections of persons on their deathbeds be considered the paradigmatic basis for morality. Since these reflections do not generally include the affirmation of any universal mo- rality—much less of rights—but rather focus on the continuity of the par- ticular communal traditions with which people have been associated, this exercise casts doubt on the value of even a heuristic rationalist defense of rights.[1]

A rationalist case for the ontology of rights of course remains available to those who wish to embrace one. But in the face of historic criticisms and contemporary doubts, the strategy is increasingly implausible.

The Teleological Critique

The teleological critique of rights criticizes the ends to which a rights-based morality leads. The paradigmatic expression of this critique may have been James Fitzjames Stephen's (1967 [1873]) rebuttal to John Stuart Mill's *On Liberty* (1977 [1854]), now regarded as one of the classics of conservative thought (Muller 1977).

A contemporary and admirer of Mill, Stephen read *On Liberty* sympathetically. "I am not the advocate of Slavery, Caste, and Hatred," Stephen writes, "nor do I deny that . . . Liberty . . . may be regarded as good." But sympathy gave way to criticism as Mill's "theories" of liberty struck Stephen as logically "unsound." Stephen's principal objection was that rights ("liberties" in Mill) cannot be "ends in themselves" since the ends to which they lead "do not typify, however vaguely, any state of society which a reasonable man ought to regard with enthusiasm or devotion." "All morality" and "all religion" operate not by respecting rights but by restricting them. It follows that "Mr. Mill's system is violated not only by every system of theology which concerns itself with morals" but also "by every known system of morality." Since "there is hardly a habit which men in general regard as good which is not acquired by a series of more or less painful and laborious acts," Stephen is compelled to ask, "Why, then, is liberty, defined as Mr. Mill defines it, to be regarded as so precious?"

This teleological criticism of rights has often been implied by those who decry the alleged licentiousness and social chaos of the societies that enshrine them. Lee Kuan Yew (Zakaria 1994) and Amitai Etzioni (1996) are two recent instances of this type of critic. But it is important not to confuse practical criticisms of rights-based societies with the theoretical rebuff. Practical criticisms are more easily countered by the proponents of rights who say, first, that the descriptions are vastly exaggerated and, second, that the cost of occasional excess is a price worth paying for liberty. The more serious criticism is that any philosophy which elevates rights to a supreme principle (i.e., as "trumps") confuses means with ends, and insofar as any society enacts this confusion it must necessarily become licentious and chaotic. Much of the fame accorded to Edmund Burke's (1986 [1790]) condemnation of the French Revolution came from his prediction of the chaos and tyranny that would follow the attempt to implement rights. He foresaw what Stephen also detected:the elevation of rights to moral ends can only destroy the moral and social fabric of a society.

The force of the teleological critique of rights is thus different from the ontological critique—and perhaps more devastating. For as Stephen shows with respect to Mill, if his moral system were to be realized it would deprive people of every system of meaning or morality beyond that of rights. But since people do desire to inhabit a social world in which meanings are at least in part hierarchically arranged and socially maintained, a society in which rights really were the highest moral good would be one in which inhabitants could lead only purposeless, anomic lives.[2]

To this criticism the proponent of rights has no effective rebuttal. After all, it merely casts a critical gaze on liberalism's affirmative case. The rationale for a liberal rights regime is that it is the best practical solution to a situation of moral pluralism. Because people disagree in their conceptions of the good (and following a century of religious warfare over such disagreements), liberalism arose as an alternative to authoritarian attempts to impose a moral scheme on dissenters. But by this very rationale the liberal must concede that rights are not the highest end, only a provisional means for reducing discord. Indeed, Mill himself does not claim that liberty is the highest good, only that it creates the conditions necessary for discovering those goods. But if this is true it amounts to conceding that rights are not in fact the highest good and can be "trumped" by even higher goods. The rights advocate is therefore caught in the awkward position of promoting a social ethic that, if successful, is ideally superseded. How then can this ethic be posited as the highest good?

Both Bentham and Marx reveal their essential sympathy with this teleological critique of rights indirectly by attempting to unmask what they propose to be the real ends lurking beneath the rhetoric of liberty. The "cry of rights," notes Bentham (1987 [1843]:73), arises when "a man has a political caprice to gratify . . . but can give no reason why it should be gratified." For Marx, the interpretation is a little more complex. "The freedom in question is that of a man treated as an isolated monad and withdrawn into himself" (Marx 1987 [1844]:146). In other words it is the "freedom" of alienated, bourgeois man suffering the effects of a society with a deeply distorted moral aim.

None of which is to say that proponents of rights in liberal regimes have no arguments to advance. They do. It is that in the absence of consensus about social goods rights-based liberalism may be the most peaceful arrangement possible. Even so, this case for rights concedes the teleological case against them: that rights of themselves are inadequate moral ends. Historically, therefore, this case has been most convincingly made only in very limited arenas, such as in certain restrictions on state interference with religion. But these instances do not show rights to be goods in themselves, only to be a plausible means for enabling people who disagree about goods to coexist in relative tranquillity. A glance at most contemporary liberal political theory (e.g., Rawls 1971; Gutman 1980) as well as many recent human rights documents (e.g. CEDAW) reveals that the impulse to promulgate rights has expanded well beyond these modest and pragmatic beginning compromises. Rights are no longer promoted as the means to other goods but as the highest goods themselves. In this way they are subject to the teleological critique.

Echoes of the Critique

Although many of the foregoing criticisms of rights have reappeared in the "Asian values" debate, it is worth noting that they have resurfaced in contemporary Western guises as well. (They have also generally been abandoned by conservatism, which has for the most part allied itself with a rights-based economic liberalism.) The two most important areas of this resurgence may be feminism and communitarianism.

Feminism arose in the West more or less in tandem with human rights and may be thought of as an instance of them. Nevertheless, some recent feminists have begun to question the appropriateness of a rights-based agenda for women. A main feminist critique is, as it has been historically, ontological and epistemological. Since Carol Gilligan's (1982) study of female moral development many have come to question the existence of an innate rationalist moral sense. They argue that the principled type of moral reasoning that underlies the assumption of universal human rights is typical of male morality but atypical of female moral reasoning. For women moral values like caring, sympathy, and relatedness take precedence over values like rights. Although the bulk of this literature focuses on substantive issues at a considerable remove from human rights, it does parallel ontological criticisms of rights by asserting that the same morality is not available to all persons simply by virtue of their humanity but is a constructed feature of social-psychological experience.

Whether based upon this epistemology or not,[3] some contemporary feminists proceed to echo the teleological criticism of rights. These feminists, sometimes called "difference theorists" (see, e.g., Rhode 1989), assert that the differences between women and men are such that the application of the same rights to both is inappropriate. To some the application of supposedly universal rights to women has the effect of undermining a specifically feminine way of being, while to others it is the impossibility of the sexes ever relating as equals that prohibits the indiscriminate application of the same moral principals to both (see, e.g., Cornell 1991, Dworkin 1987). Either way, the conclusion is the same. Women are conceived of as different from men and therefore entitled to different treatment; context—in this case gender—dictates morality.

If this branch of feminist thinking suggests the Asian argument that rights are relative to social context, it should. The arguments are formally identical, and both resurrect historic criticisms. The chapters by Lynda Bell and Lucinda Peach in this volume probe these affinities and their implications more fully, so here it can suffice simply to point out that some contemporary feminist thinking recalls the challenge to rights made by others in different contexts.

The other major contemporary movement to recall the historic criticisms of rights is the communitarians (see, e.g., Bell 1993; Etzioni 1993, 1996; Gutman 1985; Sandel 1981, 1996). They argue that persons are socially constituted or "encumbered" selves and so restate the ontological objection to rights, namely, that rights arise as a matter of social convention rather than nature.[4] Indeed, though not formally identified with the movement but a frequent philosophical source for those who are, Alisdair MacIntyre (1984) goes so far as to say that belief in human rights is on a par with belief in witches. Others in the school stress that the liberal view of autonomous individuals freely choosing their own ideals of the good life—so central to liberal doctrines of rights—is simply wrong. Individuals, they rather maintain, are socially constituted and thus "encumbered"—but hardly free.

Communitarians have also made much of the social chaos that has allegedly arisen as a consequence of the West's over-promotion of rights. Although their focus has been primarily on practical consequences rather than the rights-as-ends problem, the more theoretical criticism is sometimes broached. Thus Michael Sandel (1996) sharply criticizes what he calls the "procedural liberalism" of the U.S. This is the view that rights take precedence over all other substantive goods—a view that Sandel (echoing Stephen) tries and finds wanting.

Communitarians also draw upon another source of the criticism of rights in Western history: nineteenth-century republicanism. While neither republicanism nor an interpretation of the American as republican (rather than liberal) is essential to the communitarian argument, many draw from these sources to reinforce their social agenda.[5] Specifically, communitarians advance the argument that the United States was not founded on an ideology of rights-based liberalism but on republicanism, and did not become a decidedly rights-based liberal state until the turn of the twentieth century or so.[6] Until then rights were considered good, but neither an absolute nor the highest good. It was in fact widely acknowledged that rights could be enjoyed only in the context of a good society. Hence, the good brought by rights existed in relation to the good of society, with republicans believing that the two rose or fell together.

Whatever the historical reality of republicanism, it is used by communitarians to strike a blow against the idea that the modern state can be completely rights-based. Sandel (1996) for example asks how a rights-based state can handle religion. If it is completely neutral it must be secular. But from the standpoint of religion secularism is not neutral but anti-religion. Sandel (1996) and Bell (1993) also ask about gay marriage. If the state is neutral with respect to the life plans of its citizens as a theory of universal rights demands then it cannot prohibit gay marriage. But it cannot prohibit polygamy either, for that too involved the imposition of a moral judgment on citizens and so violates their rights. It ultimately follows that the state has no business involving itself at all in marriage. To this example Bell (1993) adds the problem of state subsidization of the arts. His question is on what grounds can the genuinely neutral rights-affirming state subsidize theater but not professional wrestling. Unless the state imposes a notion of good entertainment on the public, thus failing to respect its rights, it cannot.

Although there may be ways for the rights advocate to respond to these and similar criticisms,[7] recourse to a rights-based democracy may not be among them. As one of the most ardent contemporary republicans, Robert Bellah (1978), put the matter, a truly liberal state devolves into a parliamentary cacophony of self-interested voices and crisscrossing coalitions. What most Americans think of as a "democratic" solution to these problems is thus really a republican or communitarian solution—that is, one in which a substantial number of citizens devote themselves to a public good that transcends their own narrow interests. But to believe in a public good larger than the aggregation of individual rights is also to embrace a public philosophy larger than rights-based liberalism.

It is also interesting to note that both Sandel (1996) and Bellah (1978) single out religion as especially problematic from the standpoint of a rights-based liberal political philosophy. For it was in responding to the Wars of Religion following the Reformation that liberalism first arose triumphant. To find contemporary critics of liberalism challenging liberalism on just this substantive area is to suggest that the division between the camps is a wide one indeed.

Most of these communitarian critics of rights stop well short of endorsing the conservative label of their most articulate historic predecessors. Those most susceptible to the label even go to great lengths to reject it. Bell (1993) for example suggests a curious and not quite clear contrast between the "tradition" that he claims to favor and the "traditionalist" outlook of Edmund Burke. Regardless of the label, the ideas are familiar—and subject to the same criticisms.

A Critique of the Critique

Weaknesses in the rights camp do not mean that the opposing camp is strong. Actually, the critics of rights also confront two troublesome problems. One is that while the opponents of rights generally support a modest range of rights they give no reason for doing so. This weakness runs through the conservative tradition as well as its contemporary reincarnations. Edmund Burke may well have been a supporter of both the English and American revolutions as well as an Irish sympathizer, and he may thus have opposed the French Revolution not so much because he opposed all rights but because he feared their wholesale celebration at the expense of other goods (see, e.g., O'Brien 1986). Indeed, he writes that liberty "is good" (Burke 1986 [1790]). But why should Burke have favored any rights at all? His philosophy gives no reason for doing so. The same criticism applies to Stephen, who claimed to be no defender of caste or slavery, but who gave no reason for that position. It applies as well to feminist "difference theorists." Although they may be correct to reject the application of a universal scheme of rights to women and men, some notion of rights must underlie their feminist agenda. And the criticism applies especially to contemporary communitarians, who glibly accept the achievements of liberalism while calling for a "moratorium" on future rights (Etzioni 1993). By what rationale do they accept some (existing) rights but not other (future) rights?

All critics of rights do not succumb to this inconsistency,[8] but most do. Even those who avoid it, however, may still stumble over the apparent fact that something like a notion of human rights seems to appear as a moral maxim in many cultures. Thus, the Confucian principle of reciprocity and the Christian golden rule are each close enough approximations to Immanuel Kant's "categorical imperative" to prompt some observers to propose them as universal instances of rights-like morality. To be sure, the existence of such maxims is hardly evidence for the universality of rights, which if they have existed have also been more often violated than maintained in the several traditions that profess them. Yet, since most traditions uphold some notion of rights as goods, the burden falls on the critic to explain why this should be the case. But of course the burden weighs heavier on those who concede that rights are goods but give no justification for the concession.

This problem is also found among proponents of "Asian values." After arguing that the Western-style rights agenda is mistaken, Singapore's Kausikan (1993, 1995–96) declares that "the hard core of rights that are truly universal is smaller than many in the West are wont to pretend," and that "a focus on a more restricted but precise core of basic human rights . . . is a more productive approach." The question that he nowhere addresses, however, is by what rationale he concedes even a "hard" or "precise core" of human rights.[9]

This leads to the second criticism of most rights opponents: they offer no criteria for evaluating traditions. Since they clearly prefer traditions that are supportive of some rights, they are obviously willing to evaluate traditions by some external criteria of justice. But what are these criteria and from where do they arise, unless it is the very rationalist moral sense that they otherwise deny?

It is no out to suggest, as Walzer (1983) does, that some traditions are "deeper" and therefore more just than others. Nor can the problem be avoided by using what Bell (1993) calls "transitional arguments." (These are arguments that compare alternative cultural practices in order to choose the morally superior one.) Both strategies ultimately beg the question. Unless there is some criterion of justice independent of cultural practice it is impossible to decide which argument is "deeper" or which "transition" is superior to another (see, e.g., R. Dworkin, 1985). Once again, rights critics are forced into a rationalist corner if they wish to evaluate moral practices — which of course they do.

To these objections there are only two rejoinders. One is to plead ignorance. This is a main theme in the conservative tradition, and at least intellectually honest. Confronted with even an appealing philosophy—as most
conservatives believe some theory of rights is—the conservative tends to
worry that it might not work as expected because of unforeseen problems.
The tendency is to proceed with changes slowly lest they backfire and destroy
the goods already enjoyed. When the new idea strikes them from the start
as potentially problematic, conservatives are even less inclined to support its
implementation. The safest course is to continue with traditional ways since
the changes could be worse.

The other rejoinder is, obviously, to posit a notion of the good that can
be used to evaluate traditions. This is the strategy of Bentham and Marx—
as well as innumerable utopians throughout history. But of course by positing
a notion of the good, utopian theorists invite criticisms of their posits.

But neither rejoinder applies well to contemporary circumstances. The
world of the "Asian values" debate is hardly a static one in which, motivated
by prudence, the thoughtful leader can simply stay the conservative course.
It is rather a dynamic, ever-changing arena in which new states are born,
traditional cultures are overrun, and questions of rights or other criteria for
cultural evaluations are unavoidable. Moreover, neither feminists nor communitarians want to preserve the status quo. Whatever the value of prudence
in a more static world, it is neither an option nor normally an aim in our
world. But the utopian alternative—a society in which there is agreement
on a good that transcends rights—is hardly foreseeable either. Fukuyama
(1992) may have overstated the case for a globe bereft of alternatives to
capitalist liberalism, but few would want to return to the last time the West
experienced a serious threat to rights-based liberalism, the fascist era. Against
it liberalism prevailed for the same reasons it arose two centuries before: Not
because it was the most cogent philosophy, but because it was preferable to
the allegedly "utopian" alternative.

The strongest case for human rights, as well as for liberalism generally,
has long been this practical one: that it is superior to all alternatives. Yet it
is precisely against this case that the proponents of "Asian values" strike their
most decisive blow. For they arguably demonstrate what neither fascism nor
Marxism could, namely, that a more harmonious and prosperous society is
possible on the basis of an alternative moral philosophy.[10] To make a case
for human rights in this context requires more than a restatement of the
practical arguments. Required is rather a cogent, theoretical argument. If

such a case must be more measured than has been necessary historically, it is because the criticisms of it must now be taken into account. Even so, because the criticisms contain weaknesses too, a tempered affirmative argument can be advanced.

A Communitarian Theory of Rights

There is only one way that a theory of human rights can be reconciled with the main criticisms of them outlined above (that rights can neither be derived from a universal rationalist principle nor can stand as any society's highest good). It is to accept these criticisms as valid but to propose that more or less universal features of human experience nevertheless make a rights-like moral scheme available to people on occasions when they seek a moral alternative to their existing social traditions. If such an argument can be plausibly sketched it will address the weaknesses of the critics' accounts, namely, that they give no reason for supporting the rights they do support and that they fail to specify criteria for evaluating cultural traditions. Yet by emboldening them it will bring them closer to their opponents' camp. The result will not be a defense of rights as automatic trumps, but it will be the establishment of a framework for including rights as a criterion of justice in any discussion of cultural values. More importantly, the framework will be one that the critic of rights will be compelled to concede.

The opposite procedure—to begin with the affirmative case for human rights and then to temper it with an appreciation of cultural traditions— cannot produce the desired results. Rights advocates may want final moral authority and believe that it is available to them on a rationalist basis, but they have no rebuttal to those who simply deny the rationalist argument. Worse, even if the rationalist argument is accepted, rights activists have no way of explaining how so pristine a moral sense can lead to the more complex and contextualized notions of moral ends that humans everywhere posit. Although it is logically possible to begin by conceding the strong case for rights, the procedure stumbles into both snares of the critics and thus offers no avenue for reconciliation. Parsimony if not persuasion weigh in against this approach.

The first approach will therefore be pursued. It may be called communitarian because it builds upon the historic criticisms of rights generally endorsed by communitarians while answering their desire to support rights, but avoids the confusing connotations of other labels. Neo-conservative would fit equally well were the label not already taken (and many neo-conservatives not to have departed from the historic conservative critique of liberalism). Republican might also be used, but it risks raising confusions with the various tributaries of thought already coexisting within that tradition. Feminist is obviously too narrow. The communitarian label is therefore adopted.

The theory must begin by conceding the fundamental communitarian case: People are not primarily autonomous, rights-bearing selves, but the products and carriers of social traditions. The case should also be deepened. The traditions that mold people are unavoidably hierarchical, even necessarily coercive. They are hierarchical because, for a tradition to be meaningful, it must select from the array of possible values those that it will emphasize and so arrange them hierarchically. To value everything equally is to value nothing in particular. Then, since social traditions are not simply abstract ideas but lived social practices, the arrangement of values requires that normal social roles and institutions express them. In other words, the society must be hierarchical in ways that express and embody the group's values. Because of this hierarchy of both values and social practices, coercion—or what might appear to be coercion from the standpoint of those outside of or simply disaffected with the tradition—is unavoidable. "Coercion" is of course a strong word and no argument is here advanced that it must be especially brutal or onerous. But it does no good to pretend that a meaningful social order can avoid denying some individuals certain liberties in some situations. If people are to be socialized to embrace their culture and to socialize others to that embrace, they must be molded and mold others to it. Although this might more politely be called "education" rather than "coercion," short of the postulate that education appeals to a metaphysical logos which coercion may violate (the sort of rationalist supposition rejected here) the two are the same thing.

According to this view of persons and cultures people conceive as their highest good as participating meaningfully in and maintaining their hierarchical society. How then does a notion of rights arise—and with it the ability to criticize one's culture? The answer lies in two universal experiences: the norm of reciprocity and the idea of human equality.

The norm of reciprocity is thought to be universal (Gouldner 1960). Although it may therefore suggest rationalist foundations, inferring these is unnecessary. The pioneering theorist of the emergence of rationalist-like

qualities of thought from social experience is probably Emile Durkheim
(1965 [1917]), whose student and nephew, Marcel Mauss (1967), extended
the approach to the analysis of exchange relations. To Mauss as for later
generations of theorists, something like a norm of reciprocity is a universal
feature of social life even though it need not be derived from a priori mental
categories.

By itself, however, the norm of reciprocity cannot account for human
rights. Although the norm does dictate that interactions proceed according
to a moral logic of equivalence, which is a notion akin to rights, it typically
operates in morally structured contexts in which the exchanging participants
seek equity only according to predetermined roles. So, for example, reciprocity may govern relationships between ruler and subject, men and
women, or father and son—none of which in most contexts presume equal
rights. Indeed, certain displays of authority and deference may be considered
reciprocal insofar as the participants are fulfilling role obligations more or
less predetermined by their society. Conversely, the assertion of a universal
right by either party may actually reflect a breakdown of reciprocity—a violation of the norm—insofar as it represents a rejection of more widely
shared moral ideas about the appropriate ranking of various persons and
their mutual obligations.

However, if the norm of reciprocity is coupled with a belief in the equality
of the interacting parties, it will result in a rights-like idea of justice. Since
neither of the interacting parties in cases of equality are defined by social
circumstances to be superior or inferior to the other, the only moral criterion
to which they can appeal is the norm of reciprocity itself. But in a condition
of equality, reciprocity is but another way of saying human rights. That is,
both parties have exactly the same social privileges and social obligations as
the other, so each is obligated to treat the other as he or she expects to be
treated.

This reasoning is consistent with the usual liberal argument that the idea
of rights presupposes a notion of equality (e.g., R. Dworkin 1978). However,
most liberal inferences about the basis for notions of human equality are too
ambitious for the communitarian. Any posit of a rationalist basis for equality
is of course suspect. But even the conjecture that humans arrive at a notion
of equality by crediting one another with the "dignity" that attends each
person's need to fashion a meaningful life is overly optimistic. This kind of
conjecture smacks of a reified concept of the person that a communitarian
must deny even as it presupposes what it purports to explain. In order to

credit another with this kind of dignity, it must be assumed that persons everywhere struggle to fashion a meaningful life and recognize that others do as well. But the bulk of humanity—even the bulk of humanity in liberal societies—probably does not think of life's meaning this way. Surely most think of it as socially given rather than individually chosen. Even in the rare situations in which life's meaning does arise as an individual problem, the awareness of that problem does not by itself explain why people would be prompted to grant dignity to others for confronting it too. That extension of dignity to others presupposes universal experiences of fellow-feeling that incline persons to sympathize with one another.

The better basis for a notion of human equality may therefore be found in certain common experiences of fellow-feeling. Hobbes's (1958 [1651]) thesis that the common fear of death is such a leveler comes immediately to mind, although Mencius's (1963) belief in the universal capacity for sympathy also suffices. The important point is that equality be understood to be based upon certain experiences that really are universal—not merely rationalist posits or heuristic inferences. Since all people are cognizant of death and can empathize with suffering, such experiences may therefore be said to be universal. Based upon them (and perhaps others) a rudimentary notion of equality can be plausibly posited.

Although such experiential bases for equality are plausible and under most circumstances may be operative, they may be too weak to generate a rights conviction by themselves. It is not clear, for instance, that a Hobbesian fear of death is a sufficient basis for a belief in equality sturdy enough to support human rights. History provides too many examples of both murder and suicide justified by social values to believe that it is. The reservation is similar for Mencian compassion. Surely suffering may sometimes elicit the requisite fellow-feeling for a notion of equality to develop, but just as surely it does not uniformly do so. Again, history offers countless examples of indifference to and even infliction of suffering upon others. Enemies and oppressors may "dehumanize" their victims before inflicting harm on them—the literature on atrocities suggests they do—but history shows that this is a process that is accomplished fairly routinely. It also merits mention that neither Hobbes nor Mencius developed theories of human rights based upon their posits of fellow-feeling.

Therefore, while it is plausible to conjecture that some and perhaps most people across cultures develop ideas of human equality based upon fellow-feeling, in themselves these experiences do not suffice to establish the convictions firmly. The problem, as Max Scheler (1954 [1912]) notes, is that the persons expected to make these moral judgments are themselves socially constituted. Looking inward, they see their society and its hierarchical values. These values trump the appeal of equality, although it remains an accessible experience.

To translate common experiences into a norm of equality sturdy enough to support rights therefore requires a social value conducive to doing so. The question is: Under what conditions might such a value arise? The easiest answer is when people find it to their advantage to cooperate across cultural boundaries, that is, where they agree to disagree. Such conditions may arise in postmodern societies where individuals struggle for personal meaning, sympathize with others they assume to be similarly struggling, and thus arrive at a rough notion of the liberal right to fashion one's own life plans unhampered by others. But not too much should be made out of a scenario like this one, which either reifies the concept of persons by stripping them of their cultural moorings or describes a situation in which cultural constructions of personhood themselves paradoxically create this image of the existentially autonomous person. Better scenarios are those in which persons do understand themselves to be culturally constituted adherents of particularistic values, but also desire to cooperate across cultural boundaries for specific, limited purposes.

The paradigmatic example of this situation is that of cross-cultural exchange. In this situation cultural differences are given. Persons do not expect to agree with one another's socially constituted values but agree to see themselves in their similarities rather than their differences for the promise of mutual gain. Voltaire (quoted in Holmes 1989) may have described this situation best: "Enter the Exchange of London, that place more respectable than many a court, and you will see there agents from all nations assembled for the utility of all mankind. There the Jew, the Mohammedan, and the Christian deal with one another as if they were the same religion, and give the name of infidel only to those who go bankrupt." That this description is echoed by Karl Marx's objection to rights as a mere convention of the bourgeoisie underscores its force. Both defender and critic agree that in situations of cross cultural economic exchange the common humanity required for rights may arise.

Perhaps more importantly, this description roughly corresponds both to the classic instances of reciprocity studied by anthropologists and to the religious pluralism that marked the rise of human rights in Europe. In the

first instances an ethic of equivalent reciprocity has been found to characterize the initial contacts of different cultures when cooperation rather than
conquest was the aim. In the second instance it was precisely the desire to
halt the wars of religion that prompted Europeans to subscribe to a notion
of rights. In neither instance were rights held to be "trumps" in the sense of
being the "highest good," nor did the posit of equality go so far as to encompass a notion of "dignity" in the contemporary individualistic sense. But in
both a notion of rights arises as a compromise substitute for a moral code
when agreement about higher goods is impossible.

These instances illustrate the argument, which in short is that the foundation of human rights lies in universally available notions of equality enacted into social practice when situations call for reciprocity across cultures
differences. If this argument is accepted, then a communitarian case for
rights has been made. It is a case that bases rights on a more solid moral
foundation than their critics allow but a more fragile foundation than their
advocates allege. On the one hand human rights are said to arise from experiences that are more or less universally available to humanity. They are
therefore sturdier than mere convention. But on the other hand the enact-
ment of rights depends upon a foundation of human agreement or positive
law which can by definition be only situational rather than universal. Rights
are therefore weaker than arguments based upon natural law allow. In all,
this reasoning suggests that rights are within the universal moral repertoire
of humanity, but not universal in the rationalist sense normally credited to
them by their advocates.

A communitarian defense of rights like this one has, I believe, a certain
intuitive appeal. It makes sense of both the claim that rights are "merely"
matters of convention and the claim that they are moral trumps. It reconciles
these claims by rooting rights in agreements which, in effect, proclaim them
to be trumps. The proclamations do not alter the prior ontological or teleological status of rights—hence the critics' suspicions that they are philosophically unsound. But by codifying a moral position that is within the
universal repertoire of humanity the agreements carry more weight than
could be accorded to convention alone.

If it follows that the idea of rights is within the grasp of the bulk of
humanity based upon experience and may be enacted by agreement, it also
follows that a supra-cultural criterion for evaluating cultural traditions is also
universally available. This criterion is the ideal of equality and rights in
conditions of moral pluralism. This is not, it must be stressed, a stance that

is automatically morally superior to others within the tradition. But it is a universally available moral position from which traditions can be evaluated—and the only such universally available position. It is thus the standard that can and should be used to assess cultural traditions, even though these assessments cannot be presumed to by the last words on the matter. In this way as in others, a communitarian theory of rights gives more play to them than the critics of rights allow while simultaneously restricting their use to the advisory role of a default position. Some of the implications of this position can be sketched by way of conclusion.

Implications of the Communitarian Synthesis

The gist of this synthesis is to ask that rights not be considered as ends—much less as trumps—but only means for establishing a rough sort of justice where other ends collide. It suggests, therefore, that there is a higher good than human rights, namely, a meaningful cultural life.

This subordinate status of rights to cultural meanings can be reinforced by examining one of the instances in which rights seem to arise in their fullest: cross-cultural exchanges. These exchanges have revealed a curious phenomenon for those who assume that exchange relations based upon equality result in equal outcomes (see, Ekeh 1974, for a discussion of the different theories of exchange). For with some regularity exchange partners offer each other goods of greater value than they receive. Why should the norm of reciprocity under conditions of equality result in imbalanced exchanges, an apparent voluntary loss? The answer generally given is that the extra measure "lost" in the exchange is a contribution to the building of the relationship, which the loss does by obligating the recipient to future exchanges. But this in turn may suggest something more fundamental: that asocial equality is a condition that people find discomforting, and when in such situations they move to cement normative and hierarchical relationships within which shared meanings rather than formal equality can govern their interactions. If this is true, then the argument that an entire society can be based primarily upon a morality of rights looms as an implausibility. For people appear to be uncomfortable with such a morality and try to move beyond it.

That this is true of people is illustrated by evidence from the West. The equal rights so often touted in the West are, upon closer examination, rarely as equal in reality as they are in rhetoric. Whether an informal group of friends in the neighborhood (Whyte 1943) or even the formal equality of a jury (Hare, Borgatta, and Bales 1965), research has consistently demonstrated the quick emergence of a rigid power and prestige order. How much more farfetched is the notion of, say, equal rights before the law or in the political process? Few would maintain that every defendant in a criminal trial and every voter actually enjoy equal rights. Westerners, no less than others, inhabit of a culture in which equal rights are sharply skewed by hierarchies of values substantiated by social practices. That we say that we possess equal rights and occasionally base moral claims upon that conviction is no evidence that we typically enjoy such rights or even want to. Indeed, the belief may not be too far removed from the inhabitants of Salem maintaining that witches were in their midst.

Even more troublesome for the rights advocate is the realization that for every situation that produces a rights-like moral compromise there are others that evidence plunder and the imposition of hierarchical values. To be sure, from an external point of view a rights-like moral creed is a morally preferable solution for the interacting of divergent cultures. But from a perspective within one or another of the interacting cultures, ethnocentric and material advantage may be the more appealing ethic. To dismiss these aims as merely immoral is shortsighted. They are immoral only from the fairly narrow standpoint of universal rights. But since this standpoint is not the one to which most people are oriented most of the time, nor the one that supplies them with compelling moral ends, it is mistaken to dismiss the violation of rights for the sake of one or another socially constructed morality as immoral. The lesson that should rather be derived is the one that recognizes the moral limits and necessary fragility of an ethic human rights in a world where people rightly demand richer meanings embedded in social practices.

Even so, the rights advocate is not bereft of moral voice. Since the appeal to rights is within the universal repertoire of humanity, the assertion of rights is one that must be granted a moral hearing. This is so especially where subcultural groupings within a cultural tradition themselves resist a certain imposition of values and their corresponding behavioral requirements, or where cultural conflict itself arises. These situations offer prima facie evidence of the failure of the tradition to provide a coherent moral framework for all its members. On such occasions, there is every justification to evaluate the tradition from the universal standpoint of human rights and, assuming the differences are otherwise unreconcilable, to urge the adoption of these moral standards instead of the contested ones. Although the standard of rights cannot be a final one (and it is morally dubious, to say the least, to seek to implement them where cultural traditions remain harmonious and reasonably free of dissent), a rights-based morality clearly has a role to play in instances marred by cultural conflict and dissent. Indeed, it is the only moral vision that can be called upon.

It follows that rights-based moral reasoning has a large part to play in the pluralist nation-state. For these states by definition demand a moral scheme appropriate to cooperation across cultures and subcultures. Whereas rights advocates should appreciate that even the liberal state can in no way be completely neutral with respect to moral ends, they may nonetheless confidently call for a state that errs more on the side of rights than it does on the side of restrictions. The argument can only be partial and pragmatic, but it can be confident: the pluralist nation-state is by definition an entity that must appeal to the morality of rights since no other moral strategy is universally compelling.

More extreme implications also follow, namely, that there is no valid communitarian distinction between negative and positive, civil and social rights. A pluralist regime like the United States which is established in large part on principles of equality and rights cannot thereby justify the huge discrepancies between rich and poor that it maintains. Rights, derived not from any mystical doctrine of natural law but from the norm of reciprocity based upon common human experience, pluralist exchange, and positive law may just as easily demand equal access to health care and economic security as they do the choice of physician and entrepreneurial opportunity. The difference is not in kind or even in degree. It is solely one of realpolitik.

It is also the case that rights are an entirely legitimate criterion for justice in the international arena. To be sure, rights proponents should avoid promoting the arbitrary cultural values of the West under the guise of rights and, in particular, avoid the promotion of individualism that is so attached to Western ideas about rights. Rights as here defended by communitarian reasoning are in no way properties of individuals but are rather properties of individuals as embodiments of cultural traditions. To avoid a "clash of civilizations" (Huntington 1993), proponents of rights must be especially careful to avoid confusing what is merely one culture's conception of the person with a legitimate claim to rights. Nevertheless, it is entirely appropriate for Westerners or others to insist that a rights-based agenda, properly articulated, be a major element of and even condition for international cooperation. Indeed, the essence of human rights is now, as it should be, the

articulation of a minimal moral code that all cultures can be held to despite
their legitimate differences. As Bryan S. Turner (1993:498) put this matter
when contrasting human rights with citizenship rights, "human-right
concepts can be seen as a progressive paradigm which is relevant to a
world system. . . . The point about *human* rights is that they are extra-
governmental."

Even so, advocates of rights must be careful—more careful than they
have hitherto been—to distinguish their use of rights as a means for adju-
dicating cultural disputes or evaluating social traditions and the promotion
of rights as ends in themselves. The repertoire of rights is intuitively available
to humanity. But people also want that which makes their lives meaningful:
a coherent hierarchy of values and the social and institutional arrangements
that realize and sustain them. These values and arrangements are by their
very essence indifferent respecters of rights, and rights provide no substitute
for them.

A remark by Edmund Burke (1986 [1790]:95) about the "curious character" of his Protestant nemesis, Dr. Price, may illustrate this point. He is
"so earnest for setting up new churches," noted Burke, "and so indifferent
concerning the doctrine which may be taught in them." A minister who one
would presume would be committed to promoting a moral vision of life's
ends was identified by Burke as one solely committed to promoting the
means. Surely a humanity that on occasion justifiably demands the right to
select its church also wants that church, once selected, to disseminate the
truth as it understands it. For the meaningful life does not arise from the
selection of the church but from the doctrines of value theoretical taught
therein. And these are not "selected."

The ultimate task of social criticism is thus not to foster rights but to
fashion theories of inequality and value that are morally palatable. But rights
advocates are by definition not such theorists; nor can they be. Their goal
must rather remain the more limited one of suggesting instances in which
greater equality and more rights may be desirable across cultural divides.
Tempered by a recognition of its limitations, this goal is nevertheless a worthy
one. Indeed, it is the only universally reliable moral guide.

Endnotes

1. Nor is it effective to counter as some (e.g., Donnelly 1989) do that a close
   textual reading of Locke and other rights proponents is consistent with valuing

community. True, Locke *claimed* that his ideas were consistent with community attachments. But remarks like "all the rest of Mankind are one Community" betray how abstract the notion of community that Locke was forced to embrace in consequence of his equally abstract notion of rights. To include all of humanity into one giant community, after all, is not to value any particular community, but only community as an abstraction.

2. To this conclusion the critic, like Burke (1986 [1790]), generally appends a prediction of despotism. The reasoning is that since people cannot tolerate meaninglessness and politics abhors a vacuum, one or another tyrant or faction will quickly impose order.

3. It is of course possible to speculate that the alleged differences between female and male moralities are based upon inborn differences between the sexes. If successfully advanced such an argument would amount to a kind of biologically-based rationalism. Most follow Gilligan (1982), however, in supposing that the different moralities arise from different social-psychological experiences.

4. A main theme of Etzioni's (1993) communitarianism is that rights exist only in relation to responsibilities. To assert this, of course, is also to assert that rights arise only by social conventions which, by granting rights, also obligate the bearer to certain reciprocal social obligations. This is a very different notion of rights than Donnelly (1989) for example endorses. Donnelly is in fact quite specific in arguing that a right is not paired with an obligation on the part of the bearer but with others' obligations to grant that right. Donnelly's view can be sustained only if rights adhere to persons as persons rather than arise from convention.

5. Communitarianism and republicanism are so allied today as to lead many to conclude that they are the same thing. Yet it seems to me that the two schools are different. Communitarianism stresses the social embeddedness of persons and their natural desire for community. Republicanism, while accepting this communitarian plank, seems much more concerned with maintaining rights in a society—even sometimes seeming to believe in "natural rights"—albeit only with a corresponding emphasis on virtue and public spiritedness. This prompts most republicans to consider themselves to be defenders of what they consider to be historic liberalism (see, e.g., Galston, 1991), a posture rarely encountered among those who more self-consciously hoist the communitarian banner.

6. The dating is somewhat arbitrary. Garry Wills (1992) identifies Abraham Lincoln's Gettysburg Address as the turning point while Robert Bellah (1975) views the 1960s and 1970s as the epochal moment. Michael Sandel (1996), who has perhaps examined this shift from a republican to a liberal public philosophy most comprehensively, identifies several turning points, most of them in the early decades of the twentieth century.

7. Some version of libertarianism seems the most logical response. However, such a political philosophy makes it difficult to argue as many rights theorists do (e.g., Rawls 1971; Gutman 1980) that extensive state action is required by rights.

8. Republicans, Benthamite utilitarians, and Marxists may be immune. For republicans the immunity is purchased at the price of accepting the liberal argument that rights arise from natural law. However, they then must face the inverse problem of justifying their concern for virtue and the good society on the basis of a theory of natural rights, which in others' hands does not lead to these concerns. Both Bentham and Marx proposed comprehensive visions of the good that did not require them to concede any space for rights.

9. When I challenged him on just this point (1997, New York) Kausikan replied that he had no interest in engaging in a discussion based upon philosophical "first principals" but, as a diplomat, was simply acknowledging that core rights have been universally granted by the positive law of international documents. That reply, however, is insufficient. For he immediately follows the above-quoted remark about the "hard core of rights" being "smaller" than many believe with the statement: "Forty-five years after the Universal Declaration was adopted, many of its 30 articles are still subject to debate," that it "is not a tablet Moses brought down from the mountain," and remarks to the effect that international norms "evolve." These comments indicate that Kausikan is in fact willing to challenge even the most basic of international human rights documents, so cannot derive his belief in a "core" set of rights from them. The question thus remains: On what basis does Kausikan admit the existence of *any* universal rights?

10. It might be countered, of course, that the proponents of "Asian values" have not demonstrated this social harmony and that their violations of human rights testify to this failure. (It would be difficult to argue that they have not demonstrated prosperity, however.) But I for one am willing to concede this argument. True, Asia taken as a whole may not evidence social harmony, but neither does the West taken as a whole evidence it. The question of "Who's better?" is endlessly debatable and probably silly. Should Singapore be compared to the U.S. or Detroit? Japan with the U.S. or Italy? Suffice to say that when tallying up measures of social harmony—as well as human rights violations—many Asian states compare favorably with many Western states.

Bibliography

Bell, Daniel. 1993. *Communitarianism and its Critics.* New York: Oxford University Press.

Bellah, Robert N. 1975. *The Broken Covenant: American Civil Religion in a Time of Trial.* New York: Seabury.

————. 1978. "Religion and Legitimation in the American Republic." *Society* 15 (May/June):6–23.

Bellah, Robert N., et al. 1985. *Habits of the Heart: Individualism and Commitment in American Life*. Berkeley: University of California Press.

Bentham, Jeremy. 1987 [1843]. *Anarchical Fallacies; being an examination of the Declaration of Rights issues during the French Revolution*. In Jeremy Waldron, ed. *Nonsense Upon Stilts: Bentham, Burke, and Marx on the Rights of Man*. New York: Methuen.

Burke, Edmund. 1986 [1790]. *Reflections on the Revolution in France*. New York: Penguin.

Chan, Joseph. 1996. "The Task for Asians: To Discover Their Own Political Morality for Human Rights." *Human Rights Dialogue* 4 (March):5–6.

Cornell, Drucilla. 1991. "Sexual Difference: A Critique of MacKinnon's *Toward a Feminist Theory of the State*." *Yale Law Journal* 100 (17) (May):2250,2257.

Donnelly, Jack. 1989. *Universal Human Rights in Theory and Practice*. Ithaca: Cornell University Press.

Durkheim, Emile. 1965 [1917]. *The Elementary Forms of the Religious Life*. New York: Free Press.

Dworkin, Andrea. 1987. *Intercourse*. New York: Free Press.

Dworkin, Ronald. 1978. *Taking Rights Seriously*. Cambridge: Harvard University Press.

————. 1985. *A Matter of Principle*. Cambridge: Harvard University Press.

Ekeh, Peter. 1974. *Social Exchange Theory: The Two Traditions*. Cambridge: Harvard University Press.

Etzioni, Amitai. 1993. *The Spirit of Community: The Reinvention of American Society*. New York: Simon and Schuster.

————. 1996. *The New Golden Rule: Community and Morality in a Democratic Society*. New York: Basic Books.

Freeman, Michael. 1996. "Human Rights, Democracy, and 'Asian Values,'" *The Pacific Review* 9(3):352–366.

Fukuyama, Francis. 1992. *The End of History and the Last Man*. New York: Free Press.

Galston, William A. 1991. *Liberal Purposes: Goods, Virtues, and Diversity in the Liberal State*. New York: Cambridge University Press.

Geertz, Clifford. 1973. *The Interpretation of Cultures*. New York: Basic Books.

Gilligan, Carol. 1982. *In a Different Voice: Psychological Theory and Women's Development*. Cambridge: Harvard University Press.

Gouldner, Alvin W. 1960. "The Norm of Reciprocity." *American Sociological Review*, vol. 25.

Gutmann, Amy. 1980. *Liberal Equality*. New York: Cambridge University Press.

————. 1985. "Communitarian Critics of Liberalism." *Philosophy and Public Affairs*, vol. 14.

Hare, A. Paul, Edgar F. Borgatta, and Robert F. Bales, eds. 1965. *Small Groups: Studies in Social Interaction*. New York: Knopf.

Hobbes, Thomas. 1958 [1651]. *Leviathan*. Indianapolis: Bobbs-Merrill.

Holmes, Stephen. 1989. "The Permanent Structure of Antiliberal Thought." In Nancy L. Rosenblum, ed. *Liberalism and the Moral Life*. Cambridge: Harvard University Press.

Hom, Sharon. 1996. "Re-Positioning Human Rights Discourse on 'Asian' Perspectives." *Buffalo Journal of International Law* 3:251–276, abridged as chapter 7 of this volume.

Hume, David. 1997 [1748]. "Of the Original Contract." in Jerry Z. Muller, ed. *Conservatism: An Anthology of Social and Political Thought from David Hume to the Present*, 51–61. Princeton: Princeton University Press.

Huntington, Samuel P. 1993. "The Clash of Civilizations." *Foreign Affairs* (Summer) 72 (3).

Kausikan, Bilahari. 1993. "Asia's Different Standard." *Foreign Policy* (Fall):24–41.

———. 1995–96. "An East Asian Approach to Human Rights." *Buffalo Journal of International Law* 2(2) (Winter):263–283.

———. 1997. "Governance that Works." *Journal of Democracy* 8 (2) (April):24–33.

MacIntyre, Alisdair. 1967. *A Short History of Ethics*. New York: Routledge.

———. 1984. *After Virtue: A Study in Moral Theory*. Notre Dame: Notre Dame.

Marx, Karl. 1987 [1844]. "On the Jewish Question." In Jeremy Waldron, ed. *Nonsense Upon Stilts: Bentham, Burke, and Marx on the Rights of Man*. New York: Methuen.

Mauss, Marcel. 1967. *The Gift: Forms and Functions of Exchange in Archaic Societies*. New York: Norton.

Mencius. 1963. "The Book of Mencius." in Wing-Tsit Chan, ed. *A Source Book in Chinese Philosophy*, 51–83. Princeton: Princeton University Press.

Muller, Jerry Z. 1997. "What is Conservative Social and Political Thought?" Introduction, *Conservatism: An Anthology of Social and Political Thought from David Hume to the Present*, 3–31. Princeton: Princeton University Press.

Nisbet, Robert. 1978. "Conservatism." in Tom Bottomore and Robert Nisbet, eds. *A History of Sociological Analysis*. New York: Basic Books.

O'Brien, Conor Cruise. 1986. "The Manifesto of a Counter-Revolution." Introduction to Edmund Burke, *Reflections on the Revolution in France*, 9–81. New York: Penguin.

Rawls, John. 1971. *A Theory of Justice*. Cambridge: Harvard University Press.

———. 1985. "Justice as Fairness: Political not Metaphysical." *Philosophy and Public Affairs*, vol 14.

———. 1988. "The Priority of Right and Ideas of the Good." *Philosophy and Public Affairs*, vol. 17.

Rhode, Deborah. 1989. *Justice and Gender*. Cambridge: Harvard University Press.

Rosenblum, Nancy L. 1989. "Introduction." In Nancy L. Rosenblum, ed. *Liberalism and the Moral Life*. Cambridge: Harvard University Press.

Sandel, Michael J. 1981. *Liberalism and the Limits of Justice*. New York: Cambridge University Press.

——. 1996. *Democracy's Discontent: America in Search of a Public Philosophy*. Cambridge: Harvard University Press.

Scheler, Max. 1954 [1912]. *The Nature of Sympathy*. New Haven: Yale University Press.

Stephen, James Fitzjames. 1967 [1873]. *Liberty, Equality, Fraternity*. New York: Cambridge.

Taylor, Charles. 1999. "Conditions of an Unforced Consensus on Human Rights." in Joanne R. Bauer and Daniel A. Bell, eds. *The East Asian Challenge for Human Rights. Cambridge*: Cambridge: Cambridge University Press, 124–144.

Turner, Bryan S. 1993. "Outline of a Theory of Human Rights." *Sociology* 27(3) (August):489–512.

Waldron, Jeremy, ed. 1987. *Nonsense Upon Stilts: Bentham, Burke, and Marx on the Rights of Man*. New York: Methuen.

Walzer, Michael. 1983. *Spheres of Justice: A Defense of Pluralism and Equality*. New York: Basic Books.

Whyte, William Foote. 1943. *Street Corner Society: The Social Structure of an Italian Slum*. Chicago: University of Chicago Press.

Wills, Garry. 1992. *Lincoln at Gettysburg: The Words that Remade America*. New York: Simon & Schuster.

Zakaria, Fareed. 1994. "Culture is Destiny: A Conversation with Lee Kuan Yew." *Foreign Affairs* (March/April) 73 (2):109–126.

4 Rights Hunting in Non-Western Traditions

Steven J. Hood

In their effort to secure human rights while still preserving cultural identities, scholars have engaged in a hunt for notions of rights in non-Western traditions. I argue that such a quest is misdirected. Human rights, as currently understood in international law, are ideas rooted in the Western philosophical tradition. Using the examples of Confucianism and Islam, I suggest that they lack the philosophical foundations for a full-fledged concept of rights. The Confucian and Islamic traditions do, however, contain ideas of civic virtues like tolerance, compromise, and civility, which support good government. I conclude that non-Western thinkers must adopt rights theory from the Western liberal tradition, but can take from their own traditions ideas that support responsible rule.

Why focus on Confucian and Islamic traditions of thought? The relative worth of Confucianism and Islam in relation to human rights and democracy has been a heated topic in the last two decades. Some scholars argue that both traditions are inherently antidemocratic. They reject Western notions of democracy and form the basis of civilizations that inevitably clash with Western civilization (Huntington 1991, 1993). Others contend that Islam and Confucianism can be just as supportive of human rights as the Western tradition. It is not inherent weaknesses in Confucianism and Islam that have kept rights from being realized, but war, colonization, and economic backwardness that have slowed the development of human rights (An-Na'im 1987; Dwyer 1991). A third, relativist line of argument rejects universal claims of human rights. It suggests that non-Western cultures are obliged to reject Western notions of rights if they contradict their accepted religious or cultural norms. This argument has been especially popular among officials in some East Asian countries and in countries where Islam dominates (State Council of China 1996; Zakaria 1994; Pollis and Schwab 1979). In all these debates, Confucian and Islamic voices are the ones most often heard outside of the West. For this reason, a consideration of the prospects for justifying human rights within these traditions is appropriate.

Scholars engaged in this debate can readily point to the many fine qualities of Confucian and Islamic thought. There are profound justifications for leading moral lives within both traditions. Confucianism and Islam are not merely ways of thinking about things, they are ways of living. The identities of individuals are very much intertwined within the Confucian and Islamic views of life. It naturally follows that devout Confucians and Muslims most likely believe their ways are superior to the ways of the West. The acceptance of universal norms of human rights is a direct challenge to the authority of Confucianism and Islam, even though the two traditions are as different from each other as they are from the Western tradition. Many rightly fear that to accept human rights would be to compromise basic tenets underpinning Confucian and Islamic authority. To compromise Confucian and Muslim ways is not simply the loss of a philosophy or a religious tradition, it is the loss of identity. For the Confucian, the erosion of the family, a decline of respect for parents, and the questioning of authority are the feared results of compromising traditional ways. For the Muslim, compromise can evoke the anger of God, weaken religious authority, and damage the political goals of Islamic society. As I will argue, these fears are warranted: to accept the universality of human rights is to gut Confucianism and Islam of some of their fundamental principles.

The Twin Pillars of Modern Democracy: Rights and Virtues

Political scientists have gone to great efforts to define democracy. Many of the prominent definitions focus on democratic processes rather than the philosophical characteristics of liberal regimes (Schumpeter, 1942; Dahl, 1971; Karl and Schmitter 1991). I believe this is unfortunate because it forces political scientists to look for minimal standards of democracy such as regular elections, popular participation, free speech, and so forth. While these are all important characteristics of democratic regimes, they do not specifically address the essence of democracy. Authoritarian regimes can and sometimes do hold regular elections and tolerate free speech and popular participation in some aspects of political life. But they remain authoritarian regimes until political rights are formally established. When we use minimal definitions of democracy we leave the door open for authoritarians to declare that their regimes are free even though they may violate individual rights in other ways. For this reason, it is important to consider the philosophical basis of democracy as practiced in the West.

The contemporary notion of democracy is built upon two pillars—rights and republican virtues. Rights are distinctively Western and modern, while common notions of virtue are found in most major Western and non-Western traditions.

The Discovery of Nature and Rights

Political rights have been validated by the guarantees they give individuals in democratic societies. Rights reinforce our sense of human dignity by granting us expectations of security, prosperity, opportunity, and belonging in a polity where all are deemed equal under the law. Rights are relatively new, having sprung directly from the work of thinkers like Locke, Rosseau, Kant, and Montesquieu, and indirectly from the ancient Greeks. Rights are considered instinctual, though they had to be discovered. It is the discovery of rights that creates the most basic problem for non-Western traditions that claim to have a notion of political rights. It is also problematic for Westerners, primarily because it is too often assumed that we have always known about rights.

The discovery of rights is impossible without the discovery of nature, which necessarily precedes the discovery of rights. The discovery of nature separates us from the beasts of the field by virtue of our reason and helps us make sense of our world. It allows us to discover our universal rights as human beings since we are no longer bound to natural authority. It helps us distinguish between political rights proper and things that are claimed to be rights but are other things entirely. The chore of discovering nature falls upon philosophy for philosophy, in seeking the first things, tries to distinguish between those things that are natural and those things that are human. Prior to the discovery of nature, no distinction is made between customs or ways that are held to be the same everywhere or held to be different everywhere. As Strauss suggests, "custom or way is the prephilosophic equivalent of nature" (Strauss 1950:82–3). "Our way" is good because it is our way of doing things, because it is old, and because it is ancestral and therefore closer to the gods or the divine. In order for us to consider the question of what regime is the best regime, we have to determine first that there is a need to find a better regime. Hence we have to question the ancestral way or discover nature.

This is precisely the project that Socrates engaged in that eventually led to his trial, arrest and death (Plato 1984). He was determined that certain ideas could be questioned in a scholarly context even though the laws of the land declared such musings forbidden. For Socrates a central question was which ideas were derived from the gods (nature) and which ideas could be ascribed to reason. In other words, what role should reason play in our lives? This question is one of central importance. For Athens, such a question was not merely a philosophical query. To raise questions about whether or not a particular idea was from the gods was to question the legitimacy of the gods and therefore the very foundations which Athens was built upon. It was to challenge the way of ancestors, of natural authority, of natural law itself.

The ancient Hebrews did not cross the line from revelation to reason because they had no concept of nature as existing separate from the human world (Strauss 1950:81–82). It was a prephilosophic life. God's laws had to be kept because they were God's laws. Serious reflection on why God-given laws could be considered blasphemous and risked "splitting up the totality into phenomena" that were natural and unnatural (Strauss 1950:82). God's work was in the heavens and in the earth. All matters were, therefore, of direct relevance to God and human beings could understand only what God intended for them to understand.

This was also the view of the early Christians. But while the early Christians were not to question the role of God as lawgiver, there was room to question the role of the state vis-à-vis religion. A good Christian could be a good Christian by rendering unto Caesar what was Caesar's and rendering unto God what was God's. But showing preference for religious authority over political authority is not the same as discovering rights. Somehow reason had to be legitimized in a world where revelation accounted for everything from science to politics. Thomas Aquinas helped clear the way when he proclaimed that God's laws could be understood according to reason, not simply as demands sent down from an indifferent God (Aquinas 1945). Philosophers picked up where the Greeks left off, trying to determine where the limits of God's world and man's world lay. Over the centuries, the West came to accept that:

1. Nature is a separate phenomenon from things that are human;
2. with nature separated from the human realm, scientific inquiry is possible because human beings do not have to accept purely religious explanations of the material world;
3. with the discovery of nature, Protestant reformers could more carefully scrutinize the state for fostering policies deemed to be beneath the dignity of human beings.

In short, both religious and nonreligious scholars challenged authority from different standards, though both traditions reinforced separation of the sacred and the secular worlds.

It fell upon thinkers like Locke, Rosseau, Kant, and Montesquieu to make a clear break from traditional authoritarianism. Locke pointed out that we had to understand that our familial relations and our relationship to God was founded first and foremost on the premise that the few are better fit to rule than the majority (Locke 1988). The son obeys his father because his father controls the son's material well-being. In turn, the son respects the monarch because he has learned to respect the authority of his father. Other thinkers also believed that for people to truly be free, they must rationalize their relationship to God and eradicate all ideas that encourage unquestioned support of those in political authority over them. Only then could a liberal society based on rights emerge. Liberalism challenges traditional political authority by proclaiming that no single person or group of persons can, by nature, rule over others. On the basis of rights we are able to rule ourselves and select representatives to govern as we would have them govern.

It is common for citizens, leaders, and scholars to claim things as rights that are in many cases not rights. Rights and the language of rights carry more weight in our contemporary discussions than do virtues. Part of this stems from the fact that our virtues cannot always be backed by law. Additionally, we citizens of democracies too often believe rights are more important than virtues. There is also a simple misunderstanding of rights. People generally associate political right as the equivalent of a moral right. For this reason, it is easy to assume that any political, moral, or ethical claim is a political right. Similarly, any duty or obligation we feel a person has is often couched in rights language. This rights stereotyping is incorrect, however. Duties and obligations are often not the same things as rights. Duties and obligations can be religiously based, ethically based, culturally based, or simple preferences based on common sense. Very often, therefore, such claims are really normative judgments or statements of preference rather than formal political rights.

Out of necessity, rights do consist of duties and obligations, but more particularly, they assume something more basic. Rights are based on the fundamental assumption that all persons are ultimately equal in power, freedom, and their desire for self-preservation. As human beings, we all share the same desires for property, security, and sociality with others in order to maximize our enjoyment in living and because our lives are made easier by cooperating with others in a society bound by a social contract. In this social contract, we agree that all members of society possess basic rights—free speech, property ownership, trial by jury of our peers, religious freedom, suffrage, and so on. These rights are contractual because just as others are obliged to allow us to practice our rights providing they do not infringe upon the rights of others, we are similarly duty-bound to give others the same consideration. The key thing to remember is that rights require mutual understandings of what all people are and are not at liberty to do.

This interpretation of rights calls into question the assertion that personal rights can be suspended whenever a government official claims his Confucian responsibility of putting the interests of the state first by withdrawing free speech or other liberties that belong to individuals. It similarly raises questions about the claims of many religious and political leaders in predominantly Muslim states that religious and political expediencies are rights that are not acknowledged in the West. It is improper to refer to such a claim as a right since there is no mutual obligation on behalf of those in political authority to acknowledge the sovereignty of the individual. Rights are contractual in nature, implying equality under the law. Confucian and Islamic codes claim superior status for those in authority and thus deny the validity of debate and desirability of public discussion. For this reason, rights that are claimed by these traditions are normative judgments and preferences made known by religious and/or secular authorities, not universal rights. There is no acknowledgement of a contract based on mutual equality, freedom, or responsibility.

To summarize this discussion, the minimal requirements needed to claim a rights tradition include the following:

1. The discovery of nature, which means the acceptance of reason and rational explanations for why human beings are separate from

nature. It also means that human beings are free agents, not bound by custom, ancestral tradition, or other claims of superiority.

2. A general acceptance that authority can legitimately be challenged. The challenge to authority is a permanent feature, not merely a single episode of popular political participation. Human beings have the right to examine all moral, ethical, and political claims made by political leaders and to determine the appropriateness of each claim. Human beings are therefore free to scrutinize public policy and can do so without fear of retribution.

3. Finally, a common understanding that rights of equality, liberty, justice, and suffrage are inalienable. There is a social contract based on common consent stipulating that democracy is the best regime and that all other regimes are inferior to democracy.

Republican Virtues

While political rights are often demanded because of people's immediate desires to satisfy self interests, republican (or civic) virtues give meaning and staying power to democracy. Comparative studies that focus on political process and fail to consider civic virtues overlook much of the character and potential of democratic regimes. Robert Putnam's (1993) recent study on democracy in Italy emphasizes the importance of civic virtues to democratic effectiveness and democratic quality. Putnam argues it is not enough to suggest that political institutions shape politics or that political institutions have been shaped by historical experience. He argues institutions are also shaped by the influences of civic virtues. If citizens are virtuous, government is better able to accomplish good things. Where principles of equality, trust, tolerance, and solidarity are appreciated, government usually functions well and mutual respect is built between citizens and public servants. Nonvirtuous citizens, on the other hand, diminish the likelihood of institutions being able to make economic and political strides. Political corruption increases and pessimism abounds. The lack of civic virtue increases the possibility that democratic processes will be side-stepped and rights abused. What is left, then, is to consider what these virtues are and why they should become a focus of human rights studies.

Putnam's findings are not new. In fact, many scholars have pointed to the similarity of Putnam's writings and the work of other scholars like Robert

Bellah and Daniel Bell to Alexis de Tocqueville (Bellah 1986; Bell 1993). Tocqueville spent much time looking at the democratic disposition of citizens in the early American republic and its impact on the regime generally (Tocqueville 1966). These writers acknowledge a debt to ancient Greek philosophers and to the French philosopher Montesquieu, all who distinguished democratic systems from their despotic rivals, not on the basis of rights, but by the virtues espoused by political regimes. Moderation, tolerance, frugality, and similar virtues provided the glue that held democratic systems together, not necessarily rights (Montesquieu 1989). Similarly Rousseau was suspicious of Locke and others who he believed paid too much attention to rights at the expense of virtues that support democratic good will. He believed an enlightened people would willingly forego the self-interests associated with rights, even sacrificing "pleasures, tranquility, wealth, power, and life itself," for the preservation of good (Rousseau 1987:72–73). Furthermore, he believed virtues and rights together would create a remarkable change in human beings, transforming man from a "stupid, limited animal into an intelligent human being and a man" (Rousseau 1987:150–51).

Contemporary theorists who argue for a serious consideration of virtues suggest we make a sharp distinction between desirable and undesirable attributes of regimes. William Galston suggests that undesirable attributes include death, wanton cruelty, slavery, poverty, malnutrition, vulnerability, and humiliation. Liberal goods, therefore, must in some way represent the opposites of these undesirable things: life, normal development of basic capacities, fulfillment of interests and purposes, freedom, rationality, society, and subjective satisfactions (Galston 1991:168, 174–76). But these goods correspond closely to what nearly all regimes aspire to deliver and include basic human needs necessary for survival. How do virtues relate to these goods?

The acceptance of liberal virtues suggests people can improve their lives and behave in virtuous ways. Some virtues apply to all states such as the desirability of courage, obedience to the law, and loyalty to society. But liberal societies demand more. Individuality must be developed in the sense of fostering self-restraint, self-transcendence, tolerance, the primacy of family life in a moral society and an acknowledgment that some ways of living are better than others. At the same time liberal citizens must respect the rights of others, choose quality leaders, practice moderation, and show concern for others. Liberal leaders must be willing to find common purposes and at times insist on the reality of hard choices. These virtues, Galston argues, will help democracies narrow the gap between political principles and political practice and promote duty as a way of life (Galston 1991).

There is general agreement in Western societies that these virtues originate from two sources (Pangle 1992) One source is religious as found within the Judeo-Christian tradition, and the other source from human nature as treated in the works of Montesquieu, Rousseau, and the American founders. Within these sources we find a moral and philosophical justification for virtues citizens must possess (shame, reverence, self-control, truthfulness, justice, obedience to the law and piety) and the virtues leaders must exhibit (generosity, noble ambition, pride, justice, intelligence, and prudence) (Pangle 1992:107). It is within this pillar of democracy, the need for virtues, that Islam and Confucianism can play an important role in supporting democracy. Virtues complement rights. There is much within both Islam and Confucianism that can bolster a spirit of civic virtue to curb individual ambition, excesses of the state, and in turn help preserve rights.

In summary, moral and ethical ideas that enhance the prospects for and maintenance of democracy include the following:

1. An acknowledgement that one's personal actions have a direct influence on the well-being and happiness of others in society. There must be an acceptance of notions of right and wrong based on individual accountability.
2. A sense of moderation, tolerance, fair play, courage and frugality. Traditions that esteem principles of human dignity generally accept these ideas, which in turn bring civility to public and private life in a democracy.
3. Leaders uphold a high standard of virtue. There is a strong belief that their words and actions must provide a moral example for others to follow.

Having looked at these twin pillars of modern democracy we can now consider how Confucianism and Islam compare to these ideals.

The Confucian Tradition and Democracy

There is always a danger in labeling a society in a way that identifies it with an exclusive philosophical tradition. Yet we often refer to the Chinese tradition as a Confucian tradition. Few Chinese today know anything about Confucius. Most do not read Confucian classics and few can offer any details about Confucian philosophy. Most of what is accepted today as Confucianism consists of the revered institutions of filial piety, good human feelings, doing favors for friends, respecting hierarchy, and practicing virtue (Ebrey 1991). For this reason, the influence of early Confucianism, Neo-Confucianism, other non-Confucian philosophies, as well as contemporary philosophical debates in China are mostly of interest to intellectuals and not to everyday Chinese. The Confucian tradition in China is a vulgarized form of Confucianism roughly based on the work attributed to Confucius and Mencius (Nivison 1996:3; Madsen 1984:11–12). Hence we will spend most of our time looking at the influence of early Confucianism since it has had the most prolonged impact on Chinese politics and society.

Confucianism and Nature

Early Confucianists (beginning around 500 BCE) lacked a complex theory of metaphysics. Natural phenomena were often explained by relying on observation and traditional explanations of the supernatural. There was no clear attempt to separate natural things from human things. In large measure, studying the natural world was pushed aside as Confucians preferred to focus on human affairs without distinguishing human beings from nature.

There is general agreement that Confucius and his students believed that in ancient times sages provided perfect rule since they possessed all of the desired virtues of heaven. It was the duty of superior men to try to become like sages, even though sages were no longer found on the earth. Confucius exerted considerable effort trying to get those around him to turn back to the ancients as a source of virtuous living. He did not spend much time talking about the natural world or about human nature. His student Mencius paid some attention to the problem of human nature, proclaiming it to be good. Still, most of Mencius's efforts were directed to matters concerning personal, family, and state governance. It was left to neo-Confucianists to develop a body of metaphysical theory. During the twelfth century they borrowed heavily from Buddhism and Taoism to explain natural phenomena. But Confucians have historically shown little concern for the problems that arise in blurring distinctions between the natural and human worlds. Being eclectic, they have blended elements of legend, folk religion, Buddhism, and Taoism to explain things they did not understand (Feng 1952). They relied on ritual and faith in the ancients to know better and longed for an earlier period when truly just men walked the earth. Thus, virtue has its roots in a bygone time and can at best be copied only in part. Because the ultimate good remained hidden in the past, nature was left undiscovered, and authority was never challenged.

Confucianism's concentration on matters of filial piety and authoritarian government was not based on a formal philosophy of science and hence claimed no discovery of nature. Confucianism is not alone in failing to help the Chinese to discover nature. None of the other schools of philosophy in China asked the kinds of probing questions of nature and human existence that were common for Western philosophers to ask. Even today, the Chinese have a great interest in tapping into the energy of nature to enlighten the mind, cure disease and delay the infirmities of age. Indeed, there is a popular reliance on mysticism to explain everything from weather change to the behavior of political leaders. The primitive state of science and poor development of political philosophy led to China's thirst for both from the West. At the same time, there was little forethought about what ought to be imported. The result has been a tragic political history and near total dependence on the West's scientific accomplishments. For this reason, the discovery of nature in China is something of an imported process, coming in bits and pieces.

In other ways, however, Confucianism is a major political philosophy in the grand sense of the term: that is, Confucianism asks the related questions of what is the good life and how should one live one's life. Confucius and his students borrowed from traditional Chinese conceptions of culture, family life, and ethical and moral principles to build their political philosophy. From these they developed a world view of what ought to be. But it is a world of virtues and a rejection of individualism, hence rights. It puts family and emperor first and rejects any universal standard to question one's place in the family or in the kingdom.

The family plays a central role for Confucianism because it is within the family that children learn how to respect their father's authority and power. The promotion of filial piety in turn teaches all people to respect the authority and power of the state (Schwartz 1985:68). The importance of authority and power is best taught within the realm of *li*, or proper behavior. Children and subjects must be taught *li* through example, ceremony, ritual, and by understanding the distinctive roles each individual must live by in the family, in the village, and in society at large. These ideals coupled with knowing your proper relationship to others around you constitute the Confucian concept of public virtue (Schwartz 1985:70). Authority and power should not simply be identified with oppression. To be practiced properly, harmony will be realized within the family first and then within society. Thus moral teachings reinforce Confucian notions of authority and power. They teach an individual to cultivate *jen*, or virtue, which is necessary to truly understand one's duties and obligations.

It is the way of a gentleman to practice virtue and uprightness in all dealings outside of the home. For Confucianism, however, governing the home in a harmonious manner means the loyalty of the son to the father and the father to the son is more highly esteemed than being honest in your dealings with others outside the home (Confucius 1971:8:18).

The singular importance of understanding one's obligations to one's superiors in Confucianism is reinforced by the oft-cited five basic relationships: ruler and subject, father and son, husband and wife, elder brother and younger brother, and friend and friend. It is significant that three of these relationships are familial relationships, and Confucius and Mencius repeatedly admonished their students that demonstrating love for parents was of far greater importance than demonstrating love for a god or the emperor. The Chinese imperial state understood Confucianism to be family-first and emperor-second in this respect. This was nevertheless acceptable as the emperor came to rely on Confucian principles to keep order in society so that he did not have to take drastic measures to curb the errant behavior of bad subjects. In addition, the emperor could receive support from the people who believed the emperor esteemed the morality, benevolence, and righteousness espoused in Confucian teachings, even though the emperor may demonstrate harsh acts of repression from time to time. Because the state bureaucracy was supported by the Confucian system of examination and recruitment of scholar/rulers, the emperor was insulated from the people by civil leaders and therefore removed from the constant popular scrutiny that hands-on monarchists are often subjected to.

Reverence for Authority and the Rejection of Rights

While we often think of the benefits strong families lend to democratic societies, the same can be said of traditional family life and authoritarian regimes. The existence of strong, close-knit families and its link to authoritarianism is well founded. Confucianism sees the family as a fundamental political unit headed by a father who is unquestioned in his position as head of the household. Furthermore, the father has responsibility to nurture and take care of the needs of his children. In his *First Treatise of Government*, John Locke points out that family life is the perfect training ground for children to learn to support monarchy. Like a father, the monarch rules over his subjects who in turn offer their unquestioned devotion to the monarch as a father figure (Locke 1988: chapter IX). Confucius has a similar view of family life. And while Locke is critical of this relationship, Confucius sees the family as the most basic of any political unit in the kingdom. As long as the authority of the father remains unquestioned, people will not seriously challenge authoritarianism. But as long as Confucian authority remains unchallenged, there will be no individual rights. And rights are the primary goal of liberalism and the guarantor of harmony.

Confucianism values harmony, but harmony is not brought about by a recognition that all are equal under the law. Parental authority is not challenged in Confucianism. Locke reduces family relationships to relations of necessity on the one hand and self-interest of the father (and monarch) on the other. By examining familial ties in this way, Locke hoped we would challenge the legitimacy of paternal authority, and by extension the monarch, on the basis of better allocating necessities and luxury through individual self-interest. Conversely, Confucius and his followers teach us that children should, under all circumstances, accept paternal authority. This means overlooking the simple weaknesses of fathers as well as the serious crimes they may commit as demonstrated in the examples above. Loyalty to the father and the family is a key to understanding harmony in a Confucian society. By governing the home well, Confucius believed the kingdom would have greater harmony. Proper teaching in the home will help each person know how to act in any given situation. The very essence of the five human relationships is a code of how unequals should interact in society. Deference is always given to the elder, even, as Confucius and Mencius point out repeatedly, if the elder is wrong. The only time a subject in the kingdom may override the will of the emperor is when it becomes necessary for the subject to see to the needs of his own father first. Deference to parental and political rule assumes that some have superior status in the Confucian world. It is only after this loyalty to parents has been established that principles of morality and ethics come into play. Confucian rituals teach how each person in the realm is subject to hierarchies and behavior that assumes a correct path. Confucianism eschews self-interest if it runs into conflict with the needs and desires of a parent or the political leader.

The rights of citizenship assume duties and obligations that a Confucian world cannot justify. In a democratic society, children of a certain age have the right to leave their parents and, if they choose, to never have contact with them again. They have a right to judge their fellow citizens on crimes committed, to judge the performance of political leaders, to follow their self-interests, even though they may clash with accepted moral and ethical norms. Democratic citizenship obliges us to recognize the universality of the law in dealing with others' crimes, whether they be committed by a brother, a parent, or a political leader. Confucianism views these political attitudes with abhorrence. Loyalty to family is more important than any universally held notions of political rights and moral notions of right and wrong. For this reason, Confucianism is supportive of authoritarianism, whether it be despotic or monarchical, because there is no recognition of rights as espoused by liberalism.

Confucian Virtues and the Good Regime

It is frequently pointed out that Confucianism has never been practiced in China in its ideal form. While this is true, vulgar Confucianism has been taught by the state to shore up respect for the regime, regardless of its quality or promise. Confucian leaders are supposed to practice benevolence and reciprocity, just as a father and his child would practice these virtues in the home. There is a moralist argument at work here—leaders know better and therefore deserve respect. Chinese leaders have usually got what they wanted, very often by force. And just as clergymen in the West opposed much of the brutal repression inflicted upon the people by monarchs the church recognized as legitimate, there is no doubt that Chinese practicing Confucian principles in their home gave the emperor room to get away with behavior orthodox Confucianists deemed unvirtuous.

Wm. Theodore de Bary believes there is a liberal strain in Confucianism, especially neo-Confucianism. But what he refers to as liberalism consists of virtues rather than rights. Liberalism is the political philosophy espoused by those who call for the recognition of rights in conjunction with virtues. De Bary's notion of liberalism is actually focused more on ideas of virtue, moderation, individual enlightenment and compromise (de Bary 1983:6–9). These are the concerns of Montesquieu, the American founders and contemporary philosophers who worry Western democracies have become too reliant on rights at the expense of the ideals Tocqueville found most promising about modern democratic life (Tocqueville 1966). Hence Confucianism does emphasize a body of political virtues, but as a political philosophy it is nevertheless rights averse.

Beyond filial piety, loyalty, and basic morals, what are the virtues Confucianists espouse? While Mencius holds a rather optimistic view of human potential, Confucius is skeptical when it comes to identifying the virtues of the common man. For one thing, Confucius probably believed that the common man would not understand higher things because the common man was mostly engaged in a struggle for survival and did not take time to reflect on the things scholars did. In addition, the common man was too interested in everyday matters that were of little or no significance to superior men, or gentlemen. He believed that common people were not easily restrained and would often choose the wrong way. He considered them ill tempered, foolish, and crafty (Shils 1996:59). For this reason, we must turn to Confucius' description of the scholar not only to find virtues that made men superior in a Confucian world but also what ideals overlap into areas we would deem virtuous for the citizen of a republic.

Confucius does not indicate in his writings that he thought about the concept of a civil society. He does not spend much time on economic matters, on private property, on the people's livelihood and its relation to state affairs, nor popular discussion of state affairs. But he does deal with virtues that are often spoken of when referring to the scholar/ruler and the conduct of civil affairs. The Confucian scholar is to be benevolent. By this we assume Confucius means the leader must be kind and concerned for the welfare of others. To some degree, the morality of the people is dependent on the morality of the leaders and the scholars who advise them. "If they [the people] be led by virtue, and uniformity sought to be given them by rules of propriety, they will have a sense of shame, and moreover, will become good" (Confucius 1971:2:3). The monarch was to make "pulse and grain as abundant as water and fire" (Mencius 1970:7:B:23). Thus moral responsibility was laid at the feet of the monarch. He was not given license to do whatever he chose. Education was to be as grounded in moral substance as it was practical matters so that a scholar/ruler would not be tempted to usurp power or love power more than the well-being of the public. In fact, great leaders are those who serve according to righteousness, and if this is not possible, "relinquish office" (Mencius 1970:5:B:9).

Confucianism is generally intolerant of religion and suspicious of free thinking because both can lead men from the way. Confucius was persuaded that the common people easily turn away from and are too unreflective of the right way. For this reason, it is essential for good leaders to show the way in order for common people to live the way they should. In other words, princes and scholar/rulers have a moral obligation to keep people on paths of righteousness. Good rulers can encourage the people to live good lives. In taking the right path, no actions are as advantageous as acts of filial piety. It is therefore the role of the prince to rule over the people and the people's responsibility to support the ruler. The people are to work hard and the ruler to make his will known to men (Shils 1996:59). Leaders are to be tolerant insofar as they did not mete out harsh punishments or stray too far from the right way.

The superior man practices li, cultivates jen, and in so doing contributes to society by his mere presence. This is because a virtuous person is admired not simply for the individual development that he has experienced, but also because such a person has a desire to serve others around him and can offer wisdom and encouragement that ennoble the regime. He is tolerant of others' shortcomings, conducts all his affairs with dignity and is courageous in taking the right paths in life, no matter how unpopular doing right may be.

Confucianism can offer much in the justification of virtuous living, but it must be developed in a way that establishes virtue as a universal value and not something mainly obtainable to the few men who will rule over others. This will result in greater acceptance of rights generally and will help Confucian societies focus on common standards which much exist if democracy is not only to evolve but to thrive. Future leaders in Confucian cultures who seek to establish democracy for the first time or who strive to improve existing democracy would do much to improve the prospects of a democratic culture by speaking of Confucianism in a way that promotes republican virtues and incorporates rights into their work. Doing so will mollify the authoritarian attributes of Confucianism and build confidence in the reasonableness and dignity of democracy.

Islam and Democracy

The emergence of Islam in the seventh century had a profound influence on family and political life in the Arabic speaking world. Contrary to popular belief in the West, the Islamic tradition requires much of the believer in terms of commitment to family life and obligations to others outside the family. Too often the image Westerners have of Muslims is that of uncompromising religious extremists given to indiscriminate acts of violence. This perception has no doubt been reinforced by the many political conflicts that plague the Islamic world and the differences of how religion is practiced in the Islamic and Christian tradition.

Prior to Islam, the lot of women and children in the Arab world was brutish. If her husband died or left her, a woman was left to fend for herself and rely on the kindness of family. She had no legal recourse to seek outside help. The teachings of Mohammed brought about major changes in family life. Fathers and husbands were to take a more responsible role in family life. Women were to receive part of the dowry at the time of marriage. Women could apply for divorce, and receive an inheritance upon the death of male family members. Monogamous relationships were strongly encouraged and husbands could no longer leave a wife at his whim. Husbands were instructed to be faithful and loving towards their wives and children. The husband was called upon to be a reliable provider of food, clothing and shelter. Followers were encouraged to not only look out for the well-being of their family, but to be considerate and active in looking out for the welfare of their communities as well (Esposito 1982).

God, Nature, and the Evil of Political Philosophy

In addition to Islam being a tradition of responsibility, gentleness and compassion, Muslims are to accept all who are "children of the book," namely Christians and Jews. At the same time they are to recognize that there is but one God, Allah, and Mohammed is His prophet. Islam is the one correct way of living Allah's revealed law, though Muslims are to recognize the good in others who do not believe in the Qur'an or the teachings of Mohammed. Muslims believe in a heaven and hell, and like Jews believe that faith is demonstrated not as much by what you believe (as in the Christian tradition) but more in how you demonstrate faith by obedience to religious law. For this reason, Christians have difficulty understanding why democratic ideals cannot be easily embraced in Muslim societies. It is not merely democratic ideals that are difficult to introduce in Islamic society, however. There have been attempts to introduce other political regimes in the Muslim world, especially those pondered and debated by the philosophers of ancient Greece. But the acceptance of any secular authority presupposes the legitimacy of secular thought—philosophy. That has proven to be problematic in the case of Islam.

Christianity and Judaism both teach that the heavens and the earth were created by God, who used His power to command the elements and the elements obeyed. Islam also believes in the creation of the heavens and the earth by a divine and all-knowing being. Christians and Jews, however, have come to accept scientific understandings of nature and to conduct scientific research in accordance to scientific laws that were discovered by human beings. Few Christians and Jews understand the problem that is created by accepting both philosophical understandings of nature and the human condition on the one hand and sacred knowledge as received by revelation on the other. There are contradictions as God reveals what He will reveal about certain phenomena whereas science is based on reason and builds upon reason to manipulate nature and to learn about other things. Many generations have passed since this contradiction became apparent, giving the average believer room to practice religion and simultaneously believe in science. Thus Christians and Jews have found a way to rationalize certain attributes of religion and they are therefore comfortable with the uneven fit that exists between religion and science. But it is not as easy in the Muslim world.

The Holy Qur'an is "the Perfect Book, free from all doubt . . . " (1:2). It is eternal and unchangeable. It contains all that is needed for mankind to know how to have a fulfilling life and make it to heaven (10:58). Within its pages the Qur'an reveals that all aspects of nature and creation are a reflection of Allah's will and Allah's work (13:2–5). For this reason, Muslim students are not educated in the same manner as students are in the West. Education in the Islamic world begins with the Qur'an, whether it be language, science, theology, or jurisprudence.

But the same could be said about Christianity before there was an attempt to rationalize the Christian religious tradition. This is why the efforts of St. Thomas Aquinas (1225–1274) were so significant. The Greeks had already established precedent for discovering nature by seeking to explain things according to reason. But Christianity initially viewed this attempt as an attack on the revealed word of God. Aquinas, however, believed that in addition to the supernatural, God revealed principles and gave humans the capacity to understand these principles by reason and experience alone (Aquinas

1945: Part I, Articles 1–10). He was free to make such assertions because there was not a clear antiphilosophic bias among the ecclesiastical hierarchy. Students of theology were expected to learn both religious cannon and philosophy in the course of their studies (Fortin 1987:250).

It was not as easy for the great Muslim philosopher Alfarabi (870–950). Alfarabi was the first philosopher who attempted to bring together the religious elements of Islam with classical political philosophy. Alfarabi is credited with reclaiming classical thought and using it as a complement to revealed religion (Mahdi 1987:206). He attempted to use Platonic thought to inform Islam as a way of bringing about the best regime. His work impressed other Muslim thinkers, most notably Avicenna and Averroes, as well as the Jewish philosopher Maimonides and predictably Aquinas. But Aquinas was not as bound by religious law as were the Muslim and Jewish philosophers which enabled him to philosophize freely. Alfarabi had to be much more careful in not drawing too close a connection between his philosophy and specific passages in the Qur'an, though his attempts to merge the sacred with the secular were nevertheless apparent (Mahdi 1987:208).

There is no mistaking the important role medieval philosophy had in rationalizing the will of God and thereby developing the Western tradition of reason and political thought. Some of that credit can be attributed to Alfarabi even though his work was largely rejected by other Muslim scholars. Today we hear scholars contending that like Christianity, Islam also relies on principles of consensus and consultation on matters of religious importance and therefore holds the same promise of using reason in thinking about the temporal world, thus uncovering philosophy (Enayat 1982:129). But the strong reliance on law in the Islamic tradition creates the same prohibition on philosophy that Alfarabi and others encountered centuries ago. Hence, nature remains largely undiscovered in the Islamic tradition. Christianity was able to rationalize a spiritual and temporal world. Such a possibility is difficult in a Muslim country. A caliph may delegate temporal authority to an emir, but the spiritual authority of the caliph continues to be respected by the emir and his government (Rosenthal 1962:23).

Islamic Virtues Over Rights

The secular ruler's authority over the subject in Muslim societies is not usually considered to be absolute. Leaders are subject to the same laws that the people are. Islamic law (or the Sharia) is universal and egalitarian. The Sharia is the law for all Muslims, and ideally, all human beings (Esposito 1988:89). The Sharia transcends the family and the authority of fathers. It places duty to God highest, and then duty to others and family, thus requiring the same standards of all. Because of the egalitarian and universal nature of the Sharia, some scholars suggest there is a precedent for rule by law in the Islamic tradition, thus room for constitutional law, and a place for a legal opposition. The Sharia is an embodiment of eternal truths, but recognizes that human beings are not perfect and may stumble in their attempts to follow the law. Scholars claim that acknowledging infallible truths and the fallibility of human interpretation provides the basis of sound constitutional law (Esposito and Voll 1996:41). Indeed, constitutionalists have been able to use the Sharia to back all kinds of claims supporting rights—limited rule, limits to obedience and even election of the imamate. But while the rule of the leader is not supposed to be absolute in Islamic society, using the Sharia to back constitutional law is problematic (Lewis 1988:113–16). Regimes that rely on the Sharia are vulnerable to competing interpretations of the Sharia (Mayer 1988:209). Some key principles set forth in the Sharia could be used as a springboard to develop a philosophy of rights, but it would require a fundamental shift towards rights than is presently accepted by Muslim scholars (Mayer 1991:77). Very often, the Sharia is used to justify the denial of rights. This can be pointed out by considering what currently happens when a leader's actions go against the Sharia.

In theory, if a leader breaks the law, he has gone against Islamic law and has broken the trust for which he was installed. Under these circumstances, he places himself in jeopardy, both politically and spiritually (Lewis 1988:91). But this is not to say that leaders who commit gross errors in Muslim countries are compelled to leave office. Much of this is determined by the degree or significance of the error within the context of how others live their lives. If the ruler's actions have a detrimental effect on those trying to live the law, he is on shaky ground. But if his errors are errors in judgment, or errors that do not harm the status of Islam in society, he is often given latitude to rule as he pleases. This is justified by religious leaders who believe the political authorities are bound to make mistakes because of the complexities of politics and the fact that secular officials are not as likely to be in tune with Islamic tenets as spiritual leaders are. There is also a certain resignation that anybody who rules will make mistakes but final arbitration must be made by Allah.

But mistakes and not following Islamic law closely enough can spell political trouble. There are quietist and activist traditions within Islam. The
quietists respect authority and tend not to place as much importance on
religious orthodoxy in political affairs as does the activist tradition. The activists watch political leaders more closely. If it is determined that the political authorities are not following the religious tradition closely enough,
they rebel and attempt to replace the leadership with those who have a more
orthodox understanding of political authority and the law. Under these circumstances, activist Muslims must follow leaders who pay close attention to
the Islamic tradition (Lewis 1988:94). Much of the Islamic revivalist movement is an attempt to awaken the original excitement of the founding era of
Islam. There is a strong belief that modern society, Westernization, and colonization has contributed to the disintegration of religious fervor for Islam.
For this reason, activists call upon Muslims to purge non-Islamic elements
from their lives and from political authority. In some cases, there has been a
turn to armed struggle to bring back orthodoxy (Esposito 1988:126–27).

Many scholars are quick to point out that such behavior and reliance on
a restoration of Islamic fervor is the exception rather than the rule. They
suggest there are other attributes of the Islamic tradition that can contribute
to the establishment of rights that have been lost as we have focused our
attention to activist Muslims. These scholars argue that in addition to the
egalitarian nature of Islamic law, there is also a tradition of limited obedience
to political authority. The activist tradition in Islam does, in fact, suggest
that devout Muslims should avoid following an unrighteous leader. This is
not to suggest however, that the acceptable alternative is for them to follow
a democratic leader. To date, there is not sufficient evidence to affirm
whether or not the idea of limiting obedience to a secular leader is the same
thing as advocating an enlarged role for the individual vis-à-vis the state.

There is also a tradition of consensus building and of seeking compromise
in Islam. Indeed, consensus developed from the practice of trying to determine the intent of law. In this process, majority opinion came to matter in
decisions of jurisprudence. In the course of these decisions, individual opinion and ambition is checked (Esposito 1988:84). These time-honored traditions of allowing differing interpretations of law has given rise to the contention that the use of reason can be extended to areas of nonreligious
matters as well. It should be noted that all of the privileges referred to so far
were only allowed within the circles of those charged with interpreting Islamic tradition. There is no invitation for others to engage in these discus-

sions. Most of these concepts were developed between the ninth and four-teenth centuries. The ideas are not as interesting to those interpreting the law today as they were then. Most contemporaries are interested in discussing ethics, revelation, and campaigning against rationalism (Mayer 1991:55).

There is the suggestion, however, that Islam simply has not taken the turn that Christianity took that eventually led to the establishment of rights. At least not yet, that is. Christianity, it is pointed out, had to develop the concept of rights. These scholars suggest there exists within Islam some idea of free will, established by the concepts of consensus, compromise, and reason, and from the Qur'an. They argue the Qur'an does not specifically establish state authority nor does it call upon state authority to punish people for apostasy. The Islamic concept of universal guidance suggests human beings all have the ability to determine the right course to follow. In addition, it is argued that the Qur'an teaches that the deeds of human beings will be judged by Allah alone. For this reason, justice is determined ultimately by Allah and by universal guidance (a gift from Allah) which is the "presupposition of individual conscience" (Little, et al. 1988:79, 82). Thus there exists not only the possibility of religious tolerance, but also the separation of church and state and the divine right to self-determination via individual conscience.

Others claim that a sense of democracy and freedom is found within the Islamic tenets of kindness and mercy. Showing kindness and mercy, they say, indicates tolerance. Tolerance, being a key requirement for democracy, means that the seeds of political rights are found within the Islamic tradition (Enayat 1982:130–31).

The claim that individual conscience, tolerance, universality, and egali-tarianism of the Sharia are proofs of a latent rights tradition is significant if religious authorities interpret these concepts with a view to rights. It is a fallacy to suggest that one ought to believe something to be a particular way when it only reflects the individual desires of the person forwarding the argument. To date, there is no significant religious interpretation that has been forwarded to support these arguments. It is at best a creative interpre-tation of Islamic law that reflects more Western secularism than Islamic influence. Most often, Muslim scholars change the meaning of rights in such discussions or claim incompatibilities of interpretations. The discussion of rights is

kept at a level of idealistic abstraction, and the individual provisions become vague, equivocal, and evasive when the authors address areas where premodern Sharia rules deviate sharply from modern human rights norms. . . . [They] lack any clear theory of what rights should mean in an Islamic context or how to derive their content from the Islamic sources in a consistent and principled fashion (Mayer 1991:53–54).

We are thus left with the realization that in most cases, those claiming a compatibility between the Islamic tradition and internationally accepted standards of human rights do not speak authoritatively for Islam. Their work has been informed by the Western belief that rights are universal and can therefore be found in non-Western traditions. But without rationalizing Islamic thought, there is no solid support for rights in the Muslim world.

That is not to say that there are not principles that are useful in building a democratic society within the Islamic tradition, however. All of the ideas we have discussed above, consensus, consultation, compromise, kindness, mercy, egalitarianism, universality of the law, are all tenets that can be used in a democratic regime. One must be careful, however, in claiming that they can only be used to support democracy. Most authoritarian regimes, especially those that emphasize personal responsibility and duty, subscribe to high moral principles like these mentioned here. In order for these principles to support democracy, there must be some agreement that they can be interpreted in a way to rationalize Islamic thought enough to support rights, and to provide moral guidance for individuals so that democratizing regimes do not have to rely solely on rights to justify democracy. In this regard, these virtues give hope that rights may someday be recognized in the Muslim world. At the same time they may help satisfy Islamic concerns that the political regime must not stray from the fundamental good taught within the Islamic tradition.

Hence scholars have too often searched for rights in the Islamic tradition without realizing that rights presuppose philosophy. It is therefore more fruitful to direct attention to these principles they suggest constitute the basis of rights and reapply them in ways they can be used as republican virtues.

Conclusion

During the 1970s and early 1980s, much was made about the great divide between rich and poor countries (the so-called North-South debate) and the conflict between NATO countries and Warsaw Pact countries. These categories of analysis have subsided in importance as the political and economic promise of liberalism has swept the globe. Capitalism in its various forms and the language of human rights have found acceptance among authoritarian and democratic regimes alike. Authoritarian leaders fear the embarrassment of being the last dictator in their region of the world or the legacy of being the last authoritarian ruler of their country. This has encouraged erstwhile authoritarians to make democratic compromises leading to the acceptance of rights as espoused in the West. The appeals to authoritarian legitimacy made by leaders like Chiang Kai-shek, Chun Do-hwan, Alberto Fujimori, Augusto Pinochet, and the Sultanist-style leaders of the Middle East, are now looked at in the same way people view organized crime figures who try to foster an image of competence and community concern rather than of fear and intimidation.

While it is true we can learn from the cultures of the world it is also increasingly apparent that rights, as understood first in the West, are finding acceptance across cultural boundaries. In the process, rights are becoming a common heritage of the peoples of the world. In Confucian countries great progress has been made in embracing rights, though much remains to be done. In its present form, Confucianism does not respect the role of the individual in the regime. Its content is authoritarian and it is deeply suspicious of equality and liberty. To argue Confucianism has a rights tradition is the same as to suggest that the monarchical regimes of the West knew rights were better but for one reason or another people decided not to claim them. But there is room to work with the tradition of virtues in Confucianism and have them support rights. In the Islamic world, the call to liberalize is still new. Islam has many noble virtues that can be employed to support democratic regimes. But there is no tradition of rights belonging to Islam. As long as Muslim scholars struggle against Alfarabi's dream of providing a place for philosophy alongside religion, the possibility of political philosophy is thwarted and rights will remain buried.

Both of these traditions can learn much from the West. It was in the West that nature was first discovered, that reason came to play a role, and individualism sprung from the work of philosophers in both religious and secular settings. In the West there exist philosophical rationalizations that can break the grip of authoritarianism. In the West the hunt for rights began and it can also begin for those who desire to build a tradition of rights in Confucian and Islamic cultures. In the meantime, to look elsewhere for rights is a futile exercise that will reap only disappointment.

Bibliography

An-Na'im, Abdullah. 1987. "Islamic Law, International Relations, and Human Rights." *Cornell International Law Journal* 20(2):333–35.

Aquinas, Thomas. 1945. *Summa Theologica*, Edited by Anton C. Pegis. New York: Random House.

Bell, Daniel A. 1993. *Communitarianism and its Critics*. New York: Oxford University Press.

Bellah, Robert N. 1986. *Habits of the Heart: Individualism and Commitment in American Life*. New York: Harper and Row.

Confucius. 1971. *Confucius: Confucian Analects, The Great Learning and The Doctrine of the Mean*, Translated and Edited by James Legge. New York: Dover Publications.

Dahl, Robert A. 1971. *Polyarchy: Participation and Opposition*. New Haven: Yale University Press.

de Bary, Wm. Theodore. 1983. *The Liberal Tradition in China*. New York: Columbia University Press.

Dwyer, Kevin. 1991. *Arab Voices: The Human Rights Debate in the Middle East*. Berkeley: University of California Press.

Ebrey, Patricia. 1991. "The Chinese Family and the Spread of Confucian Values." In Gilbert Rozman, ed. *The East Asian Region: Confucian Heritage and its Modern Adaptation*. Princeton: Princeton University Press.

Enayat, Hamid. 1982. *Modern Islamic Political Thought*. Austin: University of Texas Press.

Esposito, John L. 1982. *Women In Muslim Family Law*. Syracuse: Syracuse University Press.

Esposito, John L. 1988. *Islam: The Straight Path*. Oxford: Oxford University Press.

Esposito, John L. and John O. Voll. 1996. *Islam and Democracy*. Oxford: Oxford University Press.

Feng Yu-lan. 1952. *History of Chinese Philosophy*, Volumes I and II, Translated by Derk Bodde. Princeton: Princeton University Press.

Fortin, Ernest L. 1987. "St. Thomas Aquinas," in Leo Strauss and Joseph Cropsey, eds. *History of Political Philosophy*. Chicago: University of Chicago Press.

Galston, William A. 1991. *Liberal Purposes: Goods, Virtues, and Diversity in the Liberal State*. London: Cambridge University Press.

Huntington, Samuel P. 1993. "The Clash of Civilizations?" *Foreign Affairs* (Summer 1993).

Huntington, Samuel P. 1991. *The Third Wave: Democratization in the Late Twentieth Century*. Norman, Oklahoma: University of Oklahoma Press.

Karl, Terry Lynn and Philippe C. Schmitter. 1991. "What Democracy Is . . . and Is Not." *Journal of Democracy* (Summer).

Lewis, Bernard. 1988. *The Political Language of Islam*. Chicago: University of Chicago Press.

Little, David; John Kelsay, and Abdulaziz A. Sachedina. 1988. *Human Rights and the Conflict of Cultures: Western and Islamic Perspectives on Religious Liberty*. Columbia: University of South Carolina Press.

Locke, John. 1988. *Two Treatises of Government*, Edited by Peter Laslett. New York: Cambridge University Press.

Madsen, Richard. 1984. *Morality and Power in a Chinese Village*. Berkeley: University of California Press.

Mahdi, Mushin. 1987. "Alfarabi," in Leo Strauss and Joseph Cropsey, eds. *History of Political Philosophy*. Chicago: University of Chicago Press.

Mayer, Elizabeth. 1991. *Islam and Human Rights: Tradition and Politics*. Boulder: Westview Press.

Mencius. 1970. *Mencius*, Translated by D.C. Lau. New York: Viking Penguin.

Montesquieu, Charles de Secondat. 1989. *The Spirit of the Laws*, edited by Anne Cohler, Basia Miller, and Harold Stone. Cambridge: Cambridge University Press.

Nivison, David S. 1996. *The Ways of Confucianism: Investigations in Chinese Philosophy*. Edited by Bryan W. Van Norden. Chicago: Open Court.

Pangle, Thomas L. 1992. *The Ennobling of Democracy*. Baltimore: The Johns Hopkins University Press.

Plato. 1984. *Four Texts of Socrates*, translated by Thomas G. West and Grace Starry West. Ithaca: Cornell University Press.

Pollis, Adamantia and Peter Schwab. 1979. "Human Rights: A Western Construct With Limited Applicability." In Pollis and Schwab, eds. *Human Rights: Cultural and Ideological Perspectives*, 1–15. New York: Praeger.

Putnam, Robert D. 1993. *Making Democracy Work: Civic Traditions in Modern Italy*. Princeton: Princeton University Press.

Rosenthal, Erwin I.J. 1962. *Political Thought in Medieval Islam: An Introductory Outline*. Cambridge: Cambridge University Press.

Rousseau, Jean-Jacques. 1987. *Basic Political Writings: Discourse on the Origin of Inequality and On The Social Contract*, translated by Donald A. Cress. Indianapolis: Hackett.

Schwartz, Benjamin I. 1985. *The World of Thought in Ancient China*. Cambridge: The Belknap Press of Harvard University.

Shils, Edward. 1996. "Reflections on Civil Society and Civility in Chinese Intellectual Tradition," in Tu Weiming, ed. *Confucian Tradition in East Asian Modernity: Moral Education and Economic Culture in Japan and the Four Mini Dragons*. Cambridge: Harvard University Press.

State Council of the People's Republic of China. 1996. *Human Rights and China* (November). Reprinted in *Beijing Review* (November 4, 1991).

Strauss, Leo. 1950. *Natural Right and History*. Chicago: University of Chicago Press.

Tocqueville, Alexis. 1966. *Democracy in America*, Translated by George Lawrence, Edited by J.P. Meyer. New York: Harper Perennial.

Zakaria, Fareed. 1994. "Culture Is Destiny: A Conversation With Lee Kuan Yew." *Foreign Affairs* (March/April):109–126.

Part 3

Human Rights Law and Its Limits

5 How a Liberal Jurist Defends the Bangkok Declaration

Michael W. Dowdle

Introduction

Human rights are inherently universal and inalienable. By vesting in humans, human rights vest in everyone, and hence are universal. And since they vest in humans by virtue of our humanity, society can never gain authority to recall or curtail their application, hence they are inalienable. For many, probably most, in the human rights community, this has been interpreted as meaning that one may not take cultural or other forms of situational specifics into account when deciding what political actions are acceptable within the human rights regime (see, e.g., Ayton-Shenker 1995, Donnelly 1985; see also Harries 1997; see generally Steiner and Alston 1996:192–193).

In 1993, however, the Bangkok Governmental Declaration, a joint declaration on human rights promulgated by a group of primarily East and Southeast Asian countries in Bangkok in the spring of 1993,[1] challenged this dominant interpretation of the human rights community. While not challenging the overall universality and inalienability of human rights per se, the Bangkok Declaration nevertheless states, in relevant part, that the application of human rights "must be considered in the context of a dynamic and evolving process of international norm setting, bearing in mind the significance of the national and regional particularities and various historical, cultural and religious backgrounds." It claims, in other words, that economic and other situational specifics should be taken into account in determining what particular political actions are acceptable under the international human rights regime.

As noted by Philip Alston (1994:380–381), the human rights community has yet to respond effectively to this dissident claim of the Bangkok Declaration. It is not sufficient merely to dismiss the Declaration as an instrument of bad faith. The actual mind-set of the signatories and drafters of the Bangkok Declaration does not affect the strength or lack thereof of the claims made by that Declaration. Arguments are about matters of truth, not intentions: the test for that truth does not depend on the mental state of the person making the argument. Some who read the Declaration are indeed honestly attracted to its claims (see, e.g., Alston 1994:380–381; Harries 1997). In failing to respond to the merit of the Bangkok Declaration's claims, the human rights community perpetuates a real perception within much of the third world that much of human rights discourse is really more lecture than true dialogue, and one more self-serving than public spirited (Alston 1994).

As this chapter shall show, the Bangkok Declaration's claims are actually wholly consistent with a conception of rights that enjoys much purchase in the West. In order to respond effectively to the challenges of the East Asian nations, we need to start taking their arguments seriously, and develop a more realistic description of how traditional human rights relate to other legitimate moral concerns with which they must sometimes compete.

Human Rights and Moral Demands

For most of us, violations of human rights are not just technical illegalities, they are moral wrongs, and this moral authority compels a kind of respect and obedience that we simply do not afford to, say, traffic regulations. This moral authority is clearly reflected in many of the seminal human rights instruments. The European Convention for the Protection of Human Rights and Fundamental Freedoms finds moral authority for its provisions in the "profound belief in those fundamental freedoms which are the foundation of justice and peace in the world. . . . " The Universal Declaration and the two Covenants find authority for their respective lists of rights from the fact that these rights derive from respect for the "inherent dignity of the person." The Universal Declaration finds further authority in the fact that human rights serve as the foundation of freedom, justice and peace in the world. We might refer to this kind of moral compulsion as "prescriptive effect." Note, however, that the world and its history are replete with examples of legal regimes that claimed to enjoy special correspondence with moral reality, but did not. See, e.g., Tise 1987 (noting claims to moral truth made by proponents of slavery laws). Thus, if human rights law is to truly enjoy the prescriptive effect it claims, it must correspond somehow to our own *independent* notions of what justice demands (Dworkin 1978:206–222; Hurd 1995:418). But how successful is the traditional conception of human rights as generally used by the human rights community at securing such prescriptive effect?

The human rights community commonly advances a particular conception that sees rights as "rules" that command that particular actors must always respond in particular ways to particular situations. (A more developed description of this particular conception of rights can be found in Dworkin [1978:14–28] and Hart [1961:100–110].) Such rules are characterized by the fact that they recognize no indeterminate sources of possible contrary authority. If a rule says no right turn, without articulating any exceptions, and we turn right anyway, we have by virtue of that act alone broken the rule. As an Inspector Javert might remind us, the reason *why* we turned right is of no import unless the rule (or the larger body of rules of which it is a part) articulates a relevant exception.

Human rights, we are often told, are also of this quality: a country that sacrifices freedom of the press in pursuit of economic development is said to be in violation of human rights law simply because that that law has no articulated exception which allows freedom of the press to be sacrificed for such a reason (see, e.g., Kiss 1981:291). We will refer to this particular type of rule as "hard commands," and to the particular conception of rights it evokes as "hard rights."

Some might wonder how human rights could be regarded as hard commands when the human rights instruments themselves allow for governments to legitimately abridge articulated human rights under specified conditions. Article 4 of the International Covenant on Civil and Political Rights says, for example, that "[i]n times of public emergency which threatens the life of the nation . . . the States Parties . . . may take measures derogating from their obligations under the present Covenant to the extent strictly required by the exigencies of the situation. . . . " Remember, however, that a hard command may subject itself to contrary sources of authority, but only so long as these sources are *articulated*. A hard conception of rights only denies the possibility of indeterminate (or unarticulated) exceptions, not of exceptions generally.

Hard commands can be contrasted with another kind of command, obviously called soft commands. A soft command requires that we give a particular concern sufficient weight in *deciding* what actions to take without demanding that we *act* in a certain way. In other words, a soft command recognizes that unarticulated, competing claims of authority might exist, and merely demands that the decisionmaker take its particular concern into adequate account.

Most if not all moral commands are in the form of soft commands. We can see this from the fact that for most, if not all, moral principles, we simply cannot articulate in advance all the instances in which it would acceptable for us to act in contradiction to the principle (Rawls 1971:20–21, 46–50, 46–52). Therefore, if a legal regime is to enjoy prescriptive effect, its rules also must be in the form of soft rather than hard commands. Following the terminology popularized by Ronald Dworkin (1978), we will refer to the particular soft commands upon which such a conception of rights is founded as "principles," as contrasted with "rules."

The soft-command character of rights-as-principles (or "soft rights") is clearly evident in American constitutional law. (See generally Nowak et al. [1995:994–996], Dorf [1996], Dworkin [1978].) Of course, many of the rights articulated in the Bill of Rights are indeed couched as hard rights. The first amendment, for example, reads that that "Congress shall *make no law* . . . abridging the freedom of speech [emphasis added]". Nevertheless, the actual application of these rights is much more nuanced. Congress is readily able to pass laws that abridge our ability to speak freely when and where necessity demands or prudence dictates. These include laws that forbid, for example, disclosure of state secrets; unregulated offers to sell securities; and public broadcast of obscene language (see generally Nowak, et. al. 1995:994–996). As noted by the United States Supreme Court, despite the absolute language with which these rights are framed, under standard juridical interpretation the actual application of these rights must be weighed against competing concerns:

> [W]e reject the view that freedom of speech and association . . . are "absolutes," [in the] sense that where the constitutional protection exists it must prevail. . . . Throughout its history this Court has consistently recognized at least two ways in which constitutionally pro-

tected freedom of speech is narrower than an unlimited license to talk.
On the one hand, certain forms of speech, or speech in certain contexts, has been considered outside the scope of constitutional protection. . . . On the other hand, general regulatory statutes . . . have not
been regarded as the type of law the First or Fourteenth Amendments
forbade Congress or the States to pass, when they have been found
justified by subordinating valid governmental interests, a prerequisite
to constitutionality which has necessarily involved a weighing of the
governmental interests involved . . . . (*Konigsberg v. State Bar of California*, 366 U.S. 36, 49–51 (1961)).[2]

Indeed, James Madison introduced the ninth amendment into the American
Constitution, which reads that "[t]he enumeration in the Constitution, of
certain rights, shall not be construed to deny or disparage others retained by
the people," with the express intent of preventing American rights-based
jurisprudence from adopting a hard conception of rights. In presenting the
initial draft of that amendment before the House of Representatives, he
warned that a strict, rule-based construction of our constitutional rights
would sap these rights of their moral authority, and thus of their effectiveness.
(Madison 1989; see also Waldron 1993 for a more philosophically fleshed-
out articulation of this idea.)

Moreover, the application of our constitutional rights is weighed not only
against other rights, but also against state budgetary constraints and other
incidence of administrative convenience (see, e.g, *Mathews v. Eldridge*, 424
U.S. 520, 531–532 (1976)), and sometimes even against community standards of decorum (see, e.g., *FCC v. Pacifica Foundation*, 438 US 726 (1978),
see generally Costonis 1982). This may well come as a shock to those
brought up on the rhetoric of many human rights commentators. Human
rights, we are often told, are founded on the notion that legitimate individual
concerns should not be sacrificed for simple "communitarian" interests (see
below). And yet, as we have just seen, here in the land that some claim to
be the standard-bearer for Western individualism (see, e.g., Huntington
1996:71–72, 306–307), such rights are in fact so sacrificed all the time.

Human Rights and Legal Positivism

Of course, no one could claim that a hard conception of rights is intellectually, politically, or philosophically "illegitimate." The hard conception

is frequently associated with "legal positivism" (see Dworkin 1978:14–28). Legal positivism posits a descriptive rather than a prescriptive vision of the law. According to it, the legitimacy of legal command is defined wholly by procedures for legitimacy that are articulated by the law itself (Hart 1961:100–110). While many legal positivists do recognize that law should correspond with our moral intuitions, they do not condition the law's legitimacy on such a correspondence, the way that the principled conception of right does (see, e.g., Kelsen 1966:570–572). According to positivism, unjust law is just as legal as just law. (The soft conception, by contrast, is derived from what we might call "legal liberalism," which sees a direct connection between the legitimacy of law and its morality.)

Throughout Western legal history, positivism has been as prominent a component both of Western legal history and of Western legal thought as has been liberalism. Indeed, public international law, the superstructure of which human rights law is a part, has historically been largely conceived of as positivist law (Friedmann 1964:75–77; Kelsen 1966:570–572). The particular conceptualization of human rights and hard rights reflects the positivist foundations of the international legal regime. See D'Amato 1995: 51–69.

The choice between positivist and liberal conceptions of law affects more than philosophical taxonomists, however. It also affects the way the legal regime interacts with its environment. And despite its well-established status both within Western legal thought and within public international law, there is real reason to question whether, as a practical matter, legal positivism is the more appropriate foundation for a human rights regime.

There are at least three reasons that suggest that liberalism promises a more effective human rights regime than positivism. First, the positivist foundations for human rights are not particularly strong. The seminal source for the international regime of human rights is the Universal Declaration, whose status as a positive legal instrument is open to real question (Schachter 1991:85, Henkin 1990:177–178). The two positivist documentary mainstays of that regime, the International Covenant on Civil and Political Rights, and the International Covenant on Economic, Social and Cultural Rights, are both in the form of treaties, and thus technically binding only on signatory states, and are subject to the myriad of reservations that states have attached to their signing. The other positivist foundation recognized by traditional principles of public international law, "state practice" (commonly called customary international law), is also a weak reed. Even the strongest proponents of international human rights frequently despair at the general ineffectiveness of norms of human rights in shaping actual international behavior (Schachter 1991:336–337), and such evidence as is commonly marshaled in support of such "custom" generally fails to conform to the criteria commonly used to evaluate such practices (id., Henkin 1990:180–181).

This problem is much less detrimental to a principled conception of human rights, however. A principled conception of rights can buttress weaknesses in positive legal authority by appealing to the moral foundations that underlie the positive law's legitimacy. In this way, a principled conception of rights actually gives the human rights regime a stronger basis of *institutional* authority than does a positivist conception.

Second, the positivist corpus of international human rights law is also too sparse to support an effective human rights regime. This sparseness limits human rights effectiveness in two ways. First, it limits the areas in which the human rights community can authoritatively interject itself. A fundamental axiom of law everywhere is *nullum crimen sine lege, nullum poena sine lege* ["no crime without law; no penalty without law"] (The application of this principle to public international law is discussed in D'Amato 1983.) Obviously, implicit in this axiom is a corollary that the more sparse the legal framework, the fewer matters it can authoritatively seek to regulate, and the human rights corpus is much sparser than many in the human rights community seem willing to admit. The positive human rights sources do not really address themselves very well to newer, important social areas—such as environmental protection (Philip Alston 1984:612, Nickel 1993:281) and women's empowerment (Bell [this volume], Peach [this volume])—with which many in the human rights community are becoming rightly concerned. To the extent that the human rights community wishes to credibly expand its mandate to address these and other new areas of concern, a positivist theory of rights does not offer much support.

A principled conception of human rights, on the other hand, allows for a more expansive human rights penumbra. As noted above, a principled conception of rights requires human rights law to account for all issues of political justice, not merely those crystalized in the positive human rights corpus. To the extent that "new" issues like environmental protection and women's empowerment significantly impact the pursuit of internationalized legal justice that is the ultimate goal of human rights law, these issues become legitimate concerns of the human rights community.

The spare nature of the human rights corpus, when combined with a positivist legal orientation, also prevents the development of human rights law another way. Even under the most thorough of codes, situations frequently arise in which legal commands seem to point in obscure directions or otherwise contradict one another. For this reason, the effectiveness of any legal code depends in significant part on how well it is able to resolve its inevitable gaps and potential contradictions.

To the positivist, these problems are resolved principally through a secondary set of positivist rules which govern statutory interpretation. See Hart 1961:100–110. See, e.g., Singer (1994) (giving positivist "canons of statutory interpretation" for American law), Merryman 1985:39–48 (detailing the development of such rules in civil law systems). The positive human rights corpus, however, contains no such interpretive rules. Thus, the human rights community has no positivist authority on which it can rely for filling in statutory lacunae or choosing between superficially contradictory human rights mandates (Alston 1994:380–381, D'Amato 1995:48–50, McDougal et. al, 1980:813–814). This is particularly problematic for human rights law because the broad and general language with which human rights commands are articulated makes these rights particularly vulnerable to lacunae and interpretive dispute (D'Amato 1995:48–50).

A principled conception of rights, by contrast, does not require corrective rules in order to resolve legal conflicts and ambiguities. In the past, for example, issues such as slavery, women's suffrage, black suffrage, and segregation represented exceedingly difficult issues in American constitutional law, issues the positivist framework of our law was wholly unable to resolve. But these are not hard cases today, because the moral relevance of the law leads us to believe that there is indeed a perceivable and objective distinction between just and unjust solutions even in the face of the most abstruse of legal conundrums. We found that as we discussed these hard issues, rational consensus converged on a particular solution or solutions as constituting the most just response to that situation. See also Taylor 1998, Barnhart [this volume]. Since, as we have seen, under a principled conception of rights proof of justice coincides with proof of legality, this emerging rational consensus on the demands of justice also works to identify the correct legal response to the issue.

In fact, such consensual solutions are frequently more effective in the longer run than the inherently morally arbitrary solutions imposed by positive corrective rules, both in resolving the problem at hand, and in promoting confidence in the legal system's ability to effectively address hard problems in general. For example, the United States Constitution contains several provisions giving positive legal protection to the practice of slavery (see, e.g., Article 1, Section 9; Article 4, Section 2; and Article 5). These provisions were intended to provide positive law that would foreclose debate on the legality of slavery in the United States, a debate that the founders believed would destroy the new union. Despite these provisions, however, a growing moral revulsion to slavery not only kept this debate alive, but ultimately compelled a legal conclusion to this issue that was very different from that the framers sought to enshrine. In fact, the principal effect of the framers' attempt to use legal positivism to enshrine such an inherently unjust legal demand was to lead a significant portion of the population to question the legitimacy of constitutional authority per se (Kammen 1994:96–105; see also Cover 1975). Only after the slavery question was resolved in a morally persuasive manner was the American constitution able to begin enjoying significant respect within American culture (Kammen 1994:142).

This lesson should strike a note of concern in the heart of those who seek to found particular human rights claims or interpretations solely on the soil of positivist legal argument. When one claims that such-and-such a rule can never be derogated from; or that one kind of moral concern must *always* trump some other; or that a country must solve social problem "a" before it can begin addressing social problem "b," *simply because the positive human rights documents say so*, one is employing a form of argument identical to the positive constitutional arguments employed in defense of slavery in Antebellum America. Such positivist appeals work to cheapen the law, because they provide no compelling rationale as to why anyone *should* obey or even care about what the law says. See Hurd 1995:418, Thoreau 1991:29–30.

This brings us to the third problem of positivism with regard to international human rights law. Lacking access to any compelling moral force, human rights would enjoy only such effect as can be inspired by simple fear of institutional enforcement. See, e.g., Ni Aolain 1995:106, Henkin 1990:226. Such enforcement requires fairly elaborate institutional apparati that are able to make the threat of judicial sanction seem sufficiently real in a wide enough variety of circumstances. But existing institutional mechanisms for enforcing international human rights are weak at best and the dynamics of the international arena are such that it is unlikely that these mechanisms will improve much well through the foreseeable future (Henkin 1990:205–208). This dependence on institutional enforcement forces the human rights community to seek to defend its already weak positivist fortress with weapons it simply does not have.

But in fact, institutional enforcement is not a necessary component of an effective legal system. Many legal systems have been able to exert significant disciplining effect without even the threat of institutional enforcement. These include the British constitutional system (Wade and Bradley 1993:19–30), much of the American constitutional system (Chermerinsky 1996: 28–30, Rosenfeld 1993:138–139), many other constitutional systems (Cappelletti 1971:1), and even much of the public international legal system (Henkin 1979:47, Henkin 1990:57). As noted by Justice O'Connor of the United States Supreme Court, the reason why such systems are able to exert such effect is because of their ability to appeal to our independent notions of justice:

> [The Supreme] Court cannot buy support for its decisions by spending money and, except to a minor degree, it cannot independently coerce obedience to its decrees. The Court's power lies, rather, in its legitimacy, a product of substance and perception that shows itself in the people's acceptance of the Judiciary as fit to determine what the nation's law means and to declare what it demands." (*Planned Parenthood of Southeastern Pa. v. Casey*, 505 U.S. 833, 865 [1992]).

Ultimately, the effectiveness of the human rights regime depends on its ability to attract a kind of respect that cannot be compelled by institutional threat and/or appeal to institutional authority, a fact the human rights documents themselves acknowledge in their frequent appeal to "human dignity" and other higher moral sources. Thus, rather than focusing on the institutional features of the human rights regime, as positivism forces it to do, the human rights community may do better to focus on developing more compelling descriptions of how the demands of human rights interact with the myriads of other legitimate but competing demands that countries—particularly developing countries—face.[3] This requires a liberal, rather than a positivist, conception of human rights.

A Liberal Defense of the Bangkok Declaration

Once we understand the relative advantages of applying a principled conception of rights to human rights law, we can see why the claims of the

Bangkok Declaration deserve much more serious intellectual attention than they have heretofore enjoyed. These claims are really just straightforward extrapolations from the liberal conception of rights-as-principles employed by the American and many other Western constitutional systems. Consider, first, the Bangkok Declaration's claim that the particular circumstances of a polity must be taken into account in determining how a particular right is to be applied. Different circumstances obviously are going to present us with different collections of moral concerns. Few would be morally offended, for example, if a polity presently faced with severe threat of violent inter-ethnic conflict might rationally give greater concern to the socially disruptive implications of, say, hate-speech than one not so threatened.[4] (See, e.g., Cole 1997, discussing the Houston media's voluntary decision not to report on the desegregation of Houston's commercial sector for fear of inciting white racist organizations to violence.) The Bangkok Declaration's second claim holds that as a general matter the application of international human rights must be informed by the particular "values" of the cultures to which they are being applied. Since liberal political theory does not recognize a preferred morality superior to all others, different polities can, at least as a theoretical matter, legitimately assign different but nevertheless equally "legitimate" weights to the same just principles. Obviously such difference in priority can sometimes yield different moral conclusions in polities otherwise facing a similar moral problem (see below).

The issues raised by the Bangkok Declaration extend beyond this simple reading of its text, however. In actuality, the Bangkok Declaration tenders both of these claims within the context of a larger intellectual and political debate about the proper shape of our increasingly internationalized world. Read in context, these claims invoke implications that are somewhat more iconoclastic than might otherwise be apparent, even within a principled-rights framework. In order to show compelling intellectual force for the Bangkok Declaration, we should show this force for these claims as they sit in the context of this larger debate.

The first claim, that the applications of rights must be situation-specific, evokes a subtext that reflects and derives from the particular political agenda that led the primarily East and Southeast Asian governments to issue the Bangkok Declaration in the first place. This subtext is addressed to a particular type of situational disparity: namely, the contrast between countries that are economically developed and those that are not. Reading in this light, a more fleshed-out version of this claim would proceed as follows: The international law regime has recognized that in addition to the more traditional political and civil rights that most people in the West think of when we think of "rights"—rights like free speech, freedom of religion, and equal protection, for example—there also exists a right, vesting in the nation as a whole, to pursue and enjoy the fruits of economic development.[5] Obviously, underdeveloped and developing countries have more and greater needs in this area than do economically developed countries, and some of the applications of these more traditional civil and political rights urged by the human rights community could have some level of adverse affect on an underdeveloped nation's efforts to pursue the fruits of economic development. The human rights regime should therefore be more circumspect in applying civil and political rights to developing countries than in applying them to developed countries.

It is not at all clear, however, that this particular type of disparity should affect the application of rights, and many argue that it should not. Objectors argue that the international human rights regime, to the extent it does recognize a value to economic development, also prohibits sacrifice of any articulated civil or political right in pursuit of such development. Of course simply articulated as a positivist legal claim—i.e., that such tradeoffs are forbidden simply because the law says they are forbidden (see, e.g., Donnelly 1985)—this argument invokes little moral respect. As we saw above, simply saying that "one must because the (positive) law says one must" does not by itself secure our moral confidence in the underlying justice of the law's claim. A more sophisticated form of these arguments, however, asserts that real conflict between civil and political rights and social, economic and developmental rights in fact does not exist *as a practical (or empirical) matter*, and thus that abridgement of civil and political rights is never really necessary or morally indefensible. See, e.g., Sen 1997.

Taken at its most literal, however, the empirical component of this argument is most certainly false. Take, for example, the right to due process as articulated in Articles 3(b) and 9 of the International Covenant on Civil and Political Rights. Effective protection of such rights requires professionalized and well-trained judiciary and police, which in turn requires a significant legal and criminal justice education system and, derivatively, significant financial resources to build and maintain such a system. But any money spent on judicial and police training is money that cannot be spent on, say, promoting primary education or other infrastructural projects that could significantly promote economic development. At least on the level of governmental spending, conflict between at least some civil and political rights—namely, those that need active governmental support in order to be effective—and other kinds of rights is inevitable (Berlin 1961:169–170).

One might try to avoid the inevitable conundrums of budgetary constraints by limiting one's conception of privileged civil and political rights to what are frequently called "negative" rights (see Berlin 1961:122–123, for a conceptualization of negative rights). Negative rights are rights that do not require active governmental support, but only impose limitations on state action. Free speech, for example, is arguably such a right: the state need not actively promote free speech, it need only allow it. Obviously, since protection of negative rights like freedom of speech does not demand significant resources, it would seem to conflict much less, if at all, with the more active promotion of economic development.

It is not clear, however that there is in fact no conflict between negative and more active (or "positive") rights. The social dynamics introduced by the unregulated exercise of negative rights can sometimes interfere with the positive reform efforts demanded by positive rights: A freer press, for example, could greatly facilitate mobilization of opposition to female or minority assistance programs (see, e.g., Cole 1997). Unless and until one can disprove the possibility of such interference in all cases, a proposed blanket prioritization of negative over positive rights will not and cannot enjoy prescriptive support.

Moreover, prioritizing negative over more active, positive rights would result in a human rights regime that is very different from the one we have now. Some of the core responsibilities of human rights, such as protecting women against private abuse and discrimination, and abolishing child labor and forced prostitution, clearly require active state intervention—the state cannot meet these demands simply by not participating in such crimes (Bell [this volume], Peach [this volume]).

In fact, a claim that negative rights trump other rights could well eviscerate what protections some core human rights, like women's and children's rights, currently are able to provide. For example, freedom of conscience, as articulated in article 18 of the Universal Declaration and article 18 of the International Covenant on Civil and Human Rights, is generally regarded as a "negative" right, since its protection requires little active state intervention. But freedom from gender discrimination and abuse, as articulated in the Convention on the Elimination of All Forms of Discrimination Against Women, clearly requires significant state intervention for its protection (see

UNDP 1996a), and thus could not be considered a privileged, negative right. To the extent that a particular group within a country conscientiously chooses to discriminate against and even abuse women, perhaps as a matter of religious practice or even simply as a matter of strong, reflected tradition, such abuses would have to be tolerated, and perhaps even protected, by the human rights regime that privileges negative over positive rights (Steiner and Alston 1996:254). For most of us, however, this would be unacceptable: such practices are simply incompatible with the larger moral objectives of human rights law.

Others seek to support the claim that there is never any necessary tradeoff between economic development and the protection of civil and political rights by arguing that, even if such protections might detract from this development in some isolated areas, protecting civil and political rights actually promotes economic development *overall* (see, e.g., Human Rights Watch 1992, Sen 1997). But this argument enjoys little empirical or theoretical support. Empirical studies supporting this claim are contradicted by equal numbers of studies that refute it (see Knack and Keefer 1995:223, Przeworski and Limongi 1993:51–55). Moreover, those studies that do support this claim universally fail to distinguish what we might call soft authoritarian regimes—those which evince a significant and informed commitment to matters of economic development, like Singapore and China—from those more pathological regimes in which the ruling elite's principal concern is with enriching themselves at the expense of the common weal (see, e.g., Dasgupta 1993:116–121). Supporting studies also fail to distinguish between levels of economic development (Przeworski and Limongi 1993:63–64), whereas studies that do account for levels of economic development evince strongly that the economic benefits of civil and political rights only kick in once a minimal, prior level of economic and social development has already been achieved (Inglehart 1997:184, Ethier 1997:270–271, Burkhart and Lewis-Beck 1994, Przeworski and Limongi 1993:62). Thus, even those studies suggesting that more libertarian regimes outperform authoritarian regimes *overall* do not refute the claim, discussed in further detail below, that in *certain situations, certain forms* of authoritarianism may be more effective at promoting fair economic development than those with more libertarian practices.[6] For countries in such situations, the necessity of tradeoffs are still a real possibility, and need to be accounted for somehow in the human rights regime.

Nor are the various mechanisms by civil and political rights that are said to promote overall economic development as strong or universalized as their proponents are wont to claim. One way that civil and political rights are said to promote economic development is by facilitating the free flow of information and other forms of resources, such as labor. This is said to promote economic development in two ways: by facilitating government's ability to gather information about local conditions, thus allowing the government to structure sounder strategies for economic development; and by promoting market efficiency by lowering transaction costs among market participants, facilitating the free flow of labor and other resources, and ensuring that market transactions are founded on a complete and accurate understanding of all relevant information. By contrast, authoritarian regimes are said to encourage officials to hoard information and other resources, both from the public (i.e., the free market) and from other political actors, in order to protect their power and political reputation. This, in turn, prevents effective governmental response to local scarcities and local inefficiencies, and inhibits market efficiency more generally (see, e.g, Dreze and Sen 1989, Human Rights Watch 1992).

With regard to the first part of this claim, however, not all authoritarian structures suffer from this kind of information pathology. Soft authoritarian regimes can devote considerable energy to gathering (although not necessarily to broadly publicizing) unbiased information about local conditions (see, e.g., Dowdle 1997, discussing governmental efforts in China to gathering unbiased information). For such regimes, the informational efficiencies brought about by libertarian political structures would be of little added benefit in the structuring of sound economic policy. Indeed, given the successes of the economic development programs adopted by numerous soft authoritarian regimes in East Asia, it seems difficult to assert that the leaders and bureaucrats of such regimes must suffer from any significantly greater informational deficiencies than their counterparts in more libertarian regimes at the same level of economic development (see, e.g., Yergin and Stanislaw 1999:157–26).

With regard to the second part of this claim, we need to be aware that the less the "market" in question resembles the ideal markets described by neoclassical economics, the less that market benefits from increasingly free information flows. While generally free access to some sorts of information is essential for markets to work at all, this fact alone does not mean that simply freeing up market access to more information will always result in a correspondingly significant increase in market efficiency. Market efficiency depends on a number of diverse factors, and in underdeveloped economies it can easily be the case that the market suffers from structural deficiencies—

e.g., lack of education, inadequate information technologies, inadequate enforcement, inadequate banking systems, cartelization—that prevent the market from benefiting from the particular kind of transactional efficiencies promoted by civil and political rights. An Asian Development Bank study conducted by Katrina Pistor and Philip Wellons (1999), for example, found that the greater informational efficiencies associated with "rule of law" development did not promote economic development in insufficiently-developed markets in Asia (see also Stark and Bruszt 1998:109–136, discussing this problem in the context of economic development in Hungary).

Another way that civil and political rights are said to promote development in underdeveloped economies is by reducing corruption and wasteful military spending. But there is little positive correlation between regime type and levels of corruption, once economic variables are accounted for. (See, e.g., Putnam 1993, comparing corruption in southern and northern Italy.) In fact, transitions to democracy generally result in immediate increases in corruption (Wright 1997; della Porte 1996; World Bank 1992:54). In any event, as noted by the United Nations Development Programme, cleaning up governmental waste and corruption in underdeveloped countries generally requires an expenditure of resources that is simply beyond the means of most of these countries, regardless of regime type (UNDP 1997:72–73, 107). Similarly, many developing countries, again regardless of regime type, simply cannot reduce bloated military spending—one of the principal spending inefficiencies in both developing and developed countries—without provoking a coup d'état (Colletta et. al, 1996, Londregan and Poole 1990:151).

Civil and political rights are also sometimes said to promote economic development by encouraging investor confidence in the economy. International business, it is sometimes asserted, is more comfortable investing in free and open societies than in authoritarian ones. But there is little actual support for this claim. In fact, as noted in Przeworski and Limongi (1993:61), democracy may actually discourage international investment in economically underdeveloped countries. The fact that many in the human rights community regard international business with suspicion (see Bernstein and Dicker 1994, discussing this phenomenon in the context of American trade with China following Tiananmen), suggests that many in this community in fact feel that international business is not as sensitive to human rights condition as this particular claim would have us believe.

Finally, civil and political rights are said to promote economic growth by making government more responsive to the citizenry. But this could well be a mixed bag for many economically underdeveloped polities, in which sustained economic development frequently requires the social reforms—such as elimination of price and employment supports, and gender and minority development initiatives—that are quite unpopular with the majority of citizens. A regime more insulated from popular pressures could find it easier to implement such policies than one that is more responsive (Becker 1983; Sorensen 1991:7–16; Olsen 1982:17–74; Ethier 1997:271).

In fact, when one focuses on the more underdeveloped of economies, both empirical studies and theoretical analyses are strongly arrayed in support of a conclusion that authoritarian policies can *sometimes* be more effective at promoting economic development than libertarian regimes (Ruttan 1991:284, Marsh 1979:63–64, Przeworski and Limongi 1993:63–64). There is much evidence to suggest that libertarian regimes require a certain, minimal level of prior economic and civil development in order to be effective (Pistor and Wellons 1998, Inglehart 1997, Ethier 1997). Economically underdeveloped societies generally lack the education levels and private wealth necessary to make many civil and political rights meaningful to the general population, and they lack the civil society infrastructure many believe necessary to sustain the kind of a truly pluralist society civil and political rights seek to promote (Inglehart 1997:190–215, Putnam 1993:63–82, Becker 1983). Authoritarian policies, by contrast, can better allow a regime to implement unpopular but necessary economic and social reform policies that would otherwise attract considerable political opposition in more libertarian settings. Such policies can also allow the regime to better pursue more long-term development and reform strategies by avoiding the public choice and cycling problems faced by more pluralist regimes (Sorenson 1991:7–16, Becker 1983, Olsen 1982:17–74).

None of this is to imply that authoritarian regimes are always justified in sacrificing civil or political rights in pursuit of economic development; or that one is always privileged to pursue economic development at the expense of civil and political protections; or even that civil and political protections must inevitably conflict in some way with economic development. Most authoritarian regimes are indeed run solely for the benefit of the autocrats. Nor do I mean to suggest that the abuses practiced by economically successful authoritarian regimes (such as China or Singapore) are as necessary as these regimes allege they are. But it is *possible* for such conflicts to arise, and the mere possibility of such conflict is enough to demand that we in the human rights community temper at least somewhat our ideological arrogance. We need to at least acknowledge that tradeoffs between civil and

political rights and the moral benefits associated with economic development sometimes are indeed unavoidable; that in such situations a decision
to pursue the latter at some expense to the former can be morally defensible;
if the human rights regime is to enjoy the prescriptive effect it claims.

As with the Bangkok Declaration's first claim, the Declaration's second
claim—that the application of rights should be influenced by the particular
values of the polity—also evokes a well-understood subtext. Some assert that
East Asian cultures are "communitarian," in the sense that they place more
value on the integrity of the collective society than on the integrity of the
individual within the society. They see Western-style rights—particular civil
and political rights—as inherently individualist, meaning that they value
individuals more than the collective. For this reason, they conclude, Western-
style civil and political rights are inappropriate for East Asian cultures (Huntington 1996, Peerenboom 1995, Kausikan 1993).

Unfortunately, this subtext has generally blinded us to the larger possibilities of the Bangkok Declaration's second claim. Many would agree that
the whole individualist/communitarian distinction is so tautological as to be
analytically meaningless (see, e.g., Putnam 1993:114–115; see also Dowdle
1999, for an examination of the tautological aspect of this distinction with
regard to analyses of Chinese culture). But this does not mean that polities
might not evince other patterns of value differences that, while not rationally
aligned along a communitarian/individualist spectrum, nevertheless affect
how particular rights operate within these polities. For example, Ronald
Inglehart's recent study (1997) finds that societies at different stages of industrialization evince different constellations of political values. An example
of this linkage is that while both "post-industrial" societies (such as the
United States) and developing societies (such as those that characterize East
and Southeast Asia) value environmental protection and social stability, post-
industrial societies place greater relative value in environmental protection,
whereas developing societies place greater relative value in stability (id. at
109–113). Obviously, this would effect how these different types of societies
weigh environmental rights and other human rights against legitimate interests in social stability.

Indeed, there are just too many instances where we in the United States
routinely bend particular rights to meet particular cultural variables in our
own constitutional law to take seriously claims that culture just "does not
count" in the application of human rights (Kymlicka 1995). An example of
this is the constitutional leeway we give native-American jurisdictions. With

regard to due process and equal protection, for example, the U.S. Court of Appeals for the 9th Circuit noted in 1976 that:

> the courts have been careful to construe the terms "due process" and "equal protection" as used in the Indian Bill of Rights with due regard for the historical, governmental and cultural values of an Indian tribe. As a result, these terms are not always given the same meaning as they have come to represent under the United States Constitution (*Tom v. Sutton*, 533 F.2d 1101, 1104 n.5 [9th Cir. 1976]).

In fact, in both the United States and Canada, our respect for culture differences gives native-American jurisdictions significant latitude in matters involving due process, equal protection, property rights, and governance: allowing these culturally defined jurisdictions to engage in political practices—such as requiring that public officials be members of a particular ethnic group, or employing and evoking religious symbols at governmental functions—that would be unconstitutional if done by non-ethnically-defined jurisdictions (Cohen 1982, DePalma 1998).

Some seek to avoid the implications of such cultural relativity by claiming that, even if different cultures do evince different constellations of values, the *particular* values enshrined by the human rights regime are universally respected by and in every culture. But even accepting this as true (which I do), simple correspondence of values does not guarantee corresponding application of values, since the particular *weights* assigned to these values may nevertheless vary from culture to culture. Both the United States and Canada, for example, place significant value both on free speech and on promoting equal dignity among citizens. But in the United States, public speech that promotes racist agitation—a form of what is called "group libel"—is as a general matter constitutionally protected, because in our political culture the value of freedom of speech is said to outweigh the threat such speech imposes on the libeled race's legitimate demands for equal respect. See *Brandenburg v. Ohio*, 395 U.S. 444 (1969). In Canada (and much of Western Europe), on the other hands, group libel is forbidden, because in Canada's political culture, the moral demands of equal respect in this instance are said to outweigh the moral benefits of free speech (see *R. v. Keegstra*, [1990] 3 SCR 697). (This particular divergence is examined more fully in Greenawalt 1992:15–25.)

In fact, a healthy respect for what we might call "cultural specifics" could well promote a better understanding of human rights than we currently enjoy (Alston 1994). There is a natural tendency for persons to assume that deviations from their own settled practices are inferior simply by virtue of their deviation. For example, British jurists looking at the French administrative law system in the late nineteenth and early twentieth centuries simply assumed that because that system lacked adversarial proceedings, and intermingled administrative and judicial functions, that system represented a travesty to justice (Wade and Bradley 1994:605–607). But as common law jurists grew to better understand the French system of administrative law, some British legal scholars began to argue that Britain's own emerging administrative law jurisprudence might actually have much to learn from the French model (Brown and Bell 1993:3–4).

Taking cultural specifics into account does not mean that our moral judgment must blindly acquiesce to whatever legal and political practices a particular community chooses to institute. Rather, it means that in applying that judgment to different communities, we must be sympathetic to that community's particular constellation of competencies, expectations, threats, and obstacles. In some cases, perhaps most, we will rightly reject the suspect practices. These constellations can be unique, but they are not necessarily *that* unique, and it is no doubt the case that our commonalities as fellow *Homo sapiens* far exceed our environmentally and historically imposed divergences. In some cases, however, we will find that previously suspected practices are in fact morally rational responses to a community's unique collection of path dependencies and environmental threats and obstacles, as British scholars and jurists did with regard to French administrative law. Our growing respect for the unique governance systems used by many Native American communities is an example of this. And in a few cases, we might also find that that response is rationale even in light of our own path dependencies and environmental threats and obstacles. The goals of human rights can be realized in a myriad of ways, and no one person or organization or polity or philosophy has the capacity to foresee them all. Understanding and accounting for "cultural specifics" would serve to continually remind us that there is always more to human rights than can be dreamt of by our own, inevitably limited philosophies.

Conclusion

Of course, the picture I paint of the Bangkok Declaration is not necessarily the one intended by most of its drafters or its signers. Taking economic development into account does not mean that civil and political liberties can always be sacrificed in pursuit of higher GDP, even in underdeveloped countries; and it certainly does not mean that we must defer to any and every economic justification that might be offered in defense of authoritarian oppression. Similarly, taking culture into account is not the same as "cultural relativism." It does not deny the possibility of objective and universal moral truths; it does not demand that the international community blindly defer to a regime's pronouncements as to what are really in the "best interest" of its people; and it does not damn whole peoples to perpetual authoritarian oppression due to the philosophical musings of long-dead cultural icons.

Nevertheless, the actual claims of the Bangkok Declaration still leave plenty of room for the expansion and maturation of human rights law. Economic conditions and diversities of political culture are concerns to which the human rights regime is going to have to begin paying more respect, if that regime is ever to enjoy strong prescriptive effect outside the limited confines of the human rights community. Such respect is not contrary to the notion of universal rights. Rather, it is a refinement of that notion, one that better tracks our own moral evaluation of these issues, and one that brings our conceptualization of human rights much more in line with that found in most if not all Western constitutional systems.

As even many human rights scholars have noted, the hard universalism of traditional human rights rhetoric is not particularly persuasive to persons, Western as well as Eastern, outside the human rights community (Harries 1997; D'Amato, 1995:48–50, Alston 1994:381, 389, Alston 1988:50–52). This is because it simply does not comport with our general moral understanding; it does not comport with how Western countries implement these rights in their own domestic legal systems; and it does not comport with the spirit (and necessity) of human synthesis that characterizes the rest of the public international law system. To overcome these problems, we need a more nuanced vision of universalism — one that accounts for the moral force of the Bangkok Declaration's claims without allowing human rights law to drift into the tautological irrelevance of cultural relativism.

A conception of rights that sees rights as principles rather than hard commands does just that. Principles do not provide the same comfort of certainty that hard rules do. But as suggested by John Rawls (1971) and Ronald Dworkin (1978) in the context of Anglo-American jurisprudence, they do allow us to both take into account and move beyond the fact that even the strongest of our own moral demands may not always be appropriate for other persons in other situations, without forcing us to the conclusion that all moral truth is relative and thus not worth pursuing. Such a conception provides a framework around which people who honestly disagree about particular aspects of justice can nevertheless create, through a mutual exploration of principles and experiences, a universally just regime. It is, in other words, a framework for the kind of legitimating dialogue that a liberal political philosophy demands: a dialogue from which the present human rights regime could greatly benefit. (See also Barnhart [this volume], Taylor 1999).

Acknowledgments

The author is grateful to the members of the 1997 NEH Summer Seminar for many contributions to his thinking. The author would especially like to thank Andrew J. Nathan and Michael Barnhart for their repeated reviews of the numerous earlier drafts of this article. Valuable comments on earlier drafts were also tendered by Mark Barenberg, Randle Edwards, Kent Greenawalt, Stephen Marks, Randall Peerenboom, Oscar Schachter, and Frank Upham. Many of the ideas in this article were initially forged in enlightening discussions with Ronald Dworkin, Philip Alston, Michael Dorf and Randall Peerenboom.

Endnotes

1. The Bangkok Declaration was the product of a regional preparatory held in Bangkok in March 1993 in preparation for the Second World Conference on Human Rights that was held in Vienna in June of that same year. The Bangkok Declaration was intended as a statement of the Asian Region's stance on human rights. See Steiner 1995:235, Kausikan 1993, Ghai 1994.
2. The Court has also articulated similar balancing tests for freedom of religion (see Nowak et al. 1995:1282–1284); the right of due process (see Nowak et al. 1995:553–557); the prohibition against bills of attainder (*i.e.*, legislative instruments in which the legislature seeks to usurp the role of the courts, prohibited by Article I section 9 clause 3 of the United States Constitution) (see *Nixon v. Administrator of General Services*, 443 U.S. 425 [1977]); the right to property (see *Miller v. Schoene*, 276 U.S. 272 [1928]); and the right to privacy (see *Carey v. Population Services International*, 431 U.S. 678 (1977)). Even the Court's jurisprudence on the freedom from slavery seems to involve an implicit balancing of competing juridical concerns (see Posner 1987:19).
3. In fact, such an approach has been adopted by the international labor law regime, and has—according to many—actually resulted in the development of a more effective collection of human rights standards than currently enjoyed by the more general human rights regime. See Schlossberg 1989:56–65. This

has led a number of persons, including former Red Cross President Elizabeth Dole and former New York Senator Daniel Patrick Moynihan, to recommend the International Labor Organization as a model for constructing a more effective institutional framework for human rights implementation. See "'Human Rights Priest' Urges Stronger U.S. Role in ILO," *ILO Washington Focus*, October 1992:1, 4, 6.

4. Compare "Balance of Rights," *The Irish Times*, June 30, 1998:15 (editorial supporting British ban on Protestant groups staging provocative march through Catholic neighborhood in Northern Ireland) with *National Socialist Party of America v. Skokie*, 432 U.S. 43 (1977) (U.S. Constitution protects American Nazi Party's right to march through predominantly Jewish suburb).

5. In 1987, UN General Assembly passed a resolution entitled "Declaration on the Right to Development." This right was presaged by a number of the provisions contained in the International Covenant on Economic, Social and Cultural Rights. The "right to development" was formally recognized by the UN Commission on Human Rights in 1997. See generally Steiner and Alston 1996:1110–1146.

6. Proponents of enlightened economic development frequently point to particular countries or regions in support of their claim. Sen (1997:10–11) cites the example of Botswana, for example. But I am not here arguing that enlightened economic development is always impossible. I am only suggesting that it may *sometimes* be impossible. Even accepting Botswana as an example of enlightened economic development, it is not clear how well Botswana's developmental model exports to other countries in other situations. See, e.g., Boroughs and Whitelaw 1998:52 (noting that Botswana enjoys access to significant amounts of international aid and significant natural wealth).

Bibliography

Alston, Philip. 1984. "Conjuring Up New Human Rights: A Proposal for Quality Control." *American Journal of International Law* 78 (3) (July):607–621.

Alston, Philip. 1988. "Environment, Economic Development and Human Rights: A Triangular Relationship"—Remarks of Philip Alston" (panel discussion). *Proceedings of the Annual Meeting—American Society of International Law* 82 (Annual 1988):50–55.

Alston, Philip. 1994. "The UN's Human Rights Record: From San Francisco to Vienna and Beyond." *Human Rights Quarterly* 16(2) (May):375–390.

Ayton-Shenker, Diana. 1995. *United Nations Background Note: The Challenge of Human Rights and Cultural Diversity*. March. New York: United Nations Department of Public Information DPI/1627/HR.

Becker, Gary S. 1983. "A Theory of Competition Among Pressure Groups for Political Influence." *Quarterly Journal of Economics* 98 (3) (August):371–400.

Berlin, Isaiah. 1961. "Two Concepts of Liberty." In *Four Essays on Liberty*. Oxford: Oxford University Press, 118–172.

Bernstein, Robert L. and Richard Dicker. 1994. "Human Rights First." *Foreign Policy* no. 94 (Spring):43–47.

Boroughs, Don L. and Kevin Whitelaw. 1998. "Where U.S. aid works." *U.S. News & World Report* (May 6):52.

Brown, L. Neville and John S. Bell. 1993. *French Administrative Law* 4th ed. Oxford: Clarendon Press.

Burkhart, Ross E. and Michael S. Lewis-Beck. 1994. "Comparative Democracy: The Economic Development Thesis." *American Political Science Review* 88(4) (December):903–910.

Cappelletti, Mauro. 1971. *Judicial Review in the Contemporary World*. Indianapolis: Bobbs-Merrill.

Chermerinsky, Erwin. 1996. "The Goldwater Institute and the Federalist Society—Federalism and Judicial Mandates: Statement by Professor Erwin Chermerinsky." *Arizona State Law Journal* 28(1) (Spring):17–220.

Cohen, Felix S. 1982. *Felix S. Cohen's Handbook of Federal Indian Law* 1982 ed. Charlottesville: Bobbs-Merrill Law Publishers.

Cole, Thomas. 1997. *The Strange Demise of Jim Crow*. Austin: University of Texas Press.

Colletta, Nat J., M. Kostner and I. Wiederhofer. 1996. *Case Studies in War-to Peace Transition, The Demobilization and Reintegration of Ex-Combatants in Ethiopia, Namibia and Uganda*. Washington: World Bank, Africa Technical Department Series, Discussion Paper No 331.

Costonis, John J. 1982. "Law and Aesthetics: A Critique and a Reformulation of the Dilemmas." *Michigan Law Review* 80(3) (January):355–461.

Cover, Robert. 1975. *Justice Accused: Antislavery and the Judicial Process*. New Haven: Yale University Press.

D'Amato, Anthony. 1995. "Human Rights as Part of Customary International Law: A Plea for Change of Paradigms." *Georgia Journal of International and Comparative Law* 25(1–2) (Fall–Winter):47–98.

D'Amato, Anthony. 1983. "Legal Uncertainty." *California Law Review* 71(1) (January):1–55.

Dasgupta, Partha. 1993. *An Inquiry into Well-Being and Destitution*. Oxford: Clarendon Press.

della Porte, Donatella. 1996. "Corruption and Democracy." *UNESCO Courier*. June 1996:18.

DePalma, Anthony. 1998. "Canada Pact Gives a Tribe Self-Rule for the First Time." *New York Times*. Aug. 5:A1, A10.

Donnelly, Jack. 1985. "In Search of the Unicorn: The Jurisprudence and Politics of the Right to Development." *California Western International Law Journal* 15(3) (Summer):473–509.

Dorf, Michael. 1996. "Incidental Burdens on Fundamental Rights." *Harvard Law Review* 109(6) (April):1175–1253.

Dowdle, Michael W. 1997. "The Constitutional Development and Operations of the National People's Congress." *Columbia Journal of Asian Law* 11(1) (Fall):1–125.

Dowdle, Michael W. 1999. "Heretical Laments: China and the Fallacies of 'Rule of Law.'" *Cultural Dynamics* 11(3) (November):287–314.

Drèze, Jean and Amartya Sen. 1989. *Hunger and Public Action*. Oxford: Clarendon Press.

Dworkin, Ronald. 1978. *Taking Rights Seriously*. Cambridge: Harvard University Press.

Ethier, Diane. 1997. "Democratic Consolidation: Institutional, Economic, and External Dimenstions." In Abdo I. Baaklin and Helen Desfosses, eds. *Designs for Democratic Stability: Studies in Viable Constitutionalism*. Armonk, NY: M. E. Sharpe:259–284.

Friedmann, Wolfgang. 1964. *The Changing Structure of International Law*. New York: Columbia University Press.

Ghai, Yash. 1994. "Human Rights and Governance: The Asia Debate." *Australia Yearbook of International Law*. 15:1–34.

Greenawalt, Kent. 1992. "Free Speech in the United States and Canada." *Law and Contemporary Problems* 55 (1) (Winter):5–33.

Harries, Owen. 1997. "Virtue by Other Means." *The New York Times*. Sunday, October 26, section 4:15.

Hart, H.L.A. 1961. *The Concept of Law*. Oxford: Clarendon Press.

Henkin, Louis. 1979. *How Nations Behave* 2nd ed. New York: Columbia University Press.

Henkin, Louis. 1990. *International Law: Politics, Values and Functions: General Course on Public International Law*. Boston: M. Nijhoff.

Human Rights Watch. 1992. *Indivisible Human Rights: The Relationship Between Political and Civil Rights to Survival, Subsistence and Poverty*. New York: Human Rights Watch.

Huntington, Samuel P. 1996. *The Clash of Civilizations and the Remaking of World Order*. New York: Simon and Schuster.

Hurd, Heidi M. 1995. "Interpreting Authorities." In Andrei Marmor, ed. *Law and Interpretation*. Oxford: Clarendon Press:405–432.

Inglehart, Ronald. 1997. *Modernization and Postmodernization: Cultural, Economic, and Political Change in 43 Societies*. Princeton: Princeton University Press.

Kammen, Michael. 1994. *A Machine that Would Go of Itself: The Constitution in American Culture*. New York: St. Martin's Press.

Kausikan, Bilahari. 1993. "Asia's Different Standard." *Foreign Policy* 92(2) (Fall): 24–41.

Kelsen, Hans. 1966. *Principles of International Law* (2nd ed. Robert W. Tucker, ed.). New York: Holt, Rinehart and Winston.

Kiss, Alexandre Charles. 1981. "Permissible Limitations on Rights." In Louis Henkin, ed. *The International Bill of Rights: The Covenant on Civil and Political Rights*. New York: Columbia University Press:290–310.

Knack, Stephen and Philip Keefer. 1995. "Institutions and Performance: Cross-Country Tests Using Alternative Institutional Measures." *Economics and Politics* 7(3) (November):207–228.

Kymlicka, Will. 1995. *Multicultural Citizenship: A Liberal Theory of Minority Rights*. Oxford: Oxford University Press.

Londregan, John B. and Keith J. Poole. 1990. "Poverty, the Coup Trap, and the Seizure of Executive Power." *World Politics* 42(2) (January):151–183.

Madison, James. 1989. "Speech to the House Explaining His Proposed Amendments with Notes for the Amendment Speech." In Randy E. Barnett, ed. *The Rights Retained by the People" The History and Meaning of the Ninth Amendment*. Fairfax: George Mason University Press:51–64.

Marsh, Robert. 1979. "Does Democracy Hinder Economic Development in the Latecomer Developing Nations." *Comparative Social Research*. 2:215–248.

McDougal, Myres S., Harold D. Lasswell and Lung-chu Chen. 1980. *Human Rights and World Public Order*. New Haven: Yale University Press.

Merryman, John Henry. 1985. *The Civil Law Tradition* 2nd ed. Stanford: Stanford University Press.

Ni Aolain, Fionnuala. 1995. "The Emergence of Diversity: Differences in Human Rights Jurisprudence." *Fordham International Law Journal* 19(1) (October): 101–142.

Nickel, James W. 1993. "The Human Right to a Safe Environment: Philosophical Perspectives on its Scope and Justification." *Yale Journal of International Law* 18(1) (Winter):281–295.

Nowak, John E. and Ronald D. Rotunda. 1995. *Constitutional Law* (5th ed.). St. Paul: West Publishing Co.

Olsen, Mancur. 1982. *The Rise and Decline of Nations: Economic Growth, Stagflation, and Social Rigidities*. Cambridge: Harvard University Press.

Peerenboom, Randall. P. 1995. "Rights, Interests, and the Interest in Rights in China." *Stanford Journal of International Law* 31(2) (Summer):359–386.

Pistor, Katharina and Philip A. Wellons. 1999. *The Role of Law and Legal Institutions in Asian Economic Development, 1960–1995*. Oxford: Oxford University Press.

Posner, Richard A. 1987. "The Constitution as an Economic Document." *George Washington Law Review* 56(1) (November):4–38.

Prezeworski, Adam and Fernando Limongi. 1993. "Political Regimes and Economic Growth." *Journal of Economic Perspectives* 7(3) (Summer):51–69.

Putnam, Robert D. 1993. *Making Democracy Work*. Princeton: Princeton University Press.

Rawls, John. 1971. *A Theory of Justice*. Cambridge: Belknap Press.

Rosenfeld, Michel. 1993. "Executive Autonomy, Judicial Authority and Rule of Law: Reflections on Constitutional Interpretation and the Separation of Powers." *Cardozo Law Review* 15(1–2) (October):137–174.

Ruttan, Vernon W. 1991. "What Happened to Political Development?" *Economic Development and Cultural Change* 39 (2) (January):265–292.

Schachter, Oscar. 1991. *International Law in Theory and Practice*. Boston: M. Nijhoff.

Schauer, Frederick. 1991. *Playing the Rules*. Oxford: Clarendon Press.

Schlossberg, Stephan I. 1989. "United States Participation in the ILO: Redefining the Role." *Comparative Labor Law* 11(1) (Fall):48–80.

Sen, Amartya. 1997. *Human Rights and Asian Values*. New York: Carnegie Council on Ethics and International Affairs.

Singer, Norman J. 1994. *Sutherland's Statutory Construction*. Deerpark, Il: Clark, Boardman and Callaghan.

Sorensen, Georg. 1991. *Democracy, Dictatorship and Development: Economic Development in Selected Regimes of the Third World*. London: Macmillian.

Starks, David and Laszlo Brust. 1998. *Postsocialist Pathways: Transforming Politics and Property in East Central Europe*. Cambridge (UK): Cambridge University Press.

Steiner, Henry J. and Philip Alston. 1996. *International Human Rights in Context*. Oxford: Clarendon Press.

Taylor, Charles. 1999. "Conditions of an Unforced Consensus on Human Rights." In Joanne R. Bauer and Daniel A. Bell, eds., *The East Asian Challenge for Human Rights*. New York: Cambridge University Press, pp. 124–144.

Thoreau, Henry David. 1991. "Civil Disobedience." In Hugo Adam Bedau, ed. *Civil Disobedience in Focus*. London: Routledge:28–48.

Tise, Larry E. 1987. *Proslavery: A History of the Defense of Slavery in America, 1701–1840*. Athens, GA: University of Georgia Press.

United Nations Development Programme. 1997a. *Human Development Report 1997*. New York: Oxford University Press.

United Nations Development Programme. 1997b. *Corruption and Good Governance: Discussion Paper 3*. New York: UNDP Division of Public Affairs.

Wade, E. C. S. and A. W. Bradley. 1994. *Constitutional and Administrative Law* 11th ed., A. W. Bradley and K. D. Ewing, eds. London: Longman.Group, Ltd.

Waldron, Jeremy. 1993. "A Right-based Critique of Constitutional Rights." *Oxford Journal of Legal Studies* 13(1) (Spring):18–51.

World Bank. 1992. *Governance and Development*. Washington, D.C.: World Bank.

Wright, Robin. 1997. "Democracy: Challenges and Innovations in the 1990s." *The Washington Quarterly* 20(3) (Summer):23–36.

Yergin, Daniel and Joseph Stanislaw. 1999. *The Commanding Heights: The Battle Between Government and the Marketplace that is Remaking the Modern World.* New York: Simon and Schuster.

6   Are Women Human? The Promise and Perils of "Women's Rights as Human Rights"

Lucinda Joy Peach

> My name is Nuj and I am 18 years old. I grew up in a village in Mae Sai district, a town on the northern border between Thailand and Burma. Since I was small I remember seeing women . . . wearing thick make-up and beautiful dresses, and walking in and out of the brothels that were mushrooming in the village. . . . Mae Sai so much revolved around the sex business; daughters are sold to local agents as well as agents from Bangkok. The women who work in the sex trade in Bangkok can send home a lot of money to build big houses and to buy cars. When you see people getting these things, the whole business appears quite attractive. . . . Champa is a local sex worker who has made a fortune working in Bangkok. She always came up to Mae Sai to recruit women to go south. When she asked me to work as her housekeeper in Bangkok, I decided to go with her. . . . I lived with Champa and her husband, Yonguth, who beat me and forced me to work as a prostitute. . . . Throughout the three years I worked in that massage parlour, I never received any money for my body. . . . After work, Champa would bring me back to the flat, and she locked me in the room where I could watch TV. . . . Finally I decided to escape (Skrobanek, Boonpakdi, and Janthakeero 1997:1–2).

Introduction

"In no society today do women enjoy the same opportunities as men" (United Nations 1995b:1). By and large, women around the globe have fewer resources and opportunities than men, who control the vast majority of the world's wealth and power. Women around the world are impoverished in greater proportion than men; they have less access to food, money, education, health care, and so on, than men; and they are at greater risk of harm from poverty, starvation, domestic violence, rape, and other sexual crimes (Seager 1997). As Robin Morgan explains: "Because virtually all existing countries are structured by patriarchal mentality, the standard for being human is being male—and female human beings *per se* become other,' and 'invisible' " (Morgan 1996:1). Part of the devaluation of the worth and value of females in relation to males has been the exclusion of women as both subjects and objects of the law, including international law, and especially from international human rights law (see, e.g. Charlesworth 1994:63).

These realities prompt the question of the title: "Are women human?" The issue is not a trivial one, since international human rights law was developed almost exclusively by men for men, without the participation of women and without specific attention paid to the distinctive interests and needs of females. In addition, beyond the question of whether women are part of the definition of "human" lies the question of whether all (adult) female persons can be included within the category "woman." Answering this second question involves asking whether there are commonalities among biological female persons that unite them as "women" in ways that outweigh the differences—of culture, class, ethnicity, religion, sexual orientation, geographical and social location, etc.—that divide them.

Despite these conceptual difficulties, both feminist and human rights organizations have developed strategies to improve the status of women based on international human rights law.[1] By "feminist," I mean to refer to persons who are committed to ending the subordination of women. Promoters of women's rights as human rights have tended to adopt principles of what I refer to as "liberal feminism"—such as equal rights, fairness, and justice—principles which presume—at least for legal purposes—that the commonalities between men and women and among women of varied backgrounds outweigh their differences.

The United Nations Fourth World Conference on Women held in Beijing in 1995 (Women's Conference) saw the fruition of years of campaigning by women's rights and human rights activists to identify women's rights as human rights.[2] Women's human rights was a strong theme of both the official UN Women's Conference as well as the Non-Governmental Organizations (NGO) conference held concurrently in Huairou (Chow 1996:188). The Platform for Action drafted at the Women's Conference frames women's rights "as indivisible, universal, and inalienable human rights" (United Nations 1995).[3]

At the same time that the campaign for women's rights as human rights has been evolving, critics of international human rights laws have challenged the appropriateness of linking women's rights with human rights. These critics generally fall within one of three somewhat overlapping groups. The first group I refer to as "care feminists," to distinguish them from liberal feminists who support the campaign for women's rights as human rights. Most care feminists adopt psychologist Carol Gilligan's suggestion that in contrast to men, who tend to resolve conflicts on the basis of an "ethic of justice" framed in terms of individual rights and abstract legalistic principles of fairness and justice, women tend to resolve conflicts more on the basis of an "ethic of care," which embodies principles of caring. nurturing, and maintaining relationships and connections to others (Gilligan 1982).[4] Such differences, they claim, make international human rights law ill-suited to meet the distinctive needs of women.

The second group I refer to as "cultural values critics." This is a disparate group, comprised of political and religious leaders and postmodern scholars, among others, who share the position that human rights are not in fact universal—as they are asserted to be in United Nations documents and elsewhere—but are, rather, culturally relative. Among the most vocal advocates of this challenge to universal human rights have been promoters of so-called "Asian values," the view that Asian cultures have different values than western ones, and thus should not be held to Western standards for human rights. Instead, they claim that Asian nations need to develop human rights standards that accord with their own specific social and economic needs and circumstances. In recent years, the People's Republic of China, Malaysia, and Singapore have asserted that Asian nations in particular are experiencing economic, social, and political challenges that justify restrictions on Western-style human rights. According to the Asian values argument, then, international human rights are inappropriate for nonwesterners, including women.

Among cultural values proponents are religious leaders who contend that the movement for women's rights as human rights is the product of Western, liberal, secular feminists, which, in effect, inappropriately assumes that women from radically different cultural and religious traditions are essentially the same. Somewhat similar criticisms have been articulated by a third group, which includes a number of women of color and third world feminists,[5] many of whom draw upon postmodern and/or postcolonialist perspectives.[6] Critics in this third group argue that the differences among

women are often more significant than the commonalities, given the intersectionality of gender with race, class, ethnicity, religion, sexual orientation,
and other primary determinants of identity. Thereby they undermine the
universality required to support the content of women's rights as human
rights (Mohanty 1991:70).

What all three of these somewhat distinct groups share is a critique of
the universalist assumptions in international human rights law. Care feminists critique the notion that women are really intended to be included as
human within the term "human rights," and contend that the definition of
"human" in human rights fails to accurately reflect the relational, interdependent character of female identity. Cultural values critics argue that human rights are a product of Western cultures, and dispute that they are
applicable in nonwestern cultural contexts. Postmodern and third world
feminists combine these critiques in contesting the applicability of a Western
derived and male biased legal regime which was developed in the absence
of the participation of—and largely without regard for—women from non-
western cultural traditions. In this respect, they are rightly skeptical about
the appropriateness of attempting to force "women" into the concept of
"human" as it has been defined in international human rights law.

In this essay, I will critically examine the campaign for women's rights as
human rights from a perspective that assumes the merit of at least part of
each of these critiques. Although some of these criticisms are undoubtedly
intended to maintain traditional gender roles, others raise legitimate questions about the appropriateness of using an individual rights-based strategy
to address the oppression of women without regard for their specific social
and cultural location, including, in particular, their religious heritage. My
focus is not on the central issue of the so-called "Asian values debate." Instead, I begin from the pragmatist position, described later, that the existence
or universality of human rights cannot be established in any foundationalist
or ultimate sense, but is, like human identity itself, a product of social processes. I assume that the recognition and enforcement of (at least most of)
the human rights contained in United Nations treaties may be potentially
beneficial to "human" beings (yet to be defined), regardless of their amorphous ontological status, but that the benefits must be demonstrated, rather
than assumed, as human rights activists tend to do, especially with respect
to women's rights.

The following will examine the issue of the practical benefit or efficacy
of international human rights laws for women in the context of the trafficking

of women for prostitution and sex tourism in Thailand.[7] Since this activity
involves one of the most obvious examples of the violation of women's human rights, while at the same time implicating cultural and religious norms,
especially regarding gender roles, it presents an appropriate case for testing
the practical and moral efficacy of women's human rights. Focusing on
Thailand also permits an examination of the efficacy of international human
rights law in a predominantly Buddhist culture, in contrast to the emphasis
of most recent scholarly attention on conflicts between religious and human
rights discourses in Islamic, Hindu, Christian, and traditionally African cultures.

I will begin with a fuller consideration of the challenge that feminist and
cultural values critiques present for interpreting women's rights as human
rights, and then consider the practical efficacy of women's human rights in
the specific case of the trafficking of Burmese and Thai women into prostitution and sex tourism in Thailand. After describing the limitations of international law for addressing this issue, I will propose that feminist pragmatist theory offers the basis for a better approach. Finally, I will conclude
by discussing the advantages of using a feminist pragmatist approach to empowering women involved in the sex trade in Thailand as well as women
and other "humans" more generally.

Are Women "Human"? Critiques of Women's Rights as Human Rights

Among the several different critiques of international human rights that
have been advanced, perhaps the most significant for purposes of assessing
the campaign for women's rights as human rights is the charge that the
identity of the subject of human rights is not in fact universal, as it is claimed
to be, but is instead male gendered and culturally Western. Since feminist
and cultural values critiques are based on arguments which overlap with
one another in several respects, I will discuss them together, rather than
independently.

To begin, feminist legal theorists have noted several respects in which the
law is "male." They point out that law in general was designed by men to
serve predominantly male interests. Not only does the law continue to reflect
a male bias, but it has assisted in the creation and perpetuation of women's
subordinate status (Charlesworth, et al. 1991:613). The law has historically

treated women as unworthy or incapable of being "rights holders." This male
bias also has infected international law, which feminist legal theorists have
characterized as a "thoroughly gendered system" (Charlesworth, et al. 1991:
615). As Hilary Charlesworth points out, human rights documents use men's
rights and male standards of equality as the model for the inclusion of
women's rights (Charlesworth 1994:64; Charlesworth, et al. 1991:631).[8] In
addition, "issues traditionally of concern to men become seen as general
human concerns, while 'women's concerns' are relegated to a special, limited category" (Charlesworth, et al. 1991:625). As Alice Miller, Director of
the Women's Project for the Human Rights International Law Group, points
out, "while some steps toward integrating gender have occurred within the
UN treaty system, very few institutionalized advances have taken place"
(Miller 1998:12). As a consequence, women's needs and interests are recognized only to the extent they "fit" within the pre-established regime of
international human rights.

This limitation has resulted in women's human rights activists having to
attempt to "fit" women's claims into preestablished human rights, such as
claiming that domestic violence is a form of torture or that rape is a crime
of war, rather than these claims being recognized as human rights violations
in their own right. While such strategies are creative, they also point up the
traditional absence of explicit international law protections for many harms
suffered exclusively or predominantly by women. To the extent that women's
issues diverge from "male rights" in areas such as reproduction, child rearing,
rape and domestic violence, they risk being ignored or viewed as unrecog-
nizable as human rights.

Although more recent international human rights documents that
women have participated in framing, such as the Women's Convention and
the Beijing Women's Platform, have remedied this problem to some extent,
the bias still exists. Such biases have led feminist legal scholar Kathleen
Mahoney to conclude that "international human rights law is largely meaningless to women because the definitions and development of rights are built
on the male experience and have not responded to women's needs or realities" (Mahoney 1996:838).

Two significant ways that the male bias of international human rights law
reveals itself is in its emphasis on individual rights, and in the legal division
between public and private domains. Individual legal rights principles are
based upon a conception of the subject of rights as an independent, autonomous individual male. They neglect consideration of how individuals are

embedded in family and community relationships which may significantly constrain their autonomy and individuality. This is especially true for women, who are more often defined primarily in terms of their social roles as mothers, wives, and daughters than as autonomous individuals.

Human rights law also maintains boundaries between the so-called "public sphere" of government, political, and commercial activities, which men have traditionally dominated and excluded women from, and the "private sphere" of family and domestic life, to which women have been relegated. Because the law reflects a greater concern with protecting the rights of individuals interacting with governments and state actors in the "public sphere," it generally has been blind to crimes that disproportionately effect females, such as domestic violence, marital rape, and child sexual abuse, crimes that are perpetrated behind closed doors in the "private" sphere of marriage and family life (see, e.g., Hernandez-Truyol 1995:231). International human rights law generally imposes obligations only against states and their official agents and, consequently, it cannot reach the private actors who are responsible for many human rights violations against women, especially in areas such as rape and domestic violence (Mahoney 1996:851; Thomas 1993:58; Cook 1994b:247; Romany 1994:85). Here, third world feminists have observed that international law conceives power as residing in a centralized state authority, what some critics refer to as its "statist" bias. It fails to recognize how power is actually diffused throughout multiple levels, institutions and individuals.

Another aspect of the sharp distinction between public and private in international human rights law that harms women's interests is the disproportionate emphasis on civil and political rights over and against social and economic rights. While the former are understood to be valid claims that individuals have to protect them against interference by the state in areas such as freedom of speech, religion, press, due process, etc., the latter are generally viewed as "entitlements" rather than "rights," which the state is not obligated to provide.[9] Such understandings of human rights make them of limited usefulness to the majority of women in the world, who need to improve the basic material conditions of their lives before they can take full advantage of civil and political rights.

To some extent, the force of this critique is diminished by the UN Covenant on Economic, Social, and Cultural Rights (Economic Covenant, 1966b), which provides for such basic rights as a minimum standard of living. However, many nations, including the United States (which has refused to ratify the Economic Covenant), do not accept an obligation to provide social, economic, and cultural rights. Consequently, the weight of international human rights law still falls predominantly on the side of civil and political rights rather than economic, social and political ones (Byrnes 1994:192).[10]

The public emphasis of international human rights law also makes it poorly designed to change the "private" social attitudes and values about women which perpetuate women's oppression. As Ronald Krotoszynski observes, "one cannot rewrite by legislative fiat the content of people's hearts and minds," a necessary prerequisite to altering their attitudes and behaviors through modifications in the legal order (Krotoszynski 1997:424, 436). Similarly, Leslye Obiora notes that

> Law alone seldom changes behavior. Although it is certainly a key determinant of change, it is not a panacea nor is it a brooding omnipresence in the sky. It is instead a mechanism that is integral to, and contingent on, a broader societal scheme. Against this backdrop, it is reasonable to infer that law can wield considerable influence over actions and attitudes [only] where it is accepted as legitimate authority (Obiora 1997:358).

According to these feminist critics, then, international human rights law can at best be of limited value—given its inability to alter the stereotyped, sexist, patriarchal, and sometimes misogynist views of women which ultimately must be transformed in order to create any fundamental or stable improvement in women's social and legal status.

Third world feminists add that international human rights law is not only "male," but also culturally biased in favor of privileged Western male interests, based on what feminist law professor Berta Hernandez-Truyol describes as "a white, Western/Northern European, Judeo-Christian, heterosexual, propertied, educated, male ideology" (Hernandez-Truyol 1996:651). This conception of the human was developed primarily by representatives of Western nations with little regard for the identity of peoples from nonwestern cultural traditions, especially women.[11] In addition, because international human rights law frames prohibitions on sexual discrimination in terms of principles of abstract equality (Romany 1994:93)[12]—such as those of nondiscrimination and equal rights with men (e.g. Byrnes 1994:189)—it fails to give adequate attention to the ways that women *are* different from men.

Cultural values critics argue that the human rights described in the United Nations Charter, Declarations, and other international documents are largely the product of Western European notions of rights, and do not represent any genuine international consensus. They contend that since human identity is culturally constructed, and differs from culture to culture, international human rights are inappropriately applied in nonwestern cultural contexts, especially those more focused on community and the common good than on individual rights.[13] At the Women's Conference in Beijing, the Vatican and conservative Islamic fundamentalist groups criticized clauses in the Platform for Action that claimed the universality of women's rights (Johnson 1995:A1; Dormady 1997:119). They argued that the concept is based on "a feminist imperialism that reflects disrespect for religion and culture, an overzealous individualism, and an effort to impose Western values that destroy the family and local communities" (Bunch 1996:203; see Higgins 1996:97).[14]

Third world feminists also criticize international human rights law as "essentialist" in presuming—rather than demonstrating—commonalities among all women. They argue that because the differences among women are often more significant than the commonalities, it is inappropriate to assume the universality required to characterize women as a monolithic group for purposes of human rights laws. As an example of this universalism, the section of the Beijing Platform for Action on "Human Rights of Women" claims that "The universal nature of these rights and freedoms is beyond question" (United Nations 1995a:10, para. 211). For third world feminists, it is not at all beyond question. For instance, Chandra Mohanty contends that such "application of women as a homogeneous category to women in the third world colonizes and appropriates the pluralities of the simultaneous location of different groups of women in social class and ethnic frameworks; in doing so it ultimately robs them of their historical and political *agency*" (Mohanty 1991:71–72).

A related problem, according to third world feminists, is that international law cannot address adequately the specific kinds of oppression that women experience in particular cultural contexts. This is in part because international law generally lacks respect for the integrity of local cultures. Cultural values critics emphasize that cultural differences matter as much if not more than gender differences; and that such differences are not limited to language and custom, but also involve basic understandings of what it means to be human. As Leslye Obiora argues persuasively, "insofar as the individ-

ual's formation of a sense of humanity, self, and identity is invariably contingent on a cultural context, respect for the totality of individual human
rights necessarily entails some degree of respect for the variability and specificity of culture" (Obiora 1997:279).

For instance, feminist opposition to female circumcision or genital mutilation (the very use of one term or the other is suggestive of one's normative
assessment of the practice) has been accused of having as its referent "only
the culturally Western and Westernized middle class woman, who alone can,
within the terms of our present order, come to constitute the generic
woman" (Wynter 1997:509). Similarly, Abdullahi An-Na'im observes that

> The impact of culture on human behavior is often underestimated
> precisely because it is so powerful and deeply embedded in our self-
> identity and consciousness. Our culture is so much a part of our per-
> sonality that we take for granted that our behavior patterns and rela-
> tionships to other persons and to society become the ideal norm. . . .
> Culture influences, first, the way we see the world and, further, how
> we interpret and react to the information we receive" (An-Na'im 1992:
> 23).

Religion, as a central dimension of many cultures, also may be key to
personal identity. Whereas from an outsider's perspective, a religious institution or prescription may appear clearly to be oppressive to women, it may
be central to how women within that religious tradition understand themselves and experience their subjectivity. *Purdah* within some Islamic cultures
provides a vivid illustration of this. From a "Western" perspective, the practices of veiling and secluding women are viewed as extremely oppressive to
women. But from the view of many Muslim women, the practice provides
them with certain kinds of social advantages they would not otherwise enjoy.
However, since " 'human rights' rest on a view of the individual person as
separate from, and endowed with, inalienable rights *vis-à-vis* the state or
society, respect for the integrity and basic rights of individuals dictates that
coercive cultural measures be constrained by rigorous standards" (Obiora
1997:332).

Some of these criticisms can be met with counter arguments that explain
why international human rights are still valuable for advancing women's
status, regardless of their flaws. For example, the argument that international
human rights exclude women's interests and concerns has been made partly

anachronistic by the incorporation of women and women's interests into international human rights agreements in recent years. Similarly, some of the rationales given by cultural values critics can be persuasively countered. Even though international human rights laws were largely designed by European and American men, such laws nonetheless have resonance and relevance for people from radically different cultural traditions (Coomaraswamy 1996:17; An-Na'im 1999). In addition, many nonwestern states have already ratified or otherwise consented to be bound by international human rights laws.

Less amenable to rebuttal, however, is the implication resulting from conjoining the feminist and cultural values critiques, which is that the very conception of human identity that underlies international human rights is both "male" and "Western." From this perspective, women are not "human" and international human rights law cannot effectively protect their interests, especially those from nonwestern cultural backgrounds. According to this argument, international human rights assumes a Western male subject, bearing the traditionally male-gendered characteristics of autonomous, independent, atomistic individuality (*see* Charlesworth 1994:64). As Ratna Kapur and Brenda Cossman explain:

Legal discourse constitutes subjects as legal citizens; as individuals with rights and responsibilities vis-à-vis other citizens and the state. This discourse is both universalizing and naturalizing—all legal citizens are the same (they are *equal* before the law), and all legal citizens are natural subjects (they are equal *before* the law)" (Kapur and Cossman 1996:40).

Yet women may not be defined—or define themselves—as individuals with rights in the same way as men, as care feminists have noted. Given the Western male-centered genealogy, design, content, and function of international human rights laws, then, there is reason to be skeptical that such laws are applicable to all women (Bouvard 1996:ix–xvi).

The force of these criticisms of international human rights law is that women are not "human" within the meaning of international human rights law—either because women are fundamentally different than men (who provide the model or standard for international human rights law), or because the category "women" does not constitute a sufficiently coherent and unitary basis upon which to premise human rights, or because both rights and women are so defined by culture—and cultures differ so radically—that the concept of a universal human rights for women is necessarily flawed. The merit of these critiques can be assessed by considering the effectiveness of women's international human rights in the context of trafficking of women in the sex industry in Thailand, an issue which involves both women and nonwestern cultures.

Nonhuman Women? Sex Trade Workers in Thailand

The case of Burmese and Thai women involved in the sex tourism and prostitution industries in Thailand vividly illustrates the merit of aspects of the feminist and cultural values critiques of women's human rights and the limitations of an international human rights strategy for empowering women. Although it has roots in the colonial period, the sex trade in Thailand began to take its modern form with an influx of GIs stationed in Asia during the Korean and Vietnam Wars, and has been maintained since then by the influx of foreign "tourists," many of whom come to Thailand for the sex industry alone (Hill 1991; Thitsa 1980). Since 1982, Thailand has earned more foreign currently from tourism than any other economic activity (Brock and Thistlethwaite 1996:10, 116–17; Hill 1991:136).

Human Rights Watch and other commentators have detailed the conditions under which many women from Thailand and Burma, some still teenagers, are sold by their families or otherwise coerced, manipulated, or deceived into the burgeoning sex trade in Thailand. These women are often imprisoned by a system of debt bondage which is frequently nearly impossible to "pay off." They are forced to work in impoverished conditions, physically abused, underpaid, and deprived of basic rights to liberty, freedom to leave the brothels, or to receive needed medical treatment. They are frequently arrested for violating laws against prostitution (a double standard since the "clients" and pimps are not arrested), especially upon trying to escape. They are often returned to the brothels by law enforcement personnel (or, in the case of Burmese women, returned to the Myanmar government to risk prosecution for leaving the country without permission), or subjected to prolonged detention (frequently sexually and otherwise physically abused while in detention), or both (Human Rights Watch Women's Rights Project 1995:205–229; Satha-Anand 1999; Skrobanek et al. 1997;

Skrobanek 1992). In addition to these violation on their liberty, many of these women are even deprived of the conditions necessary to protect themselves from HIV, contributing to the AIDS epidemic that is rapidly spreading throughout Thailand and more slowly within Burma.[15] The risk of HIV transmission has not deterred traffickers, but has only encouraged them to seek younger and younger women and girls, especially from the hill tribe regions, to ensure their "cleanliness" from the deadly disease (Human Rights Watch 1995:205–229; Satha-Anand 1999; Skrobanek 1992).

International law historically has been ineffective in addressing the problem of trafficking in women for prostitution and sex tourism. Several international human rights instruments call for the elimination of trafficking in women, including the Platform for Action, the Women's Convention, and the 1949 Convention on the Suppression of the Traffic in Persons and the Exploitation of the Prostitution of Others (Anti-Trafficking Convention— the main international law instrument addressing trafficking, which Thailand never signed). In any event, the Anti-Trafficking Convention is ill-defined and its enforcement mechanisms are weak. It reflects a moralistic attitude toward prostitution and is abolitionist in its approach, which commentators have largely agreed is ineffectual.[16] Consequently, the Anti-Trafficking Convention has largely failed to eliminate trafficking or prostitution or to protect women.

Some critics argue that existing international laws are poorly designed to address the kinds of human rights abuses that trafficking in women and children for the sex trade entails, while others contend that the problems lie more in the "lack of enforcement, stemming from weaknesses in the substantive international law provisions and procedures as well as a lack of political will in the face of powerful economic and social forces" (Farrior 1997:214–15). A number of additional factors, including "the international cross-border character of trafficking," the "absence of a central international authority on trafficking in women" (Coomaraswamy 1997:9) and the lack of any body vested with the primary responsibility to gather information or hear complaints concerning prostitution and trafficking in women (Byrnes 1994:208–9), contribute to the problems of using international law effectively to protect women victims of trafficking.

As Thai scholar Juree Vichit-Vadakan observes, "issues affecting the status of women are complex and so intertwined that enacting new laws will not necessarily solve the problem at hand" (Vichit-Vadakan 1994:523). In addition, law in general is structurally ill equipped to deal with moral issues, especially those involving sexual morality, and has always been ambivalent about prohibiting prostitution. Because the actual sexual activities involved in trafficking take place in private, they fall outside the scope of international law's traditional concern only with the public realm.

As a practical matter, the private character of sex work makes it difficult for the law to regulate, even at a state level, without infringing upon other human rights values such as privacy, liberty, freedom of association, reproductive freedoms, etc. In Thailand in particular, because families often collude with traffickers, the secretive character of transactions in the sex trade hides them from the view of law enforcement. In addition, the Thai government does not wish to seek negative publicity about the burgeoning sex trade taking place within and across its borders, further privatizing the issue from "public" international law regulation.

Even assuming that prostitution could be adequately addressed as an issue of international human rights, international law is ineffectual without the active participation of national governments to enforce it. Even though Thailand ratified the Universal Declaration of Human Rights in 1948, and acceded to the Women's Convention in 1983, it has refused to sign the Anti-Trafficking Convention and has failed to protect the human rights of women engaged in sex tourism and trafficking.[17] Domestic laws prohibiting prostitution have had little impact. This should not be surprising, given the impoverished economic system in Thailand which motivates the government to look the other way, and promotes the police extortion which enables sex establishments to continue in operation (Skrobanek et al. 1997:27–28; Coomaraswamy 1997:17). Further, Thai laws criminalize prostitution and fail to provide protection and services for those seeking to escape working in the industry.[18]

The global economy is another major factor in the failure of international law to suppress trafficking in Thailand, as prostitution and sex tourism bring badly needed revenues into the country (Seabrook 1996:133–34; Skrobanek 1992:124), revenues that neither women nor those benefitting from trafficking and the sex industry have any other possible way to generate. (The recent failures of Thai financial institutions can only serve to exacerbate this situation.) Dismal economic opportunities for many Thais, in combination with the (relatively) profitable sex trade industry, encourage many Thai families to sell their daughters into debt bondage in order to help maintain the rest of the family.[19]

A central problem, and one overlooked by most commentators, is the disparity between conceptions of personal identity in international law and local culture, especially with respect to female identity. This disparity is especially prominent in Buddhist cultures, where persons, especially females, are defined as embedded in social networks of family, kin, and community rather than as individuals unencumbered by social ties (Satha-Anand 1999; Vichit-Vadakan 1994:516; Zakaria 1994:113). Thai and Burmese Buddhist women in particular are socialized to be relationally and family oriented selves rather than autonomous, independent individuals. (Satha-Anand 1999:21; Brock and Thistlethwaite 1996:193–94). Without an understanding of themselves as individuals entitled to rights, Buddhist women are not able to take advantage of international human rights law.

In addition, Buddhist teachings contribute to cultural valuations of women as inferior to men, which facilitates the perpetuation of trafficking and the sex industry in Thailand. Buddhist scriptures emphasize that women are attached to the material world of the senses and emotions, in contrast to men, who are able more easily to transcend their embodied and worldly existence for spiritual goals. Women's identity is depicted as embodied and social, embedded in relationships with others, and dependent on things of this "world" (Kirsch 1985:303, 310). This conception of female identity is thought to be an important factor in the great numbers of Thai and Burmese women involved in the sex industry, as well as one of the reasons for the lack of an established female monastic order within Thailand and Sri Lanka (Satha-Anand 1999; Thitsa 1980; cf. Keyes 1984:237).[20]

The Buddhist principle of *karma*—the law of cause and effect—is understood to be responsible for a person's status in life. People who led exemplary lives in the past will be reborn in positive circumstances, and those who led dissolute, immoral lives, will be reborn to suffering and misery. In this understanding, to be a woman is the result of previous bad karma. In fact, many Buddhist scriptures state, among a number of derogatory and misogynistic comments about women, that a woman must be reborn as a man in order to achieve Enlightenment. At the same time, women's karmically inferior status serves to legitimate or even excuse their involvement in "immoral" or karmically negative activities like prostitution (Eberhardt 1988:78; Keyes 1984:224).

Since there are always opportunities to change one's karma, a person's gender is not fixed beyond this life, but can be changed to the better in a future life. Males can favorably improve their karma and make merit which satisfies their indebtedness to their parents through joining the *sangha* (order of monks), even temporarily. However, this option has not been available to women since the order of nuns died out in most Southeast Asian countries

centuries ago (see Kabilsingh 1991).[21] This in itself contributes to the den-
igration of the status of women in Buddhist cultures by providing "evidence"
of their spiritual inferiority (Eberhardt 1988:78). As Thomas Kirsch explains,
"the monk's role is the most esteemed role in Thai society and . . . women
are categorically denied admission to this role. Thus, men and women stand
in qualitatively different relations to Buddhist values and norms" (Kirsch
1985:304).

Women's "merit making" activities are generally limited to practicing
generosity by giving donations (usually money, food, and other provisions)
to temples and individual monks, and raising a son who enters the order
(Keyes 1984:229, 233). Thus, lacking other options for merit making,
women's work in the sex industry, if temporary, can be justified and remedied
based on understandings of karma and merit making as gender-differentiated
(Brock and Thistlethwaite 1996:196).

It is evident, then, how the gendered system of merit making actually
serves to encourage women's continued participation in prostitution. Thai
daughters, especially the youngest in a family, feel a strong burden of indebtedness to take care of their parents, which they can satisfy by sending
money home. Prostitutes have told researchers with pride how they can
please their parents and their communities by doing so (Skrobanek et al.
1997:23, 77–78; Vichit-Vadakan 1994:518). Family members may willfully
neglect to inquire how the money was earned, especially as it can be used
to make merit by giving lavish donations to the local temple. Seen in this
way, prostitution actually can be a karmically advantageous activity! Nonetheless, there is still a social stigma associated with prostitution that deters
many women from being able to return home and limits their opportunities
to marry and have families (Skrobanek et al. 1997:70–71; Keyes 1984:234).
Yet many families are so pleased to receive the money that they frequently
are willing to remain "willfully ignorant" about how their daughters obtained
it (id. at 69–75).[22]

Although the all-male monastic establishment does not condone the sexual exploitation of women through trafficking and coerced prostitution, it
has not formally opposed the practice either. According to Buddhist teachings, prostitution violates the prohibition on sexual misconduct, one of the
"five precepts" taken by lay Buddhists. Skrobanek et al. observe that "Buddhist monks should in principle be opposed to prostitution; but there has
been little evidence of their involvement in activities to change the attitudes
of the people" (1997:77–78). In fact, the Abbot of Rim Mon monastery told

researchers: "We must be reasonable. . . . Besides, what is wrong if the employers of the girls make merit at the local temple or visit the village?" (*id.* at 78). This attitude should not be all that surprising, given that the trafficking in women results in indirectly supporting Buddhist institutions. It facilitates the ability of males in an impoverished economy to become monastics rather than wage earners (and live without having to engage in physical labor), supported by the goods of merit making earned by the sexual labor of their sisters.

Since participation in the Sangha is socially respected, whereas participation in sex-work is not, the consequence of the gendered division of merit making is to perpetuate the male domination of society. Given this religious gendering of Thai social institutions, and its legitimation of male superiority over females, there is little incentive from within existing Thai Buddhism to improve the human rights of women involved in trafficking and the sex industry. In addition, the Buddhist religion does not itself recognize a concept of human rights (e.g. *Journal of Buddhist Ethics* 1995). In addition, as the center of Thai culture, Buddhist teachings have been the central norm shaping the nation's social institutions and legal order (Kirsch 1985:315; Reynolds 1994:435). Thus, negative Buddhist views of women have been instrumental in shaping the legal status of women in Thailand. The law in Thailand further contributes to the exploitation of sex trade workers by devaluing the status of women. Rather than serving to protect their rights, Thai law (not unlike the legal systems of many nations) until recently formalized discrimination against women, legitimating male dominance over women in marriage, divorce, and allocation of marital property.[23]

The absence of social support for females to develop identities as individuals in Thailand is reinforced by the lack of a developed legal tradition based on individual rights (McDorman 1987:927). Larger forces in Thai society and culture value harmony of social relationships, avoiding confrontations, and resolving disputes by informal means such as tolerance, community or moral pressure, or informal systems of dispute resolution rather than individual rights and rule-oriented systems involving bureaucratic institutions like courts. Social relations in Thailand are governed more by status than legal rights. Although broad generalizations are dangerous, it does seem to be the case that people in Thailand, as in other Asian countries, are less concerned with individual rights than with social duties. In fact, researchers report that neither the Thai government nor most NGO's addressing trafficking in Thailand have expressed "a great deal of interest in using

the law to combat trafficking or to seek compensation for its victims" (Skrobanek et al. 1997:94, 95).

Thus, women's own understandings of their gendered identity also serve
to inhibit the effectiveness of international human rights law in addressing
trafficking. As Satha-Anand argues, human rights cannot be asserted without
awareness to a legitimate claim to reasonable control and determination of
one's own life" (Satha-Anand 1999:211). But Burmese and Thai women's
very involvement in the sex trade suggests that at least many of them lack
such an awareness or a sense of autonomy and independent agency. Given
their socialization, it is unreasonable to expect that Thai women will even
be aware they have "human rights," never mind take action to enforce them
on their own behalf.

Buddhism also presents other obstacles to the effectiveness of using human rights law to address the trafficking problem in Thailand. Although
prostitution is believed to accumulate negative karma by reinforcing craving
and attachment to the sensual world of desire (which perpetuates bondage
to this world of *samsara* or suffering), it is not considered to be a "sin" in
Buddhism as it is in Christianity, Islam, or other religions (Brock and Thistlethwaite 1996:62–63; Murcott 1991:119–21; Keyes 1984:236).[24] The earliest Buddhist scriptures include narrative involving prostitutes, sometimes
as friends of the Buddha, whose generosity helps to sustain the Sangha (monastic order) (e.g. Murcott 1991; Rhys Davids 1989). Buddhist teachings
indicate that prostitutes can overcome the negative karma they have accu-
mulated by renouncing sex work and abiding by the precepts.

Finally, international human rights law is ill-equipped to address the problem of the trafficking of women into prostitution and sex tourism because
many women are at least "willing victims," if not voluntary agents, of their
fate. Even though many trafficked women are misled and deceived about
the type of work they are being solicited for (if not actually coerced or imprisoned), and even though it is arguable whether "free choice" can exist
when economic exigencies and lack of alternative means of equivalently
remunerative employment make prostitution an inevitable "choice" for
some women, nonetheless, many women in the sex industry are fully aware
of what they are getting involved in, continue to stay involved beyond any
contract or debt bondage arrangement, and return to their home villages to
actively recruit the participation of other women (Skrobanek et al. 1997:32–
36). Whether or not they initially "chose" to become prostitutes, "once they
occupy such roles, women more often than not adopt some measure of

control over their lives, endeavouring to improve their own and their families' material circumstances" (Thitsa 1987:37). In addition, women who have been involved in "migrant sex work"—trafficked to other countries—often play a role in the system to obtain new recruits, acting as agents and advisers for younger women (*id.* at 54–56).

This "complicity" by women in the violation of their human rights is inconsistent with the kinds of violations of human rights that international law was designed to address. Indeed, perhaps this element of complicity—whether actual or only potential—has contributed to the difficulties in getting this and other controversial issues such as female genital surgery/mutilation/circumcision and sex selective abortion on the international human rights agenda to begin with. If the so-called "victim" is participating without manifest coercion in the activity which constitutes the supposed violation, is it appropriate to say that her human rights have been violated? The answer is not obvious, especially based on the traditional conception of the bearer of human rights as an autonomous, independent individual agent. Even in those cases where trafficking is evidently the result of coercion rather than voluntary participation, law enforcement continues to be lax, in part based on the *perception* that women migrate and involve themselves in prostitution voluntarily (Skrobanek et al. 1997:98).

To summarize, given the inadequacies of international human rights laws relating to the trafficking of women (especially regarding enforcement), coupled with the Thai government's unwillingness and/or inability to adhere to its international obligations (as well as enforce its domestic laws), the dismal alternative economic opportunities to sex work, the religious and cultural impediments to trafficked women developing rights consciousness or viewing themselves as rights bearers, and the (greater or lesser) voluntariness and/or complicity of many women in the sex industry, international human rights law is unlikely to be an effective means for empowering trafficked women. The absence of the necessary conditions for protecting trafficked women's rights as human rights suggests the need to consider alternative approaches.

Toward a Feminist Pragmatist Approach to Women's Human Rights

The preceding analysis indicates some of the limitations of international human rights law for empowering women, especially in nonwestern cultural contexts. Feminist pragmatist theory offers an alternative, as yet undeveloped, approach to women's rights as human rights[25] which avoids many of the conceptual and practical problems of the liberal feminist endorsement of women's human rights as well as those of the cultural values, care feminist, and third world feminist critiques. Feminist pragmatism is rooted in the philosophy of the American Pragmatists, who included William James, John Dewey, George Herbert Mead, and Charles Peirce. American Pragmatism shares with feminism a rejection of traditional rationalist and empiricist approaches to philosophy, a commitment to the inseparability of theory and practice, a shared focus on everyday life, respect for others, an emphasis on community, an attention to the role of experience, feeling, and emotion in knowledge, an understanding of truth as contextual and relative to particular interests (what is also known as "standpoint epistemology"), and a central place given to the particular, the concrete, and the factual elements of experience, as opposed to the universal, the generalizable, and the abstract (see Radin 1990:1707; Siegfried 1991:2, 16). In the context of women's human rights, a feminist pragmatist perspective is centrally concerned with determining what approaches are likely to be practically effective for empowering women and ending women's oppression. It does not affirm or reject any particular approach based only on theoretical or ideological concerns, but is interested in "what works" to empower women.

A feminist pragmatist approach thus draws on elements from the promoters as well as the critics of women's human rights described above, while it breaks new theoretical ground. First, it rejects a wholesale abandonment of women's rights as human rights—despite its limitations—based on the recognition that this strategy may provide an effective means of improving women's status in certain situations. Rather than accept either the liberal assumption that all women can be included unproblematically within the "human" of "human rights," or the critics' assumption that women are not "human" in this sense, a feminist pragmatist approach begins with the premise that the concept of "human" in human rights is flexible enough to include women, among them nonwestern women, despite its Western male origins.

From a pragmatist perspective, in what sense can human rights be said to include women, especially nonwestern women? Not, as in the liberal view, in a way that is based on some notion of universal reason or rationality. However, the loss of an absolute foundation or grounding for human rights does not entail accepting that human rights are merely "male" rights or wholly culturally relative. As Tracy Higgins has astutely observed, "Loss of faith in objectively valid universal norms leads to cultural relativism only when coupled with a particular normative view that privileges cultural difference over cultural convergence (Higgins 1996:108–9).

As already noted, An-Na'im and others have recognized that human rights are already accepted by many nonwestern cultures, and that the potential exists for further consensus to be reached by developing indigenous cultural values and norms that are analogous to, if not identical with, human rights norms. This acceptance and potential for an overlapping consensus gives human rights a status that, if not universal, has nevertheless garnered the acceptance of a majority of the world's nations, which now share basic human rights norms, at least as members of an international community that has signed certain international law agreements.

In rejecting the applicability of international human rights laws to cultures that lack an indigenous tradition of human rights, cultural values critics frequently lack a fine-grained analysis of how "culture" is defined and, more significantly, *who* is doing the defining. Local cultural values typically have been defined by men, usually those in positions of political power and authority. Women have been excluded from participating in the formulation and establishment of most of the cultural and religious values which frequently dictate how they are to live their lives, from the most personal details of modes of dress, sexual partners, and reproductive activities, to the extent of any political participation and nondomestic labor. The argument against women's rights based on cultural values is especially unjust when women have been excluded from the establishment of those values. Consequently, the lack of an indigenous recognition of women's rights should not automatically rule out the appropriateness of a woman's human rights strategy in a particular cultural location.[26]

In addition, cultures are not homogeneous and unitary, but internally diversified, even fragmented and conflicted. Thus, it is inappropriate to treat culture as synonymous with "the state." Frequently, multiple cultures or cultural groups are clustered within the geographic boundaries of a particular state. Even a relatively culturally homogeneous nation like Japan contains different minority groups and caste divisions. Culture is thus not coextensive with political boundaries. In most parts of the world today, there is a significant amount of cultural interaction, overlap, and "borrowing," in part due to the legacy of colonialist imperialism. Further, the transnational and international arenas are also influential in shaping identity. These include both repressive and liberative forces, both the globalization of capitalist exploitation of labor as well as expanded standards of human rights. Consequently, human beings are not only members of a particular cultural group, or citizens of a particular state; they are also members of an international or global community in which they have been recognized as bearing certain human rights. As a result neither local nor national, secular nor religious, cultural nor political discourses are hegemonic in defining personal identity.

. Contrary to the claim that the concept of women's human rights is essentialist in *assuming* without demonstrating commonalities in women's experience, a feminist pragmatist approach accepts the transcultural relevance of human rights based on demonstrated commonalities in women's experience across cultures. Examples include the devaluation of women's labor, the feminization of poverty, and violence against women (see McConnell 1996:906; Okin 1994). Nonetheless, a feminist pragmatist strategy recognizes that these commonalities may take different forms in different cultural contexts, and that a too facile assumption of commonalities may mask significant differences in women's experiences that may make a human rights strategy ill-advised in a particular context (Higgins 1996:122).[27]

Since the conception of "humanness" presumed by international human rights is foreign to at least some women's identities—either their own self-understandings or as culturally constructed—two possible solutions suggest themselves: "incorporation" and "diversification." The first involves expanding the understanding of "human" in international human rights to include women from diverse cultural contexts. The second is to pursue alternative strategies for empowering women. Efforts at using the incorporation strategy have met with only qualified success, as already discussed. Although activists may ultimately succeed in expanding the scope of international human rights laws to encompass people who were not considered to be "human" when the laws were drafted, as well as harms that were not then considered to be human rights violations, this approach is very slow and may be only partially successful (An-Na'im 1992). Thus, the diversification strategy will be preferable in many circumstances.[28]

Nevertheless, despite the legitimacy of extending international human rights laws to include women from nonwestern cultures as a theoretical matter, a feminist pragmatist approach remains cautious about the advisability of doing so in all cases as a practical matter. In this respect, it accepts the cultural values perspective to the extent of agreeing that persons are constituted by culture, and so will necessarily be differently situated with respect to human rights. In particular, the Western, male conception of identity assumed by human rights discourse potentially conflicts with the social construction of female identity, especially in a traditional religious society like Thailand. Human rights law is likely to be of limited if any practical utility for women who lack consciousness of themselves as "rights bearers" (Cook 1994a:4–5; Coomaraswamy 1994:65). Consequently, a feminist pragmatist strategy recognizes the validity of women's human rights, but not as the exclusive or primary strategy, and perhaps not as an appropriate or efficacious approach in a particular case.[29] Rather, it is viewed as only one of a number of potentially applicable approaches for empowering women.

In making the determination of whether international human rights law is likely to be effective in empowering women in a particular case, a number of factors need to be considered:

1. *The specific cultural, religious, geographical, political, and socio-economic context.* This inquiry includes asking whether cultural conditions exist, such as religious or other gender ideologies, that would either subvert or facilitate the recognition and enforcement of women's human rights. Fundamentalist religions present distinctive difficulties for promoting women's rights as human rights because of their construction of female identity as divinely ordained to be subordinate to males. Since religion is a significant, if not core, aspect of identity for many women around the world, it is not appropriate to assume that conflicts between religion and women's international human rights can simply be resolved by restricting the former in favor of the latter, as some scholars have proposed (Sullivan 1992:824–29; Howland 1997). Where women's "rights" are viewed as in opposition to a religion and/or cultural custom and tradition, it may be more effective to use an alternative strategy which does not reveal itself as an external threat to the authority of that cultural or religious tradition. In addition, problems that are specific to a woman's particular culture, social and geographical location, race, class, sexual orientation, and religion cannot all be adequately addressed by an international legal strategy, no matter how carefully designed. The law is a "blunt instrument" and so international human rights law may not ad-

dress the particular manner in which women are being oppressed in a particular locale.

2. Related to the first factor is *the presence of "legal consciousness" and or "rights consciousness"* within a culture and within women in particular. An exclusively legal strategy is likely to be ineffective in significantly advancing the interests of women within cultures that are regulated more on the basis of cultural and social norms other than the rule of law. Because international human rights law basically determines the appropriate contours of human rights policy in advance, and from the "outside," and then "imposes" that conception onto a culture where it may be alien, it may be especially difficult to implement with respect to women whose identity is shaped by a sexist and patriarchal cultural tradition, especially a religious one. As the case of trafficking in Thailand illustrated, the lack of a developed legal rights tradition in a culture may make a rights-based strategy ill-suited to advancing women's status (Cook 1994a:4–5; Coomaraswamy 1994:65). As Higgins suggests, "if the self is constituted by culture, as many feminists assume, equating emancipation from external coercion with individual freedom is problematic. Instead, feminists must consider a more complex process of emancipation that involves transformation of the self" (Higgins 1996:115). If a culture does not provide the basis for women to develop "rights consciousness," that is, a sense of themselves as rights bearers, the efficacy of an approach to women's empowerment based on international legal rights will necessarily be limited.

3. Third, and related to the first factor, is whether an international human rights strategy is likely to present a *risk of backlash*. This is the danger that the use of international law may make a governing body *more* resistant to improving the status of women than if the appeal had been framed in terms of local laws and/or indigenous norms and values. The common linkage of women to the preservation and transmission of culture (Othman 1997); Kapur and Cossman 1996:45, 65)[30] may contribute to the opposition to women's human rights—especially in traditional sexist and patriarchal cultural contexts (*see* Hernandez-Truyol 1996:65). As Mahoney observes, "the accusation that human rights activists are out to destroy the culture can be a powerful tool in the hands of those who wish to maintain the status quo of female subordination" (Mahoney 1996:856).

In this circumstance as well, then, empowering women may be better effectuated by less formal, confrontational, and potentially antagonistic activities than the use of international human rights laws. The potential for backlash heightens the importance of considering whether the implementation of a women's human rights approach may result in disadvantaging the status of women in a particular locale more than it empowers them. In addition, the existence of hostility by the relevant government to "the West," to international human rights law, and/or to women's rights more generally, may limit the efficacy of a women's human rights approach.

4. Fourth, what has been *the historical experience of others using a legal or rights strategy* to forward their claims against the state, especially with respect to similar or related issues? Has an international human rights strategy been successful with respect to other issues in a particular locale? If not, why not? A feminist pragmatist approach recognizes that law is a partial solution to women's oppression even in the best of circumstances, as women's experience with domestic law reform around the world has shown (Kapur and Cossman 1996; Hoff 1991). As the proposal for an optional protocol to the Women's Convention points out, even though the Convention is the second most widely subscribed to international human rights treaty in existence, "violations of women's human rights remain widespread in all societies and cultures," and "women are not aware of their rights and have difficulty getting remedies for violations of these rights" (United Nations 1997:1).

In addition, international law solutions are limited in their very composition. Individual complaint procedures under UN human rights treaties require voluntary compliance by states (Byrnes 1994: 198–99), and a number of states attempt to avoid compliance with international law agreements, even those they do sign, especially those relating to women's rights.[31] The practical reality is that states cannot be sanctioned for their failure to protect women's rights under international law (*see* Cook 1994b:228). Further, procedures under international human rights instruments are generally *slow*, in part because exhaustion of national remedies must usually precede the implementation of international ones, which themselves often take years (Chow 1996:189). In addition, the international tribunals hearing complaints are predominantly male, which may bias the outcome of cases brought to hear violations of women's human rights. So, for example, in a state which has not signed international human rights agreements or has failed to demonstrate some will to adhere to its obligations under such agreements, pursuing a women's human rights strategy is probably not worthwhile.

Nonetheless, it is important to keep in mind that international law is potentially useful in ways that far surpass its status as *law*, that is, its ability to provide effective implementation and enforcement of treaty principles. As Miller suggests, "the promises made by governments in ratifying these treaties can be the basis for effective public education on women's rights, for advocacy on the obligations to change discriminatory laws, or for direct litigation to find laws or practices invalid" (Miller 1998:6). In addition, international law and United Nations-generated human rights law with its treaty bodies and oversight mechanisms, also provides a framework for national and local groups to organize and effectively lobby for local recognition of human rights. International human rights norms themselves may play a significant role in the development of respect for international human rights around the world, regardless of the absence of the conditions which would make such norms legally binding or enforceable.

Thus, even in those circumstances when it appears that international human rights law—especially *as law*—appears to be (or actually is) irrelevant to a particular situation of women's oppression, the actual impact of its attempted recognition, implementation, and enforcement may be far different. Nonetheless, where the power oppressing women is not centralized, as is the case with patriarchal domination, human rights law is apt to overlook the actual locus of harm.

5. A final, and perhaps most important, factor is *whether there is sufficient agreement among affected women to advocate for the recognition of a specific human right as a woman's right.* Whereas, for example, there is near unanimity among women's groups worldwide, for example, that women have a right to be free from domestic violence, the same unity does not exist regarding other issues, such as female genital surgery. This is also the case with

women's involvement in the sex trade. One of the disagreements regarding the trafficking issue is whether there can be genuinely uncoerced prostitution in a patriarchal and sexist society which devalues women, objectifies them as sex objects, and limits their economic opportunities. Radhika Coomaraswamy, the United Nations Special Rapporteur for Violence Against Women (Special Rapporteur), admits that there has been too much division over this issue, even within the women's movement, to enable a concerted international campaign to enact more effective laws concerning trafficking (Coomaraswamy 1997:14). Since prostitution continues to be the best employment possibility for many women, it is not evident whether international law should advocate an abolitionist approach to the sex industry, regardless of its violation of women's rights, or instead strive to improve the working conditions for women engaged in it.

Part of the inquiry regarding the existence of sufficient support for using a human rights strategy involves ascertaining whether women are participating in "their own oppression" by uncoerced and/or "voluntary" involvement in the very activities which constitute the violation of a human rights standard. If so, as in the case of the trafficking of women for prostitution in Thailand—as well as practices such as female genital circumcision and sex-selective abortion—it may be difficult to assess whether the women in question are suffering from "false consciousness" or instead manifesting a different cultural understanding of their "best interests." Ongoing dialogues may clarify the situation over time, and make it more apparent whether the women in question would, in fact, appreciate and benefit from the intervention of human rights laws in their lives.

If the basic preconditions for the recognition and enforcement of women's human rights are lacking in a particular situation, however, a feminist pragmatist approach considers alternative, "ground up" grassroots strategies that might be more effective than international law (Etienne 1995; Miller 1998).

Nonetheless, because trafficking in women for the sex trade *is* an international problem, involving the crossing of national borders, international law certainly has a significant role to play in combating the exploitation of women and children who are being trafficked. Coomaraswamy argues that "international standards and guidelines are the only meaningful mechanisms with which to confront" the sex trade, given their ability to coordinate interstate efforts to apprehend and prosecute traffickers (Coomaraswamy 1997:14). An international human rights approach may also provide needed education, international publicity and pressure, and a framework for coordinating the efforts of governmental bodies, NGO's, and individuals working to combat trafficking. However, for the reasons already specified, international law alone is an inadequate solution.

Basic economic empowerment and alternative modes of economic survival for the sex trade workers and their families are vitally important to ending trafficking in Thailand. International human rights laws prohibiting the trafficking in women or even specifying legal protection for economic rights cannot be effective unless and until alternative means of economic survival are available, even if international and domestic laws were enforced by the government in good faith.

Thus, practical strategies such as those proposed by the Women in Development movement to enable women to attain economic independence—such as providing education, literacy training, micro-credit, and communal land ownership—may be even more effective than women's human rights for addressing the problem of trafficking in Thailand. However, changing the economic status of large numbers of women also will require ending the sex discrimination which preserves better, higher paying jobs for men, as well as providing more economic opportunities to all people (a bleak prospect today).

As noted, the inadequacy of a legal solution to the particular problem of trafficking of women into prostitution and sex tourism results in part from the inability of law to change gender biased attitudes of individual actors. As Farrior observes, "trafficking will not end until states take steps to modify cultures that allow women and girls to be viewed as commodities to be trafficked" (Farrior 1997:229). Thus, another promising approach is cultural reinterpretation. This approach seeks to provide a cultural "ground" for the acceptance of women's rights by reinterpreting traditional gender ideologies that have been used to legitimate male domination and discrimination against women.

As a dimension or aspect of culture—which is "dynamic and changing, both internally and in response to external forces and influences" (An-Na'im 1992:432; Rao 1995:173)[32]—religion is also subject to change and reinterpretation. Thus, even if presented in terms of fixed and immutable tenets (e.g., "Natural law" or God's Commandments), religion can sometimes be

softened or modified to eliminate at least the more egregious forms of discrimination against women in that tradition.

Othman describes the merits of the scriptural reinterpretation approach:

> Having . . . promoted the emergence of locally acceptable cultural
> and national moral systems favoring recognition of women's rights,
> women and women's movements will then be in a position to advocate
> women's equality in cultural terms that are locally persuasive and au-
> thentic. They then will be able to argue that women's emancipation,
> as required by international human rights instruments such as
> CEDAW, is consistent with local and national cultural values. In this
> way, they will avoid placing themselves, or being placed by others, in
> a position where their challenge to women's subordination and their
> support for women's full enjoyment of human rights are seen as merely
> an imposition of outside Western cultural ideals (Othman 1999:188–
> 89).

Since this proposed strategy mediates between the primary or exclusive use
of an international women's human rights "external" strategy, on the one
hand, and the use of only a local or indigenous "internal" strategy, on the
other, it has more potential to be effective than a strategy which uses either
international human rights or local interventions alone. In addition, because
this strategy works within women's religious and cultural paradigms" (Othman 1999:191–92), it limits the possibilities for opposition and backlash
from conservative and anti-feminist elements within the culture, and thereby
enhances the possibilities for empowering women. It also is responsive to
the observation that "the availability of secular remedies does not eliminate
the need to the modify religious law or practice that impairs the rights of
women who remain within the religious community" (Sullivan 1992:847).
Even where international human rights law may be effective, then, there
may still be a need for this kind of strategy.

Suwanna Satha-Anand has proposed that reinterpreting sacred Buddhist
texts is a more effective strategy than international women's human rights
for addressing the trafficking of women into the sex trade in Thailand (Satha-
Anand 1999). Buddhist scriptures are an important means for disseminating
religious and cultural values at the popular level. Because Thailand does
not have a tradition of human rights, Satha-Anand claims that "cultural
empowering of women is crucial to creating more awareness of this problem

as a new rights issue in a society wherein the economic, legal, historical, and cultural conditioning are working *against* the recognition of women's rights" (Satha-Anand 1999:194). She suggests that the reinterpretation of the sexist, patriarchal, and even misogynistic elements of Buddhist texts has the potential to the transform gender ideology at the popular level.

Given the pervasive influence of religion in shaping personal and community identity in Thailand, Satha-Anand's reinterpretation strategies have the virtue of not forcing women to choose between their religiously-given identity and the independent, individualistic identity that is the subject of international human rights. Such "local" strategies more effectively address the critically important aspect of women's subjectivity that the international women's human rights approach neglects, what Satha-Anand describes as "the self-formation process of women" (Satha-Anand 1999:206). Scriptural reinterpretation is also less likely to alienate or motivate opposition from fellow citizens or government officials than international human rights strategies, which may be perceived as inappropriate meddling by Western outsiders into the integrity of local culture and tradition.

This approach is not without its own difficulties, however, as evidenced by the limited success of feminists using this strategy in other religious traditions.[33] Nonetheless, Christian churches remain, in many ways, male biased institutions. Within the Catholic Church in particular, women are still prohibited from becoming priests, and normative social roles for women continue to the be limited to the those of wife and mother, even though some space has opened up for women to work as part of their responsibility to the help maintain their families financially. Similarly, many fundamentalist and evangelical Protestant denominations continue to the relegate women to the secondary roles inside and outside of the Church.

Furthermore, without providing specific suggestions about how the reinterpreting is to the be undertaken, Satha-Anand's specific proposal appears to the be an abstract, "textual" academic exercise that will have little bearing on how Buddhist scriptures are understood by the majority of Thai Buddhists. Who is doing the reinterpreting, and for what audience? Would the reinterpreted texts be taught in school? If not, how would the reinterpretations be disseminated? Do Thai women—especially mothers and prostitutes—read Buddhist texts? If not, is it reasonable to the assume that Buddhist monks will recite reinterpreted scriptures in religious services? What other mechanisms are available within local society to transmit these new understandings to the population? More generally, it may not always be possible to empower women using a "local" cultural strategy such as textual reinterpretation, in part because of explicit religious or cultural restrictions on women's autonomy to the engage in such practices, including women's lack of basic literacy skills.

Given the limitations of each of these alternatives, the most effective approach to the empowering of women in a particular cultural context may be a multi-faceted one which uses a combination of different approaches. Combining international law with more contextualized, gender sensitive, and culturally specific and nuanced approaches to the securing of women's needs and interests globally can undoubtedly be more effective than pursuing an international human rights strategy alone.

Indeed, Skrobanek, et al.'s research led them to the conclude that, in addition to the greater enforcement of criminal laws against traffickers, combating the sex trade requires government agencies to play a role in raising awareness, educating communities about the facts of trafficking and prostitution, providing counseling for women, creating alternative employment opportunities, and providing assistance to the victims (Skrobanek et al. 1997:79). NGO's in Thailand in fact are using multiple strategies to address trafficking. For example, the group EMPOWER (Education Means Protection of Women Engaged in Recreation) provides education in Thai and English and a health class on AIDS. It also produces a newsletter and drama-activities in order to strengthen the position of prostitutes. Some NGO's are engaged in grassroots-level information campaigns designed to educate trafficking victims at both points of departure and entry about destination countries, their rights and responsibilities for support and assistance, along with the situations of violence and abuse that may arise. Some NGOs have also established resource centers to provide assistance (Coomaraswamy 1997:21).[34] Once such basic survival strategies have been provided, the rights consciousness necessary to make international human rights law effective becomes a far more realistic possibility.

Conclusion: Women Are Both Human and Women

In the "final" analysis, then, are women "human"? From a feminist pragmatist perspective, the answer might best be characterized as "yes, but . . . " That is, women should be included within the "human" of human rights to the extent that international human rights law provides an effective approach for empowering them. However, as the feminist and cultural values critics discussed here have demonstrated, women's rights as human rights is a partial and incomplete strategy at best. If applied unreflectively, without regard to the differences of gender and cultural context, international human rights can be ineffective, if not positively damaging, to the interests and well being of the women it purports to assist.

Among the many limitations and criticisms of international human rights discourse considered here, one of the most significant is its failure to recognize and address the role of culture, especially religion, in shaping personal identity and subjectivity. A legal rights strategy is unlikely to be effective in empowering women who lack "rights consciousness" and some sense of themselves as agents of their own lives. These observations should not be interpreted as demonstrating that international women's human rights are morally inappropriate, an illegitimate interference with the cultural integrity of women who do not "think like we do." Instead, they suggest that international human rights law may be an inappropriate strategy for empowering women where the conditions for its effective implementation and enforcement are lacking.

Although the analysis of international human rights presented here has focused on gender and cultural differences, it has broader applicability in suggesting that a pragmatist analysis should be undertaken in order to the assess the feasibility of using international human rights more generally. For if the subjects of international human rights law do not regard themselves as "rights bearers" or have a "legal" or "rights" consciousness, or if their cultural traditions do not recognize law and individual rights as important mechanisms for meeting basic human needs and interests, then international human rights law is likely to be ineffective. Thus, *any* human rights campaign would benefit from the pragmatist analysis proposed here.

Endnotes

1. The literature addressing human rights from feminist perspectives is fairly recent, but burgeoning rapidly (see, e.g., Cook 1994; Peters and Wolper 1995; Bunch 1995a; Bunch 1995b; Heyzer 1995; Wetzel 1993; Symposium, *Brooklyn Journal of International Law* 1996; Symposium, *Case Western Reserve Law Review* 1997; Human Rights Watch Women's Rights Project 1995; Amnesty International 1995).

2. Although framing women's rights as human rights is a fairly recent strategy, the UN has prohibited discrimination based on sex since the UN Charter was

ratified (see UN 1945: arts. 1(3), 13(1)(b), 55(c), and 76(c), and this prohibition has been repeated in the Universal Declaration of Human Rights (UN 1948), the International Covenant on Economic, Social, and Cultural Rights, arts. 2(2), 3 (UN 1966b), and the International Covenant on Civil and Political Rights, arts. 2(1), 3, 23(4), 26 (UN 1966a).

3. The Vienna Declaration and Programme of Action adopted in June 1993 by the World Conference on Human Rights specifies that "human rights of women and of the girl-child are an inalienable and indivisible part of universal human rights" (UN 1993).

4. Gilligan observed a gender difference in her research on how adolescents and others responded to a number of hypothetical moral dilemmas. Whereas the males in her study tended to resolve moral problems in accordance with an "ethics of justice," characterized by a concern with individual rights, abstract principles of justice, and adversarial relations, Gilligan found that the females tended to rely on "an ethics of care," which assumes that persons are socially interdependent rather than independent (Gilligan 1982).

5. The term "third world feminist" is defined by Chandra Mohanty (1991) as a perspective which recognizes both that gender cannot be defined "in any trans-historical, unitary way" (Mohanty 1991:5), that neither Western nor Third World women constitute any unitary or coherent interest group, that the lives of women of color are defined by the intersectionality of gender, racial, class, and often colonial or imperial domination, and cannot be reduced to a single factor, and that women "need to build our politics around the struggles of the most exploited peoples of the world" (Mohanty 1991:10).

6. The term "postmodern" is used to describe theorists who are interested in challenging the Enlightenment's essentialist and foundationalist assumptions, especially of universalism, rationalism, and humanism, as well as the universal principles, norms, and assumptions, and categories of thought that perpetuate dichotomies such as male and female, and the hierarchies of power and privilege that accompany them (Mouffe 1992; Nicholson 1992; Butler 1992). "Post-colonial" is used to describe a perspective that focuses on the way that culture and identity have been shaped by colonialism and imperialism (Mohanty 1991).

7. The United Nations has defined "trafficking" as including "the purposes of sexual exploitation, pornography, prostitution and sex tourism" (United Nations 1995a: para. 230 [n]).

8. In her view, "unless the experiences of women contribute directly to the main-stream international legal order, beginning with women's equal representation in law-making forums, international human rights law loses its claim to universal applicability; it should be more accurately characterized as international men's rights law" (Charlesworth 1995:105).

9. This is certainly the case in the United States, where the rights enumerated in the Constitution and Bill of Rights largely have been interpreted as restricted only to the so-called "negative" rights which individuals have against state interference with their civil and political liberties, rather than extending to encompass also "positive" rights which would require the state to provide individuals with social and economic goods.

10. In part, this reflects the greater power and authority within the UN of so-called "first world" or developed, mostly Western, nations as opposed to "third world" or developing nations and governments governed by socialist rather than capitalist political systems, for whom securing economic, social, and cultural rights has been a more fundamental agenda (Higgins 1996:93). In fact, the very decision by the UN to establish an Economic Covenant separate from the Covenant on Civil and Political Rights was in part the result of objections by a number of states to recognizing social and economic benefits as legal "rights" that states are affirmatively obligated by positive law to provide (Boutros-Ghali 1995:43).

11. Even traditional male human rights advocates admit that international human rights law was developed on the basis of Western, Enlightenment, male-centered conceptions of persons as autonomous and independent, distinct from the community and endowed with inalienable individual rights (Donnelly 1989:9–14).

12. As Rebecca Cook notes, under the definition of "discrimination" in the Women's Convention, "a law that makes no express distinction on the basis of sex in its language cannot be impugned under this definition despite its having a discriminatory effect" (Cook 1994b:235).

13. For instance, during his visit to the United States in October, 1997, Chinese Premier Jiang Zemin responded in a debate with President Clinton by claiming that China and the U.S. have different "historical and cultural traditions" and that "the concepts on democracy, on human rights, and on freedoms" are relative (Harris 1997:A17).

14. In Sudan, "Muslim women are being told that patriarchy is not what is hindering them, but international law as part of Western ideas is the real obstacle to women" (Halim 1994:406). Elsewhere in Africa, "women's groups working to reform discriminatory laws and practices are dismissed by some governments 'as misguided elite women aping Western concepts' " (Cook 1994a:18).

15. A news article in April 1996 reported that Thailand may have 800,000 people infected with HIV and Myanmar may have 400,000 (WIN News 1996:60). A study of prostitutes in Chiang Mai, Thailand, conducted in 1992 by the Red Cross and World Health Organization, found that four out of every five prostitutes tested were HIV-positive. It is estimated that 50 to 80 percent of the prostitutes in Thailand are infected (Brock and Thistlethwaite 1996:144).

16. As research on the sex trade in Thailand indicates, anti-prostitution laws may actually encourage trafficking by making it more profitable on a black market, and enabling traffickers to avoid legal obligations to repatriate women if they are arrested (Skrobanek et al. 1997:102).

17. On December 12, 1996, the UN General Assembly called upon countries of origin, transit, and destination to take a number of steps to outlaw and eliminate the trafficking of women and girl children, including implementing the Beijing Platform for Action. It requested member nations to the Women's Convention to submit statistics and information regarding trafficking in their annual reports to CEDAW and the Committee on the Rights of the Child. The absence of Thailand among the thirty countries submitting reports suggests that its government lacks the political will to enforce international human rights norms (United Nations General Assembly Report 1997:11, n. 2). Thailand has also failed to submit its second and third periodic reports to CEDAW (due, respectively, in September, 1990 and 1994) as required for signatories to that document and to the Platform. These practices are consistent with what one legal scholar characterizes as a general tendency of the Thai government to tolerate a discrepancy between formal legal regulations and actual practice (McDorman 1987:923–24).

18. Thailand has had a law prohibiting the trafficking in girls or women for prostitution since 1928, with the "Prostitution Control Law" being the relevant statute from 1960 until 1996. Prior to that time, however, prostitution was legal and brothels were legally registered at the beginning of the twentieth century. The 1960 Act imposed a double standard by prohibiting the selling of sex, but not its purchase. In 1996, a new Prevention and Suppression of Prostitution Act was passed. Intended to focus on punishing those involved in the commercial sexual exploitation of minors, it imposes special penalties for using coercion to involve others into the sex industry, but does not address abuses of persons already in the industry.

19. The link between the Thai economy and prostitution is the result of a number of national and international influences, including "complicity between foreign investors and native companies to hold down the rates of pay for female labor" (Thitsa 1980:13). As Siriporn Skrobanek notes, the trafficking in women and the sex tourism industry in Thailand "are a reflection of the sad reality of an international society which aims at economic growth and maximizing profit by exploiting powerless groups in poor countries" (Skrobanek 1992:129).

20. Keyes argues that the most "salient" image for women who become prostitutes is still that of the nurturing mother, rather than those of women as sex objects or sexual temptresses or mistresses (Keyes 1984:237).

21. The female order has not been reintroduced in Thailand, in part because of the opposition of the male monastic establishment (even though male orders

have been reintroduced in several other Buddhist countries after having disappeared).

22. For example, upon learning the actual facts of how their daughters were actually employed at a local Thai community public education event at which some local former prostitutes testified, some family members attending expressed anger and hostility toward the organizers and witnesses, illustrating the "collusive unknowing that sometimes unites families with agents, traffickers and exploiters" (Skrobanek et al. 1997:82).

23. Women's equal right to divorce was not legalized until 1976, when the Civil and Commercial Code provisions governing family matters were amended to remove such legal disabilities of women (Thitsa 1980:7).

24. The Pali word for prostitute is *vesi* or *vesiya*, meaning "a woman of low caste, a prostitute, a harlot" (Murcott 1991:119). However, one of the *Therigatha* (part of canon of Buddhist scriptures, meaning "Songs of Sisters" or "Poems of the Nuns," purported to be written records of the Buddha's first female disciples)—popular stories that are one of the main modes for disseminating Buddhist principles and values from the monastic level to the laity—tells the story of Ambapali. After serving many previous lives in hell for having cursed a monk, she was finally reborn as a beautiful woman who became a very wealthy courtesan. She gave birth to a son who became a devout disciple of the Buddha, as did she herself. After her son attained ultimate enlightenment, she entered the order and attained *arhatship* (realization) (Murcott 1991:131–34; Truong 1990:136). The story contains no negative opprobrium directed at Ambapali for being a prostitute. To the contrary, it relates that the Buddha accepted Ambapali's invitation for him and his disciples to dine with her the day after he preached in a nearby town, and she built a hermitage on her property for the Sangha (community of Buddhist monastics) (Murcott 1991:130).

25. A few feminist theorists have explored the potential of pragmatism for feminist theorizing, but none, to my knowledge, have addressed human rights specifically (see, e.g. Radin 1990; Rorty 1991; Fraser 1991; Siegfried 1990; Siegfried 1991).

26. Thus, Abdullahi An-Na'im's conclusion that "the interpretation and practical application of [human rights laws] in the context of a particular society should be determined by the moral standards of that society" (1999:37) is especially inappropriate with respect to women's human rights, which, for the most part, have not been recognized.

27. As Karen Engle points out, both women's rights and human rights organizations have not been able to successfully incorporate the "Exotic Other Female" into their analyses (Engle 1995). Without doing so, however, women's human rights jurisprudence will remain either essentialist—assuming all women are alike—

or exclusionary—refusing to include women who do not agree with "our values."

28. Even the UN has recognized, at least on occasion, the propriety of forwarding alternative strategies to advance women's interests. For example, the World Conference of the International Women's Year in Mexico City in 1975 focused on "the underdevelopment of socio-economic structures in most areas of the world as the major cause of women's inferior position" (Boutros-Ghali 1995:85). Similarly, the World Conference of the United Nations Decade for Women, held in Copenhagen in 1980, "adopted a Programme of Action which stressed even more strongly the links between economic development and improvement in the status of women" (*id.* at 86). For the most part, however, the international human rights community has focused on legal rights as the primary strategy for promoting human dignity and freedom from oppression.

29. This feminist pragmatist approach shares some, but not all, of the elements of an "anti-essentialist" feminist perspective, which views both gender and human rights to be contingent products of particular cultures, and consequently focuses on specific contexts of women's oppression rather than presuming universality (Higgins 1996:102–3).

30. Muslim women, for example, "become charged as the 'guardians' for the maintenance of important cultural values and of the society's moral integrity as a whole" (Othman 1997:36). This is also true in Hindu societies (*see* Kapur and Cossman 1996:45, 65).

31. As an example, more states have entered reservations (that is, objections to certain provisions) to the Women's Convention than any other human rights convention.

32. As Arati Rao explains, "culture is a series of constantly contested and negotiated social practices whose meanings are influenced by the power and status of their interpreters and participants" (Rao 1995:173).

33. Christian women have succeeded in many denominations in making significant changes toward gender equality within their churches based, at least in part, upon Biblical reinterpretations. Such changes have ranged from eliminating male-biased terminology from hymns and liturgy to the opening up the avenues for women to participate in the Church, including leadership positions, to the denomination formally addressing issues of fundamental concern to the women, such as reproductive rights, domestic violence, the feminization of poverty, etc.

34. Without some kind of coordinated, adequately funded and staffed effort, however, it is hard to the imagine such an information strategy having much of an impact on most of the women involved in the sex trade in Thailand, especially those being trafficked into the country from Burma or other location.

Bibliography

Amnesty International. 1995. *Its About Time! Human Rights are Women's Right.* New York: Amnesty International.

An-Na'im, Abdullahi. 1992. "Toward a Cross-Cultural Approach to Defining International Standards of Human Rights" In An-Na'im, ed. *Human Rights in Cross-Cultural Perspectives: A Quest for Consensus*, 19–43. Philadelphia: University of Pennsylvania Press.

———. 1999. "The Cultural Mediation of Human Rights Implementation: Al-Arqam Case in Malaysia." In Joanne R. Bauer and Daniel A. Bell, eds. *The East Asian Challenge for Human Rights.* Cambridge: Cambridge University Press.

Boutros-Ghali, Boutros. 1995. "Introduction," *The United Nations and Human Rights 1954–1995.* New York: United Nations Reproduction Section.

Bouvard, Marguerite Guzman. 1996. *Women Reshaping Human Rights: How Extraordinary Activists Are Changing the World.* Wilmington, DE: Scholarly Resources, Inc.

Brock, Rita Nakashima and Susan Brooks Thistlethwaite. 1996. *Casting Stones: Prostitution and Liberation in Asia and the United States.* Minneapolis: Fortress Press.

Brooklyn Journal of International Law Editorial Staff. 1991. "Symposium Introduction." *Brooklyn Journal of International Law*, 21:899–913.

Bunch, Charlotte. 1995a. "Women's Human Rights and Development: A Global Agenda for the 21st Century," in Noleen Heyzer, ed. *Commitment to the World's Women: Perspectives on Development for Beijing and Beyond*, 159–63. New York: UNIFEM, 159–63.

———. 1995b. "The Global Campaign for Women's Human Rights: Where Next After Vienna?" *St. John's Law Review* 69:171–78.

Bunch, Charlotte and Susana Fried. 1996. "Beijing '95: Moving Women's Human Rights From Margin to Center." *Signs: Journal of Women and Culture* 22(1):200–204.

Butler, Judith. 1990. *Gender Trouble: Feminism and the Subversion of Identity.* New York: Routledge.

Byrnes, Andrew. 1994. "Toward More Effective Enforcement of Women's Human Rights through the Use of International Human Rights Law and Procedures." In Rebecca Cook, ed. *Human Rights of Women: National and International Perspectives*, 189–227. Philadelphia: University of Pennsylvania Press.

Case Western Reserve Law Review Editorial Staff. 1997. "Colloquium: Bridging Society, Culture, and Law: The Issue of Female Circumcision." *Case Western Reserve Law Review* 47(2):263–52.

Charlesworth, Hilary. 1994. "What Are 'Women's International Human Rights?" In Rebecca Cook, ed. *Human Rights of Women: National and International Perspectives*, 58–84. Philadelphia: University of Pennsylvania Press.

———. 1995. "Human Rights as Men's Rights." In Julie Peters and Andrea Wolper, eds. *Women's Rights, Human Rights: International Feminist Perspectives*, 103–113. New York: Routledge.

———, Christine Chinkin and Shelley Wright. 1991. "Feminist Approaches to International Law." *American Journal of International Law* 85:613–645.

Chow, Esther Ngan-ling. 1996. "Making Waves, Moving Mountains: Reflections on Beijing '95 and Beyond." *Signs: Journal of Women in Culture* 22(1):185–92.

Cook, Rebecca. 1994a. "Women's International Human Rights Law: The Way Forward." In Rebecca Cook, ed. *Human Rights of Women: National and International Perspectives*. 3–38. Philadelphia: University of Pennsylvania Press.

———. 1994b. "State Accountability Under the Convention on the Elimination of All Forms of Discrimination Against Women." In Rebecca Cook, ed. *Human Rights of Women: National and International Perspectives*. 228–256. Philadelphia: University of Pennsylvania Press.

Coomaraswamy, Radhika. 1994. "To Bellow Like a Cow: Women, Ethnicity, and the Discourse of Rights." In Rebecca Cook, ed. *Human Rights of Women: National and International Perspectives*, 39–57. Philadelphia: University of Pennsylvania Press.

———. 1996. *Report of the Special Rapporteur on Violence Against Women, Its Causes and Consequences, Ms. Radhika Coomaraswamy, submitted in accordance with Commission on Human Rights Resolution 1995/85*. United Nations Commission on Human Rights, 52rd Session, Item 9a, E/CN.4/1996/53, 1996.

———. 1997. *Report of the Special Rapporteur on Violence Against Women, Its Causes and Consequences*. United Nations Commission on Human Rights, 53rd Session, Item 9a, E/CN.4/1997/47, 1997. http://193.135.156.15/html/menu4/chrrep/4797.htm (downloaded 10/16/97).

Crenshaw, Kimberle. 1991. "Mapping the Margins: Intersectionality, Identity Politics, and Violence Against Women of Color." *Stanford Law Review* 43:1241–99.

Donnelly, Jack. 1989. *Universal Human Rights in Theory and Practice*.Ithaca, NY: Cornell University Press.

Dormady, Valerie. 1997. "Women's Rights in International Law: A Prediction Concerning the Legal Impact of the United Nations' Fourth World Conference on Women." *Vanderbilt Journal of Transnational Law* 30:97–134.

Eberhardt, Nancy. 1988. "Introduction," in N. Eberhardt, ed. *Gender, Power, and the Construction of the Moral Order: Studies from the Thai Periphery*. Madison, WI: Center for Southeast Asian Studies.

Engle, Karen. 1995. "Female Subjects of Public International Law: Human Rights and the Exotic Other Female." In Dan Danielson and Karen Engle, eds. *After Identity: A Reader in Law and Culture*, 210–28. New York: Routledge.

Etienne, Margareth. 1995. "Addressing Gender-Based Violence in an International Context," *Harvard Women's Law Journal* 8:39–70.

Farrior, Stephanie. 1997. "The International Law on Trafficking in Women and Children for Prostitution: Making it Live Up to its Potential." *Harvard Human Rights Journal* 10:213–255.

Fraser, Nancy. 1991. "From Irony to Prophecy to Politics: A Response to Richard Rorty." *Michigan Quarterly Review* 30(2):59–66.

Gilligan, Carol. 1982. *In a Different Voice: Psychological Theory and Women's Development*. Cambridge: Harvard University Press.

Halim, Asma Mohamed Abdel. 1994. "Challenges to the Application of International Women's Human Rights in the Sudan." In Rebecca Cook, ed. *Human Rights of Women: National and International Perspectives*, 397–421. Philadelphia: University of Pennsylvania Press.

Harris, John. 1997. "U.S.-China Pacts Reached in Shadow of Discord on Rights." *Washington Post* (December 30), A1, A17.

Hernandez-Truyol, Berta Esperanza. 1995. "Concluding Remarks—Making Women Visible: Setting An Agenda for the Twenty-First Century." *St. John's Law Review* 69:231–54.

———. 1996. "Women's Rights as Human Rights—Rules, Realities, and the Role of Culture: A Formula for Reform." *Brooklyn Journal of International Law* 21:605–678.

Heyzer, Noleen, ed. 1995. *A Commitment to the World's Women: Perspectives on Development for Beijing and Beyond*. New York: UNIFEM.

Higgins, Tracy. 1996. "Anti-Essentialism, Relativism, and Human Rights." *Harvard Women's Law Journal* 19:89–126.

Hill, Catherine. 1991. "Planning for Prostitution: An Analysis of Thailand's Sex Industry," in Meredeth Turshen and Briavel Holcomb, eds. *Women's Lives and Public Policy* 133–44. Westport, CT: Greenwood Press.

Hoff, Joan. 1991. *Law, Gender, and Injustice*. New York: New York University Press.

Howland, Courtney. 1997. "The Challenge of Religious Fundamentalism to the Liberty and Equality Rights of Women: An Analysis Under the United Nations Charter." *Columbia Journal of Transnational Law* 35(2):271–377.

Human Rights Watch Women's Rights Project. 1995. *Human Rights Watch Global Report on Women's Human Rights*. New York: Human Rights Watch.

Johnson, Ian. 1995. "Unprecedented Protest, Yet Great Promise." *Baltimore Sun* (Sept. 6):A1.

Journal of Buddhist Ethics. 1995. *Conference on Human Rights*. http://noether. vassar.edu/~Epanfili/.jbe (October 2–5).

Kabilsingh, Chatsumarn. 1991. *Thai Women in Buddhism*. Berkeley, CA: Parallax Press.

Kapur, Ratna and Brenda Cossman. 1996. *Subversive Sites: Feminist Engagements with Law in India*. New Delhi: Sage Publications.

Keyes, Charles. 1984. "Mother or Mistress But Never a Monk: Buddhist Notions of Female Gender in Rural Thailand." *American Ethnologist* 11:223–241.

Kirsch, Thomas. 1982. "Buddhism, Sex-Roles and the Thai Economy." In Penny Van Esterik, ed. *Women of Southeast Asia*. (Northern Illinois University: Center for Southeast Asian Studies, Occasional Paper No. 9, 1982.

———. 1985. "Text and Context: Buddhist Sex Roles/Culture of Gender Revisited." *American Ethnologist* 12:302–320.

Krotoszynski, Ronald. 1997. "Building Bridges and Overcoming Barricades: Exploring the Limits of Law as an Agent of Transformational Social Change." *Case Western Reserve Law Review*, 47:423–444.

Mahoney, Kathleen. 1996. "Theoretical Perspectives on Women's Human Rights and Strategies For Their Implementation." *Brooklyn Journal of International Law* 21:799–856.

McConnell, Moira. 1996. "Violence Against Women: Beyond the Limits of the Law." *Brooklyn Journal of International Law* 21:899–913.

McDorman, Ted. 1987–88. "The Teaching of the Law of Thailand." *Dalhousie Law Journal* 11:915–30.

Miller, Alice. 1998. "NGO's and Human Rights." Paper on file with the author at American University.

Mohanty, Chandra. 1991. "Introduction: Cartographies of Struggle Third World Women and the Politics of Feminism." In Chandra Mohanty, Ann Russo and Lourdes Torres, eds. *Third World Women and the Politics of Feminism*. Bloomington: Indiana University Press.

Morgan, Robin. 1996. *Sisterhood is Global*. New York: Feminist Press.

Mouffe, Chantal. 1992. "Feminism, Citizenship, and Radical Democratic Politics." In Judith Butler and Joan Scott, eds. *Feminists Theorize the Political*. New York: Routledge, 369–384.

Muntarbhorn, Vitit. 1996. "Human Rights In Thailand." In Leslie Palmer, ed. *State and Law in Eastern Asia*, 103–40. Aldershot, Great Britain: Dartmouth Publishing Company Limited.

Murcott, Susan. 1991. *The First Buddhist Women: Translations and Commentaries on the Therigatha*. Berkeley, CA: Parallax Press.

Nicholson, Linda. 1992. "Feminism and the Politics of Postmodernism." *boundary 2*, 19(2):53–69.

Obiora, L. Amiede. 1997. "Bridges and Barricades: Rethinking Polemics and Intransigence in the Campaign Against Female Circumcision." *Case Western Reserve Law Review* 47:275–378.

Okin, Susan Moller. 1994. "Gender Inequality and Cultural Differences." *Political Theory* 22(1):5–24.

Othman, Norani. 1999. "Grounding Human Rights Arguments in Non-Western Culture: Shari'a and the Citizenship Rights of Women in a Modern Islamic Nation-

State." In Joanne R. Bauer and Daniel A. Bell, eds. *The East Asian Challenge for Human Rights*. Cambridge: Cambridge University Press, 169–92.

Peters, Julie and Andrea Wolper, eds. 1995. *Women's Rights, Human Rights: International Feminist Perspective*. New York: Routledge.

Pruitt-Hamm, Bruce. 1994. "Humanitarian Intervention in Southeast Asia in the Post-Cold War World: Dilemmas in the Definition and Design of International Law." *Pacific Rim Law and Policy Journal* 3(1):183–226.

Radin, Margaret Jane. 1990. "The Pragmatist and the feminist." *Southern California Law Review* 63:1699–1726.

Rao, Arati. 1995. "The Politics of Gender and Culture in International Human Rights Discourse." In Julie Peters and Andrea Wolper, eds. *Women's Rights, Human Rights: International Feminist Perspectives*, 167–75. New York: Routledge.

Reynolds, Frank. 1994. "Dhamma in Dispute: The Interactions of Religion and Law in Thailand." *Law & Society Review* 28(3):433–52.

Rhys Davids, C.A.F., and K.R. Norman, trans. 1989. *Poems of Early Buddhist Nuns*. Oxford, Great Britain: Pali Text Society.

Romany, Celina. 1994. "State Responsibility Goes Private: A Feminist Critique of the Public/Private Distinction in International Human Rights Law." In Rebecca Cook, ed. *Human Rights of Women: National and International Perspectives*, 85–115. Philadelphia: University of Pennsylvania Press.

Rorty, Richard. 1991. "Feminism and Pragmatism." *Michigan Quarterly Review* 30(2) (Spring):231–58.

Satha-Anand, Suwanna. 1999. "Thai Prostitution, Buddhism and 'New Rights' in Southeast Asia." In Joanne R. Bauer and Daniel A. Bell, eds. *The East Asian Challenge for Human Rights*. Cambridge: Cambridge University Press, 193–211.

Seabrook, Jeremy. 1996. *Travels in the Skin Trade: Tourism and the Sex Industry*. London: Pluto Press.

Seager, Joni. 1997. *The State of Women in the World Atlas*. New York: Penguin Books USA, Inc. (revised ed.).

Siegfried, Charlene Haddock. 1990. *William Jame's Radical Reconstruction of Philosophy*. Albany: State University of New York Press.

———. 1991. "Where Are All the Feminist Pragmatists?" *Hypatia* 6(1):1–19.

Skrobanek, Siriporn. 1992. "Exotic, Subservient and Trapped: Confronting Prostitution and Traffic in Women in Southeast Asia." In Margaret Schuler, ed. *Freedom From Violence: Women's Strategies From Around the World*, 121–137. New York: UNIFEM.

———, Nattaya Boonpakdi, and Chutima Janthakeero. 1997. *The Traffic in Women: Human Realities of the International Sex Trade*. New York: Zed Books Ltd.

Spelman, Elizabeth. 1988. *Inessential Woman: Problems of Exclusion in Feminist Thought*. Boston: Beacon Press.

Sullivan, Donna. 1992. "Gender Equality and Religious Freedom: Toward a Framework for Conflict Resolution." *International Law and Politics* 24:795–856.

Symposium. 1997. *Case Western Reserve Law Review* 47:275–378.

Thitsa, Khin. 1980. *Providence and Prostitution: Image and Reality for Women in Buddhist Thailand.* London: CHANGE International Reports.

———. 1987. "Nuns, Mediums and Prostitutes in Chiengmai: a Study of Some Marginal Categories of Women." In Centre of South-East Asian Studies, *Women and Development in South-East Asia* I. Great Britain: University of Canterbury.

———. 1995. "Conclusion." In Julie Peters and Andrea Wolper, eds. *Women's Rights, Human Rights: International Feminist Perspectives,* 356–59. New York: Routledge.

Thomas, Dorothy. 1993. "Domestic Violence as a Human Rights Issue." In *Human Rights Quarterly* 15:36–62.

Truong, Thanh-Dam. 1990. *Sex, Money and Morality: Prostitution and Tourism in Southeast Asia.* Atlantic Highlands, NJ: Zed Books Ltd.

United Nations. 1945. *United Nations Charter.* Excerpted in United Nations. 1995. *The United Nations and Human Rights.* 143–46. New York: United Nations.

———. 1948. *Universal Declaration of Human Rights.* G.A. Res. 217, UN Doc. A/810, at 71, arts. 2, 16(1).

———. 1966a. *International Covenant on Civil and Political Rights.* 999 U.N.T.S. 171, 173, 174, 179, 179.

———. 1966b. *International Covenant on Economic, Social, and Cultural Rights.* 993 U.N.T.S. 3, 5, 5.

———. 1981. Convention on the Elimination of Discrimination Against Women, 18 Dec. 1979, UN GAOR Supp. 34th Sess., No. 21 (A/34/46) at 193, UN Doc. A/RES.34/180 (entry into force 3 Sept. 1981).

———. 1989. *United Nations Multilateral Treaty Series,* deposited with the Secretary General, Status as of Dec. 31, 1989, at 171 UN Doc. ST/LEG/SER. E/8 (1989).

———. 1992. Convention on the Elimination of Discrimination Against Women, Committee on the Elimination of Discrimination Against Women, 11th Session, New York (20–31 January), *General Recommendation No. 19,* CEDAWC/1992/L.1/Add.15 (29 January 1992).

———. 1993a. *Declaration on the Elimination of Violence Against Women.* G.A. Res. 104, UN GAOR, 48th Sess., Supp. No. 49, at 217, U.N. Doc. A/RES/48/104.

———. 1993b. *Vienna Declaration and Programme of Action adopted at the World Conference on Human Rights,* A/CONF.57/24 (25 June, 1993). *The United Nations and Human Rights* (New York: United Nations, 1995), pp. 448–464.

———. 1995a. *Beijing Declaration and Draft Platform for Action,* UN Doc. A/CONF.177/20 (1995).

————. 1995b. *Development Programming Human Development Report.* New York: United Nations Press.

————. 1995c. *The United Nations and Human Rights.* New York: United Nations.

————. 1995d. *Report of the Fourth World Conference on Women* (Beijing, 4–15 September 1995), resolution adopted by the UN General Assembly at the 16th plenary meeting (15 September 1995).

————. 1996. *Women in Thailand: A Country Profile.* New York: United Nations.

————. 1997. Division for the Advancement of Women, "What is an Optional Protocol?" HTTP://www.un.org/dpcsd/daw.

United Nations General Assembly. 1997. *Report of the Secretary-General, Traffic in Women and Girls.* A/52/355, Sept. 17, 1997, 52d session (posted on internet gopher://gopher.un.org:70/00/sec/d. a/ga52nd/A-52-355).

Van Esterik, Penny. 1982. "Laywomen in Theravada Buddhism." In P. Van Esterik, ed. *Women of Southeast Asia.* Northern Illinois University: Center for Southeast Asian Studies, Occasional Paper No. 9.

Vichit-Vadakan, Juree. 1994. "Women and the Family in Thailand in the Midst of Social Change." *Law & Society Review* 28(3):515–24.

Wetzel, Janice Wood. 1993 *The World of Women: In Pursuit of Human Rights.* Houndsmill, N.J.: MacMillan Press.

Williams, Patricia. 1991. *Alchemy of Race and Rights.* Cambridge: Harvard University Press.

Women's International Network News Editorial Staff. 1996. "Thailand: New Information on Traffic in Women." *Women's International Network News* 23 (Winter):59.

Wynter, Sylvia. 1997. "'Genital Mutilation' or 'Symbolic Birth?' Female Circumcision, Lost Origins, and the Aculturalism of Feminist/Western Thought." *Case Western Reserve Law Review* 47:501–52.

Zakaria, Fareed. 1994. "Culture is Destiny: A Conversation with Lee Kuan Yew," *Foreign Affairs* 73(2) (March/April):109–125.

7 Re-Positioning Human Rights Discourse on "Asian" Perspectives

Sharon K. Hom

Within multiple global power configurations mapped along developed/developing countries, and North/South divide, ongoing statist "Asian" human rights debates predominantly line up on an East/West axis, characterized by competing universalism and relativism as core oppositional normative and empirical claims. The Western understanding of universal human rights generally references and emphasizes a vision of civil and political rights shaped by a liberal Western tradition. The challenge of East Asian states to this understanding of human rights has cultural, political, and economic dimensions. Underlying the charges of Western cultural imperialism is a post-colonialist legacy, and a suspicion that assertions of Western universal human rights are pretexts for intervention in the domestic affairs of other countries. Thus, "what appears, from the Western perspective, to be a noble campaign for universal rights is interpreted from an Asian perspective as cultural imperialism."[1] The charge of cultural imperialism is also made from the economically smug position of nation-states who are widely touted as "high performance" economies who have engineered the economic miracle of rising GNPs that has apparently made many developed countries nervous.

These engineers of "economic miracles" are in turn criticized by human rights activists and scholars for an ideological subterfuge that attempts to mask their authoritarianism behind culturalist relativism claims and for their assertion of a false dilemma between civil and political rights and economic and social rights.[2] At the same time that the Asian "economic miracle" is heralded by Asian governments and Western observers, voices such as NGOs, dissident, religious, labor and others suggest that beneath the "miracles," there are human costs, among them labor rights protection, child labor, industrial safety conditions, poor living conditions, low wages and underpayment, gender-based sexual harassment, violence, abuse, and discrimination, that have been rendered invisible or marginalized by statist perspectives. In a public petition to the Chinese leaders, a Beijing religious group points to the poverty and suffering of the peasants, and the basic economic and housing problems facing urban residents:

> These are all problems that cannot be ignored. The cries of the impoverished and deprived have already reached to the heavens, and yet little attention is being paid to the sufferings of common people. . . . We should be able to live with dignity and our rights should be protected and guaranteed, for a society's wealth belongs to all its people and to respect the honor and ambition of each and every person is an essential condition for the advancement of society![3]

When judged against a more inclusive assessment of this "representation" on all their citizens, the claims of Asian nation-states to represent the best interests of their citizens is suspect. The invocation of "Asian" culture or a "different" standard as legitimation for a culturally relativist human rights claim is thus suspect, partial, and problematic.

This essay offers some observations, and suggests several locations from which some of the more dominant statist human rights debates can be fruitfully repositioned. As specific sources for encouraging more inclusive and human-centered discourses and implementation approaches, I cite the evolution of the human development concept, draw upon insights from domestic and international women's/human rights strategies, and turn up the volume on domestic Chinese women's rights and Chinese dissident voices within and outside China as a reminder of localized sites of struggles. Throughout this commentary, I include references to a range of constructive strategies for human rights work pursued by diverse Asian NGO groups and international human rights activists and organizations.

Interrogating "Asian" Human Rights Debates

Ambassador Bilahari Kausikan, re-presenting the "East Asian" perspective, echoes previous defenses of Asia's "different standard," and emphasizes the governmental and relativist position set forth in the Bangkok Declaration. Acknowledging the universality of human rights, he argues that rights, justice, and order are obtained in different ways at different times in the context of a diversity of historical experiences, cultures, and social and political arrangements for a particular nation. With a gesture toward diversity, he also notes that these debates over the proper approach to human rights are not just between Asia and the West, but also between and within Asian countries.[4] In assessing the challenges even with these diversity caveats of Asian governments, it's also important to keep in mind, "when we consider Asian objections to the human rights doctrine on the ground that it entails the domination of Asia by the West, not only that it entails domination of some Asians by others, but also that this domination is not culturally acceptable to those who are dominated."[5] While commending the governments' recognition of the rights of women and children, and affirming the universality, indivisibility, and interdependence of rights, an NGO response to the Bangkok Declaration also stated: "Yet the Final Draft Declaration, in several significant respects reflects the continued attempts by many governments of the Asia-Pacific region to avoid their human rights obligations, to put the state before the people and to avoid acknowledging their obligations to account for their failures in the promotion and protection for human rights."

Furthermore, there are some tricky slippages in Ambassador Kausikan's defense of Asia's "different standard" that should give one pause. "Asian" as reflected in this official narrative emphasizes "Asian" collective and community notions as basic values and consensus building in opposition to "Western" individualistic rights and adversarial legal institutions and social relations. However, Ambassador Kausikan also points to the diversity of Asian cultures and approaches and criticizes the insensitivity of Western responses for their insensitivity to "the nuances of different Asian" voices. He thus speaks of a monolithic "West" and a monolithic "American" response in particular, within an implicitly polar debate. Yet "Western," like "Asian," is really an idea, a cultural concept of identity, historically situated and contingent. Despite the calls for more complex dialogue and mutual understanding by Asian government leaders, the "West" is thus ironically reified and positioned as a convenient, monolithic oppositional target.

Ambassador Kausikan also marshals the diversity of Western voices and internal critical voices to support the morally superior, common sense, "Asian" position. He is thus invoking the critiques of scholars, writers, and news media, nongovernmental voices, to support his assertion of a position that privileges the governmental perspective. If one were to seriously argue for sensitivity and the rejection of double standards, then let's all aspire toward a clarity of definitions and sensitivity toward the nuances and diversity in the perceived "other" positions. And if we are to move beyond the current statist gridlock in East Asian human rights discourse, we need to stop conflating implicitly or explicitly the voice of the state, even a paternalistic competent one, with the diversity of voices of the individual citizens of a state, international and local nongovernmental organizations, intergovernmental and multilateral bodies. Ambassador Kausikan has suggested that the real question is what works. I would add: What is working—for whom? Who decides what is "working"? Or to put an official Chinese pragmatic spin on it, what "mice" do we want to catch?[6] When there are assertions of "difference," particularly by privileged actors in positions of power, we should ask: who benefits from these assertions of difference? Who asserts these differences/? On whose behalf? Whose voices and experiences are marginalized, rendered invisible to ensure the clarity of an oppositional East/West, universalist/relativist paradigm? What issues are foreclosed by claims of imperialism?

In addition to the challenge of engaging the full range of human rights voices on the regional, international, or local level, a dislodging of statist human rights discourse would also require critical attention to the task of identifying appropriate sources for determining the content of human rights, and the unavoidably culturally overdetermined task of "reading" the content for its meaning and intent, perhaps the problem of postmodernist interpretation. Michael Davis has identified as sources for determining aspirations and assessing human rights implementation the following: international declarations, constitutions, legislation and white papers, peace charters, NGO reports, human rights manifestoes, academic or legal discourse. Davis suggests a discourse approach that asks who is saying what, for what purposes or values, through what channels, and with what effects. Applying this to China, he concludes there is a disjuncture between rights promised and the actuality of the situation that reflects the "pathology of an underdeveloped constitutional order."[7] He identifies a rectangular relationship between dissidents, NGOs, foreign governments, and China in human rights lobbying. However, I suggest that it would be helpful to distinguish between dialogue as a process of discovery, and "dialogue" as unilateral positional assertions of already formulated views. China's "discourse with the outside world" discussed by Davis and much of the discourse of nation-states "with" each other, belongs it seems to me in the latter category.

Davis's discourse approach and a focus on process, institutions, and values analysis are helpful for moving toward a more dynamic understanding of rights implementation. To build upon this approach, I would suggest more critical attention to a fuller range of international actors such as transnationals, the role of language itself, the role of multiple audiences, the role of the "narrator"/interpreter of these sources and these processes, and the discontinuities between content, the "readings" engendered, and the discursive negotiations that create or legitimate new values and concepts. More analytical attention needs to be paid to language as a site for discursive and political contests. For example, despite similar sounding "vocabulary" of human rights discourse, when one moves beyond an implicit focus on civil and political rights discourse and looks at the indivisibility of rights addressed by development policymakers or women's rights activists and theorists, it becomes apparent that 'vocabulary" is a key site for ideological and political power/empowerment battles. One example was the drafting debates surrounding the bracketed language of the draft Platform of Action for the Fourth World Conference on Women and the objections raised by the Holy See, Muslim, and Catholic countries to the use of terms like "family," "sex," or "gender," to refer to any arrangement other than a heterosexual relationship of marriage.[8]

In her symposium essay, Christina Cerna, an attorney with the Organization of American States, focuses on specific speeches of Asian leaders as useful sources of "explanations" of Asian's different definition and content of human rights to Western and European audiences. Cerna suggests that there appears to be no difference in definitions of human rights between Western and Asian rights and that the differences lie in implementation approaches. In response to the Indonesian governmental assertion of national implementation approaches, Cerna attempts to suggest a middle ground: only in cases where there is no national implementation should the international community play a role and technical assistance should be provided only to countries with the political will to democratize.[9] However, this "reading" also invests the "speaking" of government leaders with more explanatory and communication intent than a more cynical "reading" of geopolitical posturing would suggest.

Furthermore, in the context of this international "explanation," and Indonesia's position as chair of the Non-Aligned Movement ("NAM"), certainly the audience is not only Western and European audiences, but also the 108 member states of NAM. And given domestic media coverage, the audience would also include the citizens of these states and the "speaking" of these government leaders would be an encoded message reinforcing the primacy of the government's privileged position as claimed representative of the interests of its citizens. Finally, the balancing of international intervention with national implementation suggested by Cerna sidesteps some hard questions: Who and how does this body decide that the national implementation is inadequate or nonexistent? Who and how will "political will to democratize" be measured or identified? For example, in the context of China, an assessment looking exclusively to the political will of the regime in power might lead to the dismissal of consideration of any technical assistance initiatives that might contribute to creating the conditions necessary for democracy. Cerna's approach thus implicitly illustrates the necessity of developing multilayered approaches that focus on multiple actors and sources of social change.

As historical background for his analysis of the role of legal rhetoric in Chinese social change, Professor Dellapena first recounts a conventional narrative of China's legal tradition, its characteristics and some continuities of this tradition under the Communist rule: the resort to *guanxi* (relationships), a preference for informal settlement of disputes, a Marxist ideological hostility to law as a tool of the elite, and the lack of a specially trained cadre of judges, lawyers, and prosecutors. He then argues that the demands of the student leaders during the 1989 Democracy Movement for democracy and an end to corruption through a rule of law were ignored by the Western press and misunderstood by China's leaders, both in light of the condition of these "octogenarians" and these traditional Chinese attitudes toward law. He concludes by calling for more effective use of rhetoric in communicating our concerns about the rule of law to China's leaders. While I agree that "we in the West" have not done a good job of understanding events in China, this must be viewed in the context of a long history of more than a hundred years of U.S.-China (mis)understanding. In the context of broader Asian debates on human rights approaches, the China case also underscores the importance of understanding the interrelated class, political, and gender aspects of domestic human rights rhetoric and strategies played out on an international screen. What has become increasingly clear is that the bloodshed on June 4 was also the result of a political failure of leadership and tragic strategic mistakes on everyone's part.

There is also another possible "reading" of the communication between Chinese student leaders and China's leaders. Rather than "misunderstanding" the student demands, perhaps the octogenarians understood very well the "message" the students were communicating. Bunkered behind the compound walls of Zhongnanhai, the Chinese leaders accurately read this message as a challenge to their power, to the autocratic power of the Party, and a demand for a rule of law that would undermine their privileged position outside and above the law. The entrenched efforts of the Party leaders to protect its power at all costs has consequences beyond China's borders. As Liu Qing states so powerfully:

> The continued survival and progress of dissidents is not only crucial to the future of Chinese society, but is equally important to the maintenance of international peace and stability. No matter how you look at it, the existence of dissidents in China attests to the diversity of opinion in China; it is no longer the silent and obedient society it was considered. Although these voices remain weak. they still serve to hold the autocratic system in check to some extent. if some dissidents are allowed to continue their efforts, then the foundation for democracy and human rights in China will gradually be established. The international community must not ignore or forget China's dismal human rights record. After all, it is not a good thing for the world when the rulers of a country of 1.2 billion people with a rapidly expanding economy view the values of democracy and human rights as antithetical to their interests.[10]

Challenges of the New(Old) Global Dis-Order

To de-center the state from its current privileged discursive position in human rights debates, we need to open the aperture to bring into political focus a global legacy of rampant militarism, environmental degradation, and pervasive social and economic inequality.[11] One tactic is to refocus on historical situated human beings, and to foreground the "human" in human rights that can often get lost in geopolitical contests between states or in the focus on selective quantitative macroeconomic indicators of growth and progress. Contrary to the Western liberal faith in the idea and inevitability of progress, the century just ended did not produce a "modern world" that could be described as peaceful, advanced, or morally just in human and ecological terms. Contrary to conventional media narratives that chart international politics as the business of ambassadors, presidents, legislators, and other government actors, the gendered dimensions of international politics and the intersection of gender, peace, security, and economic justice has been exposed and analyzed.[12]

In 1990, of the world's 5.3 billion people, 2.63 billion were women; more than half (55%) of the world's women live in Asia. As the gap between rich and poor widens, the picture of poverty, dislocation, suffering, and inequality clearly has a woman's face. "Women still constitute 70% of the world's poor and two-thirds of the world's illiterates. They occupy 14% of managerial and administrative jobs, 10% of parliamentary seats and 6% of the cabinet positions." Of the world's 18 million refugees, more than three-quarters are women and their dependent children. Despite several world conferences,[13] the adoption of the Nairobi Forward Looking Strategies, and the Convention for the Elimination of All Forms of Discrimination Against Women (CEDAW), while there has been progress in some regions or countries, across different economic and social systems, women continue to be excluded from access to political and economic decisionmaking, and suffer due to "domestic" violence, gender-based war crimes, violations of women's human rights and bodily integrity, and political persecution and discrimination.[14]

While the statistics cited can not begin to adequately convey the accompanying human suffering and costs of human rights abuses, they do underscore the urgent need for radical change in the long-standing premises of social, economic, and political life and for more effective responses. The Platform of Action adopted by the 1995 Fourth World Conference on Women governmental meeting, calls upon governments to take strategic action in the following critical areas of concern: poverty, education, health care, violence against women, economic structures and policies, decisionmaking at all levels, human rights, media stereotypes and access, management of natural resources and safeguarding of the environment, and the rights of the girl child. The Platform emphasized as in past international statements that the elimination of these abuses are crucial for the future and possibility of achieving a peaceful, stable, and equitable world.[15]

Beginning in 1990, the United Nations Development Programme (UNDP) has published an annual Human Development Report ranking all countries according to their "level of development." The first report introduced the concept of human development and its measurement. Subsequent reports focused on the role of international trade and markets in development, the introduction of an expanded concept of security to include human security, and the relationship between gender and development. As an alternative to the per capita income indicator used by the World Bank in its annual World Development Report, UNDP introduced a new indicator for these annual reports, the human development index (HDI). The HDI has four components: productivity, equity, sustainability, and empowerment of people. The HDI "measures the average achievement of a country in basic human capabilities. The HDI indicates whether people lead a long and healthy life, are educated and knowledgeable and enjoy a decent standard of living."[16] As the evolving international development policy consensus reflects, "[d]evelopment patterns that perpetuate today's inequities are neither sustainable nor worth sustaining."[17]

In the face of pervasive social injustice, human suffering and environmental destruction created by interrelated global, regional, and domestic factors, and powerful economic and political international actors, Asian nation-states continue to speak and argue in the anachronistic register of the nineteenth century, while positioning themselves as benevolent patriarchs. When international actors now include multilateral institutions, transnational corporations or multinational corporations, and local, regional and international NGOs, as well as international financial institutions such as the World Bank and the International Monetary Fund, how can a privileged statist human rights narrative be justified in the face of the impact of these powerful nonstate actors both on the reconfiguration of the global (dis)order and in re-mapping the human and natural landscape?

Human Rights Beyond State-Centered Paradigms

The experience of Asian NGOs illustrates some of the opportunities for collaboration between human rights scholars, professionals, and grassroots activists, as well as some of the challenges in working across differences in experience, class, and expertise. In recent years there has been an "explosion" of Asian NGOS, both quantitatively and qualitatively, that address the problems of militarization, intolerable poverty, permanent environmental degradation, the exploitation of women, children, and religious or ethnic minorities, and the abuses of prevailing authoritarian regimes.[18] Clarence J. Dias has identified three strands of the Asian human rights movement: struggles against authoritarian political regimes; delivery of basic services and education programs to the rural poor; and focus on national development programs. Although these activists did not explicitly start out with a human rights agenda, they quickly turned to human rights activism as a means to (1) empower the impoverished; (2) secure accountability of those who wield power and control over resources; (3) increase participation of the oppressed; and (4) assert values such as social and ethical values that should underlie restructuring of asocial orders.

Dias also identifies three main categories of people involved in the human rights activism in Asia: intellectuals, professionals, and activists. He describes the approach of the legal elite of working within the existing law in "test cases" and in "public interest litigation" to redress violations of civil and political rights, and the tensions of this liberal approach with the goals of activists who view reform as part of a social change and structural transformation process. Specific action strategies that intellectuals, professionals, and activists collaborated upon include campaigns such as the Infant Formula campaign; international coalitions such as the International Coalition for Justice in Bhopal; solidarity and protest organizations such as Greenpeace; lobbying groups such as the Asia Pacific Forum on Women, Law and development; regional networks such as the Asian Regional Council on Human Rights; and social movements such as the women's movement, the environment movement, and the consumer movement.[19]

Like intellectuals and political dissidents advocating human rights in Asia, Chinese dissidents, and intellectuals are and will continue to be key actors in human rights advocacy and democracy reform in China. In order to identify possible opportunities for alliance-building across different political systems and cultural contexts in working with domestic Chinese groups, we need to understand the context, obstacles, and opportunities facing Chinese NGOs or human rights/women's advocates attempting organizational strategies situated within a politically authoritarian regime.[20] In trying to understand the role of Chinese NGOs in the context of an emerging civil sector in China, a rigid model of NGOs would not address the complex relationship between domestic and international NGOs and the tensions that can arise in developing multiple and simultaneous local, regional, and global intervention strategies. Under the legal framework established by the 1989 Regulations for the Registration and Management of Social Groups, associations, scholarly groups, federations, research associations, foundations, and promotional groups must register and be operationally linked to a governmental administrative unit (*guakao danwei*). The search for Chinese "NGOs" that fit the characteristics of foreign NGOs is thus problematic given this restrictive and pervasive oversight and supervision framework.

An examination of the role of the All China Women's Federation (ACWF) within China and in the international arena during the preparatory process leading up to the 1995 Fourth World Conference on Women provides some interesting insights regarding the role of Chinese NGOs and their relationship to international human rights approaches. As the mass organization arm of the Party that acts to implement Party policies and to inform decisionmaking on the needs and interests of women, the ACWF (Fulian), occupies a difficult position in carrying out its dual functions. The ACWF serves both as the propaganda arm of the Party, and the "service" counseling and advocacy arm for women. At the same time, it is increasingly clear to outside observers that the ACWF does not speak with a monolithic voice for "Chinese women," nor is it free from internal criticism.[21] One of the current challenges facing the ACWF is the articulation and development of a role for itself as an "independent" women's NGO despite its Party affiliation. In this process, the ACWF is negotiating the perceptions of international NGOs, the diverse perspectives and roles of provincial and local fulians (women's associations) and the theoretical assessments emerging from the growing number Chinese women's studies centers,[22] and its own relationship to the various organs of state power.

As the preparatory process leading up to and the Fourth World Conference and NGO Forum reflected, Chinese women found themselves in exciting and difficult positions. Within the context of existing Chinese political, legal, and cultural constraints, Chinese women had to negotiate the tensions and opportunities of international human rights exchanges. For many of them, this was the first time they heard the expression, "women's rights are human rights." It was also the first opportunity for many Chinese women to network with counterparts from all over the world. Their silences during the Conference and the Forum, as well as their voices, and their reflections provide important lessons for the possibility and difficulties of building networks and human rights strategies that draw upon on international approaches.

One Chinese journalist, Chuan Renyuan, noted:

Consciously or unconsciously, they put themselves into the role of official spokespeople, enthusiastically explaining the "great progress made by women of our country" and arguing with "certain foreigners with ill-intentions." China lacks an understanding of human rights; it is even more lacking in comprehension of feminism. Today, we should not only struggle with the authorities to achieve the human rights and

women's rights that we need, but also with the men and women who
are permeated by several thousand years of feudal culture and decades
of Party culture.[23]

Chuan Renyuan concludes with the observation that more women in
China now dare to openly call themselves "feminists." As Chinese women
"cross" with greater frequency literal or symbolic national borders, the official efforts to enclose Chinese women within nationalistic discourses have
been only partially successful despite the public acceptance by women of
spokesperson roles during the Conference. As reflections by Chinese women
underscore, no matter what the present obstacles, the opening up of discursive spaces during this recent period and the seizing of opportunities presented by women to engage in activist research, to use the newly established
women's centers to build a supportive place for investigation of social problems, to create networks within and outside of China, cherish the rich mem-
ories of new friends, and exposure to new ideas and approaches, will have
ongoing impact that will be increasingly difficult to measure.[24] I am not
suggesting gender analysis or feminism (in whatever formulation), as the
exclusive or primary framework for a Chinese human rights analysis. However, because gender issues remain under-theorized in Chinese domestic
human rights discourse, I suggest a gender perspective to call for more work
on integrating gender issues theoretically and strategically into overall human rights strategies.[25]

However, it is not only the discourse of nation-states that needs to be
critically challenged. In the wake of the widespread attention and self-
examination of the 50th anniversary of the United Nations, the history of its
global stewardship and international governance has also been criticized.
Peter Vale has argued that we do not need more reformist thinking. Instead,
he urges us to ask "first order questions" — questions necessary to reconcep-
tualizing the very nature of international society and a new role for the
United Nations.[26] Like Chandra Mohanty and other Third World feminists,[27] Vale calls for a reconceptualization of the discursive maps that shape
the definitions and contexts of global political struggles. He points to the
contingency of discursive and material constructs and argues for the possibility of our transforming existing discourses and material realities: The structures that dominate our lives, including our approach to the UN, are only
as permanent as we make them. Crucial features of life, such as democracy,
nations, sovereignty, capitalism, the Cold War, and even the UN, have con-

crete manifestations, but are nevertheless constructs of the human mind. They are but theories, which at times certainly make us, but are also made by us.[28]

In discursive human rights debates, as Vale suggests, we need to continue to question the inevitability of dominant narratives, constructs and the circumstances that give rise to these narratives. As cultures are erased and created by globalization and emerging cultures are contested and negotiated, what does it mean to speak monolithically of an "Asian" culture even if tempered by nods to diversity? What country entering "modernity" has escaped the imprints of the imperialist and colonialist enterprise? How can we reenvision the critical negotiation of cultures in ways that transcend essentialist or nativist claims of "tradition" and that address this complex colonialist history? Is it possible to expose the opportunistic misuse of "tradition" by authoritarian power-holders and at the same time reappropriate "tradition" as one source of identity and community? What kinds of multiple and simultaneous local, regional, and international strategies can be explored?

I raise these questions not to try to address them in this brief commentary, but to suggest examples of questions that resist neat discursive frameworks such as tradition/modernity, West/East native/foreign, and local/international and that shifts the focus beyond a privileged statist perspective. As we theorize and implement alternative approaches to human rights work, we need to keep all the diverse global and local actors in our strategic line of vision. In this brief review of some aspects of these Asian human rights debates, I have pointed to the difficulties of reading across ideological, political, cultural terrain, suggested the importance of opening the aperture on the range of international human rights actors, and urged a more critical interrogation of the discursive strategies and statist assumptions of human rights debates.

In the face of assertions of the diversity of history, culture, language, and political and economic systems, by governmental and nongovernmental voices, we are still left with the challenges and opportunities of negotiating the twin dangers of the universalist-edging-into-imperialist position and a morally bankrupt absolute relativism. Yet we cannot position ourselves safely outside of this human rights landscape as neutral observers or disinterested scholars. The intellectual and ethico-political challenge facing human rights scholars is to create more empowering discursive spaces, and to contribute to more human-centered structures and processes that will promote social and economic justice. Human rights are ultimately about justice, and the contest continues over content, meaning, and implementation. Against a backdrop of global human rights debates shaped by the geopolitical power maneuvers of nation-states and transnationals, justice is often manipulated or marginalized. "Politics is driven by power, more or less constrained by justice. Power works by pretending to be just. In thinking about human rights, we should distinguish between what justice requires and what those with power demand."[29]

Human rights is too important to be left exclusively to governments.

Acknowledgments

This is an abridged and slightly edited version of an article with the same title published in The Buffalo Journal of International Law 3(1) (Summer 1996):209–234. The abridgements consist of the deletion and shortening of footnotes. The paper comments on a symposium, "East Asian Approaches to Human Rights," which appeared in The Buffalo Journal of International Law 2(2) (Winter 1995–96), and which consisted of essays by Christine M. Cerna, Michael C. Davis, Joseph W. Dellapena, and Ambassador Bilahari Kausikan. I thank Professor Dellapena and the editors of the Journal for the invitation to develop this commentary from my informal remarks delivered at the Asian Perspectives on Human Rights Panel, ASIL Annual Meeting, April 6, 1995, and published in 89 ASIL Proc. 146 (1995). Also thanks to Penny Andrews and Pamela Goldberg for reading and commenting on an early draft and my research assistant Melissa Fraser for helpful manuscript preparation work.

Endnotes

1. Michael Freeman, "Human Rights: Asia and the West," in James T. H. Tang, ed. Human Rights and International Relations in the Asia Pacific (London: Cassell, 1995), p. 14.
2. See e.g. Li Xiaorong, "'Asian Values' & the Universality of Human Rights," China Rights Forum (September 1996):32–36.
3. Beijing Protestant Holy Spirit Association, "A Word for the Poor, May 20, 1995," translated in China Rights Forum (Summer 1995):14.
4. Bilahari Kim Hee P.S. Kausikan, "An East Asian Approach to Human Rights," The Buffalo Journal of International Law 2(2) (Winter 1995–96):263–282.
5. Freeman, "Human Rights," p. 15.

6. In a pragmatic assertion of how to decide a correct policy, Deng Xiaoping has stated: "It doesn't matter whether it's a black cat, or a white cat, as long as it catches mice."

7. Michael C. Davis, "Human Rights in Asia: China and The Bangkok Declaration," *The Buffalo Journal of International Law* 2(2) (Winter 1995–96):218–220.

8. See Sharon K. Hom and Xin Chunying, eds, *English-Chinese Lexicon of Women and the Law* (YingHan funü yü falü cihui shiyi) (Beijing: UNESCO and China Translation and Publishing Corp., 1995), for an example of an attempt to focus on some of the cross-cultural, linguistic, and political translation issues embedded in key human rights/women's rights terms and concepts.

9. Christina M. Cerna, "East Asian Approaches to Human Rights," *The Buffalo Journal of International Law* 2(2) (Winter 1995–96):201–213.

10. Liu Qing, "Devoted to Democracy and Human Rights: the Development of the Dissident Movement," *China Rights Forum* (Winter 1995):4–7.

11. In 1992, the richest 20% of the world's developed countries had incomes 60 times greater than the poorest 20%. The marginalized, those excluded from the economic and social goods of development, represent over 80% of the global community. *UNDP Human Development Report* (New York: Oxford University Press, 1992). In 1997, stark disparities between the rich and poor persisted: the richest 20% had 86% shares of the world GDP. *UNDP Human Development Report*. New York: Oxford University Press, 1999.

12. See, for example, Cynthia Enloe, *Making Feminist Sense of International Politics: Bananas, Beaches, and Bases* (Berkeley: University of California Press, 1990), J. Ann Tickner, *Gender in International Relations: Feminist Perspectives on Achieving Global Security* (New York: Columbia University Press, 1992), Rebecca Grant and Kathleen Newland, ed. *Gender and International Relations* (Bloomington: Indiana University Press, 1991).

13. World Conference on Women in Nairobi (1985), Rio Earth Summit (1992), World Conference on Human Rights in Vienna (1993), Cairo International Conference on Population and Development (1994), 1995 World Summit on Social Development in Copenhagen.

14. Data in this paragraph are drawn from *The World's Women: Trends and Statistics 1970–1990* (New York: United Nations, 1991), p. 11; *UNDP Human Development Report* (New York: Oxford University Press, 1995), p. 14 (source of the direct quotation in the paragraph); U.S. Committee for Refugees, *1993 World Refugee Survey* (Washington, D.C.: U.S. Committee for Refugees, 1993); Charlotte Bunch and Niamh Reilly, *Demanding Accountability: The Global Campaign for Women's Human Rights* (New Brunswick, N.J.: Center for Women's Global Leadership, 1994); and Katarina Tomasevski, *Women and Human*

Rights (London: Zed Books, 1993). The figure for refugees does not include an additional 25 million internally displaced and persons in "refugee-like status." But as Pamela Goldberg points out, exact figures are also difficult to ascertain due to the fluidity of refugee populations, the instability of living conditions of refugees, the lack of resources, and a general disinclination to disaggregate statistics on refugee populations by gender or age. Pamela Goldberg. "Where in the World is There Safety for Me?" in Julie Peters and Andrea Wolper, ed. *Women's Rights, Human Rights: International Feminist Perspectives* (New York: Routledge, 1995), pp. 345–355. For discussions of refugee issues and demography of refugee populations, see also Susan Forbes-Martin, *Refugee Women* (London: Zed Books, 1992).

15. Report of Fourth World Conference on Women (Beijing, 4–15 September 4–15, 1995). A/Conf. 177/20 October 17, 1995. For a summary of the Platform, see Donna Sullivan. "Envisioning Women's Human Rights: What Was Achieved in Beijing?" *China Rights Forum* (Winter 1995):19–23. For an analysis of the Platform in the context of the history of the world's women's rights movement, see Charlotte Bunch, Mallika Dutt, and Susannah Fried. Beijing '95: A Global Referendum on the Human Rights of Women. Center for Women's Global Leadership on line at: cwgl@igc.org

16. *Human Development Report 1995* (New York: Oxford University Press, 1995), p. 73.

17. *Human Development Report 1994* (New York: Oxford University Press, 1994), p. 19.

18. For a listing of local, national, and regional NGOS or people's organizations (groups formed by sectors of society, e.g. peasants, laborers, fisher folk, women), see Asian Regional Resource Centre for Human Rights Education (ARRC), *A Directory of Asian Organizations Related to Human Rights Education Work* (March 1993). Contact Address: P.O. Box 26, Bugthongland P.O. Bangkok 10242, Thailand. Fax: (662) 374–0464.

19. Clarence J. Dias, "The Role of Human Rights NGOs in Asia," in Graziano Battistella, ed. *Human Rights of Migrant Workers: Agenda for NGOs* (Quezon City, Philippines: The Scalabrini Migration Center, 1993), pp. 13–16.

20. Sharon K. Hom and Sophia Woodman, "Going to Beijing With Open Eyes: Preparing for the World Conference on Women," *China Rights Forum* (Spring 1995):18–21, and Sharon K. Hom, "Economic Reform and Social and Economic Rights in China: Strategy Brainstorming Across Cultures," in Margaret A. Schuler, ed. *From Basic Needs to Basic Rights: Women's Claims to Human Rights* (Washington, D.C.: Institute for Women, Law, and Development, 1995), pp. 147–151.

21. See e.g. Li Xiaojiang, "Economic Reform and the Awakening of Chinese Women's Consciousness," in Christina K. Gilmartin et al., ed. *Engendering*

China: Women, Culture, and the State (Cambridge: Harvard University Press, 1994), pp. 360–382.

22. See e.g. Tao Chen, "Zhongguo funü jiefang yundung zouqianlema? (Is the Chinese women's movement moving forward?)" in *Tansuo yü zhengming* 6 (1993):23–27 and Tao Jianmin, "Shehui jinbu yü funü jiefang (Social progress and women's liberation)" in *Tansuo yü zhengming* 6 (1993):28–32.

23. Chuan Renyuan, "Overshadowing Feminism: Thoughts on the Beijing Women's Conference," *China Rights Forum* (Winter 1995):16–18.

24. See *Reflections & Resonances: Stories of Women Involved in International Preparatory Activities for the 1995 NGO Forum on Women* (in Chinese and English) (Beijing: Ford Foundation, March 1995).

25. See Human Rights in China, "Report Prepared for Fourth World Conference on Women," New York, June 1995; and Amnesty International, *Women in China: Imprisoned and Abused for Dissent* (London: Amnesty International, 1995).

26. Peter Vale, "Engaging the World's Marginalized and Promoting Global Change: Challenges for the United Nations at Fifty," *Harvard International Law Journal* 30(2) (Spring 1995):283–294.

27. Chandra Talpade Mohanty, "Cartographies of Struggle: Third World Women and the Politics of Feminism," in Chandra Talpade Mohanty, Ann Russo, Lourdes Torres, ed. *Third World Women and the Politics of Feminism* (Bloomington, Indiana: Indiana University Press, 1991):1–50.

28. Vale, "Engaging," pp. 288–289.

29. Freeman, "Human Rights," p. 23. In quoting Freeman, I am using "power" in this context to refer to the power of governments, multinationals, and other institutions of concentrated economic and political power. I distinguish this from the inherent power in each individual, or every civil or community group to challenge these dominant structures and to reenvision other social orders.

Part 4

Rights Discourse and Power Relations

8 Human Rights and the Discourse on Universality

A Chinese Historical Perspective

Xiaoqun Xu

Since the Tiananmen Square incident on June 4, 1989, and the end of the Cold War, the issue of human rights has been a matter of contention in the relationship between China and the West, especially the United States. The Chinese government has argued that the human rights standards the West uses to measure non-Western countries are derived from Western history and culture and not necessarily applicable to and workable in those societies. To criticize the practices in non-Western countries while employing the Western model would reflect the attempt of the West (especially the U.S.) to impose its own values and political system upon non-Western countries and assert hegemony in the world. It is to be noted that while supporting the "Asian values" argument put forward by some Asian governments, Beijing actually emphasizes that since each country (presumably even within Asia) has its own history, culture, tradition, social conditions, and development stages, there is no abstract and universal model of realizing human rights.[1] On the other hand, Western critics of China's human rights record have insisted that human rights are universal and dismissed the "Asian values" argument as "phony," an excuse for Beijing and other Asian governments not to respect human rights in their countries.[2]

In my view, the contention about whether human rights are universal or culture-specific is real (*cf.* Bauer and Bell 1999; Bell 1996; An-Na'im, 1992). To assert human rights as universal and denounce the Asian values argument as phony is a discourse, as is the argument itself. The discourse on universality is not new. In fact it has a familiar ring, reminding one of similar discourses in modern Chinese history. Rather than simply to dismiss the Asian values (or Chinese values) argument, it might be instructive to look into the historical conditions under which the current debate and similar discourses in the past arose and to analyze the interaction between discourse and politics that reflect power relations in societies and among nations.

This essay introduces three historical cases in Republican China (1912–1949) where the universality of Christianity, Western medicine, and Western judicial system, in relation to Chinese culture and tradition, were contested. The first case was the Christian missionary accommodation in the 1920s to Chinese nationalism by arguing that Christianity was not intrinsically Western but universal and that to Christianize China was not to Westernize it. The second was the conflict between Western medicine and Chinese native medicine in the 1920s and the 1930s. Western-style Chinese doctors argued that unscientific native medicine should be abolished to make room for modern medicine that was not Western but universal science, while native physicians claimed to represent national essence and portrayed Western-style doctors as helping the cultural invasion of Western imperialism by destroying native medicine. The third was the acceptance by the Republican governments of the rule of law and judicial independence as guiding principles for the judicial reform during 1912–1937, although these principles were not realized in practice. (For detailed discussions of the three cases, see Xu 1997a, 1997b, 1997c). As the discourses and practices of religion, science, and justice represent some of the most important aspects of modern world history and bear on the issue of relativism and universalism, I will consider how the three cases may inform our understanding of and approach to the current debate on universalism vs relativism in human rights discourse.

Christian Religion and Chinese Culture

When Protestant missionaries arrived in China in the 1830s, they had some preconceived notions about the depravity of the heathen people. The difference made by the Industrial Revolution between Western nations and Asian societies in technology and material culture reinforced their sense of superiority. They considered their mission as a matter of not only making converts but also changing, after the Western model, the whole society and culture the missionary encountered. In the words of Elijah C. Bridgman of the American Board of Foreign Missions, the editor of *Chinese Repository*, the objective of the Christian missions "is to take the lead in remolding society, in purifying it and in forming it on the basis of those principles of the Christian religion" (*Chinese Repository* 4[5]:204–205). As early as 1835, therefore, Protestant missionaries defined their task as a multifaceted one including preaching the gospel, establishing schools, promoting philanthropic work (especially medical missions), and publishing both Christian literature and materials on Western civilization in general (*Chinese Repository* 3[12]:559–570). Those more "secular" lines of work as an integral part of the missionary enterprise in China were predicated on the assumption about inferiority and backwardness of Chinese culture and society. Bridgman told his readers that while informing them about China, "[w]e have no very strong expectations of finding much that will rival the arts and sciences, and various institutions of the Western nations" (*Chinese Repository* 1[1]:3).

Although this assumption did not change in its basic tenet from the 1830s through the early twentieth century, missionaries of the latter date, especially liberal-minded ones, were less ambitious and less certain about their moral power to remold Chinese culture and society. Notably, something of a turning point was reached around the time of the First World War. "Missionaries in the earlier period wrote with a firm conviction that *all* they had to offer of civilization and religious practices was suited to China." But such attitudes changed discernibly during and after the war (CR 1926:767–768).

Several factors accounted for the change. First of all, a tension always existed in the missionary mind between his evangelical mission and his civilizing task—what William Hutchison calls "Christ and Culture" dilemma (1987). The tension was heightened by the rise of modernist theology and Social Gospel which tended to be more sympathetic to native cultures, by the development of cultural anthropology in the West from the late nineteenth century onward which studied the merits and functions of different cultures within their own contexts, and by the man-made catastrophe of the First World War which left many Westerners in deep doubts about the superiority of Western civilization.

The most important factor was the Chinese nationalist movement in the 1920s. The decade witnessed the Anti-Christian movement of 1922–24, the Movement to Restore Educational Rights of 1924–28, the May Thirtieth movement of 1925, the Northern Expedition of 1926–28, all of which were underpinned by a fervent nationalist and anti-imperialist sentiment among urban Chinese. Missionaries were a prime target of Chinese nationalist attacks and faced with one of the biggest challenges they had encountered in China. An important aspect of the crisis was the predicament in which Chinese Christians found themselves. They were denounced as China's traitors who had been so denationalized as to accept the role of "running dogs of Western imperialism." They suffered various forms of harassment, persecution, and even death (NCH 1/15/1927:61–62; 5/14/1927:284; NCCAR 1927:38; Derr 1927). As missionaries noted,"many Chinese intellectuals concluded that it was quite impossible to be both a patriot and a Christian" (Lyall 1965). Eager to demonstrate their adherence to Christian faith rather than dependence upon Western missionaries, Chinese Christians cried out for making the Church and its message more Chinese.

An increasing assertion of Chinese leadership in the Christian enterprise and the missionary accommodation to it had been under way. The founding of the National Christian Council (NCC) of China in 1922 was an important signpost for this development. Designed to foster Christian unity and coordinate the work of various missions and churches, the council also worked for an indigenous Chinese church. In the organization itself Chinese Christian leaders were heavily represented. The Chairman of the council was a Chinese Christian, Dr. David Z. T. Yui. One of the two vice-chairman, two of the four secretaries, and eleven of the twenty-one executive committee members were Chinese (NCH 5/13/1922:458–459; NCCAR 1923). Moreover, Chinese Christians envisioned an indigenous Chinese Church not only in terms of its leadership but also its message. Maintaining that an indigenous Chinese Church entailed Chinese expression of Christian spirituality, Dr. Yui called for a promotion of more profound scholarship on Chinese culture among both missionaries and Chinese Christians (Yui 1926).

It was under these circumstances that missionaries began to examine their attitudes toward Chinese culture. They recognized that they were at least partly responsible for the Chinese resentment against depicting China as an uncivilized country, since they had presented "the seamy side and the bizarre in an effort to secure aid" from home churches (CR 1924:695).

Significantly, these missionaries made a new assessment of Chinese religions. Chinese ancestor worship, the prime target of early missionary criticism which had been at the heart of the Rites Controversy of the eighteenth century, was now viewed in a different light as being nonreligious and thus compatible with Christianity (CR 1924:597; WCMN 1925:31–34). Some missionaries chose to go further. T. W. Douglas James of the British Presbyterian Mission held that Chinese ancestor worship as a social custom had become a symbol of continuity of human life. This aspect of human behavior was also embodied in Christianity such as the Apostles' Creed and the belief in the Communion of Saints (CR 1926:340). On this last point, E. R. Hughes explicitly equated Confucianism with Christianity. The essence of Christianity, he explained, was the Family and Filial Piety—God and his son, Jesus Christ, glorifying each other by fidelity and reciprocity (CR 1925:84).

Some missionaries claimed that Buddhism, in its search for spiritual freedom, would pave the way for the advance of Christianity (CR 1923:334). In fact all Chinese religions and particularly Confucianism were now viewed positively as the Chinese search for the eternal truth. Magic, ancestor worship, Taoism, Buddhism, and Confucianism were all steps toward the truth. "The ethical teachings of Confucianism must find their place along side the ethical teachings of Christ" (CR 1926:490–493). Missionaries noted that the similarity between Christian principles and the Chinese ethical principles lay in the Confucian emphasis on the individual's development and expression of his character in immediate social relations. The Chinese idea of supreme being was found very similar to the Christian ethical concept of God (CR 1926:427, 796–812).

At the same time missionaries considered Western civilization wanting as a moral example. Some missionaries had long recognized and openly admitted that Western civilization was not necessarily the working-out or manifestation of Christianity. They now earnestly emphasized that it was incidental that Christianity came to China dressed in the form of Western civilization, and that the missionary had the task to separate the two and reveal the true and intrinsic message of Christianity. The China Council of the Presbyterian Church in the U.S.A. resolved in 1924 that "[I]t is unquestionably desirable, especially in view of the present Chinese sensitiveness toward the West, to magnify the distinctively *Christian* and minimize the distinctively *Western* elements in all departments of our work" (CCPC 1924).

Missionaries repeatedly stated that they did not intend to cast China into a Western mold by way of the missionary endeavor. In Edward James's words, "Christianity is not national; nor is it limited to any one type of culture; . . . Chinese culture will always remain Chinese, but it will become Christian Chinese culture" (CR 1925:372). A group of seventy-two Methodist Episcopal Missionaries announced in 1925 that "there is as yet no nation nor civilization which perfectly exemplifies Christ's teachings. We are, therefore, not in China as the propagandists of any particular type of civilization" (NCH 10/10/1925:46). Henry T. Hodgkin, the secretary of the National Christian Council, stated: "We do not wish to turn China from her own inner life. . . . If the impact of the West is merely to make China a copy of the West it would be bad for both the world and China" (CR 1923:65). Writing in 1927 and pondering "why missionaries in China," Bishop George B. Grose of the American Methodist Episcopal Mission admitted that missionaries were no longer moved, as they had been thirty years ago, by the call to evangelize the world in the present generation. They were no longer moved by the conviction that the Western civilization was essential to the higher happiness of the world (WCMN 1927:11–12). A missionary reevaluation of Chinese culture had taken place.

As a religion, Christianity meets a spiritual need of human beings, but obviously it is not the only religion performing such a function. There are alternatives to it, namely, other religions from Islam to Buddhism to other less-known religious beliefs and practices. In other words, if religion is a universal phenomenon in human history, its manifestation varies from society to society and even within societies. The claim of universality by missionaries regarding Christianity represented a particular world view that privileges Christian religion as the only truth or the only path to truth in the universe. Similar claim of course has been made by other religions too. Moreover, since Christianity is monotheism, its claim of universality is accompanied by or predicated upon its exclusion of other cultural and religious traditions deemed incompatible with it. It is in this twin claim of exclusiveness and universality that lay the origins of the contempt for and rejection of non-Christian culture on the part of Christian missionaries. Viewing from this perspective, the missionary acceptance in the 1920s of Chinese culture as something worthy of knowing and cherishing could not be complete and had to be subordinate to the supremacy of Christianity. Indeed, the missionary reevaluation of Chinese culture, largely forced by the political environment of Chinese nationalism, was based on a search for compatibility of Chinese culture and Christianity and was attended by an articulate concern that an indigenous Chinese Church with Chinese expression of the faith might lose its Christian character.

Another paradox is that Protestant missionaries, while claiming the universality of Christianity, insisted on distinguishing between Catholicism and Protestantism and the differences among Protestant denominations. In this regard, it is many Chinese Christians who seemed to be more thoroughly universalistic. To them, denominational trappings, just like Western civilization, were incidental rather than intrinsic to Christianity. The National Christian Council of China, at its founding in 1922, issued a manifesto that read in part:

> Denominationalism is based upon differences, the historical significance of which, however real and vital to the missionaries from the West, are not shared by us Chinese, and is a source of confusion, bewilderment and inefficiency. . . . We believe that an unjust economic order, an unrighteous political regime, unfair treatment of any human being, or of any groups is unacceptable to the righteous and loving God (TIR 1922).

Here Chinese Christians proved to be entirely capable of thinking and speaking in universalistic terms—a universality that was defined by their understanding of Christianity. At the same time, however, their universalism was qualified by a concern to make Christian church and message more Chinese. In fact, Chinese Christians' wide-ranging social concerns and agenda and their sympathy with Social Gospelers and modernist theology in the theological controversy within the missionary movement reflected the strong influence of Confucianism, whether they were conscious of it or not. The call for Chinese expression of Christianity clearly indicates that even these Chinese who became committed to a Western-originated religion and its universalistic claim could not cut themselves off from their cultural environment.

Western Medicine and Native Medicine

In early-twentieth-century China the medical profession comprised two radically different schools—Western and native. The difference in philosophy, theory, and technique led to a conflict between the two, which was intensified by the quickened pace of modernization during the Republican period. By their education and training, Western-style doctors naturally looked down upon native medicine. They advocated national salvation through science and denounced native medicine as superstitious, unscientific, and an impediment to the development of medical science in China. Most of them were confident that given its backwardness native medicine would die of natural causes with the inexorable advance of modern medical science. But by the mid-1920s Western-style doctors became alarmed by the increasing pressure that native medical practitioners brought to bear upon the government through demands for official recognition of native medical education. Mere bias against native medicine was, therefore, translated into an institutional agenda.

A high point of the confrontation between the two camps came in 1929 under the Guomindang (GMD) government. The Provisional Regulations on Doctors (*Yishi zhanxing tiaoli*) enacted by the Ministry of Health in January of that year covered only Western-style doctors without mentioning native medicine (Zhang 1990, Croizier 1968). In February the Central Health Committee (*Zhongyang weisheng weiyuanhui*) (CHC), which was appointed by the Ministry from among government health officials and leaders of Western medical associations around the country, held its meeting in Nanjing. An important item on the agenda was to decide how to deal with native medicine. Yu Yunxiu of the Association of Medical Practitioners in Shanghai, an organization of Western-style doctors, was a major voice in favor of its abolition: "so long as the old medicine is not abolished, the people's thinking will not change, the cause of new medicine can not advance, the administration of health care can not develop." He laid out a step-by-step plan to abolish native medicine. To the shock and anger of native medical practitioners, the main points of Yu's proposal were adopted by the meeting (YC 1929:9; QYTZLH 1931:9–11; Shi 1990).

Western-style doctors justified their demand for abolishing native medicine by expounding a key word—science. They asserted that Western medicine was based on scientific research and experiment; whereas native medicine was based on mysticism (*xuanxue*) (Pang 1933). They refused to accept the sanctity of native medicine on the ground that it was Chinese tradition and had a long history. They denied that native medicine had a theoretical basis. Yu Yunxiu laughed at the argument that Chinese bodies could be best cured by Chinese drugs. All drugs were produced by the earth, and all human beings were conditioned by the same nature. Drugs that cure were blind to the difference between East and West (Yu 1928).

Western-style doctors were irritated by the line drawn between *zhongyi* (Chinese medicine) and *xiyi* (Western medicine). They opposed the identification of their practice with the Western and equated it with the new and scientific instead. They pointed out that Western medicine also had a history of evolving from an unscientific to a scientific stage. That modern medicine happened to have developed in the West did not mean it was exclusively Western, for medical science was universal (Wang 1935). In medicine there was no difference between the Chinese and the Western, but only between the new and the old (Yu 1928). At the same time that Western-style doctors opposed people calling them and their practice *xiyi*, they consciously referred to native medicine and its practitioners as *jiuyi* (old medicine or old-fashioned physicians). Indeed, they asserted that native medicine did not even deserve the word "medicine" (*yi*) and should be more accurately called "black magic" (*wushu* or *xieshu*) (YP 1930:6, 9; 1932:2–3).

To the rhetorical and institutionalized attack by Western-style doctors, native physicians responded with an all-out counteroffensive. They established a national organization to lead their cause; they mobilized native drug trade and the Chinese merchant community at large for moral support; they lobbied the government to swing the official policy toward native medicine, taking advantage of the division of opinions within the GMD regime. A crucial part of native physicians' defense by offense was their propaganda campaign using cultural nationalism as a counter-discourse against the discourse of Western medicine being universal science.

Native physicians understood that at a time when China was struggling to modernize, they could not go against the banner of science. Their argument, not insincere at least for some of them, was that native physicians were willing and ready to move toward science but the "abolitionists" were denying native medicine the opportunity to become scientific (*kexue hua*). By far the most powerful argument native physicians advanced was that native medicine was part of China's national essence and that the fate of native medicine and drugs involved the principles of nationalism and of the people's livelihood—two of the Three Principles of the People which were the official ideology of the GMD government. The whole movement to oppose the CHC resolution in 1929 was organized around this theme. The slogans at the national conference of native medical and drug trade associations summed it up: "Promote native medicine to prevent cultural invasion (*wenhua qinlue*) and promote native drugs to prevent economic invasion (*jingji qinlue*)," and "to promote native medicine is to protect China's culture and economy, and to oppose the [CHC] resolution is to oppose imperialism" (QYTZLH 1931:38, 39). Native physicians accused Western-style doctors of trying to ruin the Chinese nation by destroying its national heritage and of serving imperialist interests by making China dependent upon imported Western medicinal products at a boundless cost.

Native physicians spared no effort to highlight the foreignness of Western medicine and the Chineseness of native medicine. As the name of native medicine assumed an exaggerated importance for native medicine's perception and legitimacy, native physicians began by 1929 to refer to native medicine as "national medicine" (*guoyi*) and native drugs as "national drugs" (*guoyao*). In December 1929 the National Federation of [native] Medical and Pharmaceutical Associations resolved that all establishments of native medicine and drugs, such as associations, schools, stores, call themselves *guoyi* and *guoyao* instead of *zhongyi* (Chinese medicine) and *zhongyao* (Chinese drug) (QYTZLH 1931:49). Native physicians' rhetorical offensive, combined with lobbying the government and mobilizing popular support, eventually paid off. The legitimacy of native medicine was legally established by 1937.

As a science, Western medicine is different in nature from Christianity. It is universal in meeting a social need for curing human illness. Yet it need not be exclusive either. Throughout history there have been alternatives to Western medicine (in its modern form), one of which is Chinese native medicine. That these two kinds of medicine are not mutually exclusive and can be complementary has been proven in the medical practice in China and elsewhere. Insofar as any medicine that cures human illness is universally valid, both Western and native medicine are universal.

In the 1920s and 1930s, however, motivated by group interests and professional bias, Western-style Chinese doctors asserted that only Western medicine was universally valid and that native medicine was worse than useless. They employed a master discourse of "science"as a magic weapon to attack native medicine and claimed to be fighting for the public interests. Significantly, such a discourse was based upon certain notions popular in the West, especially the notion that Western culture and technology represented the progressive, the scientific, and the universal in a unilinear, teleological scheme of things. Needless to say, the colonialist argument was precisely that the Western expansion was an unfolding of God's plan in the interests of all humankind. Similarly, Western-style Chinese doctors argued that their group interests coincided with the public interests of Chinese nation since they, and only they, were the agency of the advancement of medical science in China.

Chinese native physicians proved to be equally resourceful. Riding on the tide of Chinese nationalism, they claimed to represent national essence or national tradition. They tried to define the struggle between Western medicine and native medicine in their own terms, that is, rather than a fight between scientific progress and backwardness, they defined the conflict as one between the preservation of national essence and the invasion of Western imperialism. In this counter-discourse native physicians emerged as agency of Chinese modernization (to make native medicine scientific) as well as defenders of Chinese nation. Western-style doctors were portrayed as traitors to national legacy and the Chinese nation itself. It may be argued that native physicians also engaged in a universalistic discourse—they universalized their practice and interests on a national scale as opposed to Western-style doctors universalizing theirs on a world scale. The moral of this story is that universalistic discourse always involves certain interests and outlooks which are not universal, and that different social groups in Republican China were capable of using such discourses to defend their own interests.

Human Rights and Chinese Judiciary

Human rights or rights of man (renquan) as a concept entered Chinese vocabulary and public discourse around the turn of the twentieth century (Svensson 1996). When the Qing Dynasty, in an effort to save itself, started the judicial reform aiming at a modern Chinese judiciary in 1907, the ideas that bear directly on the reform were the rule of law, due process, and judicial independence. Although the term renquan was not always invoked explicitly, some aspects of human rights were inherent in these principles, such as trial by jury, no arbitrary arrest, no detention without public trial, etc. The draft criminal law and the draft civil law of 1910 were clearly proposed with such assumptions. The draft criminal code included the provisions on trial by jury and legal representation by lawyers, both having been unheard of before in Chinese judicial practices.

In January 1912, on the heel of the founding of the Republic, a group of Shanghai lawyers decided to form a bar association. In their petition to the Governor of Shanghai, they justified their move by saying that they wanted to establish a lawyers' association to "protect the people's rights (renmin quanli) and to spread the spirit of the rule of law throughout of the country" (SB 1/7/1912:5). To invoke public interests and nationalist purposes to advance group interests was nothing new in early-twentieth-century China, but the use of such phrases as protecting the people's rights and spreading the spirit of the rule of law was significant.

Lawyers remained committed to human rights throughout the Republican era as they continued to push for the rule of law and judicial independence. Sometimes the notion of human rights was explicitly invoked. In October 1930 the GMD Shanghai Municipal Party Headquarters (MPH) Mass Training Committee sent the Shanghai Bar a notice saying that the association was a "correct and healthy" one, but that it had failed to apply for permission from and to register with the party committee as required by the regulations on social associations. It asked the Bar to comply immediately. In response, the SBA wrote to the committee arguing that the Bar was different in nature from other social associations:

In performing its duty the profession is subject to no direction or supervision of any superior offices, so as to maintain its spirit of professional independence and allow lawyers to protect human rights (*renquan*) according to the law, in the same fashion as parliament members in session are subject to no outside interference (SLGB 1931:132–133).

This correspondence demonstrates the Shanghai Bar's professional and political sophistication. It went beyond the question of getting permission from the MPH, which the Bar would have no problem doing successfully. Instead, it articulated the legitimacy of the legal profession and its professional association in such broad terms as professional independence and protection of human rights. Although the GMD party organ insisted on and eventually succeeded in having the Bar register with a party office, it did not challenge these principles in theory.

In fact the Republican governments frequently used such vocabularies as human rights (or the people's rights), the rule of law, and judicial independence in their public announcements. In December 1912, for instance, the Ministry of Justice issued an order banning a traditional social practice where senior monks would apply corporal punishment against wayward junior monks. It stressed that such practice "violates the Provisional Constitution and tramples upon human rights, which the Republican era cannot tolerate" (ZG 12/1/9/1912). In 1913–1915 Yuan Shikai, the authoritarian president of the Republic, issued several directives emphasizing the importance of judicial independence (ZG 12/29/1913; 4/30/1915). In March 1913 Xu Shiying, the Minister of Justice, issued directives to all high courts, district courts, and procuratorates, saying that in the Republic the rule of law was the most important thing to be upheld and that judicial officials should neither abandon their duty, nor abuse their office. Within four months Xu issued another directive with the same message (ZG 1/11/1915). In March 1914 Yuan Shikai personally issued an order, prepared by Sun Baoqi, the Prime Minister, and Liang Qichao, the Minister of Justice, to prohibit judges from joining political parties, on the ground that the judicial system was to ensure the people's rights and that judges should rise above personal, selfish opinions and uphold "the spirit of judicial independence" (ZGFH 36:4). In January 1915 the prohibition of party affiliation was extended to cover county magistrates who exercised judicial powers (ZG 1/11/1915). The government also barred military personnel and the police from joining political organizations and parties (ZGFH 36:3–4, 9, 12–13).

After the GMD came to power in 1927, the judicial reform continued. While the GMD placed great emphasis on the necessity of the party dominance over the judicial system, it never renounced the rule of law and judicial independence in public discourse. The opposite was true. On July 14, 1927, Wang Chonghui assumed the office of Minister of Justice in Nanjing and Hu Hanmin, the chairman of the Central Political Council, delivered a speech at the ceremony. Since the founding of the National Government in Guangzhou (July 1925), said Hu, the nationalist revolution had been guided by the GMD party doctrine. As the military government had become the tutelage government, it was now the GMD's responsibility to move the country from lawlessness to the rule of law. He commended Wang's commitment to abolishing unequal treaties and urged him to spread the GMD party's spirit of the rule of law (FP 8/7/1927:4).

Just as GMD officials could speak in the same breath of the rule of law and the party dominance, they had no difficulty paying homage to judicial independence in public discourse. The Manifesto of the National Judicial Conference of 1935 declared:

The foundation of establishing the Republic of China are the three principles of the people and five-power constitution, and judicial independence is the basis for carrying out the principles and implementing constitutional government. In enforcing law, balance has to be maintained, and in protecting human rights, appropriateness has to be sought. All matters, from maintaining public order and good social custom to securing individuals' rights and obligations, depend upon the working of judicial organs. Advanced countries in the world,

no matter what form of government, have to take judicial independence as the unshakable golden rule if they want to maintain the spirit
of the rule of law (QSHH 1935).

This was an acknowledgment of the rule of law and judicial independence
and their function in protecting human rights as a universal principle. The
GMD government apparently accepted Western nations ("advanced countries in the world") as the model in this regard. Indeed, the legal journals of
that time often saw references made by officials as well as scholars to human
rights (*renquan*) in discussions of judicial issues.

The judicial reform during 1912–1937 resulted in limited success, however. The goal of establishing courts in all counties throughout the country,
which was considered the institutional guarantee of judicial independence,
was never accomplished. Moreover, the GMD theory of partyizing the judiciary was a mockery of the principle. Since the GMD reduced judicial
independence to the establishment of a court system independent of administration, the contradiction between party dominance and judicial independence did not exist for GMD officials.

As political concepts and judicial practices, the rule of law and judicial
independence are extremely important for realizing human rights in China.
But in the Republican era they operated in the international context of an
unequal relationship between the Chinese government and foreign powers
as well as the domestic context of evolving social and political forces in
China. It is clear that neither the Beiyang regimes (1912–1927) nor the
Nanjing government (1927–1949) had true understanding of and total commitment to liberalism, including protection of human rights, embodied in
the Western political system and judicial practices. That they carried out
judicial reform at all was due to historical circumstances. They were motivated by a general desire to modernize China and a specific objective to
abolish extraterritoriality, a privilege by which foreigners enjoyed immunity
to Chinese laws and judicial process. In the commercial treaties of 1902 and
1903, Great Britain, the U.S., and Japan promised that given the Chinese
government's desire to reform the judicial system "to bring it in accord with
that of Western Nations," they would relinquish extraterritoriality "when the
state of the Chinese laws, the arrangement for their administration, and other
considerations" warranted such actions (MacMurray 1973). A modernized
Chinese judiciary tailored after the Western model would deprive foreign
powers of their justification for maintaining extraterritoriality—an objective

constantly on the minds of legal reformers from late Qing to the Republican period (Meijer 1976; Reynolds 1993; Williams 1922). This objective explains both the acceptance of the rule of law and judicial independence in principle and the less than total commitment to them on the part of the Republican state.

Informed Chinese, particularly legal professionals, had a better understanding of these principles and were eager to see their realization in judicial practices. Not insignificantly, they saw the parallel between the establishment of Western-style judicial system and practices and the advancement of their professional interests or group interests. Equally significant was that they would use the demand of the foreign powers for judicial reform in return for the abolition of extraterritoriality to push the government to adhere to the rule of law and judicial independence. This explains in part the acceptance of these principles by the Chinese government as it was constantly reminded of them. In other words, Chinese lawyers and the Republican state accepted the principles with different motives and varying degrees of commitment.

For their part, the foreign powers that demanded China carry out judicial reform in the early twentieth century did not feel the need to shy away from the word "Western." Rather, they specifically asked the Chinese government to bring Chinese judiciary "in accord with that of Western Nations." That things Western were universally good and applicable anywhere in the world was simply assumed. The niceties that missionaries felt necessary to display in the 1920s such as highlighting the Christian aspect and downplaying the Western aspect of their enterprise were not a concern to these foreign governments at that time. Finally, to make the story complete and to appreciate the dimension of judicial reform and extraterritoriality in Republican China as a matter of power relations between China and foreign powers, let us note that the extraterritoriality was eventually relinquished by the U.S. and Great Britain in 1943, not because China's judicial reform had achieved expected results, but because China had become an ally in the Pacific War against the Japanese Empire (Fishel 1952).

Human Rights and Universalistic Discourse Today

The claim of universality is based on the premise that what is advocated and promoted is universally good to humankind and is universally desired or needed by human beings across cultures and national boundaries. Yet, as we have seen, the claim has always been put forward by historical actors with specific purposes and particular interests that are not always universal. The above three cases point to several important dimensions of universalistic discourse that are relevant to the current debate. Discourse has/is power. And discourse takes place in the context of complex interplay between group interests and public interests, between social groups and the Chinese state, and between the Chinese government and foreign powers, all underpinned by varying power relations among them and relative power resources available to them under particular historical circumstances. Power can be political, economic, military, cultural, or a combination thereof. Discourse interacts with such power relations and power resources by way of reinforcing or co-opting or resisting them. Indeed, in such interactions discourse itself becomes a power resource. It is from this perspective that the current debate on human rights and Asian values may be considered.

The concept of human rights or natural rights of man originated in Western societies (Cranston 1973; Robertson 1982; Henkin 1978). While the history of the notion is complex and not to be traced here, its best-known and most familiar expressions are found in the writings of John Locke, the English Bill of Rights (1689), the Virginia Bill of Rights (1776), the American Declaration of Independence (1776), the American Bill of Rights (1791), and the French Declaration of the Rights of Man and Citizen (1789). In these historical documents and related discourses, human rights were understood primarily as civil and political rights (Cranston 1973). Although its specific content remains controversial and evolving, the general principle of respecting human rights has gained wide recognition as universally desirable in all societies since the end of the Second World War. The principle is spelled out in the United Nations Charter of 1945, the Universal Declaration on Human Rights of 1948, and the International Covenant on Civil and Political Rights of 1966 (Cranston, 1973; Robertson 1982; Sieghart 1983; Cassese 1990).

Human rights, however, are not only universal but also historical. Rather than being abstract principle, the notion of human rights always has historical content and it can be meaningful only when applied to real persons in concrete historical situations. The triumph in Western societies of the notion of civil and political rights as natural rights of man both accompanied and reflected the historical change in political and economic power relations in those societies, i.e. the rise of middle class (bourgeoisie) and capitalism and the demise of the landed aristocracy and the divine right. The efforts to prioritize civil and political rights to the neglect of social and economic rights as human rights underscored the interests and power of this new elite associated with capitalism in those countries. This orientation became an intellectual and sociopolitical tradition there. It is no surprise that not until 1965, at the demand of developing countries, was the International Covenant on Social, Economic, and Cultural Rights adopted by the United Nations and thus the concept of human rights widened to cover social and economic rights (the United States has not signed the document) (Robertson 1982; Cranston 1973).

Since the late sixties, the West has been moving from an exclusive concern with civil liberty in rhetoric to a practical attention to economic equality and social welfare—hence the term "welfare state." As Louis Henkin put it, "capitalism has conceded to welfare at least in practice" (Henkin 1978). Even in theory some Western scholars such as A. H. Robertson have called for a recognition of the desirability and necessity of both political-civil rights and economic-social-cultural rights for a full realization of the human personality (Robertson 1982).

On the other hand, the discourse that privileges political and civil rights is still dominant in the West (Gordon 1998). Argued philosophically, for instance, Maurice Cranston's position against listing social and economic rights as human rights resonates with the basic tenet of the conservative ideology in American politics: "Since those rights [political and civil rights] are for the most part rights against government interference with a man's activities, a large part of the legislation needed has to do no more than restrain the government's own executive arm. This is no longer the case when we turn to 'the right to work,' 'the right to social security,' and so forth. For a government to provide social security it needs to do more than make laws; it has to have access to great capital wealth, and many governments in the world today are still poor" (Cranston 1973). This philosophy would explain why, for instance, American cigarette companies are able to make huge profit at the expense of public health including children's health and now target smokers and potential smokers in the developing countries when they face increasing opposition within the United States. For the same reason, gun control legislation can be opposed as restriction on civil liberty while what happens to victims of gun violence is not considered a human rights issue. As Joy Gordon observed, "claims of human rights rhetorically work in a manner which is not unlike a holy war: as a claim of absolute righteousness which ironically can come to operate at the expense of simple decency. We can look at the asymmetry of the standard notion of human rights and see this easily. For example, someone who is homeless and begging on the streets, but has the right to hire a lawyer for $300 an hour or buy network television time, suffers no violation of his or her human rights" (Gordon 1998). In no small part, therefore, the history of human rights concept in the West and the present power relations within Western societies such as the U.S. account for the fact that Western critics continue to use civil and political rights as the sole or primary measure of human rights conditions in non-Western countries.

More importantly, the Western emphasis on political and civil rights in the current discourse on human rights is to be understood as part of international politics in a changing world. The human rights discourse entered the international relations and the U.S. foreign policy in the mid-1970s because it was considered as "a powerful antidote to the ideological force of Communism," i.e. as a Cold War weapon (Newberg 1980). Yet, if the human rights discourse had some utility in dealing with Eastern Europe and the Soviet Union, it could have hardly been a useful political weapon in Asia, Africa, and Latin America. In the Cold War era the United States supported many governments around the world that were no less authoritarian than the People's Republic of China (PRC), as long as those governments were anti-Communist, following the American global strategy and serving the American interests in the Cold War. Only with the end of the Cold War, and with the democratization in such Asian societies as South Korea, Taiwan, and Mongolia, as well as in Eastern European countries and the former Soviet Union, has it become possible to use the human rights issue as a political weapon in dealing with the PRC. This is why human rights have become an important issue in the relations between China and the West only in recent years.

China needs to be dealt with at all because the recent rapid growth of Chinese economy has been contributing to a reconfiguration of international power relations. Every national government has its own opinion about what the post-Cold War world order ought to be like, but no nation can be certain what it will be like. In view of China's economic development, Western nations have become especially concerned about what China as a rising power will mean to the world. The anxiety seems to be even greater as long as China remains different in its political system. Because of this preoccupation with China's political system in view of its increasing economic power, in addition to the history of human rights concept in the West, Western critics have ignored or downplayed the improvement in China's human rights situation in the past decade, especially in the area of social and economic rights, and focus their criticism on Chinese political and civil rights that fall short of the Western standards.

Intimately related to the changing power relations is the West's desire to claim moral superiority. It is a great historical irony that Western nations that once colonized, and contributed to the impoverishment of, Asian and African countries in the past now claim a moral superiority in insisting that these countries are not up to the standards of Western democracies (it is a double irony that some flagrant human rights abuses do exist in some of those countries, but that is another issue). The desire to claim moral victory was particularly ironic in the case of the controversy surrounding Hong Kong's return to Chinese sovereignty. In the nineteenth century and much of the twentieth century the colonial discourse was based on "othering" native peoples who were colonized. The people of Hong Kong were, therefore, not considered desiring and deserving an elected government, not before the signing of the Sino-British Joint Communique in 1984 and not until after the June Fourth and on the eve of Hong Kong's turnover to China. Nowadays an opposite side of the "othering" seems to be at work for political reasons: People in non-Western countries are declared the same as people in Western societies—they should enjoy exactly the same political and civil rights as Westerners do, no matter in what social, cultural, and economic situations they are.

In that sense, human rights defined in Western terms are preached very much as a new gospel from the West. The missionary zeal of the United States to remake the world in its own image has found a new manifestation in the human rights issue. The way to spread this gospel is strikingly similar to that of Christian missionaries in the 1920s—claiming that to use the Western standards (the exclusive concern with political and civil rights) to measure human rights situation in China is not to Westernize China but for China to accept universal standards. But unlike the missionaries of the 1920s, Western critics today make no allowance for Chinese culture and tradition and do not take into account the concrete political and socioeconomic conditions in China.

For its part, Beijing's resistance to the imposition of Western model in the human rights debate also stems from the changing international power relations. For one thing, China is no longer a semicolonial country under

Western dominance as Republican China was. In contrast to Republican governments that had to beg foreign powers to relinquish extraterritoriality, the PRC asserts full sovereignty over the mainland and opposes outside "interference." While the post-Mao judicial reform is improving the human rights situation in this regard, the judicial practice in the PRC as a whole has not met the international standards defined by the West (Lawyers Committee for Human Rights 1996). Nor has its political system changed to a Western-type democracy. Yet, Beijing does not feel it imperative to accept the Western norms or conform to such norms at a pace that Western nations desire. One reason is that no Chinese leaders want to be criticized by their internal political rivals for capitulating to the Western pressure, just as politicians in the West often utter tough words regarding China only to score points in domestic politics. An interaction between domestic politics and international politics exists.

Another aspect of such interaction is that while extremely concerned with their power and privilege in the name of stability, Chinese leaders are sensitive to the issue of moral superiority which concerns their legitimacy. Once upon a time the Chinese Communists trumpeted Marxism-Leninism-Mao Zedong Thought as the universal truth applicable everywhere in the world — a universalistic discourse. But China never had the capacity to impose this universalistic view outside its border. The collapse of socialist system in Eastern Europe and the Soviet Union and the post-Mao retreat by way of reform into quasi-capitalist economy in China have led to the moral bankruptcy of the Chinese Communist Party (CCP) ideology. The Chinese government's official formulations of "the preliminary stage of socialism" and "socialism with a Chinese character," while not devoid of theoretical contradictions, are certainly a retreat from the universalistic view of Marxism. From a vulnerable ideological position, Chinese leaders are reluctant to carry out political reform at the dictation of the West, which would further undermine their power and legitimacy. Instead of seeking equivalency in the Chinese tradition to the Western concept of human rights as some Chinese and Western scholars are trying to do, Beijing insists that the Western type of democracy and civil liberty is unsuitable to China's national conditions. Needless to say, such an assertion has yet to be proven. Yet, the CCP leaders could not afford to be proven wrong as power-holders, for it would mean the end of their monopoly of power; nor could they afford to be proven right as governmental leaders, for the political and social chaos assumed to result from such changes would be costly to the country. They opt for an approach that seems to ensure their hold on power and the country's economic growth and gradual political change. It remains to be seen whether such an approach is viable in the long run.

Conclusion

Modern world history has witnessed several universalistic discourses in tandem with large social, economic, and political movements, including Christianity, modern sciences, Western liberalism and colonialism, and Marxism. As far as China is concerned, it has been exposed to all these after the crumbling-down of Confucianism as official ideology which may be considered a universalistic discourse as well. A complex interaction among these discourses and between them and social-political forces has made the history of twentieth-century China.

Human rights discourse is the latest universalistic discourse on the world stage with a globalizing force. As an outgrowth of Western liberalism, it cannot be easily separated from the expansion of Western economic, political, military, and cultural power in the rest of the world. Universalistic discourse is often benign in its rhetoric and even in its intention, but in practice it can be and often is aggressive and conquering, with unfortunate results, as modern world history has amply demonstrated. For this reason, a counter-discourse of relativism, in alliance with nationalism, often serves as a resisting force against it. As alluded to earlier, nationalism is also a universalistic discourse but on a national scale, and it can be aggressive and conquering too. Yet, it becomes more viable in the face of a universalistic discourse/agenda on a world scale and in the form of resisting an imposition of such discourse and agenda.

At this day and age of postmodern and postcolonial consciousness, the human rights issue has naturally become a focal point of international debate. Not surprisingly, it is also part of international power politics. When the human rights discourse is carried on as international politics, its usefulness is limited in promoting and realizing full protection of human rights in the world. Yet, it would probably be naive to expect an absence of power politics in any international debate and discourse. In the human rights area we may witness the continuing interactions and negotiations among genuine humanitarian concerns, domestic political agendas, and international power-relation considerations of various social groups and national govern-

ments in the foreseeable future. Perhaps that is the way it is; at least that is
the way modern world history has been. For individuals and groups in the
international community, especially academics and NGOs, the difficult task
is to work together to promote full human rights in all societies while guard-
ing against potentially imperialistic and counter-productive imposition. After
all, even when human rights are universally valued, they still have to be
realized in a diverse world, that is, in individual societies with different
cultures and historical conditions. Even if different societies and cultures
are to be more or less homogenized in the globalization process, that should
ideally mean a convergence of the best cultural elements of all societies and
a narrowing of the gap between the economically developed and the underdeveloped. And if the highest ideal of humankind is for the world to
evolve into a community of universal peace and harmony (*datong*) where
human dignity of all persons is respected and preserved, by definition such
a world cannot be forced.

Endnotes

1.   In his 1997 visit to the U.S. Jiang Zemin, the president of the People's Republic
      of China, reiterated the view that China is entitled to its own values and its
      own definition of good government, and that the most fundamental human
      rights in China is to ensure adequate food and clothing for the 1.2 billion
      Chinese people (*Time* 10/27/1997:56; 11/10/1997:73). In an interview in early
      1997, Zhu Muzhi, chairman of the China Society for Human Rights Studies
      and the president of the Chinese Association for Cultural Exchanges with For-
      eign Countries, had the following to say: "Various countries are faced with
      different conditions and thus adopt different political systems and patterns.
      Therefore, no country should attempt to impose its own approach or political
      system or pattern on another country. Neither can they accuse other countries
      of lacking democracy simply because they choose a different pattern or
      method" (*Beijing Review* 40 [7–8]:14). For the more vehement refutation from
      Beijing of human rights abuses in China and the counter-accusation of the
      Western intention to assert hegemony can be found in Chinese official news-
      papers (RRH 3/5/ 1997:2; 3/14/1997:1–2; 3/17/1997:4; 4/10/1997:6; 4/16/
      1997:1). For the view of other Asian governments, that of the Singaporean
      government is representative. (See "Culture Is Destiny":1994; Kausikan 1995–
      96, 1996).
2.   See, for example, the comments made by Winston Lord, former U.S. Ambas-
      sador to the PRC and former Assistant Secretary of State for Asian Affairs, in
      an interview with Jim Lehrer on "News Hour" on PBS, Oct. 29, 1997.

Bibliography

An-Na'im, Abdullahi Ahmed. 1992. *Human Rights in Cross-Cultural Perspectives: A Quest for Consensus*. Philadelphia: University of Pennsylvania Press.

Bates, M. Searle. 1974. "The Theology of American Missionaries in China, 1900–1950." In John K. Fairbank, ed. *The Missionary Enterprise in China and America*, 138–139, 157–158. Cambridge: Harvard University Press.

Bauer, Joanne R. and Daniel A. Bell, eds. 1999. *The East Asian Challenge for Human Rights*. Cambridge: Cambridge University Press.

Beijing Review, 1997. Volume 40:7–8 (February 17–March 2).

Bell, Daniel A. 1996. "The East Asian Challenge to Human Rights: Reflections on An East West Dialogue." *Human Rights Quarterly* 18:641–667.

Cameron, Meribeth. 1930. *The Reform Movement in China, 1898–1912*. Stanford: Stanford University Press.

Cassese, Antonio. 1990. *Human Rights in a Changing World*. Philadelphia: Temple University Press.

Chinese Recorder (CR), 1923, 1924, 1925, 1926.

Chinese Repository, 1832, 1835.

Cranston, Maurice. 1973. *What Are Human Rights*. New York: Taplinger.

Croizier, Ralph. 1968. *Traditional Medicine in Modern China*. Cambridge: Harvard University Press.

"Culture is Destiny: A Conversation with Lee Kuan Yew." 1994. *Foreign Affairs*. Vol. 72(2):109–126.

Derr, Rev. Charles H. 1927. "American Presbyterian Mission Chenchow-Hengchow Station Letter, August 1." the Archives, the Missionary Research Library, New York.

Falu Pinglun (FP) (Law Review). 1927. Beijing.

The Fifth Annual Meeting China Council of the Presbyterian Church in the U.S.A. (CCPC). 1924. Shanghai.

Fishel, Wesley R. 1952. *The End of Extraterritoriality in China*. Berkeley: University of California Press.

Gordon, Joy. 1998. "The Concept of Human Rights: the History and Meaning of Its Politicization." *Brooklyn Journal of International Law*, Volume 23, Number 3:691–791.

Henkin, Louis. 1978. *The Rights of Man Today*. Boulder, CO: Westview Press.

Hutchison, William R. 1987. *Errand to the World: American Protestant Thought and Foreign Missions*. Cambridge: Harvard University Press.

Kausikan, Bilahari. 1995–96. "An East Asian Approach to Human Rights." *The Buffalo Journal of International Law*, 2(2):263–283.

———. 1996. "Asia's Different Standard." *Foreign Policy*, Volume 24:41.

Lawyers Committee for Human Rights. 1996. *Opening to Reform: An Analysis of China's Revised Criminal Procedure Law*. New York.

Lyall, Leslie T. 1965. *A Passion for the Impossible: The China Inland Mission, 1865–1965*. London: Hodder and Stoughton.

MacMurray, John V.A., ed. 1974. *Treaties and Agreements with and Concerning China, 1894–1919*. New York: Howard Fertig.

Meijer, Marinus J. 1976. *The Introduction of Modern Criminal Law in China*. Arlington, VA: University Publications of America.

National Christian Council Annual Report (NCCAR). 1923, 1924, 1925, 1926. Shanghai.

Newberg, Paula R., ed. 1980. *The Politics of Human Rights*. New York: New York University Press.

North China Herald (NCH). 1922, 1925, 1927.

Pang, Jingzhou. 1933. *Shanghai Jishi Nianlai Yiyao Niaokan* (An overview of Shanghai's Medicine In recent ten years). Shanghai: Zhonguo kexue gongsi.

Quanguo Sifa Huiyi Huibian (QSHH) (A compilation of the National Judicial Conference proceedings). 1935. Nanjing.

Quanguo Yiyao Tuanti Zong Lianhehui Huibian (QYTZLH) (Collected proceedings of the National Federation of Medical and Pharmaceutical Associations). 1931. Shanghai.

Renmin Ribao Haiwaiban (RRH) (The People's Daily Overseas Edition). 1997.

Reynolds, Douglas R. 1993. *China, 1898–1912: The Xinzheng Revolution and Japan*. Cambridge: Harvard University Press.

Robertson, A. H. 1982. *Human Rights in the World*. Manchester: Manchester University Press.

Shanghai Lüshi Gonghui Baogaoshu (SLGB) (The report of the Shanghai Bar Association). 1931. Shanghai.

Shi, Quansheng. 1990. *Zhonghua Minguo Wenhua Shi* (A cultural history of the Republic of China). Changchun: Jilin wenshi chubanshe.

Shi Bao (SB) (Eastern Times). 1912. Shanghai.

Sieghart, Paul. 1983. *The International Law of Human Rights*. Oxford: Clarendon Press.

Svensson, Marina. 1996. *The Chinese Conception of Human Rights: The Debate on Human Rights in China, 1898–1949*. Lund, Sweden: Studentlitteratur's Printing Office.

Time magazine, October 27, 1997; November 10, 1997.

"Two Important Resolutions" (TIR). 1922. A.L. Warnshuis Papers. the Archives, Missionary Research Library, New York.

Wang, Qizhang. 1935. *Ershi Nianlai Zhongguo Yishi Zouyi* (Comments on China's medical affairs in recent twenty years). Shanghai: Zhengliao yibaoshe.

West China Missionary News (WCMN). 1927. Chengdu.

Williams, Benjamin H. 1922. "Extraterritoriality in China." *China Weekly Review*, Volume 21, Number 12:450.

Xu, Xiaoqun. 1997a. "The Fate of Judicial Independence in Republican China, 1912–1937." *The China Quarterly*, Volume 149 (March):1–28.

———. 1997b. "National Essence vs. Science: Chinese Native Physicians" Fight for Legitimacy, 1912–1937." *Modern Asian Studies* 31(4) (October):847–878.

———. 1997c. "The Dilemma of Accommodation: Reconciling Christianity and Chinese Culture in the 1920s." *The Historian*, 60(1) (Fall):21–38.

Yijie Chunqiu (YC) (Spring and Autumn of the Medical Circle). 1929. Shanghai.

Yiyao Pinglun (YP) (Medical Review). 1930, 1932.

Yu, Yunxiu. 1928. *Yixue Geming Lun Chuji* (On the Medicial Revolution, first volume). Shanghai: Yishi yanjiushi.

Yui, David Z. T. 1926. "The Need of the Christian Movement in China." *Educational Review* 18(2):232–238.

Zhang, Zaitong, et al. 1990. *Minguo Yiyao Weisheng Fagui Xuanbian, 1912–1948* (Selected compilation of laws and regulations on medicine and health during the Republic, 1912–1948). Jinan: Shandong daxue chubanshe.

Zhengfu Gongbao (ZG) (Government bulletin). 1912, 1913, 1915. Beijing.

Zhengfu Gongbao Fenlei Huibian (ZGFH) (Government bulletin compiled by categories)

9   Jihad Over Human Rights, Human Rights as Jihad

Clash of Universals

Farhat Haq

Among the more powerful aggregates of contemporary vocabulary is the West. The term evokes an image of strength and superiority. It presupposes the notion of uniform geographic entity, encompassing numerous ethnic and social substrata. Privileged by historical development, it created and then dominated the modern era. It is ranked over and above but also over and against all others who are labeled, and also libeled, as "non-Western" (Lawrence 1989:41). Some in the West have portrayed Islamic resistance to universal human rights as part of a jihad against the West. In the Islamic world, some have portrayed the Western promotion of Human Rights as a jihad against Islam. In this essay I want to explicate some of the political dynamics behind the two-way "jihad" over human rights and then, briefly, examine the possibilities of a moral dialogue deploying jihad in the service of universalizing human rights. I have concluded that fundamentalist Islam and the West share more in common than is usually appreciated in terms of both human rights values and of absolutist attitudes that frustrate dialogue. It should, however, be noted that I am very pessimistic about the possibilities of such dialogue over issues touching on women's rights because Muslim women have become such a charged symbol in civilizational battles between Islam and the West.

Islamic Resistance to Western Jihad

Abu Al'a al-Maududi (1903–1979), a South Asian who founded the Jammatt-I-Islami, an Islamic fundamentalist movement, is a major theore-

tician of modern Islamic political thought. His writings are enormously influential in shaping what have come to be labeled fundamentalist Islamic
movements throughout the Muslim world (Kepel 1993, Binder 1988,
Lawrence 1989, Salamé 1994, 'Inayat 1986). Though not a traditional Islamic scholar, Maududi's clear prose, logical style, trenchant criticism of
"Western" values, and insistence on the superiority of the Islamic system
endeared him to many among the new generation of intelligentsia throughout the Muslim world. One of the most important contributions of Maududi
(and those who were influenced by his writings such as Sayyid Qutb of
Egypt) was to formulate an Islamic political lexicon that could respond to
Western claims of superior political systems and also become the language
of opposition to Muslim nation-states and their policy failures. By the end
of the nineteenth century there were hardly any geographic parts of the
Muslim world not dominated by the West. There were a variety of Muslim
responses to Western hegemony, but the Islamic fundamentalists attempted
to provide the most comprehensive "Islamic " response to the "Western
threat." The fundamentalists "share the conviction that Islam is engaged in
a kulturkampf with Western imperialism . . . The reassertion of Islam is a
rejection of Western dominance, of Western culture, and of the identity
which the West would impose upon Muslims" (Binder 1988:175).

Defending Islam against the onslaught of Western imperialism was one
of the key concerns of Islamic fundamentalist scholars as is clear from the
following passage written by Maududi to defend Islamic concept of jihad:

Modern Europe has decried many achievements of Islam and has accused it of many crimes, one of which is that Islam was spread through
the power of the sword. Europe has leveled this criticism at a time when
Islam has lost its political ascendancy. The sword of Islam has been rusty
for a long time but it is the sword of Europe that has become bloodied
through its efforts to swallow up all the weak nations of the world. How
can Europeans, who are behind all the bloodshed in the world, accuse
Islam of belligerency? European domination has put the world of Islam on trial. Some of us have tried to defend Islam by adopting Western standards, and have tried to expunge things that offend Western
sensibilities. The real spirit of Jihad demands that the Muslim community resist the greatest tyrannical powers in the world. Those who
struggle to end oppression and establish a just society, provide God's
people with peace and security, and struggle to improve humanity are
the ones who are engaged in true jihad (Maududi 1965:10).

Thus, Islamic fundamentalists do not reject the concept of human rights; instead, they vehemently reject the idea of Western human rights. In a 1974 speech, Maududi made the following contribution to a jihad over human rights:

People in the West have the habit of attributing every beneficial development in the world to themselves. For example, it is vociferously claimed that the world first derived the concept of basic human rights from the Magna Carta of Britain which was drawn up six hundred years *after* [my italics] the ascent of Islam. But the truth is that until the seventeenth century no one dreamt of arguing that the Magna Carta contained the principles of trial by jury, habeas corpus and control by Parliament of the right to taxation. If the people who drafted the Magna Carta were living today they would be greatly surprised to be told that their document enshrined these ideals and principles. (Maududi 1983:15)

Maududi goes on to argue that principles enshrined in the United Nation's Declaration of Universal Human Rights are "just expressions of pious hopes. They have no sanctions behind them, no force, physical or moral, to enforce them. Despite all the high-sounding resolutions of the United Nations, human rights continue to be violated and trampled upon" (Maududi 1980:15). Thus, for Maududi, Islamic human rights are given by God and as such they have much greater moral appeal than Western secular human rights: "In Western democracy, the people are sovereign; in Islam, sovereignty is vested in God and the people are His caliphs or representatives. In the former the people make their own laws; in the latter they have to follow and obey the laws (shari'a) given by God through His Prophet" (Maududi 1980:10).

Modernity of Tradition

Until the 1970s the "conventional wisdom" among social scientists was that "modernization" was inevitable and that along with modernization came secularization of societies. Although in the last twenty years there has been a good deal of scholarship on the much more complex role of religion in modern and post-modern societies (Lawrence 1989), many have continued to view religious fundamentalism as an attempt to return to strictly traditional religious values. But Islamic fundamentalism is a modern phenomenon. When Muslim collective identities were taken for granted there was no need to self-consciously and insistently proclaim the importance and superiority of Islam. A striking difference between living a life of a Muslim at the present time compared with the situation of a century ago is thus the pervasive need to think about what it means to be a Muslim. As Eickelman and Piscatori point out in their recent study of politics in Islamic societies (1996):

> Objectification is the process by which basic questions come to the fore in the consciousness of large numbers of believers: "What is my religion?" Why is it important to my life?" and "How do my beliefs guide my conduct?" Objectification does not presuppose the notion that religion is uniform or a monolithic entity (although it is precisely that for some thinkers). These explicit, widely shared, and "objective" questions are modern queries that increasingly shape the discourse and practice of Muslims in all social classes, even as some legitimize their actions and beliefs by asserting that they advocate a return to purportedly authentic traditions" (38).

The claim that Islam provides a better framework for human rights ought to be placed in this context. In the last fifty years there has been a great deal of literature produced in the Muslim world that aims to demonstrate not only an "Islamic human rights" but an "Islamic economy," "Islamic sciences," and "Islamic democracy." Most of this literature is produced not by the traditional scholars of Islam (the ulama) but rather by the lay intellectuals who have been described as "Muslim fundamentalists." Maududi became one of the main exponents of this "objectified" Islam but many modern Islamic figures ranging from Imam Khomeini in Iran to Sayyid Qutb of Egypt have worked toward crafting a coherent Islamic ideological system. For the Muslim fundamentalist, the onslaught of a host of challenges from varied sources could only be countered by "systematically" demonstrating the weaknesses of Western systems and explicating the inherent superiority of the Islamic system.

There are striking similarities in the vision, in the vocabulary, and in the tactics of persons as different as Maulana Maududi, the founder of a Sunni reformist party, and Imam Khomeini, the leading Shia figure of the twentieth century. The similarities are due to the tendency of twentieth-century fundamentalist movements to assert that Islam presents a comprehensive solution to all social, economic and political problems of Muslim societies. For example the Jammatt-I-Islami calls itself an ideological party and argues that Pakistan is an ideological state. By claiming that Islam is a complete ideological system, the Jammatt is seeking to convey a twofold impression: first, that Islam offers complete and righteous programs of principles and activity that provide guidance to Muslims in their economic, social, and civic lives; and second, that Islam as a complete ideological system contains an "inner logic" which is both superior to, and incompatible with, any other system. Thus the Jammatt and other reformist movements in the Muslim world tend toward mutually exclusive self-definition vis-à-vis what they view as rival ideological systems: nationalism, liberalism, Marxism, and Socialism. As Lawrence (1989) aptly points out, the Islamic fundamentalists "espouse an ideology but not a theology, and perhaps one of their enduring values is to force others who use a variety of terms in trying to account for the Muslim world to recognize the chasm that separates theology—a handmaid of philosophy that searches for a cohesive integration of all aspects of life—and ideology—a handmaid of power that looks for ways to authenticate those who have been rendered powerless by forces which they only dimly understand" (16).

By the 1970s many Islamic fundamentalist leaders began to react to the label "traditionalist" and started to draw distinctions between modernization and Westernization. They argued that they were eager proponents of technical modernization for their societies but did not think that in the process they must also import Western values. For example, Ayatollah Khomeini (1902–1989) maintained that "the claim that Islam is against modern innovations . . . [is] nothing but an idiotic accusation. For, if by manifestations of civilization it is meant technical innovations, new products, new inventions, and advanced industrial techniques which aid in the progress of mankind, then never has Islam, or any other monotheist religion, opposed their adoption" (Eickleman and Piscatori 1996:22). But it is not only in the realm of science and technology that the Islamic fundamentalists are modern. Their desire to turn Islam into a complete ideological system that creates an alternative to other modern ideologies such as liberalism and socialism was also a twentieth-century phenomenon.

Indeed the Islamic fundamentalists adopt the vocabularies and concerns of the very Western ideologies they oppose. The conception of Islam as a comprehensive ideological system is a response to Western imperialism and as such it is a "modern" idea. The term used for ideology, "nazira," is a modern non-Quranic term. The following passage from a speech by Maulana Maududi, delivered at Aligarh University in 1940, is most revealing in demonstrating the bases of his belief that Islam is a comprehensive ideological system:

> The world has never been introduced to an ideological state. In the olden days people were only aware of government by a certain family or privileged groups. Christianity provided a blurry outline of this idea but it did not have the complete ideological system upon which an ideological state could be built. The French Revolution provided a glimpse of this notion (ideological state) but it became lost in the darkness of nationalism. Communism popularized this concept, it even attempted to establish a state based on this idea but eventually the Communist states also succumbed to the pernicious influence of nationalism. From the very beginning up to now, Islam is the only system of thought that provided a pure ideological system without a trace of nationalism.

What is striking about this passage is that none of Maududi's examples of an ideological state is derived from Islamic history. Many of the Islamic fundamentalist movements have completely internalized key Western institutions, of which the most important is the "party" — with a formal hierarchy of positions, reports, subscriptions, meetings, minutes, files, programs, campaigns, leaflets, and so on. Even the creation of parallel women's organization betrays the modern "need" to include women.

For Islamic fundamentalists a secular modern nation-state is the greatest threat to the existence of human rights. In the 1940s, when nationalist forces gained strength and the possibility of an independent Indian and Pakistani "nation-state" loomed large, Maududi provided a critique of the modern nation state and presented a model of an "Islamic state." He argued that the modern nation-state was intrusive and authoritarian:

> In the modern world there is no limit to the scope and power of the state. In the cultural sphere, the individual rights are no longer a primary factor; the state, for collective welfare, can institute all kinds of

reform. It can dictate what script to use, what kind of dress to wear, when to get married. Under such a ubiquitous state, the very idea of fundamental rights becomes meaningless. For example, the written guarantee of fundamental rights have not protected the Negroes from brutal treatment in the United States.

Maududi compares such an authoritarian nation-state to an Islamic state in which "universal fundamental rights for humanity are to be observed and respected in all circumstances. For example, human blood is sacred and may not be spilled without strong justification; it is not permissible to oppress women, children, old people, the sick or the wounded; women's honor and chastity must be respected; the hungry must be fed, the naked clothed and the wounded or diseased treated medically irrespective of whether they belong to the Islamic community or are from amongst its enemies" (Maududi 1980:10).

In short, Islamic fundamentalists do not reject the idea of human rights. Theirs is an attempt to reject the Western form and provenance of the human rights idea in order to preserve the Islamic sense of identity and superiority, while at the same time asserting some of the same values as "Islamic" both because these values are inherent within Islam and, more importantly, because these values are intentionally prestigious. For example the Iranian Foreign Ministry responded to a highly critical report of the UN Human Rights Commission not by rejecting the human rights framework as simply an imperialist ploy, but by reaffirming its importance:

Based on the supreme teachings of Islam, the Islamic Republic of Iran considers respect for human rights and the lofty character of mankind in all material and spiritual dimensions as a fundamental duty for all governments. According to this belief, the Islamic Republic of Iran, without paying attention to any propaganda and hue and cry, will continue its efforts to strengthen the principles which guarantee support for the rights of all citizens. As the majority of the countries of the world stressed in the course of the international conference on human rights (i.e. Vienna), the only way to lend real support to human rights and promote such principles throughout the world is to end the practices of having double standards and exploiting human rights issues for political objectives (Halliday 1995:158).

Clash of Civilizations: Jihad Over Human Rights

For Western scholars and human rights activists in Muslim countries the rise of political Islam and its formulation of alternative "Islamic human rights" poses an important challenge to their work. (Lawyers Committee for Human Rights 1997). Ann Mayer (1991) provides the most comprehensive critique of the "conservative" Islamic formulations of human rights. Her book is important because she discusses in detail several examples of Islamic human rights and also because she is often cited by others interested in the relationship between Islam and human rights. The discursive terrain Mayer and Maududi occupy is one of consistency (philosophical for Mayer and theological for Maududi), exclusivity (only Western or only Islamic), and incommensurability between the West and Islam. Mayer dismisses any possibility of carving out a meaningful framework of human rights from the shari'a because of lack of individualism in Muslim cultures, primacy of revelation over reason, and focus on human duties rather than human rights. Mayer asserts that the entire political and constitutional structure of the current Muslim world had to be transplanted from the West and that any attempts to formulate Islamic human rights only result in frivolous notions of entitlements such as the right not to be ridiculed (1991:68).

Mayer objects to an Islamic-based human rights framework on the grounds that the premodern shari'a is an inadequate basis for a satisfactory international human rights scheme. Yet the Iranian constitution of 1980 has sections guaranteeing individual human rights though the Council of Guardians (Article 91), intended to ensure that all legislation is in accordance with "Islam and the Constitution." The constitution appears to both acknowledge the absolute sovereignty of God and allows for popular sovereignty. Articles of the Constitution "affirm the traditional concept of the absolute sovereignty of Allah (Principles 2 and 56), while accommodating the very different idea of popular sovereignty in conceding the people's right to determine their own 'destiny' (Principle 3:8) and allowing for occasional referenda (Principle 59) and popularly elected assembly (Principle 62)" (Eickleman and Piscatori 1996:28). Thus, to dismiss the Iranian constitution as "premodern" is both inaccurate and damaging to possibilities of dialogue between the West and the Islamic world.

A second objection raised by Mayer about the Islamic articulation of human rights is that these schemes fail to point out a consistent philosophical framework for their rights scheme. But we should ask: Is philosophical consistency important for reasonable implementation of human rights? Rather than bemoaning the lack of philosophical consistency in these articulations, the proponents of international human rights ought to take some solace in the fact that the Islamic groups are not simply rejecting human rights, an important indication of the moral pull exercised by the very notion of universal human rights. The proponents of universal human rights make two mistakes regarding Islamic fundamentalist movements. First they overestimate the influence of fundamentalist movements over the people in Muslim countries. Many Western observers simply assume that "masses are already devout traditional Muslims and that the political invocation of Islam is a manifestation of mass politics" (Binder 1988:80). But with one possible exception (The Islamic Front in Algeria), fundamentalist parties have generally not received popular support. The fundamentalist movements attempt to play the role of cultural brokers representing "Muslim Traditions" to the West but ironically they reject many of the existing cultural practices among Muslims as repugnant because they are "un-Islamic." Many Muslims may also profess respect for the convictions of the fundamentalists but feel a cultural distance from them (MacLeod 1991).

Muslim fundamentalists are a minority in numbers in their societies but they have set the terms of debate regarding the Islamic identity of Muslim societies. A recent publication by the Lawyers Committee for Human Rights in the Middle East and North America draws a conclusion about the role of political Islam: "At present, political Islam is the most effective political force in the Arab world. . . . It is not the most popular religious group among the Muslim population" (Lawyers Committee 1997:159–160). The statement may appear contradictory but it refers to a basic fact about contemporary Muslim politics. The ability to present a coherent "Islamic" ideology, effective use of print media, and a lack of any competing force capable of providing a systematic alternative doctrine, have enabled them to dominate the discourse on politics and identity. This fact requires both taking seriously the alternative formulations of Islamic fundamentalist groups and taking solace in the fact of cultural diversity in the Islamic world. By attempting to craft an Islamic framework for human rights, the fundamentalists are both affirming the validity of human rights discourse and challenging its Western accent.

Thus it is a mistake to dismiss these alternative articulations of human rights as a hoax because the framework is not based on modern, secular or coherent philosophical foundations. It is equally a mistake simply to embrace the fundamentalist articulations as legitimate because they are authentic or traditional representations of Islamic societies. There are possibilities of fruitful dialogue between the proponents of universal human rights and the Islamic fundamentalists. As I have suggested, the making of tradition is a political process. Both the flexibility of Islamic "tradition" and its hold over the believers must be appreciated in order to see the possibilities of moving toward a more meaningful dialogue with the Muslim world. The plurality and ambiguity of Islamic values and symbols allow for a link with the past and room for change. "Since values take on symbolic form, the parameters of the culture appear to remain intact while the renewal and transformation of values are in fact taking place. Thus, the constancy of traditions and shared myths is affirmed, even while change of belief and value are underway and traditions are reinvented" (Eickleman and Piscatori 1996:28). The proponents of universal human rights ought to delight in the fact that the language of human rights have become so prevalent, but they must also prepare for a "multilingual" conversation with even those most "other" of the contemporary world: the Muslim fundamentalists.

Cultural Wars and the Politics of Gender

When it comes to the possibility of dialogue over women's rights within Islam, I am much less optimistic. Fundamentalist parties such as the Ikwan in Egypt and the Jammatt-I-Islami in Pakistan have come to accept some elements of civil and political rights. Their experiences with arbitrary arrests, suppression of their publications, and general desirability of a democratic government for many Muslims have led them to claim that Islam contains such elements of freedom, justice, and equality, and thus there is no essential clash between an Islamic state and these human rights. This is not the case when it comes to the question of gender equality.

In my view there are three important obstacles to such dialogue. First, the role and status of Muslim women has become a charged symbol in the "cultural wars" between the Muslim world and the West. In response to the increasing scrutiny of "oppression" of Muslim women by the Western media, a great deal of literature is produced by Muslim men and women to demonstrate the "honor" and "respect" accorded to women in Islam. Even Muslim feminists like Fatima Mernissi (1975) who have provided a scathing critique of patriarchal practices of Muslim societies have accused Western feminists of not understanding the particular circumstances of women in non-Western societies. The second obstacle is the presence of authoritarian nation-states in most of the Muslim world. For Western feminists the most serious shortcoming of law in general and international human rights law in particular is the distinction between the private and the public and thus, for example, the "right to privacy can be interpreted as protecting from scrutiny the major sites for the oppression of women: home and family" (Charlesworth 1994:73). There is a demand then for a more activist state which could successfully intervene in the private sphere to expand the protection of such laws to women. In fact, since cultural practices are seen as an important site of oppression of women, the state has to play a much greater role in molding civil society. In the 1950s and 1960s many government introduced policies to "modernize" women, including changes in family laws, providing educational and employment opportunities for women, and at times mandating elimination of veiling. The Shah of Iran and Ataturk of Turkey are the two best-known examples of authoritarian governments that imposed reforms from the top to change the role and status of women. Such intrusive approaches to "modernizing women" from above raises several difficult issues regarding cultural autonomy, tensions between democratic values and the "liberation of women," and the consequences of the paternalistic embrace of women by an authoritarian state.

The Iranian example illustrates the complex nature of this issue. In the 1930s Reza Shah launched a modernization campaign which included a ban on the "chador" (the Iranian version of the veil). "After 1936, cinema houses and public baths closed to women wearing the veil. Law forbade bus and taxi drivers to accept veiled women as passengers. To enforce the regulations, the police roamed the streets to snatch scarves from the heads of women still trying to observe hejab or Islamic dress" (Mackey 1996:183). In the 1950s and 1960s the Shah of Iran (son of Reza Shah) continued the campaign to modernize women and promulgated the Family Protection Act to strengthen women's rights in the areas of marriage and divorce. In the early 1970s the chador had become a symbol of protest against the shah's regime and the Family Protection Act had become a favorite target of criticism by Khomeini. By 1980 the Khomeini government had imposed hejab on the entire female population. "In less than half a century, Reza Shah's police, who beat women for wearing the chador, had been replaced by

Khomeini's police, who beat women for not wearing the veil" (Mackey 1996: 298). Khomeini's government also repealed the Family Protection Act.

If we conclude the story at this point, many proponents of women's rights may say that the excesses of Reza Shah's attempt to eliminate the chador were regrettable but that both of the shah's policies were more in favor of women's rights than the current Islamic fundamentalist regime in Iran. But if we use education and employment as two variables shaping women's status, then Iranian women might be judged as better off under the current government. In 1994, thirty percent of government employees and forty percent of university students were women compared to twelve percent in 1978 (Ghazi 1994). Moreover "some of the reforms first proposed by the shah have been reintroduced by the Islamic Republic since 1991—a reinvigorated family planning program, state-sponsored prenuptial contracts that give women the right to initiate divorce proceedings, and greater opportunities in the workplace and in higher education" (Eickleman and Piscatori 1996:93). Thus, this example illustrates the highly politicized nature of women's rights' discourse in the Muslim world.

The third obstacle in the way of a fruitful dialogue on the issue of women's equality is the cultural centrality of the family in the Muslim world. For Islamic fundamentalists, the adoption of the Western model of the family is to commit cultural suicide. For Maududi the proper sexual division of labor was foundational. In his book *Purdah and the Status of Women in Islam* (which has been widely translated and disseminated throughout the Muslim world), he asserts that "the problem of man and woman's mutual relationship is indeed the most fundamental problem of civilization, and on its right and rational solution lays the proper foundation of culture and civilization. . . . Earning a livelihood for the family, supporting and protecting it, and carrying out the laborious sorts of social duties should be the responsibility of the man. . . . Bringing up children, looking after the domestic affairs and making home-life sweet, pleasant and peaceful should be entrusted to the woman" (1993:121–122).

According to Islamic thought, "The family is a primary unit for ritual observance as well as an influential site of religious and secular education and the transmission of religion and worldly knowledge from one generation to the next. It serves as locus for developing notions of trust, authority, and responsibility. In short, the family and its primary expression in domestic space, the household is frequently taken as a microcosm of the desired moral order" (Eickleman and Piscatori 1996:83). A challenge to and a critique of this "desired moral order" provokes deep anxieties. I hope the following two examples from South Asia can throw some light on the differences.

The first example comes from India, the by-now famous Shah Bano case in which a seventy-year-old divorcee sued her husband for a maintenance allowance under the Indian civil code. But Muslim personal law and the shari'a do not grant alimony after divorce. For many Muslims, especially Muslim men (most accounts I have read of this from a Muslim perspective are by men) the case became a symbol of cultural and religious protection for a religious minority in the plural and secular state of India. For Indian feminists the case demonstrated the patriarchal state's willingness to sacrifice women's interest to appease an important constituency (the Muslim vote has been important for the Congress party, for example). The decision generated many responses from supporters and opponents of the Indian Supreme Court's decision. One such response was by a Muslim professor of law who wrote a lengthy book explaining the judgment from the Islamic perspective. The book concludes by complaining that "Islamic system of management of human relation, with regard to the position of women, has been most blatantly mis-interpreted and maligned by a number of people" (Akhtar 1994:386). But it was my reaction to one of the footnotes in the book that may throw some light on the different perceptions of family. The footnote provides a detailed account of the sons and daughters of Shah Bano and the second wife. It tells us that Shah Bano's youngest son is forty years old and that all of her sons are "well settled," but that the second wife has one son and six younger daughters. My first reaction to the footnote was one of irritation: why was the author providing unnecessary information. It did not matter how many children she or the second wife had. But then, when if I shifted my "cultural lenses" a bit, I found that it may matter. The relationship between the husband and the wife may not be the only primary relation in a Muslim Indian household. Financially independent sons must contribute to the maintenance of an elderly parent. Having daughters is a greater financial burden due to the dowry custom. Thus, the financial need for the second wife was greater than Shah Bano's need.

Shah Bano's case was understood quite differently by Western feminists. The most important "facts" were that a seventy year old women was being denied a very small amount of alimony. For Indian feminists, many of them non-Muslims, the most important "facts" were that the government had abandoned women's interests and that they found themselves in an uncomfortable alliance with a Hindu fundamentalist party (the BJP). Thus, the

Shah Bano case is rife with "cultural misunderstanding" from many different angles.

The second example of misunderstanding of women's and family issues comes from Pakistan. In 1996 Asma Jahangir, a well-known human rights lawyer argued in front of the Supreme Court for a young woman who had escaped her family because they did not agree on her choice of a mate. The case was widely debated in the Pakistani media and in households. I had a remarkable conversation with a senior advocate of the Supreme Court of Pakistan about this case. He had impeccable liberal credentials. He had fought for the democratic movement and had even gone to jail for the cause. He had strongly fought for independence of the judiciary and protection of civil and political rights. He had done pro bono work for a women falsely accused under the Islamic codes in 1983. But he was vehemently against Asma Jahangir on this case. He shared a pamphlet he had written about this issue in which he quoted demographic data from Europe to show the increase in single-parent families and rates of divorce. For him the most troubling aspect of this case was that the institution of the family was being represented as "oppressive." "What about the love, protection, the intimacy and the connection that is provided by the family too?" he asked. He claimed that the case shows the dangers of imposing Western cultural practices on Muslim families.

These two examples are not meant to suggest that the response from these two Muslim males is the only valid one, but rather to suggest the great distance between the two positions: "For Muslims, the boundaries are drawn between the good family and the corrupted one; for feminists, between the empowered woman and the subjugated one. Little is neutral in these moral debates, and they form part of the complexity of Muslim politics" (Eickleman and Piscatori 1996:81).

Conclusion

While there is more room for dialogue than we thought on the general human rights idea, the issue of women's rights presents greater difficulty for such a dialogue. Given the extreme politicization of human rights discourse, especially in the realm of women's rights, what are the costs and benefits of adopting human rights language to improve the conditions of Muslim women? In other words, how useful a tool is the Convention on the Elimination of All Forms of Discrimination against Women (CEDAW, adopted by the UN in 1979) in providing equity for Muslim women? My tentative answer to this question is that casting women's rights in human rights language is not very effective. The rights language assumes a world of autonomous individuals and "promises equality to women who attempt to conform to a male model, and offers little to those who do not" (Charlesworth 1994:64). Secondly, the cultural and political dominance of the West means that the use of Western rights based language for the liberation of women will always be vulnerable to the charges of lacking cultural authenticity. The infamous Asma case in Pakistan is a good illustration of this problem. Thirdly, I am deeply skeptical of the efficacy of progressive cultural changes mandated by authoritarian nation-states.

Bibliography

Akhtar, Saleem. 1994. *Shah Bano Judgement in Islamic Perspective: A Socio-Legal Study*. New Delhi: Kitab Bhavan.

An-Na'im, Abdullah Ahmed. 1992. *Human Rights in Cross Cultural Perspectives: A Quest for Consensus*. Philadelphia: University of Pennsylvania Press.

Binder, Leonard. 1988. *Islamic Liberalism: A Critique of Development Ideologies*. Chicago: The University of Chicago Press.

Charlesworth, Hilary. 1994. "What Are 'Women's International Human Rights'?" In *Human Rights of Women: National and International Perspectives*, ed. Rebecca J. Cook. Philadelphia: University of Pennsylvania Press.

Eickelman, Dale F. and James Piscatori. 1996. *Muslim Politics*. Princeton: Princeton University Press.

Esposito, John L. 1982. *Women in Muslim Family Law*. Syracuse: Syracuse University Press.

Ghazi, Katayon. 1994. "Iran Offers an Islamic Way to Improve the Lot of Women." *New York Times*, December 21, p. A11.

Halliday, Fred. 1995. "Relativism and Universalism in Human Rights: The Case of the Islamic Middle East," *Political Studies* 53:152–167.

'Inayat, Hamid. 1982. *Modern Islamic Political Thought*. Austin: University of Texas Press.

Kepel, Gilles. 1993. *Muslim Extremism in Egypt: The Prophet and the Pharaoh*. Berkeley: University of California Press.

Lawrence, Bruce. 1989. *Defenders of God: The Fundamentalist Revolt against the Modern Age*. New York: Harper and Row.

Lawyers Committee For Human Rights. 1997. *Islam and Justice: Debating the Future of Human Rights in the Middle East and North Africa.* New York: Lawyers Committee for Human Rights.

Mackey, Sandra. 1996. *The Iranians: Persia, Islam and the Soul of a Nation.* New York: Penguin.

MacLeod, Arlene Elowe. 1991. *Accommodating Protest: Working Women, the New Veiling, and Change in Cairo.* New York: Columbia University Press.

Maududi, Abu Al'a. 1965. *Jihad in Islam.* Lahore: Islamic Publications.

———. 1980. *The Islamic Human Rights.* Leicester: The Islamic Foundation.

———. 1983. *Islami Riyast* (The Islamic State). Lahore: Islamic Publications.

———. 1993. *Purdah and the Status of Women in Islam.* Lahore: Islamic Publications.

Mayer, Ann Elizabeth. 1995. *Islam and Human Rights: Tradition and Politics.* 2d ed. Boulder: Westview.

Mernissi, Fatima. 1975. *Beyond the Veil.* New York: John Wiley.

Salamé, Ghassane, ed. 1994. *Democracy without Democrats? The Renewal of Politics in the Muslim World.* New York: I.B. Tauris.

Tétreault, Mary Ann. 1993. "Civil Society in Kuwait: Protected Spaces and Women's Rights," *Middle East Journal* 2 (2) (Spring):275–291.

Wadud-Muhsin, Amina. 1992. *Qur'an and Woman.* Kuala Lumpur: Penerbit FajarBakti Sdn Bhd.

10 Universalization of the Rejection of Human Rights

Russia's Case

Dmitry Shlapentokh

Human Rights as a Cultural Construct

There is no doubt that there is a notion of "human rights," i.e., the basic preconditions of human existence which exist regardless of the political culture and the time. As a matter of fact, these are the preconditions of the survival of any living creature. These basic human rights include food, shelter, and concern for health and personal safety. The lack of these rights has been a concern of the human species from the dawn of its existence.

From this perspective, there are human rights which are indeed universal. Yet when present-day political scientists use the term they have a different idea in mind. They usually refer to the rights which became the essential elements of the American and French Declarations, i.e., those human rights which became the essential elements of the political culture of modern Western capitalism. In a sort of oversimplistic way, these principles could be defined in the following way.

First was the equality of the people before the law, i.e., the notion that "all people are born equal." The second notion was the assumption that power should not be imposed upon the citizens and that those who are ruled should elect those who rule. The American and French Revolutions both universalized these principles. Indeed, the American Declaration promulgated the idea that this was nothing but self-evident truth. Yet human rights in their present Western interpretation were not self-evident truths for millenniums of human history. In other words, human rights in their present Western reading were the product of a long process of historical development and therefore were historically and socially constructed.

The idea of the equality of the people before the law—the notion that all people were born equal—had evolved over the course of time. The ancient Greeks had implicitly rejected the notion of the equality of the people. In Aristotle's view, the people were unequal by their nature, and those who became slaves were predisposed to be slaves by their nature. Only the Stoics, who lived several centuries after Aristotle, came to the conclusion about the existence of "natural rights," i.e., the equality of the people as biological beings, in their "natural" capacity.[1] In their view it was only social conditions which divided people into slaves and free people. Christianity actually capitalized on the Stoics' notion, and the representatives of the rising middle class resurrected it in a new form in the dawn of the modern era when they began to assume that "natural rights" render people equal, not only in heaven but on earth as well.[2] The French and American Revolutions finally made "human rights," i.e., the principles of Western political culture, a global issue. Moreover, by the nineteenth century, the notion of human rights ("liberties") had been internalized by the majority of the people in Western countries.

Of course, one could argue that human rights in their Western reading, with the attachment of political democracy as one of the major manifestations of them, could hardly be an integral part of the life of the average Westerners, especially those in the lower classes. One could point here to the political passivity, with only a few representatives of the Western populace playing any role in the country's political life. One also could point here to the statements of political analysts, especially those with leftist political leanings, that the power actually belongs to a few members of the elite, and the meaning of the Western political system could hardly be regarded as being internalized by the majority of the Western population (Foss and Larkin 1986:43–48). Consequently, they could argue that the principles of Western democracy are essentially foreign to the majority of the Western population. This assumption could have some good points, but only if one of the most important aspects of Western civilization is disregarded—that which is intimately related to human rights in their Western reading, and here I mean the legalistic implications of "human rights."

Indeed, the very foundation of modern Western civilization is the assumption that people are equal before the law. In this context they have certain rights which they employ in dealing with others (e.g., the buying and selling of goods and services) and in dealing with society (here marriage is also nothing but a contract which is legally consummated only when the parties involved have legalized their relationship through the contract) and the state. As a matter of fact, the Western state is based on the assumption of the "social contract." The legalistic web entangles all of the relationships of the majority, or at least a large number, of the members of modern Western society. The legalistic aspect of the culture ("everything in writing, please") is intimately connected with the development of the institution of private property, the legalistic web which is enmeshed in it, and the ideas of human rights (e.g., political freedom and democracy). It was the adherence to the written agreement (contract), permeating not only the relationships between individuals but also the relationships between individuals and the state, which constituted the most sacred aspect of the Western political culture. Thus, while the emergence of human rights had been caused by the development of Western capitalism, the attachment to human rights in the West is not limited to the political and economic elite. It is shared by a majority of the people, and from this perspective human rights as a political notion became universalized and became an essential aspect of the national character. It became internalized on an individual level, and a disregard for human rights (the legally valid agreement between the people) became unthinkable for Western man. The idea of human rights as a fair contractual obligation was so deeply internalized in discourse that even the radical and revolutionary movements, whose representatives targeted the complete destruction of the prevailing political and social order, might sound quite "legalistic" when they proclaimed that they were fighting for "social justice," implicitly for a fair contract.

While human rights were internalized and universalized by a considerable portion of the Western population, the idea of human rights also had great international appeal for non-Western countries, and this was due to the global domination of the West, which had become unquestionable since the second part of the nineteenth century. It is clear that the ideas of human rights and political liberties were eagerly accepted by the downtrodden masses, whose fighting for "social justice" (the revolutionary defined new social contract) had tended to be translated, as was the case with Marxism, into the eschatology of the revolutionary millennium (Furet 1988). "Human rights," as the symbol of the battle cry for the liberation of the downtrodden masses was one of the reasons for the popularity of political democracy in the beginning of the century. Yet it was not the only reason. The popularity of human rights was due to the global dominance of the West (Winks 1969). It is clear that it was the economic, political, and ultimately military predominance of the West that had made human rights attractive for quite a few. Even some of the conservative politicians were fascinated with "human rights." As a matter of fact, the spread of European colonial empires over the globe was the reason why some of them were so eager to don the external trappings of Western "human rights."

The case of Japan is a good example (Beasley 1987). The democratic traditions were rather weak in the context of the country's political discourse, and the ease with which democracy was later swept under the carpet demonstrated this clearly. Yet the guns of Admiral Perry convinced the Japanese elite that without the political gadget called democracy the country of the rising sun would be transformed into the country of the sunset. It was this internalization of the idea of human rights by the majority of the Western population, the transforming of them into an integral part of their national identity, and the global domination of the West which had provided a powerful push for viewing the Western idea of human rights as universally applicable by the second half of the nineteenth century. Yet the expansion of the West faced not only the acceptance of the Western political paradigm by the non-Western political elite, as was the case with Japan (it might be added in this respect that the idea of human rights had been accepted not for its own sake but actually for opposite goals—the building of a mighty empire), but resistance.

The resistance had come explicitly from those non-Western societies who had a problem with adopting human rights in their Western reading because of their social and political traditions. This usually occurred in societies where the capitalist ethos and the legalistic underpinning of the discourse had been downplayed. In such cases the aristocratic elite was unable to accept the legalistic aspects of a social contract which was likely to undermine their position as well as the institution of the patriarchal monarchy. It would also be an oversimplification to assume that the idea of human rights was rejected exclusively by the political elite. As a matter of fact, the majority of the people in these societies were peasants. Their Gemeinschaft social and economic discourse was also deeply hostile to "human rights," which they related to the development of capitalism, or to be precise, the market economy. For them, political liberties were either irrelevant or even harmful. In their minds they cherished not the design of a democratic society but that of a society with a powerful and wise master. The traditional non-Western societies substantiated their discarding of Western human rights by the trend in Western thought which opposed the principles of the American and French declarations. This opposite trend had become evident in Western thought by the late nineteenth century, exactly the time by which the West had achieved its unquestionable hegemony. Indeed, the very spread of the idea of human rights and its further crystallization was only one side of the Western discourse.

The Problem with Human Rights in Modern Western Discourse

What is called Western human rights (i.e., equality before the law and political democracy) was not only historically constructed (i.e., it had emerged after the prolonged development of Western capitalism) but actually had been completely integrated into only a limited segment of Western civilization, mostly the Anglo-Saxon countries. Here the principles of the Enlightenment which articulated the idea of human rights had never been seriously challenged, and they were completely implemented in real political and social discourse. Here these principles not only had been perfected throughout the nineteenth century (e.g., the sections of the population engaged in the democratic process had grown constantly throughout the century) but had been universalized through global expansion. Here the role of England was most important. Her colonial expansion not only brought democratic ideas to the non-Western nations but also implicitly related the democratic institutions with imperial power and splendor in the minds of the non-Western elite.

While England and America elaborated and applied the notion of what was called Western human rights, the situation was much more complex in other parts of the Western world. In the French Enlightenment, democracy was just one among many forms of government. Even for Rousseau, the power of the people in its fullness could be exercised only in the smaller countries. Indeed, in his idea of the social contract, which is usually viewed as the design for democratic government, the philosopher stressed the rights of society rather than the rights of the individual, with strong authoritarian overtones. It is not surprising that in this political milieu the French Revolution, in almost Orwellian fashion, translated the "Declaration of Rights" into a state of permanent terror. The German Enlightenment was not concerned with political freedoms at all. Moreover, the Romantic reaction in the beginning of the nineteenth century expressed criticism of the capitalistic order, its legalistic underpinnings, and implicitly "human rights." In their praise of the Middle Ages, the Romantics stated that equality before the law and political democracy actually was a sham for it served only to secure the power of the middle classes over the workers. Socialism, which also stemmed ideologically from Romanticism in many ways, followed this line. It is clear that socialism appealed to the idea of the "social contract" and for this reason implicitly made references to legalistic discourse and the idea of human rights. Yet the antilegalistic, the anti-Gesellschaft aspect of socialism also was evident, for the proponents of socialism, while attacking the "exploitive" contracts of Western capitalism, actually attacked the notion of any contract at all. Here they implicitly discarded the legalistic underpinnings of Western society and the notion of human rights which was enmeshed in it.

The Romantic reaction and the rise of socialism did not undermine the Gesellschaft underpinnings of Western society. Yet these new trends started to deform legalistic capitalism, especially in the countries where the Gesellschaft traditions were not strong. There was a visible trend in some societies toward what would in the future be called a corporate state where political liberties would be exchanged for economic security. This was clearly the case with Germany in the beginning of the country's existence as a unified state. As military alliances were formed and the prospect of war loomed ahead, ideas which emphasized the necessity of a strong leader who would not be accountable to the electorate increasingly began to circulate.

Colonial expansion had led to a renewed popularity of racism, which placed the colonial people completely outside of the legalistic Western discourse. The mistreatment of these people started to be justified on the grounds that political liberties should be applicable only to Europeans. This notion which deuniversalized the Western idea of human rights went along with the deuniversalization of world history. The assumption of most of the philosophers of the Enlightenment that all nations had to follow the same road had been discarded, and the notion of "civilization" was born which implied that the building elements of one civilization would not necessarily be applicable to the others. Thus by the end of the nineteenth century one could see contradictory trends in the global intellectual and geopolitical discourse in regard to Western values and what is called "human rights." On one hand, the human rights which finally had been shaped up during the eighteenth century were in the process of being expanded and universalized due to the global predominance of the West. On the other hand, the principles of the eighteenth century began to be challenged in the context of Western civilization. Paradoxically, one could state that what would in the future be called "non-Western" values were already a part of the Western discourse by the late nineteenth century.

This reaction to the principle of the American Declaration inside of Western culture provided the additional rationale for those non-Western elite who rejected the Western concept of "human rights." It could be argued that they rejected the democratic principles, either directly or indirectly, not just because they failed to fit into their culture but because they believed these principles were completely unworkable. Indeed, the members of this non-Western elite could argue that the West itself had started to abandon them, and what had been regarded as "reactionary" and "non-Western" in the beginning of the century became more and more up to date and more and more integrated in the Western political and intellectual discourse. This not only provided the non-Western elite with the sense of the inapplicability of human rights to the native culture but universalized their countries' cultural and political experience. In this context, the political system's absolute rejection of human rights was not only regarded as being appropriate for this or that culture, but also there were plans to spread it all over the globe. Indeed, here the authoritarian/totalitarian and antilegalistic Gemeinschaft culture had a messianic drive in the same way that the spread of human rights was regarded as the messianic mission of some of the countries of the West (e.g., Great Britain and America).

Thus the major point of this essay could be boiled down to the following: Not only could Western human rights be rejected as irrelevant for this or that country or civilization, but a country/civilization could proclaim its rejection of Western human rights in the form of a messianic drive, just as the liberal capitalist democracies of the West supported human rights with messianic zeal. In this drive the representatives of these countries/civilizations assumed that all people are "essentially the same" and for this reason should be similar to them. To change their "wrong" legalistic discourse (human rights) to "true" Gemeinschaft discourse which discarded "human rights," these messianic assumptions became an essential part of these people's national character, as was the case with human rights for the liberal capitalist democracies of the West. To deprive the people of these nations of their messianic denial of human rights (considered "liberation" in the eyes of Western observers) could lead to a deep spiritual crisis. As a matter of fact, it could endanger the very existence of this given civilization.

Russia and the Problem of Human Rights

The Russians of the late nineteenth century present an interesting case. To start with, the Russian intellectuals of that time were quite in tune with European developments, and in their works one can easily find ideas reflecting their reaction to the traditions of the Enlightenment in its liberal reading with its emphasis on human rights as a universalized experience. Similar to many other countries of both West and East who started to challenge the universal principles of the Enlightenment, the Russians emphasized the difference between cultures (i.e., Russia and the West). At the same time, they not only proclaimed their culture superior to that of the liberal nations of the West with their emphasis on human rights but also assumed that this should assure them of a leading position in the global community. The West should not lead them—they should lead the West. In their assertion of the differences between the cultures, they elaborated upon the notions already known in the Romantic discourse, those which later would be quite popular among Western philosophers such as Oswald Spengler, historians such as Arnold Toynbee, and recently Huntington, as well as others who emphasized cultural specificity as the framework for historical existence.[3]

Their criticism of the legalistic discourse of the modern capitalist West was also similar to that of a variety of critics of modern capitalism, from the socialists to the existentialists, which asserts that the concern with the legalistic formalities of human rights either conceals the domination of the economic elite (the socialists' criticism) or deprives individuals of intimacy and real concern for the well-being of others (the point of the existentialists).

The Russian intellectuals of the late nineteenth century preaching of strong authority and what would in the future be called a totalitarian state were also quite in tune with new trends. These ideas, for example, started to become in vogue among European intellectuals near the end of the nineteenth century and flourished during the twentieth century.

The late-nineteenth-century Russian intellectuals are important, and just because their questioning of the universal validity of human rights fits well in the intellectual discourse of Western Europe. There is another reason: it was only in Russia, among other European nations, that the discarding of human rights became deeply integrated in the fabric of national life and became inseparable from the national identity. Indeed, with all of the prevailing Gemeinschaft criticism of legalistic capitalism, with all of the praise of the authoritarian/totalitarian rulers, and even with all of the attempts in the twentieth century to reverse the democratic traditions of the eighteenth and nineteenth centuries, the legalistic discourse (hence, human rights) was too entrenched in the fabric of European life. Private property existed even among the most ferocious European dictatorships (e.g., the regime of the National Socialists in Germany), and for this reason the notion of contract had never been completely eradicated. This also explains why this criticism of democracy and legalistic discourse was mostly related to the intellectual discourse and was unable to take deep roots in real life. This was the reason why even Germany, after years of National Socialism, could return to legalistic normalcy. The racist Gemeinschaft coating was completely washed away as though it had never existed, and the legalistic foundation of the society with human rights as the cornerstone was restored. The case with Russia was altogether different.

Russia has enjoyed a unique quality in her political and intellectual discourse. On the one hand, since the reign of Peter the Great and especially since the outbreak of the French Revolution, the growing numbers of the country's political and intellectual elite (in the broad meaning of the word) had identified themselves with the West and saw the country's path as following the Western political scenario (Walicki 1987). The fascination with the French Revolution, which was especially strong by the beginning of the twentieth century, was one of the best proofs of this, for the French Revolution had traditionally been seen as one of the symbols of the West (Shlapentokh 1997). From this stemmed the idea, which had been gaining momentum since the very end of the nineteenth century, especially after the outbreak of the 1905 Revolution, that Russia would be democratic in the future. In this context, the French Revolution was more a symbol of the triumph of democracy than of terror and revolutionary dictatorship. It was not so much the principles of "1793" but the principles of "1789" which had defined in the eyes of the majority the principles of the French Revolution.

Yet Westernism, i.e., the assumption that Russia would follow the road of the West (and Westernizers represented the gamut of Russian political movements from liberals to radicals of all persuasions), had no relationship to the real economic and social backdrop of the Russian society, which was more Oriental than Western in its very nature. The institution of private property had been underdeveloped throughout the entire period of the Russian ancient regime. This was especially the case with land, which made Russia actually closer to the countries of Oriental despotism than to European society. This was a point of George Plekhanov, one of the founders of the Russian social democracy (Plekhanov 1923–27:15, 33). The situation had profoundly affected the majority of the Russian population—the peasantry.

The specificity of the Russian peasantry, which constituted the vast majority of the Russian population until the mass industrialization and urbanization of Stalin's time, was that they were not farmers in the Western sense of the word. Throughout the entire history of imperial Russia, the peasantry lived in communes. In this case, the land was not the individual property of the peasant but the property of the commune. The peasants did not even have the land as cultivators for any length of time. As a matter of fact, the commune divided and redivided the land periodically, depending on the number of males in the peasant households. Private property and consequently the legalistic discourse were not only foreign to peasant life but actually hostile to it. This actually defined the peasants' approach to "human rights." Instead of a democratic government, they wished to have a stronger master and derided the idea of the election of a supreme ruler. Instead of legal and contractual obligations, they preferred the Gemeinschaft type of relationships based on family and community ties. And they were proud, not so much of their liberty, if any, but of their orthodox religion. Their conflict with the landlords and bureaucracy was not due to the fact that the peasantry wished for freedoms which had been denied by the imperial bureaucracy but because of another quite pragmatic reason: the peasantry hated to pay taxes to the authorities and see their sons sent to the army. They also had cravings for the landlords' land (Pipes 1990). The peasants' outlook, taken holistically, was shared (in various degrees) by the majority of the other groups in Russian society. For this very reason, the Gemeinschaft disrespect for legalistic discourse had been deeply integrated in the culture of both the lower and upper classes, and here it became an essential part of the national character.

For this reason, as was admitted by Sergei Kovalev, the leading Russian human rights activist, "Some of the specific features of national tradition indeed do not help to entrench the respect for human rights in the country"(quoted in *Russkie Izvestiia* 1998). Blended with the traditional Russian messianism, which had been an essential aspect of the country's life since the dawn of modern history, Russian culture recast the rejection of human rights in a particular way. Reinforced with the traditional Russian messianism, the rejection of human rights became not just a part of the nation's self image, an integral element of what is called "the Russian soul," but an essential aspect, in the eyes of quite a few Russian intellectuals, of the country's manifest destiny. If the extension of human rights in a global setting was viewed by Americans as the necessary precondition for the progress of humanity, the rejection of human rights (or legalistic discourse in general) in global terms was seen by Russians as a necessary step toward achieving the point of omega, and it was here that Russia should play a decisive role in universalizing its own political and social experience. The importance of the Russian experience resided in the fact of messianic deuniversalization of human rights and in organic integration of this notion in national identity, particularly in the second half of the nineteenth century when these major elements of national philosophy were shaped.

While discussing the problem of human rights in Russian thought, our study focuses on the conservative Slavophiles. The point here is that this group of intellectuals did not represent just themselves but actually epitomized the Russian culture in general, in the holistic sense of the word. The universalistic meaning of the conservative thought could be seen in the fact that conservative ideas were often in tune with what had been preached by the radicals, who supposedly were their archenemies.

Conservative Discourse as a Symbol of National Character

Conservative Slavophilism is important not only because its major paradigms would later be incorporated in the Soviet regime. Nationalistic Slavophilism has represented the Russian culture (in the holistic sense of the word) more than any other strain of ideology, especially as this culture was manifested in the late nineteenth century. Indeed, the conservative views of the world could be easily detected in the views of their supposed archrivals — the radicals. The dominant brand of Russian nineteenth-century radicalism known as Populism was deeply hostile to the legalistic discourse and, consequently, to human rights in their contemporary Western reading. Most Populists praised the peasant commune, where the collectivistic feeling and real concern for each other required no legalistic framework or formal respect for mutual "rights" in their modern Western meaning. Indeed, the assortment of radicals (from exiled revolutionaries to popular writers), who were loosely affiliated with the radical movement, would juxtapose life "according to truth" (po pravde) with life according to the law in the Western meaning. Life according to the truth (i.e., life according to the dictums of Gemeinschaft culture) led to following a deep moral call, whereas life according to the law (formal adherence to human rights in their modern Western reading) implied merely a lack of concern for the fate of fellow human beings at best and in most cases actually implied the subjugation of the weak and unfortunate by those who were economically strong. In this context, democracy and its legalistic niceties did not mean much, and it was not surprising that some of the radicals joined the conservative intellectuals in openly proclaiming the authoritarian/totalitarian government (this term, of course, was not used at that time) as the system most appropriate for Russia and implicitly for the rest of the world.[4]

Similar to some of the conservatives, the radicals hailed force as the way of dealing with rivals and were convinced that the moral inferiority of their rivals would be translated into military weakness. The holistic similarities of the radicals and the conservatives, and subsequently the conservative view as a characteristic of the entire Russian culture, were apparent: the radicals sounded quite similar to the conservative intellectuals, while the conservative intellectuals often sounded like carbon copies of the radicals. Dostoevsky, quite a conservative thinker by the end of his life, noted sarcastically while commenting on the political liberties (human rights) in the West in general and France in particular:

> What is liberty? What is freedom? Equal freedom for each and all to do as they please within the limits of the law. When may a man do as he pleases? When he has a million. What is the man without a million? The man without a million is not one who does all that he pleases, but rather one with whom one does all that one pleases. And what follows from this? It follows that besides liberty there is still equality, or more precisely equality before the law. Only one thing can be said about this equality before the law. That is, as it is now put into practice, each Frenchman can and ought to consider it a personal insult (quoted in Walicki 1987:74).

The radicals followed the conservative intellectuals not only in their praise of the Gemeinschaft discourse and strong government and their frequent praise of force as the way of dealing with rivals but also in their actually contemptuous approach to the West. To be sure, the radicals found a good point in the French Revolution, the historical arch-symbol of the West in the minds of Russian intellectuals of all persuasions, not because it laid the foundation for the contemporary West but because it praised the terror, and it was here the radicals were often eager to follow suit. At the same time, the radicals, similar to the conservatives, totally rejected the revolution's major historical outcome—a capitalist society based on the principles of "1789," a society of Western human rights. The radicals followed the conservative intellectuals even in their most extravagant theoretical constructions and preached the deuniversalization of human rights (i.e., humanity not only should follow Russia but actually should be transformed to live in the Russian way) with messianic zeal.

As a matter of fact, Nikolai Fedorov, whose extravagant theories will be discussed below, was an intellectual hybrid who combined a radical's fascination with science, bordering upon semireligious worship, and revolutionary utopianism with the Russian messianism so dear to the conservative mind, with his belief that Russia was to play a special role in leading humanity to the omega of total salvation. He emphasized that this salvation could be achieved only if Westerners would totally abnegate their unhealthy traditions and way of life. Thus the similarity between the conservative and radical intellectual currents shows clearly that the conservative philosophers, including those with the most extravagant views, were not outsiders, and their views represented well the intellectual trends in the Russian culture in the late nineteenth century in general and the Russian approach to the problem of human rights in particular.

The Views of Four Intellectuals

In the present essay, the focus is on the views of several key Russian conservative intellectuals. While all of them discarded Western liberties and believed that the biggest part, if not all, of humanity should be transformed in the Russian way, each of them found special reasons to be proud of Russia's authoritarian tradition and the Gemeinschaft discourse which was inseparable from orthodox Christianity. For Tolstoy, who had a strong nationalistic feeling in the beginning of his long life, and Nikolai Danilevsky, the philosopher and political scientist, Russian superiority over the West had manifested itself in the ability to crush the foreigners. For Konstantin

Leont'ev, the essayist and philosopher, the strong autocracy made Russians more colorful and interesting people, which differentiated them from the flat and mediocre modern Westerners. For Nikolai Fedorov, an eccentric philosopher, the absence of human rights in the Western reading provided Russians with the ability to lead humanity in the grand project of the conquest of nature and victory over death. Indeed, more than anybody else's, his philosophy manifested messianic deuniversalization of human rights in Russian culture.

An analysis of these authors is to be the focus of my essay. At the same time, it will also dwell on the specifics of the Soviet interpretation of the Slavophile paradigms in respect to human rights and the problems which the integration of Western political discourse faced in post-Soviet Russia.

Tolstoy: The Case of Christian Collectivism

Tolstoy represented Slavophilism which, while maintaining the Gemeinschaft nature of Russian society, stressed that these characteristics had ensured Russia's strength in the confrontation with the West. In Tolstoy's view, the emotional bond between Russians was much stronger than the legal obligations of the people of the West. The idea of the West as being legalistic in its social discourse and Russia as being Christian or altruistic in the manifestation of its social interaction was related in the writer's mind with Russia as being emotional while the West was rational. In Tolstoy's view, the rationalism and dry legalism made Western people cruel, yet weak in their confrontations with Russians. While Tolstoy believed that Russians were superior to the Westerners due to their Christian nature, he also assumed that Christianity would finally triumph and the global community would be implicitly Russified to resemble the noble Christian-type heroes of his novels.

It seems that Tolstoy had developed these notions about the Western nations early on. In his early years, Tolstoy seems to have been under the strong influence of Rousseau (Troyat 1967:170), a Romantic philosopher who was quite fashionable in the middle of the nineteenth century. At that time, the philosopher's message was recast. In the eighteenth century, he was viewed mostly as the author of the social contract, which emphasized the rational judicial bonds between individuals and the state and among individuals. By the beginning of the nineteenth century, Rousseau was viewed as one of the major philosophers of the Romantic reaction. In this context, the message of his philosophy was quite different. Here it was stated that the philosopher emphasized that the judicial contract between people could hardly lead to a real human bond. It was a different type of bond which should be the foundation of the human community—the bond of the heart—and this could be found only among the simple folk. The simple people lived by their hearts and from this perspective were quite different from the rational calculating elite.

Tolstoy was fascinated with Rousseau, and this was possibly one of the reasons why he decided to visit France, the place where the great man had spent most of his life. While in Paris, Tolstoy saw an execution in which the criminal was guillotined (Troyat 1967:167). This event had a most profound impact on him. It was so profound that he remembered it well, even to the very end of his life when in his "Confession"[5] he tried to present to humanity the philosophy to follow.

Tolstoy, who had spent time in the army and had participated in the Crimean War, was not much shocked at the very ugliness of death. However, the execution was a killing of a different nature: in the war it was "emotional" killing; in the execution it was judicial killing. And the response of the crowd had an even greater impact on the young officer. The judicial killing was quite different in Tolstoy's mind from the spontaneous killing on the battle-field. Indeed, in Tolstoy's view, killing on the battlefield is more "natural" and less repugnant for it is the result of an emotional outburst. It could be done even by people with kind hearts. Tolstoy also viewed war implicitly as being caused by impersonal forces, as the manifestation of the spirit of violence, and here he was under the influence of Joseph de Maistre.[6]

The execution, however, took place by order of the court. Here Tolstoy understood the very nature of the execution as it was interpreted by Western judicial practice. The human being had an implicit contract with the other members of society to follow certain rules, and when he broke the contract the society had deprived him of his life. The cold implacability with which the judicial system functioned demonstrated clearly, in Tolstoy's view, the rational/pragmatic nature of the bonds among the people in Western society. The procedure showed clearly that the bonds between the people based on the judicial definition of their rights (the human rights in their Western meaning) were weak, and the state could easily dispose of those whom it regarded as being useless or dangerous. Here the Gesellschaft nature of human relationships was quite different from what was in Tolstoy's mind the nature of human relationships praised by Rousseau—relationships based on emotional bonds. The execution demonstrated to Tolstoy the superficiality of the liberalism of the Western state and the weakness of the ties between the state and the individual based on cold judicial norms. Here the execution confirmed in the eyes of Tolstoy what he had already found in the work of Rousseau.[7]

At the same time, the public aspect of the execution led to Tolstoy's greatest shock. The crowd that had come to see the execution arrived of their own free will. There were children in the crowd, and their parents had explained to them the reason for the execution (i.e., the breaking of the civil contract) and how "humanely" the guillotine operated. The view of the "awful crowd" had a most profound impact on Tolstoy (Troyat 1967:167). It proved to him not only the implicit falseness of the bond between the Western state and its citizens but also the implicit falseness of the relationship between the citizens of the West. It became clear to Tolstoy that relationships between people of the West were based exclusively on mutual interests and that there were no real bonds among them. All manifestations of politeness and friendliness were merely illusion. They were not friends, bonded by actual affection, but merely strangers, perhaps even enemies. The law did not so much guarantee their rights as it prevented them from being engaged in permanent war against each other. There were no internal restraints in their behavior, and as soon as the formal restraints the law enforced had fallen, they manifested their unrestrained individualism. It was this individualism which had made the Western man cruel and actually inhumane. At the same time, the same individualism weakened the unity of the Western people, and they would be unable to withstand a confrontation with people of a different mold.

The Christianity of the Russians manifested itself not in formal rituals but in the spontaneity of their character. It was emotional gravitation to each other and spontaneous, emotionally laden collectivism which marked the Russian national character. Their relationship was based, Tolstoy implied, not on the legal restraints of judicially defined human rights as they were understood by the West, but on the emotional and deeply internalized love for their fellow human beings. These Christian-type Gemeinschaft relationships defined Russian relationships—their relationships with each other as well as their relationships with the external world, including cases when they faced external threats. The Christian character of the Russian people and their absolute rejection of the formal legalistic bonds ensured their deep attachment to each other and thus their special strong sense of patriotism. The formal-legalistic patriotism of the West, based on the social contract of free individuals, could not stand against the emotionally loaded collectivistic character of the Russians. And this was the reason, in Tolstoy's view, why Russians had always prevailed against the West. He also implied that the West did not understand this very nature of the Russian national character. The Western people had assumed that since Russians had no "freedom" (human rights) they were nothing but slaves, a society with no internal co-hesiveness, and would be therefore easily be defeated by the West. This was implicitly, in Tolstoy's view, the case with Napoleon, who visualized himself as the great leader of the free West and who mistakenly expected that victory over the Russians would be easy.

Tolstoy's vision of the motivation for the invasion was controversial. Some scholars assumed that Tolstoy regarded the invasion of Russia as motivated by impersonal drives, and here Tolstoy was under the strong influence of Joseph De Maistre. On the other hand, it is clear that Tolstoy saw other roots for Napoleon's invasion. It is clear that for him Napoleon's invasion was the manifestation of Western individualism. The absence of internal restraints in the "free" individuals was a powerful impetus for self-aggrandizement. The invasion provided the opportunity for Western people to achieve fame and power. They strove to achieve this without any regard for the life of their fellow human beings. Tolstoy presented this vision of the Western people in his War and Peace.

Napoleon was a prime example of the brutal Western man. He was an individualist par excellence and easily sent millions of people to their deaths in battle (Tolstoy 1968 2:247). His marshals and soldiers were people with the same traits (Ibid. 2:413–14). Ambition, lust for fame, and greed were given free reign, for war had relieved them of judicial restraints. As soon as the judicial restraints had been lifted, they lost any sense of community with their fellow humans and thought that their brutal individualistic elan would lead them to easy victory over the Russians.

It seems that their views were justified in the sense that Russians, as Christian people, were hardly fit to be prime military material. A good ex-ample here was the peasant Karataev, chosen to be the epitome of the Rus-sian national character or at least to manifest one side of the Christian es-sence of the Russian soul. The reader of the book found Karataev to be a prisoner of war. He did not resist but took his position with humility and sort of cheerfulness. It seems that in a sort of twisted way he enjoyed being a prisoner. It was implied that this was due to Karataev's Christian approach to life. He saw in his position sort of an imitation of the suffering of Christ, and this provided him comfort. To make the resemblance between him and Christ almost identical, Tolstoy led Karataev to his death. En route, Karataev was unable to follow the other prisoners and French soldiers killed him. Karataev accepted death without resistance in the Christian manner. This Christian type of abnegation was not the only characteristic of the Russian people. The Christian approach to life, which implied the forsaking of one's personality, also implied love for one's fellow human beings, especially for those who had espoused the same Christian values, and this made the Russians formidable fighters who would defeat the French.

The Christian Russians had no negative feelings toward the Westerners. Their emotional collectivistic compassion did not alienate the people through legalistically defined rights but emphasized, through the negation of the notion of rights, the holistic unity of humanity. Russians, as the case of Bezukhov demonstrated clearly, were anxious to reciprocate the latent Christian feelings of the Westerners. Yet they felt the strongest feelings, of course, toward their fellow Russians, fellow Christians. The absence of rights as legally defined notions bound Russians together in a family type of unity. Here social distinctions did not play the role that they often played in the West. Indeed, in Tolstoy's work there was not even a hint of animosity between the peasants and their landlords. Consequently, a family type of unity, not antagonism, existed between the soldiers and the officers. This mutual abnegation was translated not only into a Christian type of passivity but also into the ease with which the Russian soldiers died in battle. In this case, they sacrificed their lives not for abstract human beings but defined these human beings primarily as Russians. And this Christian type of spirit made Russians, Tolstoy implied, indestructible on the battlefield. Indeed, the Russian Christian peasant soldiers had withstood, according to Tolstoy, the charge of the French on Borodino, the village near Moscow where the major confrontation between the Russian and French troops took place. The Russian retreat was due not to defeat but to a calculated decision. The French, Western men, had not been able to crush the Russians, and the French entrance into Moscow was actually the beginning of their defeat.

Indeed, Tolstoy implied, the unity of the French troops, like the unity of Western society, was not an organic, deeply internalized mutual bond of affection. It was the contractual unity of people who had been united for fulfillment of the personal goal of mutual aggrandizement and plunder. The ties between these people were either quite weak or actually nonexistent. And it was not surprising, in this case, that as soon as these Western people came to the conclusion that they would not be able to achieve this goal, their unity collapsed. This was implicitly how Tolstoy either explained the route of the French army just after the French troops had occupied Moscow or how he at least partially explained the nature of this route. Indeed, it was the absence of the internal Gemeinschaft bond which led to the almost immediate disintegration of the French army. Their external cohesiveness, similar to the cohesiveness of Western society in general, became an illusion, and the army was transformed into a horde of individuals who openly exhibited a lack of interest in each other in their pursuit of individual salvation.

It is clear that Tolstoy was quite proud of the power of the Russian soldiers who prevailed over the Westerners because of the superiority of the Christian Gemeinschaft humanism over the cold legalistic West. Yet the military victory was not at all in Tolstoy's mind when he thought about the interaction between the Russians and the Westerners in the long run. He believed this would be a spiritual victory which would lead to the spiritual transformation of the Westerners—their conversion into true Christians and, implicitly, their Russification.

The Russians did feel animosity toward the French. They could experience rage in the heat of battle. But as soon as the outburst of emotion was over, they not only felt no rage but were even compassionate toward those upon whom they had inflicted suffering in the battle. Moreover, they even felt a sort of guilt. The intensity of the Christian feelings in the Russian soul is so strong that it could even influence the cruel Western man.

Indeed, Tolstoy believed that Westerners and Russians are basically similar, despite their differences in national character and culture, in the holistic meaning of the word. All are human beings, "brothers in Christ," and the intensity of the Christian feeling radiating from the Russians would finally transform the Westerners. They would be Christianized and implicitly Russified, for Russians more than any other people on the globe, in the writer's view, manifested Christian spirituality, the deep emotional (but not formal legalistic) brotherhood of the people. Indeed, Tolstoy believed that each Russian could relate to a Russified/spiritualized Westerner on a deep existential level.

This was the case with P'er Bezukhov, one of the major heroes of the book. He was captured by the French and was suspected with the other prisoners of setting Moscow on fire. Together with the other suspected prisoners, Bezukhov was tried by a drumhead court with one of the French marshals as the chairman. The marshal looked at Bezukhov and was ready to pass judgment. As was the case with the other prisoners, it was most likely that Bezukhov would be condemned to death. Yet the marshal's eyes met Bezukhov's eyes, and a deep existential contact took place. The intensity of the Bezukhov's Christian feelings was so strong that they were apparent even to the French marshal, and he felt on a subconscious level that he was similar to Bezukhov, that they were all mortal human beings. The marshal identified with Bezukhov, and he spared his life. This action of the French marshal had broad and far-reaching implications. It demonstrated implicitly that spiritualization and Russification was not only achievable but was already happening; i.e., an increasing number of Westerners had begun to understand the falseness of the legalistic Western culture and accept the spiritual Russian values.

To sum up, it is certain that Tolstoy was convinced that the Russians would finally triumph in their confrontation with the Westerners, due to the Christian underpinning of their national character. Yet it was not military preponderance or reliance on military force which would secure the spread of Russian ideas. The point here, according to Tolstoy, was that the Russian idea is nothing but the Christian idea of love and compassion, and the writer became more convinced of this as he aged and his fame grew. He was certain that this idea would inevitably spread globally, providing the final transformation of humanity in the "Tolstovian way," i.e., nonviolently.

Nikolai Ia. Danilevsky: Christian Values as Inborn Instinct

In Danilevsky's case the Russian benign characteristics had become biological rather than the result of the Russian attachment to the Orthodox branch of Christianity. At the same time, these benign biological characteristics had ensured a dominant global position for the Russians and the other people who were close to them (i.e., other Slavic people and Asiatic people).

Danilevsky started his intellectual career as a radical (Vucinich 1976:97), and similar to the other radicals he had been influenced by Social Darwinism. When he left the conservative camp he duly incorporated Social Darwinism in his new philosophy. His point was that Russian benign characteristics and their military strength vis-à-vis the West were not the result of orthodoxy but rather the biological nature of the Slavic people. Sharply dividing the Westerners from the Slavs, Danilevsky insisted that Westerners were intrinsically bloodthirsty whereas Slavs were people with biologically intrinsic kindness. He also implicitly connected these characteristics and implicitly connected Western traits with their political and social organizations. In his view, the Western concern for political liberties was nothing but a manifestation of Western individualism. Individualism in its turn was essential for Western life for it provided a way of dividing the individuals and social groups and states for endless conflict. Danilevsky had traced this conflict from the dawn of European history. He saw its manifestation in the extermination of heretics and later in the terror of the French Revolution (Danilevsky 1885:119). In all cases, the call for freedom and liberties was just the assertion of one personality or group at the expense of another. As a matter of fact, these groups and personalities were pitilessly exterminated.

While the West had been intrinsically aggressive in the struggle for freedom (actually the subjugation of others) as one of the manifestations of Western traits, the benign nature of the Slavic East was reflected, among other things, in the Russian disregard for individualism and embracing of spontaneous, emotional collectivism where the love for fellow human beings was not derived from cold legal obligations (love could hardly be postulated in legal terms) but was a spontaneous flow from the kind Slavic heart (ibid.: 199).

Since dry legalistic discourse was foreign to the Slavic soul, Russians had never thought about benefits when they decided to help the unfortunate. Napoleon's campaign against Russia was a case in point. According to Danilevsky Napoleon did not actually constitute a real danger for Russia; Russians should be able to find a common language with him and share the domination over Europe and possibly over the world (Ibid.:40–41). This sort of arrangement would be perfectly legal in the context of international law; they were legalistically right, yet they were morally wrong. Russians, contrary to the Westerners, could not accept the notion that they should suppress other nations. This would contradict the very essence of their Slavic soul. For this very reason, a Russian alliance with Napoleon did not work. Moreover, Russian conflict with Napoleon was so protracted because of their desire to help the Europeans. The Russian czar should have been able simply to drive Napoleon from Russia and strike an alliance with him on new terms. Yet the Russian czar had proceeded with the war, and the reason was simple: he wanted to liberate Europe. Europeans, however, had responded to Russia with continuous hostility, and this was understandable, in Danilevsky's view: they were absolutely biologically incompatible with Russians. The biologically intrinsic kindness would not make Russians weak in their confrontation with the West. In Danilevsky's view, this kindness would be translated into toughness which would make Russians formidable fighters. Western conquerors (such as Napoleon) had failed to conquer the Russians because the Russians as a different ethnic group could not be easily defeated as was the case in a war waged by one European power against another. At the same time, the Russians could translate their biological difference from the Westerners into cultural difference with collectivism as a hallmark. This collectivistic spirit and general hostility to the West had made Russians natural allies of the Asian people, and united with them the Russians would be invincible not only in repelling a Western onslaught but also in imposing its domination over Westerners. At that point Danilevsky was so engrossed in proving Russia's military superiority that he had forgotten not only about Russia's intrinsic meakness but also about her revulsion in regard to conquest.

Military preponderance over the Westerners was apparently much more important for Danilevsky than for Tolstoy. Contrary to Tolstoy, he did not envisage the transformation of Westerners into Russians. Yet a Russian victory over the West was not to be regarded as the building of a Western type of empire (i.e., a political and international construction in which Russia as the master would dominate the West for political and material benefits). He viewed the Russian goal in dealing with the West as protecting humanity (foremost of all, the Slavic and Asiatic people) against Western predatory expansion. Danilevsky implied that the military preponderance of Russia would eventually lead to absorbing not only the Slavic people but also the Asians in a sort of Eurasian community. In this case, the values shared by Russians would be deeply internalized by the majority of humanity, if not by all of it (it is clear that Danilevsky had little hope of transforming most of the Westerners).

Konstantin N. Leont'ev: Despotism as a Symbol of Beauty

Leont'ev was certainly an interesting case, for he believed the Russian strength was caused not by the benign love-embracing spirit, not by the orthodox harmony (sobornost'/symphony) between the people and collectivism, but by absolute submission to the collective will and the power of the leader. It might be said that Leont'ev, more than any other Russian thinker of the imperial period, could be regarded as a totalitarian. Yet, while praising the absolute submission to authority of collectivity and, even more, to the ruler, Leont'ev asserted that the personality would not disappear in this system. To the contrary, a much stronger personality would be forged. This individuality, while existing in total submersion in collectivity, would constitute a certain and peculiar type of harmony with collectivism. A peculiar type of harmony would be achieved, and here Leont'ev could still be placed in the context of the Slavophile tradition. He would be, of course, close to Danilevsky. Still he should be placed apart from him: For Danilevsky Russian military might was the major point of concern, whereas for Leont'ev it was the aesthetic quality of the Russian autocracy and implicitly the totalitarian regime of the future which would make Russia great and the West repugnant. Still, Leont'ev was similar to Danilevsky from another point of view in that he assumed that the Russian experience would be internationalized, and in the long run the "Russian idea" (which Leont'ev actually defined as the totalitarian state) would triumph globally.

Leont'ev believed that the Russian advantage over the West was not the result of special cultural traditions. He did not make much of the fact that Russians, contrary to the people of the West, were orthodox Christians. Here he was quite different from the traditional Slavophiles for whom the Russian orthodoxy was not just a historical trait which could have been attached to any nation. Many Slavophiles implied that orthodoxy was divinely given, and the very fact that Russians were orthodox showed that they were chosen by God, and the entire business of conversion into orthodoxy was an act of divine revelation of some sort. For Leont'ev, Russia was not much different from the West. As a matter of fact, the West had enjoyed greatness in the past at the time when modern liberties, or "human rights," had been foreign to Western society (of course Leont'ev did not use such a term as human rights). The West was a great civilization when the West had been run by strong rulers and when individuals were submerged in castes, dissolved in corporate bodies, and of course were absolutely submissive to the rulers. The greatness of the West was manifested in the great personalities which the West was able to produce at that time. These were personalities of extraordinary human qualities, and their creativity was manifested not only in great works of art but also in their behavior. Most of these people were libertines, were bloodthirsty, and in general had no moral scruples whatsoever. Yet it was their very amorality which would have been impossible without the healthy authoritarian underpinning of the Western culture and which made them and the period in which they lived worthy of consideration.

The great traditions of the Western culture did not die, even when the idea of human rights (political liberties and the idea of equality of the people before the law) began to emerge in Western political discourse. Leont'ev even implied that Western culture had actually reached its acme at that time. He praised not only the great masters of the Renaissance but even the perverted rulers and found the greatest delight in the cynical streak in the philosophy of the Enlightenment (Leont'ev 1912–13 6:34), the terrorists of the French Revolution (54), Napoleon's despotism (219), and the ease with which he disposed of millions to satisfy his lust for glory and power. Yet as the events passed, the very essence of the French Revolution had revealed itself. Unfortunately, in Leont'ev's view, this essence was not the manifestation of the great terrorism and brutality which would have preserved the aesthetic glory of Western civilization, but the principles of 1789, the principles of political liberties (human rights) which had finally become entrenched in Western society. The rights of the citizens were upheld, democracy triumphed, and this, from Leont'ev's view, was the end. He saw Western society as being run by neat, law-abiding, and hardworking philistines, and this sort of people and this sort of discourse were, for him, the death knell for Western culture, for the brutality, perversion, and amorality had disappeared from life, replaced by the mediocrity of the modern West (29).

At the same time, Russia was fortunate. The country's luck was not due, in Leont'ev's view, to the blessing of Christianity in its orthodox form. Leont'ev saw even less benefit in Slavic racial characteristics. Indeed, he was rather skeptical in regard to this. The country's major advantage was its backwardness. Leont'ev did not elaborate upon how Russia was able to achieve this. He implied that possibly it might be due to the benign influence of the Mongol yoke. It had inculcated the country with a good dose of respect for strong power, and even the influence of the West was unable to erase it completely. The Russian autocracy and, in many respects, the entire fabric of Russian society had been premodern and anti-Western in its very essence. The individual in Russia had no rights and had been submerged in collectivity, entrapped in the bureaucratic web, and enslaved by the autocracy. As a matter of fact, autocratic Russia was quite close to what would be the socialist society.

Leont'ev felt sort of ambivalent toward socialism. On one hand, socialism was the enemy of the Russian autocracy to which Leont'ev was deeply attached. Socialists also promised that the coming socialist society would be even more democratic, therefore ugly in Leont'ev's view, than the existing

Western regimes. Yet Leont'ev, with his prophetic vision, stated that the triumph of socialism would create a society much more despotic than any of the present and past rulers could imagine. For this very reason, Leont'ev gave Russian socialism a sort of twisted blessing (186). So, whatever was the way of the Weltgeist, it was most likely that Russia would emerge as an authoritarian or totalitarian state. Of course, Leont'ev did not use the term, but those characteristics of the society which he liked and which he projected for Russia fit well the description of totalitarian societies in modern political thought.

So it was most likely that Russia would be an anti-democratic state, and it was precisely this which would make Russia great, for she was able to produce a great culture and great personalities. Leont'ev also added that besides the aesthetic qualities, the strong power of the autocracy made Russia militarily strong. One reason for this was that Russia's rejection of Western liberalism made her quite similar to the Asian countries. (Leont'ev definitely felt a sort of attachment to the East.) The reason for the mutual gravitation was clear. The Asian countries felt the same revulsion for Western democracy as Russia. United with Asia, Russia would not only be able to repulse the Western onslaught but possibly could impose her domination over the West. Despite all of his belief that Russia would prevail in the conflict with the West and his praise of the wholesomeness of the country's authoritarian tradition, Leont'ev often looked into the future with premonition. Indeed, he occasionally expressed doubt that Russia would be able to withstand the temptation, and Western liberalism would be able to pollute the Russian culture with its democratic values. Nothing good would result from this. Not only would Russia be transformed into an ugly liberal regime of the West — Leont'ev implied that it could be even more ugly than the regimes of the West — but the country would definitely lose its spirit of resistance and would perish. Leont'ev implied that in this case the major threat for Russia would come not from the West, which together with Russia would fall when confronted by the Chinese, whose superiority would be unchallenged due to their preservation of the traditions of Oriental despotism.

Yet even in this scenario in which the hordes of Asiatics conquered and absorbed most of the world, Leont'ev's view enjoyed a sort of twisted global optimism. Indeed, the major point of Leont'ev's philosophy was the "ugliness" of liberal democracy as major evil. The transformation of humanity to a "beautiful" totalitarian society could be done by the Asiatics. In this case, the "Russian idea" in the process of the cultural and historical transmutation would be transformed into the "Chinese idea," and while Weltgeist might change the external appearance of the "Russian idea" (the aesthetic "truth" of totalitarian discourse), its global predominance and the absorption of all of humanity would be guaranteed. In this Leont'ev might find some sort of consolation.

Nikolai F. Fedorov: The Case of Millenarian Totalitarianism

Nikolai Fedorov is a good example of a Russian philosopher who viewed the absence of human rights in their Western reading as the major reason for Russia's special role. In Fedorov's view, it was the Russians who would unite humanity for the grand design of the resurrection of the dead and the spreading of humanity over the cosmos. Fedorov apparently is not the most original among the discussed philosophers, but he is important for another reason. More than any other philosopher discussed in our study, Fedorov demonstrated the essential aspect in the late nineteenth century of the discarding of human rights (in the Western reading) by the Russians. Fedorov emphasized that the anti-Western discourse should not be limited to Russians or their allied Slavs and Asians. It should expand beyond the confinement of living humanity to have truly global and cosmic dimensions.

Fedorov's philosophy should be placed in the Russian as well as the European context. On one hand, Fedorov's ideas were apparently derived from Russian historical tradition. Religion was a key element in Russian political culture. Russians were the only independent orthodox people, and perhaps they related their Russianness with orthodoxy more than did other orthodox Europeans (e.g., Serbians). The idea of death and resurrection is the existential foundation of Christianity, and it was not accidental that this idea was central in Russian intellectual discourse. On the other hand, Fedorov's ideas were a product of European thought. Indeed, the nineteenth century was a time of belief in science. It was expected that science could solve all of the problems of society. Some of the Western thinkers assumed that the ideal society would be a society of scholars. Comte could be an example of such an approach. Thus Fedorov's teaching was mostly derived from Russian tradition, reinforced by the traditions of European thought.

The point of Fedorov's philosophy was the assumption that the project of resurrection could be achieved only if the Russian czardom dominated the globe. He assumed that autocracy as a global force was the only real prerequisite for this grand project and that dominating the West would be the only major stumbling block. Clearly the existence of Western society with its human rights (e.g., Western individualism) was seen by Fedorov as a major problem for the accomplishment of his plans.

Fedorov's negative view of Western individualism was due to his assumption that humanity could start immediately to think about the resurrection of the dead. He believed that humanity already enjoyed the technological and scientific capabilities to engage in preparation for the project, except for the Western people with their obsessive individualism. Fedorov derived the problems of the Western individualism and individualism as the phenomenon par excellence from the Western person's disbelief in the resurrection and abandoning of their dead parents.

Indeed, as Fedorov implied, the logic of the Western people was as follows. They assumed that they would die and their life is just a transitory phenomenon. They also implied that the spirit could not live separately from the flesh. Consequently they regarded the life of their flesh as the most important and Epicureanism as the only real philosophy of life. The point of Epicureanism, Fedorov implied, was to achieve maximum pleasure, and in his view it was sex which provided maximum pleasure for the individual. And it was not surprising that it was sexuality which had become the focal point of Western culture since the dawn of the modern era. Fedorov saw sexuality as the underpinning of all types of activities of Western individuals, mostly, of course, male, for they, more than the females, had been driven by sexual desire all of their lives.[8] In Fedorov's view, all aspects of activity in Western civilization were derived from sexual desire. Culture and art had played, in this context, the role of the coloring of the feathers in birds and the fur of animals. The attractive colors of the male bird were designed by nature to attract the female bird. In the same fashion, the art of Western man had been created to attract the opposite sex. Industry was also developed to provide the Western male with items such as clothes which would make him more attractive to the opposite sex. The same could be said in regard to female fashions, for the females' concern with their apparel was also due to their desire to arouse the males.

The political construction of the Western world was also a derivative of sexuality. Wars, for example, in Fedorov's vision, were the result of Western men's desire to protect their females from competing males and to ensure, in case of success of the military company, the acquisition of new sexual domains, to enlarge and expand their sexual access. Thus it is not surprising that Fedorov viewed human rights as "sexual rights," which could be placed in the context of social/sexual discourse in two ways. First, "human rights," individual liberties, and contractual obligations were needed to shirk any responsibilities to society, which was viewed here in the holistic sense as the community of living and dead. The end of the responsibilities was in this case mostly interpreted as the end of responsibilities to "the dead fathers." Their "living sons" abandoned them in order to engage in sexual pursuits. "Human rights," or liberties in their Western reading, were needed to ensure the possessive rights of the males, their sexual access. Secondly, the liberties were needed for expanding the sexual domain and intensifying the sexual pleasures to the extreme.

In the philosopher's view, the entire history of Western civilization was nothing but the expansion of individualism and shirking of responsibility. The beginning of the liberation, as Western thought interpreted it, was for Fedorov nothing but constant degeneration. For Fedorov, the Renaissance was the beginning of the end. The point here was that the Renaissance had marked the beginning of the departure from Christianity, which was based on principles foreign to modern civilizations. Indeed, the point of Christianity was concern with duty and sacrifice and disregard for earthly pleasures, sexual pursuit first of all. Christianity was also focused on death and the resurrection.

The Renaissance was the beginning of the end of this tradition, and it was the terrestrial instead of the celestial world which became the central focus of human discourse. Flesh and implicitly sex started to emerge as the central aspect of concern. The eighteenth century with its philosophy of Enlightenment had made the great leap forward in this abandonment of the duty-death-resurrection philosophy of life and departure to the philosophy of rights-liberty-flesh-sex oriented life (Fedorov 1906 1:495). In the philosopher's view, the striving of the protagonists of the Enlightenment for liberties had a deep sexual orientation and was marked by extreme individualism (Young 1979:25). The French monarchy was, in his view, the last symbol of the Middle Ages. As an institution, it was deeply connected with the church and its idea that life should not be striving for pleasure but sacrifice and collaboration with God in his labor to achieve the cosmic millennium and final resurrection of the "dead fathers." It is clear that Fedorov assumed that the ancient regime was oriented toward resurrection, even when its protagonists were not aware of the regime's metaphysical goal. The drive for political liberties was actually nothing but a drive for sexual liberties, the end of erotic inhibitions. There was another sexual implication of the philosophy of Enlightenment. Fedorov implied that the philosophy of the Enlightenment was drenched in witticism and cynicism. This manifestation of the ideas of the Enlightenment was also not accidental. Witticism/cynicism had liberated the people from restraints and provided the appropriate setting for immorality manifested in lecherous behavior. Witticism also was the way that the male attracted the female. In Fedorov's view, the French salons were the places where both male and female had found a receptive setting to find mates, to find sex objects. The terrestrial pleasures of present life had been the point of omega where the duties toward the "dead fathers" had been abandoned. Even more, the French monarchy, which had been a political and social symbol of this duty toward the "dead fathers," was the point of ridicule and hatred. One could construct here the conflict between the ancient regime and the new spirit of Enlightenment almost in Freudian terms. It was conflict between "libido" (the philosophy of Enlightenment in which the drive for political liberation was nothing but a drive for sexual liberation) and "superego," the French monarchy, the ancient regime as a set of institutions and norms focused on sacrifice and concern with society as a holistic unity of the living and the dead.

In the conflict, it was the "libido" of terrestrial eroticism which had finally triumphed over the restrictive "superego" of the ancient regime, and this conflict was known in history under the name of the French Revolution. The Revolution was a manifestation of terrestrial sexuality and logically was at odds with the duty toward dead fathers. The French revolutionaries had actually hated the "dead fathers" who reminded them of their duty toward the dead and, of course, about their own perishability. It is not surprising in this case that the French Revolution was marked by the destruction of the churches, cemeteries, libraries, and archives (Fedorov 1906 1:522).

While the West had been obsessed with the sexual drive, which it had presented as a drive for freedom, Russia was a country from a different mold. The point here was that Russians were driven not by sexual pleasures but by their love for their parents. This had changed the entire Russian approach to life. While the Western person had emphasized liberty and legally defined rights, the Russians had emphasized duty and sacrifice. It was clear why it was a focus of their discourse: without the emphasis on duty, the great work of resurrection of the "dead fathers" would not be achieved, and it goes without saying that personal immortality would not be achieved and the entire history would be meaningless.

For Fedorov the reason that humanity was not engaged in the great work of resurrection was a simple one: it was sexual pursuit, and it was directly related to political liberties. For this very reason, he thought that the czardom was not only the key to Russian political culture but the key to global salvation as well. In his view, the czardom was to control the entire globe. Fedorov, of course, preferred that the unification would be peaceful, yet he thought that war could be regarded as a possible solution of the problem. This Russian army should be, of course, "Christ loving," and Fedorov insisted that rewards should be given for sparing lives, not for the number killed (300). Of course, in Fedorov's view the global conquest by the Russians would not be similar to the European empires. The point here is that while Europeans looked at the empire in the context of the domination/possessive philosophy derived from their sexual pursuits, the Russians had a different attitude. They looked at their global expansion not as the creation of an empire but as the incorporation of the people of the earth into the family. For Fedorov, Russia itself was not a state in the European sense but a family, or to be precise it was a metaphysical family, i.e., the organizational design for fulfilling the ultimate goal of humanity—the resurrection of the "dead fathers."

Fedorov saw the global domination by the czar and, implicitly, the end of the Western human rights (political liberties in the Western reading) as the major prerequisite or at least one of the most important preconditions for the achievement of his plans. On the surface, he had visualized the traditional Slavophile type of family state. In the Slavophile view, at least in the view of the traditional Slavophiles at the beginning of the nineteenth century, a family type of state should be Christian and loving and emphasize affectionate relationships between subjects and their ruler. Fedorov's approach was quite different in that respect. He saw the future society as highly regimented and similar to the army. As a matter of fact, he regarded the army as a model for social organization (Fedorov 1913 2:462). The totalitarian streak of Fedorov's philosophy, the absolute submission of the individual to the power of collectivity, was to deindividualize and desexualize him, to transform his life and the life of society. Then, individuals and society as a whole would be led to achieve the final end of history, to expel death (in Fedorov's vision, the only enemy).

Inspired, or coerced if necessary, the individual would be engaged in almost around the clock work to prepare for the resurrection. This insistence on almost sleepless and sexless life stemmed both from Fedorov's personal life (he spent only a few hours in sleep—he hated sleep for it reminded him of death) and from his philosophy. Indeed, he believed that the Western workers insisted on limited working hours because of their desire not to be involved in the "common task" of working toward the resurrection. He implicitly connected this striving for a limited working day with the desire of the European workers and citizens in general for political liberties, which were connected in Fedorov's mind with Western sexual obsessions. One could reconstruct how Fedorov viewed the life of a unified humanity led by Russia.

It is clear that Fedorov believed that most of the people should be engaged in ordinary toil, mostly in the countryside, until the omega was achieved and complete mastery over nature replaced ordinary agriculture with a new futuristic way of obtaining food. Federov did not regard this providing of substance to the people as the major goal of the society and the major goal of unified humanity. The major goal was the resurrection and total control over nature. The point of Fedorov's approach was that resurrection was to be physical, in flesh and bones, not a symbolical resurrection. Human beings would be just reassembled from their remains, and their spirituality was also to be reconstructed from the spiritual remains, so to speak. For this reason, Fedorov assumed that society should have natural centers—the cemetery, the library, the museum, and laboratory.

The cemetery was the place where the remains of the dead were located. Consequently, they were to be taken care of and preserved, for they would be needed for the actual reassembling of the human body. Fedorov believed that particles of the dead had been scattered, not only all over the earth but all over the cosmos, so the complete resurrection would be the enterprise which would require major technological improvement and would be relegated to the future.

The library and the museum in Fedorov's project would occupy a place secondary to that of the cemetery. The point here was that the resurrection would require not just a physical reconstruction of the body but a complete reconstruction of the human being in its entirety, and it would be the library and the museum where one could find the spiritual traces of the perished human being.[9] Books and artifacts were the spiritual particles which could be reassembled in the same way as the physical particles.

The final place of concentration should be the laboratory. Fedorov discarded all or at least the bulk of the current science, both natural and social sciences. The point here, of course, was the fact that science had been oriented in the wrong way with wrong values (i.e., the political/sexual liberation of humanity). The problem with science was not that it was oriented to the human body; the crux of the problem was that it was oriented to the body as a transient phenomenon, as perishable flesh trying to snatch morsels of sexual pleasure while sliding toward the abyss of eternal death. In the context of the new universal metaphysical theocracy led by the Russian czar and inspired by advisers such as Fedorov, science would change its direction completely. Its new goal would be to investigate the problem of death, to discover how death could be overcome and the "dead fathers" resurrected, and to enable humanity to enjoy eternal life, spreading itself all over cosmic space. And the philosopher envisaged the time when an immense army of resurrected humans, presumably led by the Russian czar, would start "the conquest of the entire Universe, from the nearby solar systems to those planets which are not detectable even by the strongest telescope" (Fedorov 1913 2:632).

It is clear that in this case the "Russian truth," i.e., the discarding of legalistic discord and human rights as a derivation (all of which Fedorov had hated with a fierce intensity) would have truly universalistic meaning. What could be more universalistic than the spread of "Russian ideas," the Russian form of Christianity (indeed, the only true form of Christianity in Fedorov's view), all over the cosmos by resurrected humans who apparently would be spiritually Christianized/Russified in the process of their resurrection?

Human Rights in Context: From Imperial to Soviet Ideology

Thus, the key elements of the philosophy of Russian conservative intellectuals were the discarding of Western society and, consequently, the modern Western notion of human rights, and this rejection was the rejection of the Western model as universally applicable. These ideas of the conservative thinkers were not just those of a still-limited group of intellectuals, but represented well the Russian culture in the late nineteenth century which cut across the political spectrum This explains why the conservatives and the majority of the radical intellectuals, despite their external sharp differences, were essentially the same. This nationalistic animus did not make the Russian nationalistic discourse with its rejection of human rights in their Western reading particularly special.

As a matter of fact, it could be seen from the late nineteenth century on in many cultures which had started to resist the Western domination. Even those countries which had originally accepted the Western legalistic culture, with human rights as its essential aspect, as being inevitable for those who wished to enter into the modern era and reap its benefits (the might and imperial splendor, first of all) had started to reconsider their views in many respects. The universality of the Western legalistic discourse was beginning to be challenged. Here Japan could be an example. The country had absorbed Westernization wholeheartedly during the Meiji Restoration, and the economic aspects of its modernization had continued unabated into the twentieth century. Yet in the political and especially the intellectual realm, a reverse movement could be detected, and if this reverse momentum did not lead to complete negation of the Western experience (i.e., if capitalism and therefore the legalistic discourse were not completely obliterated), it seriously deformed it. It certainly was not the principles of the American or French Declarations which inspired the samurai in their charges in the jungles of Malaysia or in the bombing of Pearl Harbor. The same could be said about Japan's major European ally whose tank armies were hardly led by the spirit of the French or American Declaration while traversing the plains of Eurasia. Here one could see not just the discarding of human rights (in the modern meaning) as universally applicable but an actual attempt to universalize the discarding of many aspects of the liberal Western discourse. Yet in this universalization of the discarding of human rights neither the Japanese nor the Germans were absolutely universalistic. Here the point was not that the capitalist legalism was not absolutely eradicated (even in Nazi Germany, private property was still the very foundation of society, even though the institution of private property had been deformed by the Gemeinschat rationale of the totalitarian state). The point was different.

The German National Socialists were convinced of the superiority of their race and the political and social machinery which emanated from the Aryan folk. It was this machinery which they believed would ensure their global predominance. Yet they did not intend to push others to accept the dictums of the Aryan culture. That, according to the Nazis, would have been an impossible undertaking. "Untermenschen" could and most likely would retain their attachments to the "rotten" democracy, and it was this which would lead them to destruction. The story with the Russian nationalists in the late nineteenth century and to some degree with the entire Russian intellectual milieu (for the conservative nationalists, as was stated above, represented the Russian culture in general) was that they were indeed pure universalists.

In their view the Russian culture with its implicit disregard for human rights was not just the best for Russia, not just the force which would ensure the country's military predominance in the case of conflict with the West, but the principle which was morally superior to the legalistic discourse with human rights as the point of departure. The Russians believed they were mighty because they were the only people of Christ, the people of "truth" ("pravdy"), whose deep and sincere concern for the human being was infinitely higher from a moral standpoint and (as was the case with Leont'ev) infinitely aesthetically superior to the societal principles which upheld the democracies of the West. The moral and so to speak salvational implications of the "truth" (the praise of the "truth" as opposed to the ugliness of "non-truth," the legalistic discourse of the modern West, is even entwined in Leont'ev's praise of the aesthetic implications of totalitarian discourse) and the cosmic implications of the "truth" in Fedorov's teaching implied that the Russian "truth" should be truly universalized. It should not be limited to Russians, even though they considered themselves "a chosen people"[10] and for this reason, they should receive special credit for discovering the "truth." Indeed the Russian "truth" should secure global domination for Russia, not so much as the strongest power but as the most moral people. (In point of fact, the assumption that Russia should dominate others only on the basis of force, in the fashion of Westerners, would be repugnant to quite a few of the nationalistic intellectuals.) The Russian "truth" should be deeply internalized by all or at least the majority of the nations of the globe. In fact they should be "Russified" in the process of accepting the idea of an autocratic and collectivistic Gemeinschaft society as the only morally applicable society, as the only way of salvation.

In the process of "Russification," the process of being incorporated in a grand orthodox community of humanity in which other creeds would be just particular cases of the totality of the orthodox "truth," the nations of the earth, including the West, or at least the majority of humanity should shake reject the fallacies of the Western legalistic culture with human rights as its essential aspect. While some of the present-day supporters of the idea of human rights (actually the Gesellschaft society) are firmly convinced that the world will be lost unless it follows the dictum of Americanization, the Russian thinkers of the late nineteenth century were equally convinced that their creed of the discarding of human rights should be universalized. In both cases, the preaching of the universalism of these respective creeds was important because these statements were not just fleeting cultural phenomena—they had important implications for the respective traditions and corresponding values which were shared to various degrees by a considerable portion of both the elite and the masses.

The nationalistic statements of the Russian intellectuals which dominated the Russian culture in the late nineteenth century had started to undergo important changes by the beginning of the twentieth century. The revolutionary shakeups of 1905 and 1917 had convinced quite a few of the Russian intellectuals that the country was experiencing its own version of the French Revolution. The external similarities of many aspects of the political events in Russia and those in revolutionary France had convinced growing numbers of the Russian intellectuals that Russia was "France," i.e., a Western country. This sense of belonging to the West was reinforced not only by the magnetism of Western Europe's supremacy, which had reached its acme by the beginning of the twentieth century, but also by the continuous erosion of the patriarchal economy and the social structure which was the economic foundation for the Gemeinschaft nationalism of the nineteenth century which had discarded the notion of political democracy with human rights as an essential component of it. While the assumption that the old autocracy had no universal appeal and was hardly even suited for Russia started to spread—even the monarchists had started to abandon this idea—there were signs that the degree to which Russian society had been transformed into the Western order had been overestimated. This could be seen not just in the still-dominant patriarchal type of economy in the country's life (most of the peasantry, the majority of the population, still lived in communes) but in the ideological manifestation of Russian Westernism, particularly in its representatives' approach to the French Revolution, the principles of 1789.

The point here was not in their vision of terror, as some historians have claimed. In their view, the radical attachment to the French terror was an essential sign of the fragility of the democratic tradition. One may challenge this proposition. Indeed, the idea of terror was not central in the Russian radicals' appeal to the French Revolution. The majority of them had emphasized that while the way the revolutionary populace could deal with its enemies was an important reason for them to turn to the French example, more important was the democratic tradition of the French Revolution. Here the intellectuals, especially those who were on the far left of the political spectrum, stated that their appreciation of the democratic tradition of the French Revolution did not mean that they should stop with capitalist democracy. It was, of course, better for the masses than the autocracy, yet it was still limited to benefitting mostly the upper classes of the society. The goal of the Russian Revolution in this cases was not just to achieve formal liberties for the people (human rights) but to surpass them in the highest form of democracy. The sense that the Russian Revolution should surpass the limits of the French Revolution and the capitalist society created by the revolution had demonstrated the weakness of the Gesellschaft elements in the Russian culture, and consequently the Gemeinschaft Russian nationalism could easily reenter the stage as the major player. This indeed happened during the 1917 Revolution.

The collapse of the czardom was viewed by quite a few of the Russian liberals and especially by the Western liberals as the beginning of a new era. In their view, Russia should henceforth be a democratic society where mutual respect for human rights would be the basis for social interaction. Yet something different occurred. The Russian society did not plunge into the process of forging a Western democracy, with human rights as the cornerstone of the social interaction. Instead there was a great boost to anarchy. The Bolsheviks who had come to power in October/November 1917 claimed that they represented the workers and the peasants. They also claimed that they belonged to the West, following the footsteps of the French Revolution. Indeed, they claimed that they were "super Western" in the sense that they would spur the worldwide proletarian revolution which was a logical outcome of the development of Western civilization. They also continued to insist, following the logic of the development of Western civilization, that they would bring freedom (human rights) to Russia and ultimately to the global community. The only difference would be that in Soviet Russia and in the future global Soviet community the freedom (human rights) would be real, whereas they were a sham in the modern West. Yet while asserting that they would push Russia and the entire globe to the creation of a civilization of great freedom, the Bolsheviks actually acted in many ways similar to the most conservative Russian nationalists who lamented the anarchy and disintegration of the Russian empire. Indeed, while decimating the rank and file of their political enemies, the Bolsheviks disciplined the masses and forged by terror a powerful Red Army. This was not missed by some acute observers among the Bolshevik opponents who stated with satisfaction that they had not seen such disciplined forces since the

beginning of World War I and praised the Bolsheviks for achieving what
they had not been able to achieve (Rapoport 1930:242–47). By the end of
the Civil War when the Bolsheviks had reassembled the Russian empire,
some of the Whites had indeed come to the conclusion that the Bolsheviks,
regardless of their slogans and intentions, had actually accomplished the
program of the Russian nationalists who were most concerned with preserving Russian "united and indivisible."

After the end of the Civil War (1921), the Bolshevik government launched
the NEP (New Economic Policy) which legitimized some private property.
NEP made Russia look "more normal" from the perspective of some of the
Russian nationalists. At the same time, the continuous antidemocratic rule of
the regime and the messianic overtones in their dealings with the West provided additional support for their statements that Soviet Russia actually had a
nationalistic and authoritarian tradition and the Soviet brand of Marxism was
nothing but a transmogrified Russian messianic nationalism. This was the
conviction of Nikolai V. Ustrialov (1890–1938), who proclaimed that the
Bolshevik government actually had abandoned Marxism with its concern
for the worldwide proletariat and had been converted to hardcore Russian
nationalism.[11] Ustrialov was quite right in his observations, for Russian nationalism became one of the key elements in the official Soviet discourse
during the 1920s and by the 1930s had become quite important in the
official ideology. As a matter of fact, the official Soviet ideology had openly
praised Russian nationalism and regarded the Russian rulers such as Peter
the Great and Ivan the Terrible as great leaders. While Russian nationalism
(similar in many ways to the traditional nationalism from the imperial past
with all of its traditional views on human rights) had played an important
role in the ideological discourse, the Soviet Russian nationalism was not a
carbon copy of the Russian nationalism of the imperial past. The point here
was not only that Russian nationalism was conditioned by Marxism. There
were also other reasons why Russian nationalism, while retaining its basic
premises, had been deformed by other ideological trends, those which were
broader than the traditional prerevolutionary Russian nationalism.

The Soviet Regime and the Slavophile Legacy

In the pre-World War II period in the USSR, the Russians had found
themselves not only isolated from the majority of the Slavic nations in many

ways but at odds with most of them, just because they belonged to the capitalist world while the Soviet Union was a country of a different political system. Although the Soviet Union was formally recognized by scores of Western powers, it was still the outcast of the global community. At the same time, the Soviet Union had achieved internal cohesiveness in the sense that official propaganda had emphasized that after the eradication of the "exploiters," the toilers of the USSR were bound together by feelings of unity, for all of them had been citizens of the "first country of workers and peasants." The propaganda further emphasized that the people of the Soviet Union, both Slavic and non-Slavic groups, had lived together for centuries in one state and for this reason had a strong influence upon each other. This historical tradition had been blended with the assumption that all citizens of the USSR should be bound together for social as well as historical reasons. In this context, Marxism was "nationalized," and a new quasi-ethnic and quasi-cultural entity had emerged. The official Soviet publications referred to the "Soviet people," and emigres just called Soviet Russia "Eurasia"—a unique blend of cultures and civilizations in its own right. At the end of World War II when the USSR extended its geopolitical presence into Eastern and Central Europe, the Slavophile identity reemerged in a new form. Indeed, most of the people of the area were Slavic, and the reinvented Slavophilism helped to justify their incorporation into the Soviet empire. Yet the focus was still on the Soviet/Eurasian identity.

The Soviet leaders had vehemently rejected the idea that they had ever abandoned Marxism as their ideological banner, and indeed Marxism was essential for them to legitimize themselves through the revolution and the new order created in the wake of it. Marxism was the product of Western culture, and the acceptance of Marxism implied an adherence to democratic principles. Indeed, through the entire Soviet history, the leaders emphasized that they did not confront Western civilization with its democratic principles but just surpassed it. In their view, the Soviet Union had achieved much more in the liberation of the people than had been done by the capitalist West. The USSR, in this case, was not just "Western" but a "super-Western" civilization, the future of the global community. Yet Marxism with its Westernizing essence was just the external layer of the official Soviet political philosophy. It was Russian nationalism, drawn from the late-nineteenth-century nationalistic Slavophilism, which was the real operational philosophy of the regime, and the symbols of this philosophy were widely scattered in the ideological discourse of the Soviet regime. It was emphasized that the legalistic freedom in the West was just a sham, and it was actually the freedom for the stronger to devour the weak.

In a broader political/philosophical context, it was the license for the elite to exploit and abuse the masses. Soviet propaganda stated that this was because the West was capitalistic and implicitly would be changed in the case of socialist transformation in the future. Yet these statements were read in quite a different context: the problem was not with capitalism but with Western civilization, per se. On the other hand, in the Soviet political discourse, formal freedoms had been replaced by the real bonds and care which were derived from the Slavophile notion, taken from Christian principles, of the Russian soul which needed no formal call of duty or legalistic coercion to help fellow human beings. This special type of "Soviet nation" and "Soviet people" was the major reason for the Soviet Union's invincibility and successful claim to global predominance. In its praise of sheer force, Soviet propaganda had actually forsaken the idea of the loveliness and friendliness of the Russian/Soviet character and often implicitly praised the brutal force of which Russians/Soviets should be proud, because it had ensured their past, present, and future glory. And it was not surprising that Soviet ideology had often glorified such brutal Russian czars as Ivan the Terrible and Peter the Great, often repeating word for word (without, of course, quoting) the philosophical paradigms of Danilevsky and Leont'ev.

At the same time, the Soviet ideologies emphasized that the global Soviet domination would not rest purely on force. Moreover, the absorption of the rest of humanity into the Soviet block would not result in the creation of a Western type of empire where the differences between the conquered and the conquerors would be maintained for the sake of exploitation but the other countries would be thoroughly Sovietized and for this reason would be merged with the other Soviet people.

Finally, in the promises to provide, not just for the Soviet people but for all of humanity, the vision of the ultimate conquest of nature and the cosmos (this was reflected in the Soviet Union's achievements in the exploration of space) and the spreading of Sovietized humanity all over the universe, Soviet ideology actually followed the line of Fedorovian metaphysical messianism.

It was true that Westernism with its adherence to Western liberties was popular among the Soviet people. Yet one should be quite cautious in interpreting their vision of the West. For most of the populace, liberty in itself did not mean much. The West was great, not because it provided human rights but because the liberties were translated in the mind of the starving

Soviet citizens into the abundance of consumer goods and a high standard of living in general. Even for quite a few of the Russian intellectuals, who were sincere in their hatred of the controlling and abusive Soviet bureaucracy, the political freedoms or human rights were often implicitly connected with high social position or at least with recognition, as was the case with writers, poets, and scholars. The Western interpretation of human rights, with its legalistic underpinnings and the contractual nature of formal obligations, was in its very essence foreign to the vast majority of even the most staunchly Westernized Russian intellectuals, who still lived in the existential context of the Russian Gemeinschaft culture, even though they had experienced absolute alienation from the regime, as was the case with some of the country's minorities (e.g., the Jews). Indeed, they could not develop a Western mentality in a culture where there were neither middle classes nor a legalistic/contractual tradition. In this context, it was not surprising that Gorbachev's reforms which introduced Western liberties into Russia led to a result quite different from that for which the leaders had planned. In some respects, the Russians replayed the scenario of 1917 when the end of the czardom had led not to the emergence of a civil society with emphasis on human rights but to a strong push for the antisocial process. Having been deprived of the Gemeinschaft cohesiveness, the society did not acquire the Gesellschaft social contract. The post-Soviet Russians had abandoned their traditional Russian nationalism with its messianic drive enmeshed in the Marxist web and tried to replace it with the Western (mostly in its American reading) messianic drive for legalistic culture (human rights). Yet this encounter with Western capitalism and its ideological shibboleth was a disaster. Society was unable to transform itself into a new viable Western-type system but started to fall apart.

The Problems of Human Rights in Post-Soviet Russia

The privatization (economic freedom) was translated into the looting of the state resources by a few bureaucrats and out-and-out criminals, criminality of all sorts arose, and prostitution became one of the most profitable professions. The army crumbled, together with the culture and the empire itself. What had been part of the national identity and a point of pride was no more. Gone was the imperialistic élan and belief in the superiority of the Russian/Soviet-Eurasian civilization. The Mir space station is a pathetic symbol of the Russian dream to lead humanity to the stars.

It would be, of course, a gross oversimplification to assume that the Russians are totally discarding the post-Soviet experience and want to go back to the Soviet past. There is no doubt that the majority of post-Soviet Russians do not want to get rid of the institution of private property completely. While private property as pertains to big business and natural resources could be questioned by quite a few of the Russians, only those on the fringe would question the principle of private property for small enterprises, shops, and apartments. The principles are the foundation of the ideology of the middle classes, and indeed the middle classes have started to emerge in Russia, especially in the big cities. This has started to bring to the country's social and intellectual milieu the notion of respect for the law, the legalistic discourse on which the entire modern liberal capitalism was founded. And from here, from this foundation, respect for human rights in the Western meaning could take hold. The social contract, with human rights as its essential element, would expand its space to embrace relationships between citizens on a broader scale, not just those in their business discourse. From this, the sense of a new community and a new Gesellschaft nationalism could emerge with a new sense of the country's identity. And human rights (i.e., political liberties) could be integrated into the views of the new Russians, as is presently the case with the vast majority of the countries of the West. Yet this scenario would not materialize, most likely because depriving the Russians of their anti-Western values—where the absence of human rights in their Western reading was regarded not just as a symbol of their national identity, not just what made them different from the West, but what, in their view, had secured for them the leading role in the human history— has led (and this, of course, could be quite paradoxical for Western social scientists) to an identity problem for quite a few post-Soviet Russians. The present conditions most probably will not lead to the creation of a new Russia, a viable and democratic state. The democratic tradition might fail to develop, or in the worst-case scenario, a Russia deprived of any sense of national cohesiveness could fall apart, as the USSR had done.

To start with, the development of the middle classes and the introduction of the idea of equality before the law led to full-fledged human rights only after a prolonged process in the West. Even more so, the rise of the middle classes and the disintegration of the old medieval Gemeinschaft society led to exacerbation of the social and political tension, and the early rise of capitalism in the West was witness not just to a rise of democratic movements but to a drive for authoritarian rule as a protection against antisocial drives in society.[12]

In this situation, the desire to preserve personal security and property rights (the essential human rights in Western political discourse) has pushed a considerable portion of the emerging middle classes to search for an authoritarian solution.[13] The popularity of General Lebed, who in May 1998 won an important local election and who openly praised Chilean dictator Augusto Pinochet, could be a proof of the weakness of the legalistic restraints in the post-Soviet political culture. It is even more significant that Yeltsin, after having used armored troops in his clash with Parliament in 1993, was later elected. Vladimir Putin came to power after a brutal onslaught on Chechnya. His authoritarian brutality was the major reason for his popularity. This shows that the majority of Russians saw violence as a legitimate way of dealing with the opposition. Even more potentially threatening is the fact that the ideas of human rights have started to be compartmentalized. While the Western political culture in Moscow might have a considerable number of supporters, this number has dwindled in other regions where nationalism and openly Nazi ideas are quite in vogue (Umlaud 1997). This regionalizing of human rights is a sign not only that human rights in their Western meaning have not been internalized by a considerable portion of the Russian population, but it also demonstrates the fragility of the country and the potential for further fragmentation of the national identity which could lead to the disintegration of Russia proper. In this warlord atmosphere, the country could follow the road of Qing China, which was also unable to withstand the collision with the West.

It goes without saying that it is impossible to make any precise prediction about Russian society. Yet it is clear that Russia could be a good example of how attempting to make abrupt changes in the values which have sustained a country for its entire modern history, regardless of political changes, could lead to serious trouble or even to complete demise of the civilization.

Endnotes

1. This vision of the "natural conditions" of the human being was incorporated in the Stoics' cosmology with their vision of the universe in the condition of permanent rotation. On the Stoics' vision of the cosmos, see David E. Hahn, *The Origins of Stoic Cosmology* (Columbus: Ohio State University Press, 1977); Shmuel Sambursky, *Physics of the Stoics* (Westport: Greenwood Press, 1973).
2. The idea of "natural law" was first developed in Holland, and *De jure belli ac pacis* (Concerning the Law of War and Peace) by Hugo Grotius (1583–1645) could be regarded as one of the first works on the subject. On Dutch culture

of Grotius' time, see: Johan Huizinga, *Dutch Civilization in the Seventeenth Century and Other Essays* (New York: Harper and Row, 1969).

3. See, for example: Adda B. Bozeman, *The Future of Law in a Multicultural World* (Princeton: Princeton University Press, 1971); Alex Inkeles, *National Character: A Psycho-Social Perspective* (New Brunswick and London: Transaction Publishers, 1997). These works also provide a good review of the notion of national character as it was viewed in the contemporary sociological literature.)

4. Peter Tkachev could be an example of a Russian radical with strong authoritarian/totalitarian streaks in his political philosophy. On Tkachev see: Deborah Hardy, *Peter Tkachev, The Critic as Jacobin* (Seattle and London: University of Washington Press, 1977).

5. It might be added that other Russians who witnessed the event had experienced the same shock: *Russkoe Slovo*, June 22, 1909.

6. The philosopher was popular in the late-nineteenth-century Russia, and articles about him were published in Russian magazines. See for example: P. M. Ev., "Zhozef de Mestr i ego politicheskie doktriny," *Russkii Vestnik*, May 1889; A. A. Savin, "Zhosef de Mestr," *Vestnik Evropy*, January 1900.

7. This interpretation of the philosopher was popular in late-nineteenth-century Russia. See: V. Ger'e, "Poniatie o narode u Russo," *Russkaia Mysl'*, No. 5, 8, 1882.

8. It is clear that from this perspective Fedorov was, to some extent, a precursor of both Freud and Adorno.

9. The importance of libraries in the grand work of the resurrection was the reason why Fedorov assumed that all books should be saved. Lev Tolstoy had a different view, and this was one of the reasons why Fedorov was sharply at odds with Tolstoy by the end of his life. See: N. Skatov, *Dalekoe i blizkoe* (Moscow: Sovremenik, 1981), p. 212.

10. In their stress that they were chosen not because of the superiority of their material culture or sheer power but because of their moral superiority, the Russians might be compared well only to the Jews. It is clear from this perspective why Martin Buber, the Jewish philosopher who envisaged Israel as being the moral beacon for humanity, looked with sympathy upon the views of Dostoyevsky who saw the Russians as showing the pathway for humanity— Martin Buber, *Israel and the World: Essays in a Time of Crisis* (New York: Schocken Books, 1963, pp. 203–206, 210).

11. On Ustrialov's work, see: *Rossiia u Okna Vagona* (Harbin: Tipografiia Kitaiskoi Vostochnoi Zheleznoi Dorogi, 1926); *Pod znakom revoliutsii: sbornik statei* (Harbin: Izdatel'stvo "Russkaia Zhizn'," 1925); *V bor'be za Rossiiu: Sbornik Statei* (Orange, CT: Antiquary, 1987).

12. Here is a reference to Hobbes who preached what we could call the totalitarian state. In his preaching of Leviathan, Hobbes actually followed the dictums of the society which was in the process of the transformation from a Gemeinschaft to a Gesellschaft society.

13. In present-day Russia the legalistic discourse is still a small island in the sea of lawlessness and semilawlessness. Indeed, it is not law but the protection of a Mafia type of structure ("roof-krysha") which is required to do business. On the role of organized crime in Russia, see: Vladimir Shlapentokh, "Early Feudalism: The Best Parallel for Contemporary Russia," *Europe-Asia Studies*, May 1998.

On the corruption and crime in Russia, see also: Zbigniew Brzezinski, "Russia Stumbles Toward Reform," *Wall Street Journal*, April 7, 1998. The author of the piece was also quite critical about the Western help to Russia and stated in this respect that a "very high percentage of the billions of dollars sent to Moscow since 1991 has been literally stolen."

Bibliography

Beasley, W. E. 1987. *Japanese Imperialism, 1894–1945*. Oxford: Clarendon Press.

Bozeman, Adda B. 1971. *The Future of Law in a Multicultural World*. Princeton: Princeton University Press.

Brzezinski, Zbigniew. 1988. "Russia Stumbles Toward Reform," *Wall Street Journal*, April 7.

Buber, Martin. 1963. *Israel and the World: Essays in a Time of Crisis*. New York: Schocken Books.

Danilevsky, Nikolai Ia. 1885. *Rossiia i Evropa*. St. Petersburg: Tipografiia brat'ev Panteleevykh.

Ev. P. M. 1889. "Zhozef de Mestr i ego politicheskie doktriny," *Russkii Vestnik*, May.

Fedorov, Nikolai F. 1906. *Filosofiia obschago dela*, 2 vols. Vernyi: Tipografiia Semirechenskogo Oblastnogo Pravleniia.

Fedorov, Nikolai F. 1913. *Filosofiia obschago dela*, 2 vols. Moscow: n.p.

Foss, Daniel A. and Ralph Larkin. 1986. *Beyond Revolution*. South Hadley: Bergin & Garvey Publishers.

Furet, Francois. 1988. *Revolutionary France: 1770–1880*. Oxford and Cambridge: Blackwell.

Ger'e, Vladimir. 1982. "Poniatie o narode u Russo," *Russkaia Mysl'*, No. 5, 8.

Hahn, David E. 1977. *The Origins of Stoic Cosmology*. Columbus: Ohio State University Press.

Hardy, Deborah. 1977. *Peter Tkachev, The Critic as Jacobin*. Seattle and London: University of Washington Press.

Huizinga, Johan. n.d. *Dutch Civilization in the Seventeenth Century and Other Essays*. New York: Harper and Row.

Inkeles, Alex. 1997. *National Character: A Psycho-Social Perspective*. New Brunswick and London: Transaction Publishers.

Leont'ev, Konstantin. 1912–1913. *Sobranie Sochinenii*, 9 vols. St Petersburg: Deiateli; Moscow: Izdanie V. M. Sablina.

Plekhanov, G. V. 1923–1927. *Sochineniia*, 23 vols. Moscow: Gosudarstvennoe izdatel'stvo Politcheskoi Literatury.

Pipes, Richard. 1990. *The Russian Revolution*. New York: Knopf.

Rapoport, Iu. I. 1930. "U krasnykh i u belykh," *Arkhiv Russkoi Revoliutsii* vol. 30.

Russkie Izvestiia, April 15, 1998.

Russkoe Slovo, June 22, 1909.

Sambursky, Shmuel. 1973. *Physics of the Stoics*. Westport: Greenwood Press.

Savin, A. A. 1900. "Zhosef de Mestr," *Vestnik Evropy*, January.

Shlapentokh, Dmitry. 1997. *The French Revolution and the Russian Anti-Democratic Tradition*. New Brunswick: Transaction.

Shlapentokh, Vladimir. 1998. "Early Feudalism: The Best Parallel for Contemporary Russia," *Europe-Asia Studies*, May.

Skatov, N. 1981. *Dalekoe i blizkoe*. Moscow: Sovremenik.

Tolstoy, Lev. 1968. *Voina i Mir*, 2 vols. Moscow: Khudozhestvennaia Literatura.

Troyat, Henri. 1967. *Tolstoy*. Garden City: Doubleday.

Umlaud, Andreas. 1997. "The Post-Soviet Russian Extreme Right, *The Problem of Post-Communism*, July/August.

Ustrialov, Peter. 1925. *Pod znakom revoliutsii: sbornik statei*. Harbin: Izdatel'stvo "Russkaia Zhizn".

Ustrialov, Peter. 1926. *Rossiia u Okna Vagona*. Harbin: Tipografiia Kitaiskoi Vostochnoi Zheleznoi Dorogi.

Ustrialov, Peter. 1987. *V bor'be za Rossiiu: Sbornik Statei*. Orange, CT: Antiquary.

Vucinich, A. 1976. *Social Thought in Tsarist Russia: The Question for General Science of Society, 1861–1917*. Chicago and London: University of Chicago Press.

Walicki, Andrzej. 1987. *Legal Philosophies of Russian Liberalism*. Oxford: Clarendon Press.

Winks, Robin W. 1969. *The Age of Imperialism*. Englewood Cliffs: Prentice-Hall.

Young, George. 1979. *Nikolai Fedorov: An Introduction*. Belmont: Nordland Publishing Company.

11 Ethnicity and Human Rights in Contemporary Democracies

Israel and Other Cases

Ilan Peleg

Over the past quarter century we have witnessed an unde-
niable, persistent process of democratization in the world. This process began in Southern Europe in the 1970s (Greece, Portugal, Spain), spread to
South and Central America, and then to Eastern Europe, Africa, the former
Soviet Union, and finally Asia. The main form of the democratization process has been the institutionalization of general and free elections in countries which traditionally did not have them. Yet, many of the new democracies—as well as some of the old ones—did not adopt, in law or in practice,
the liberal principles of respect to civil and human rights. With the emergence of many "illiberal democracies" (Zakaria 1997), the process of democratization has been more extensive than intensive, wider than deeper,
and in many ways incomplete.

While this essay is not a comprehensive survey of illiberal democracies,
it promotes the argument that many such political systems are flawed "communal democracies," countries where a dominant community, often ethnically defined, rules over subordinate group(s) by using the power of the
majority and the machinery of the state. In such situations, the inevitable
result is the negation of equal rights to individuals and groups alike, even if
the overall democratic character of the regime is maintained, and even when
essential democratic practices (e.g. regular elections) are kept.

What I call "communal democracies" bring into sharp relief the dilemma
of collective (or community) rights vs. individually based equal rights. To
demonstrate this dilemma empirically, I will dwell on the case of Israel,

although the Israeli case is by no means the only or the worse case of "communal democracy." In fact, to open the way toward generalization, I will refer to additional cases. In dwelling on a variety of cases, I will try to demonstrate that communal democracies have the capacity to move toward liberal or toward consensus democracy, both rights-enhancing constitutional orders. The Israeli case will facilitate the identification of the conditions under which such development might occur.

Communality and Rights

The past several decades have been dominated, to a large extent, by two political forces. The first force is that of nationalism, ethnicity, or what one author called "communal assertiveness" (Lustick 1979). This force reflects the collectivist drive of a community interested in promoting its interests. In its radical forms, the force was described as fundamentalist, hypernationalist, and so forth. The second force is that of civil and human rights; it emphasizes the prerogatives of the individual in society, and sometimes even against society.

These two forces—called here the "communal agenda" and the "rights agenda"—have often competed for domination within many political systems. While the first has typically made claims based on the exclusive, paramount or superior interest of a particular ethnic, religious, cultural, or even ideological group—viewing it as clearly delineated from other groups within society—the second has based its claims on the demand for equal rights for all individuals within society. This clash of forces has reflected the inherent tension between the claim for universal human rights, on the one hand, and the assertion that rights are relative, contextual, culturally determined, and not necessarily equal, on the other hand.

The tension between these alternative agendas within contemporary polities—community rights vs. individual rights—has been heightened in view of the fact that most countries today are culturally diverse. Thus, while the number of states in today's world is fewer than 200, the number of ethnic groups exceeds 5,000 (Kymlicka 1995:1; Laczko 1994; Gurr 1993; Nielsson 1985). In very few countries (notably Iceland and the two Koreas) can we speak of genuine cultural homogeneity of the entire population.

The cultural diversity, with its natural claim for collective rights, lives uncomfortably with the worldwide, emerging argument for the universality of human rights, formulated within the traditional liberal thought as based on the rights of the *individual*. In fact, liberals tend to believe that collective rights are inherently in conflict with individual rights (Kymlicka 1995:7). Moreover, in different parts of the world, notably in Asia and in the Middle East, the universal applicability of human rights has been challenged and often fiercely assaulted in the name of cultural differentiation.

Indeed, even if one tends to endorse universal standards on normative grounds—that is, even if one views such standards as morally justified and ethically desirable—one must acknowledge, on empirical grounds, that different societies not only emphasize different rights but often have altogether divergent approaches to the very concept of rights.

This essay is an inquiry into the relationship between culture and human rights, and particularly the tension that often emerges between them in the contemporary world. Special attention will be given to the impact that culture may have on human rights, particularly through the regime type that it tends to produce. The empirical focus will be on Israel, especially since the Israeli case—with the unabashed claim of the State for being both Jewish (that is, culturally unique) and democratic (that is, committed to human rights)—emphasizes the tensions between the universal and the particular. At the same time, frequent allusions will be made to other contemporary democracies in order to emphasize the general problematique of the tension between communality and individual rights, rather than the peculiarities and idiosyncrasies of the Israeli case. My theoretical interest is, primarily, in the inherently uneasy relationships between communal interests and universal, individual human rights, a condition which characterizes numerous democracies in the contemporary world.

Conceptual Discussion

Among different regime types, democracy is particularly interesting for the study of the relationships among culture, ethnic diversity, and human rights. In totalitarian regimes, where the government implements a well-defined, comprehensive ideological program through monopolistic control over all aspects of life and politics, there is almost no place for any human rights, and the impact of cultural diversity on such rights would, thus, be limited. Even in an authoritarian environment, where governmental control is limited to the "political" and is not rooted in a revolutionary ideology, the space left for the pursuit of human rights is necessarily limited. Although the ethnic factor in such regimes could be decisive, the stable and generally low status of human rights makes the study of culture, ethnicity, and rights less than central.

In modern democracies, on the other hand, civil and human rights are more often than not at the core of the political game, frequently competing against alternative ideological, political and even communal forces. Thus, even in the United States, the quintessential "liberal democracy" (see below), the right of a woman to an abortion is challenged by the ideological conviction of the Right-to-Life movement that "life begins at conception," the freedom from religious coercion is challenged by what some view as the right of individuals or even the community to pray (even in public spaces), and the right of disadvantaged minorities for the benefits of affirmative action designed to erase past wrongs is challenged in the name of universal individual equality.

It is the argument of this essay that in no other polity is the tension between the universality of individual equality and the right of the community to define itself (and act on behalf of that definition) more pronounced than in a polity that is both democratic and ethnically divided. In fact, the deeper the ethnic divide—and the stronger the commitment to democracy—the more central is the place of civil and human rights in the political life of the country and the fiercer is the struggle over these rights. The general hypothesis is, then, that the human rights situation in a society would be strongly influenced by the "ethnic factor" in it (that is, whether a society is ethnically unified or pluralistic, and the depth of its ethnic divisions). Thus, a polity characterized by deep, competitive group solidarities based on ethnic, linguistic, racial, or religious identities (Esman 1973:49) would, in all likelihood, experience major conflict between the "rights" forces and the "communal" forces. The balance emerging from that confrontation would be determined by the regime type adopted by the polity. Thus, culture and ethnicity interact with human rights through regime type.

In deeply divided, multiethnic societies there is, typically, but not inevitably, an ongoing, fierce competition between political forces associated with the "communal agenda"—those who represent or claim to represent the ethnic majority—and groups that champion the "rights agenda," often formulated in terms of universal standards of civil and human rights. The "rights" forces, typically, include significant elements within the ethnic minority, more marginal elements within the ethnic majority, and human rights activists within the international community. In the final analysis, the fundamental source of conflict within a deeply divided, multiethnic polity is the commitment of divergent elements within the polity to alternative sets of values.

In this essay, the focus will be on multiethnic societies and, particularly biethnic democracies, and the potential tension existing within them between their self-definition as polities and their civil and human rights situation. Among multiethnic democracies, we can identify countries such as the new states of Lithuania and Macedonia, and the older states of Pakistan, Switzerland, Spain, and even the United Kingdom; interesting bi-ethnic democracies include Belgium, Canada, Croatia, Georgia, the Kyrgyz Republic, Latvia, pre-1974 Cyprus, Estonia, Finland, Slovakia, and Ukraine, as well as pre-1975 Lebanon, New Zealand, Sri Lanka, and Turkey. In this article, the *empirical focus* will be (although not exclusively) on what I would call Israel Proper, that is, Israel without the Occupied Territories. The Israeli case fits the category of "a biethnic democracy" rather well (Peleg and Seliktar 1989). Allusion to other cases will often be made.

One of the characteristics of most biethnic societies, including biethnic democracies, is that sources of power tend to be unevenly divided between the constituent ethnic groups. The sources of unevenness could be a demographic imbalance between the groups, differentials in control over economic resources, a gap in educational levels, and so forth. The central political game in biethnic societies is often played around the determination of the dominant ethnic group to sustain and even enhance the ethnic gaps, and the countervailing struggle of the "subordinate" group to close the existing ethnic gap. This interethnic struggle often determines the status of human rights within the polity, and the potential for changing it in the direction of either expansion or contraction.

A key factor in the dialogue surrounding ethnicity and human rights in biethnic democracies, a dialogue that is often both verbal and violent, is the fundamental attitude adopted by the dominant ethnic group toward the subordinate group within the polity. Although numerous individual actions and policies constitute the fundamental attitude of the dominant ethnic group, one can, for analytical purposes, distinguish between two general approaches:

1 *The domination approach*: the essence of this approach is to be found in the determination of the more powerful ethnic group to perpetuate or

even enhance its domination within the polity (see Lustick 1980, on the Israeli case). Although domination is easier to sustain in a totalitarian or authoritarian context, especially when an ethnically based ruling elite tightly controls the state machinery, domination is also possible in a democracy, if and when the ruling group represents the ethnic majority, and is willing to use its position on behalf of that majority. Democracies are open to ethnic domination especially in the absence of a viable constitution, a comprehensive Bill of Rights, and institutions (e.g. Supreme Court) willing and able to enforce these;

2 *The accommodation approach* (Lustick 1979), is fundamentally different from the domination approach. It is characterized by the active efforts by the dominant ethnic group to produce an interethnic compromise by equalizing opportunities for all groups and individuals within the polity. Thus, under the overall "umbrella" of accommodation, attitudinal tolerance could be encouraged, power-sharing institutions established, territorial autonomy recognized, linguistic and religious opportunities given, and so forth. All of these measures and even measures which give minorities relative advantage — e.g. disproportional parliamentary representation (Cypriot Turks prior to 1974) — are usually designed to enhance long-term stability within the polity as a whole.

From the perspectives of this essay it is essential to emphasize that the overall strategies of domination or accommodation are directly and intimately connected to the status of civil and human rights in biethnic societies. Thus, the use of the majority power to perpetuate control via enhancement of ethnic gaps within deeply divided societies is often (a) incompatible with genuine commitment to human rights (since it gives advantages to individuals on the basis of ethnicity), and (b) could prove, in the long run, counterproductive, destabilizing, and damaging to the interests of the ethnic majority. A biethnic democracy governed by the "domination principle," could easily become a democracy by name only, a mere procedural democracy.

Accommodationist policies, on the other hand, are designed to restrain the "tyranny of the majority" and create political opportunities for political participation to all (Lijphart 1977). Such policies, which require the commitment, imagination, and courage of the elites leading the dominant ethnic group, are in principle compatible with a civil and human rights agenda. In fact, while plurality of ethnicities within a sharply divided polity could easily prevent the implementation of a comprehensive human rights agenda, accommodationist policies, and they alone, can save a multiethnic democracy from an eventual downfall.

This general, theoretical analysis of the policies that might be adopted by an ethnic majority vis-à-vis an ethnic minority indicates that not all democracies are alike. They differ in many ways, not the least in the ways in which they treat rights. While some democracies grant all rights on individual basis (and refuse, as a matter of principle, to grant any special rights for or impose special duties on groups), other democracies might grant rights and impose duties on the basis of group membership, thus opening the door to differential treatment of individuals. For the sake of analyzing the impact of different types of democracy on the conditions of human rights in a multiethnic society, I would distinguish between (a) liberal democracy; (b) consensus democracy; and (c) communal democracy.

Liberal democracy is a regime which is both "democratic" and "liberal." It is "a political system marked not only by free and fair elections, but also by the rule of law, a separation of powers, and the protection of basic liberties of speech, assembly, religion, and property" (Zakaria 1997:22). Thus, side by side with a set of institutions and procedures designed to guarantee the rule of the majority, liberal democracy grants citizens extensive rights in an equal, universal, and comprehensive manner. In a liberal democracy, these rights are individually granted, are considered philosophically "inalienable," and are usually protected by a written constitution and a bill of rights, as well as by a court whose main function is to protect these rights. Liberal democracy is "practiced" today in both the United States and the United Kingdom, although in different forms.

Liberal democracy of the type described here is particularly suited for ethnically homogeneous societies or societies where ethnicity is largely privatized, as in the United States. In deeply divided societies, where the fundamental social and political division is along ethnic lines—as in Belgium or in Canada, for example—claims for *group rights* are likely to overwhelm the basic principle of liberal democracy that rights are granted to individuals and individuals alone.

In order to maintain the democratic form of government *despite* deep ethnic division, many contemporary democracies have adopted a form of government which Arend Lijphart initially called consociational democracy (Lijphart 1977) and then *consensus democracy* (Lijphart 1984). Lijphart believes that consensus democracy is well suited to what he calls "plural societies," where homogeneity is lacking. Furthermore, he thinks that "in plural societies . . . majority rule spells majority dictatorship and civil strife rather than democracy" (1984:23). Lijphart's consensus model calls for, *inter alia*, "special representation to certain minorities in the second chamber or upper house" (25), territorial and nonterritorial federalism (as in Switzerland and Belgium, respectively) and decentralization (28–29), written constitution which guarantees minority veto over amendments (29–30), and other means designed to restrain the majority by forcing it to share, disperse, distribute, and delegate power (30).

Although Lijphart focuses on the overall character of consensus democracies, his analysis is directly relevant for the status of civil and human rights in such states. In ethnically divided societies, there ought to be a multidimensional effort designed specifically to limit the power of the majority. If such an effort is lacking, massive violations of civil and human rights of minorities—as groups and individuals—would occur.

To tie together the categorization of regime types (Liberal vs. Consensus Democracy) and that of the fundamental attitude of the majority toward the minority (Domination vs. Accommodation), I would like to argue now that while in a liberal democracy (based on a homogenous society) the domination/accommodation issue is at least in principle irrelevant, in a consensus democracy (based on ethnically divided societies) it is at the very center of the political game, and it has huge implications for civil and human rights. In consensus democracy, civil and human rights could flourish if and only if the dominant majority aggressively pursues accommodationist policies. Such policies could include education for tolerance, as well as legal and practical guarantees for equal opportunities for minorities, in addition to permanent constitutionally established institutions designed to protect the interest of the minority. While in majoritarian liberal democracy—the Westminster Model—special attention to minority rights is unacceptable (and, presumably, unnecessary), they are the very soul of a consensus democracy and the guarantor of its long-term survival. Moreover, in pursuing stability, consensus democracies may grant minorities preferred status. Thus, Canada recognizes Quebec as a "distinct society," while the Turkish Cypriots were granted 30 percent of the seats in the pre-1974 parliament, well over their proportion within the population.

In addition to "liberal" and "consensus" democracies, there might be a place for identifying a third, traditionally unrecognized type of democracy: *communal democracy*. In 1970, Belgium adopted a series of constitutional amendments which created a French cultural council and a Dutch cultural council charged with legislating on cultural and educational matters for the two major Belgian communities. One constitutional expert maintained that Belgium thus became "a communal state" (Senelle 1978:139).

Since the Belgian solution was based on equality, and was agreed upon mutually rather than enforced by a dominant political power, the Belgian communal state fits the consensus model perfectly. On the other hand, if in an ethnically divided society one of the ethnic groups establishes political control, grants itself preferential status within the polity, and does so without the consent of the minority—we clearly move beyond the confines of "consensus democracy" toward a new terrain of regime type and a new "rights" situation.

I would call a regime which maintains the fundamental rules of democracy—free and fair elections, periodic transfer of power in accordance with the wishes of the voters, etc.—but which does not promote interethnic accommodation despite the deep societal divide, a *communal democracy*. In a communal democracy, the fundamentals of democracy may be maintained even beyond the electoral process itself (thus, free press and the rule of law could be accepted), but the dominant group is actively using its superior power—which is typically unrestrained in an effective way by a constitution, bill of rights, a political culture, or a constitutional court—to promote its exclusive interests against the interests of the minority. Thus *illiberal democracy* based on "communal" considerations is established: while the government is more-or-less democratically elected, it systematically deprives at least some of its citizens of their basic rights and freedoms (Zakaria 1997:22). It often does so in the name of communal considerations, which it takes upon itself to represent.

Sammy Smooha (1990) introduced the notion of "ethnic democracy" to the discourse of democracy. For him, this is a form of government in which there is an "institutionalized dominance over the state by one of the ethnic groups," along with "political and civil rights to individuals and certain collective rights to minorities" (1990:391). The reason I prefer to use "communal democracy" rather than "ethnic democracy" is that the institutionalized dominance by the control group *may or may not be based on ethnic criterion*. In pre-twentieth century England and the U.S., both democracies, dominant groups excluded others on the basis of race, property, gender, and so forth.

Be that as it may, in communal democracy—of which ethnic democracy is but a subset (although possibly the most common one)—the state, con-

trolled by a dominant group which speaks in the name of the largest community or a larger principle (Peled 1992) — is using a variety of bureaucratic,
political and even judicial means (Barzilai 1998) to promote the exclusive
interests of the dominant group. It is important to note that in what I call
"communal democracy," democracy *per se*, however perfect, does not prevent human rights violations on great scale. In fact, strict majoritarian democracy without a written constitution in a sharply divided society (that is,
a combination of the Westminster Model and plural society) is a recipe for
wholesale violations of human rights.

A number of examples of "communal democracies" come to mind. I will
deal below in some detail with the Israeli case, where the State has viewed
itself from the start and was even declared by the UN as "a Jewish state"
and, yet, simultaneously committed itself to be fully democratic. Additional
examples of communal democracies include countries such as Sri Lanka,
some East European states (e.g. Slovakia), the new Baltic countries (Estonia,
Latvia, Lithuania), most former Soviet and Yugoslav republics, Nigeria, and
Turkey.

In general, it is the case that states which define themselves as representing one particular segment of their population — one identifiable "community" (be it ethnic, religious, cultural, etc.) — tend to be nondemocratic.
Yet, such states may become democratic by instituting periodic elections,
allowing competition between alternative elites, etc. Moreover, and very
important for this essay, "communal democracies" can move, with time,
toward *liberal* democracy or *consensus* democracy.

What I call "communal democracy" often represents hegemonic control
over the state machinery by a particular group, used and abused for its own
benefit. In a multiethnic polity, the hegemonic model is one in which the
dominant ethnocultural "core nation" (Brubaker 1996) *uses the State as an
instrument for the establishment, enhancement, and perpetuation of its exclusivist control over the public sphere, to the exclusion of all other groups.* While
Smooha calls such a model "ethnic democracy," his *assumption* that democracy (in any of its definitions) is, in fact, sustainable in such a state,
especially in the long run, ought to be critically examined, both in principle
and empirically.

The hegemonic model is based on the notion of the transformation of
the state from a *neutral* arena for the struggle between conflicting interests
within society (an ideal type notion which is rarely achieved in reality) to
an arena *expropriated* for the exclusivist use of a single ethnocultural group.

My concept of the hegemonic-ethnic state is, at least in part, *Gramscian*, insofar as there is within the dominant ethnic majority an *hegemonically unchallenged assumption that the state is the exclusive domain of the "core nation."* This assumption, shared by elites and masses alike, makes it unlikely if not entirely impossible for members of the ethnic majority to view "their" state as nondemocratic. Hegemonic ethnicity, having been internalized, is perceived as "natural," making the use and abuse of state power for exclusive ethnic goals normal and noncontroversial.

What I call "hegemonic statehood" is "a relatively hegemonic situation in which a given cultural definition of reality dominates the society at large" (Aronoff, 1989:xiv) and, equally important, has *decisive impact on all of the state institutions.*

It is important to note that the hegemonic state and all its agents view themselves as acting on behalf of the "core nation." Yet, hegemonic statehood runs into serious difficulties with any notion of genuine democracy if and when substantial number of citizens are not, in fact, members of the core nation.

The democratic problem of hegemonic statehood is that it is based on the *intersection of two extremely powerful social forces* which in this particular regime form—hegemonic statehood—reinforce each other to the detriment of genuine democracy. The first force is the ethnic or national force, reflecting individuals' supreme allegiance, commitment and loyalty to "their" particular group. The second force is the enormous power of the modern state. When these two forces intersect, in an ethnically divided society, the modern state—bureaucratized, militarized, and armed to the teeth with regulations and with weapons—becomes an *unprecedentedly potent instrument in negating minority rights.*

Following Theda Skocpol (Evans, Rueschemeyer and Skocpol, 1985:21) my approach to the State—within the framework of hegemonic statism— follows that of de Tocqueville. The brilliant Frenchman's two masterpieces, *The Old Regime and the French Revolution* and the better-known *Democracy in America*, emphasize the importance of the state within societies. States matter because of their overall patterns of activity, their affect on organizational configurations, their encouragement of certain collective political actions (but not others), and so forth (Evans et al.:21).

In today's world, in contrast to the one known to de Tocqueville, the state, with its centralized control over education, enormous economic and military resources, dominance over mass media and communication, and now computerized capabilities, is a political instrument of unparalleled strength in human history. When this instrument is *monopolized by an ethnic majority against an ethnic minority*, democratic norms are, inevitably, violated.

The theory of the relationship between hegemonic statehood and democracy rests, then, on several propositions:

A The combination of passionate ethnic force and centralized state power in a deeply divided society creates a controlling sociopolitical reality, likely to overwhelm all other countervailing realities (e.g. claims for individual or minority rights, humanitarian instincts within the majority);

B This overwhelming sociopolitical reality—hegemonic statehood—is *bound to seriously damage the quality of democracy* within the polity, and possibly suffocate and destroy democracy altogether;

C Contrary to common perception, hegemonic statehood is not only fatal to its "natural" victims—members of the ethnic minorities within the state—but also its alleged beneficiaries, members of the ethnic majority. Democracy is, simply put, indivisible: once it is destroyed in one part of the polity (that is, in the majority-minority relationships), its pathology is likely to spread, cancer-like, to other parts of the body politic.

The determination and possible destruction of democracy in hegemonic states is particularly likely when several conditions prevail. *First*, the "core nation"—the demographic majority in control of the state—enjoys multi-dimensional superiority in all important socioeconomic areas: level of education, technological knowhow, control over the means of production, etc. *Second*, there is a deep, bitter, violent historical conflict between the ethnic groups in the state. *Third*, the state lacks—sometimes by design (Peleg, 1998)—a constitutional order, political culture or legal tradition supportive of equal treatment under the law, due process, and protection against arbitrary action by the state itself, the government in office, or the majority. *Fourth*, the majority within the dominant ethnic group is, fundamentally, intolerant (Shamir and Sullivan 1983). *Fifth*, there is no significant international pressure on the majority to treat the minority with fairness and in accordance with democratic principles.

In an ethnically divided society, as in politics in general, the role of the *political elite* is crucial. The elite of the ethnocultural majority can push the majority, although not easily, in the direction of full equality, minority protection, and genuine democratization. Nevertheless, the temptation of using the minority for the purpose of generating political support, especially via "scapegoating," is often irresistible for majority politicians. Moreover, the push toward total ethnic domination in what, after all, members of the majority view as *their* state, could prove, in reality, irresistible, a historical inevitability. Ethnic politicians are not known for their inclination to commit suicide: they usually jump *on* the train, not *under* it.

Ironically, the existence of democracy within the ethnic majority and the establishment of procedural democracy in the polity as a whole—both compatible with ethnic statehood—may prove dysfunctional in terms of the development of *genuine* democracy within the polity. The reason is that in such a situation, majority politicians are likely to gain, sustain, and enhance power by either using actively the "ethnic card" or, at the least, refusing to appear "soft" on the minority by initiating a program for dismantling the hegemonic, ethnicized state.

Be that as it may, a divided society with an ethnic historical conflict, and elite commitment to democracy which is, at best, *secondary* to its commitment to the ethnic interest (and desire to stay in power) is likely to lead to *low-quality, flawed democracy*. Such flawed democracy is unlikely to achieve the reasonably moderate conditions of Diamond, Linz and Lipset: meaningful competition for power will be limited by constraints on the minority and "disloyal" elements within the majority, inclusive participation will be outlawed or at least realistically unachieveable, and liberties will be violated by law or through practice (Kretzmer 1990). Most importantly, these deviations are not the result of personalities but inevitable problems linked to and flowing from the *very structure of the hegemonic state itself.*

In fact, the problems associated with ethnic statehood are so deeply rooted in the very essence of the system that, more often than not, they are not even recognized for what, in fact, they are—major deviations from democratic principles—by the majority within the dominant ethnic group. Moreover, a vibrant but nevertheless procedural democracy—periodic election, free press, freedom of association—often *camouflage the low level of democracy* in the ethnicized state.

Hegemonic statehood, it should be noted, is an inherently unstable condition, especially when compared to the two accommodationist models presented before. The tension between the self-proclaimed "ethnic" nature of the state, on the one hand, and its commitment, however *pro forma*, to "democracy," is a source of constant, often unrelenting pressure. So how is this inherent tension to be resolved?

There are several possibilities:

A *Status Quo*. Despite the tension between the ethnic nature of the polity and democratic forces, the hegemonic state succeeds in maintaining its low-quality democracy;

B *Moderate, "cosmetic" changes toward increasing democratization* are introduced, gradually dismantling the most flagrant violations of the democratic credo;

C *Radical revision toward genuine democracy* is implemented by transforming the ethnic or communal state to either a liberal or consociational democracy;

D *Relatively mild changes toward further ethnicization* of the state are carried out by strengthening its ethnically hegemonic institutions;

E *Radical action* is taken by the ethnic elite toward the transformation of the multiethnic state to a *purely ethnic state* or an Apartheid State via harsh means such as mass expulsions, ethnic cleansings, and even full-fledged genocides.

As often is the case, *within the hegemonic structure one finds the seeds of its very own destruction*, and, all things being equal, the more aggressive hegemonic statehood is, the quicker will it destroy itself. By its very nature, the hegemonic state radicalizes its victims, politicizes them, and forces them to organize effective resistance, often with the support of the world community.

Despite the high stakes involved in hegemonic statism, it is often the case that hegemonic states cannot change their nature. Often the very essence of the polity is defined by its ethnicity, so that to change its ethnic definition would be a form of collective suicide. While solutions to excessive ethnicity and unreasonable hegemony could be found, the majority in its blindness, sense of powerfulness, and insensitivity may not be psychologically open to deal with them.

The full understanding of Hegemonic Statehood, requires a focus on the *definition of citizenship* (as well as the various forms of citizenship) within hegemonic states. There are, I would argue, two types of citizenships in an ethnically hegemonic state (Peled 1992; Peled and Shafir 1996; Shafir and Peled 1998): *full and real citizenship* and *formal and nominal citizenship*. While both types of citizenship include the enjoyment of basic rights and liberties, only members of the dominant majority receive full and real citizenship, a status which enables them to legitimately participate in determining the public good (Peled 1992). Membership in the *ethnos*, not mere residence in a country, or even the holding of its identity card and/or passport, determines whether a person enjoys full or partial citizenship, and whether he or she has real or nominal, maximal or minimal rights. The struggle of the minority is to transform its status from that of nominal citizenship to that of real one.

The majority, on the other hand, is likely to insist on its hegemony, and even its exclusivity, in all matters of the public good. A state defining itself ethnically is unlikely to allow "its" nonethnics a free and equal access to the public good. While there is a perception that such policy requires coercive means, democratic means (and even more often semidemocratic ones) can often achieve the same goals and with a lower cost. A unified ethnic majority can easily exclude a minority by using such means as elections, referenda, coalition-building, parliamentary votes, and supreme court decisions. Thus, the goal of appropriating all power over state institutions for the majority and excluding the minority of all significant power could be achieved via means that most within the ethnic majority, and maybe even many within the international community, would view as politically and legally legitimate.

The dimensions of hegemonic statehood are many and diverse. They typically include, but are not limited to the following areas of public policy:

1. the dominance of the majority's language;
2. control over the educational system (including that of the minority);
3. hegemony over all mass media;
4. land control in order to effectively marginalize the minority (Yiftachel 1997, 1998)
5. careful supervision of immigration, emigration, and citizenship in the polity, so as to enhance the demographic advantage of the dominant group;
6. control of the national iconography, enshrined symbols, and collective memory (including museums and monuments, as well as names of places) (Zerubavel 1995; Benvenisti forthcoming; Azaryahu 1995);
7. public employment.

All of these and many other areas are zealously controlled by the hegemonic state. The more zealous and inflexible the policy, the more likely is the crisis in the relations between majority and minority and the more severe it is likely to be. Moreover, the larger number of marginalized citizens, both in absolute numbers and in percentage of the total population, the more likely and severe the crisis.

In terms of the *quality of democracy*, the larger the number of dominated "citizens," and the more marginalized they are, the less democratic the polity is. Modern democracy requires, especially in its liberal form, congruence between citizenship and rights. The ethnically hegemonic state not only violates this principle, *its entire raison d'être is the violation of this principle.* As such, it cannot be but marginally democratic.

The Case of Israel

As a "communal democracy," with hegemonic characteristics, Israel is an interesting case. All the theoretical distinctions introduced before are reflected in numerous ways in the Israeli case. There is an ongoing internal struggle between nationalists ("communalists" or "hegemonists," in the terminology of this article) and civil libertarians, the country is a deeply divided society (between Arabs and Jews) where the majority has dominated the minority for years. The occupation of the West Bank and Gaza has intensified this struggle, as did the Arab-Israeli conflict in general. The State has established a myriad of institutions and policies designed to guarantee the continued domination of the majority. Accommodationist policies have not been pursued energetically, if at all.

Nevertheless, what makes the Israeli case fascinating and highly relevant for numerous other ethnically divided polities is that over the last thirty years or so there has been a more serious effort on the part of important elements within the majority to strengthen the "rights agenda," mostly at the expense of the "communal agenda." These efforts will be highlighted in this section, and emphasis will be put on the chances that Israel's communal democracy would evolve into a liberal or consensus democracy.

The conditions for the evolution of civil and human rights in Israel are very complex, yet not unpromising. There are a few general characteristics of the Israeli polity that are of great relevance for the possibility of the country's "communal democracy" evolving in the direction of either "liberal" or "consensus" democracy, resulting (in either case) in the enhancement of human rights.

First, Israel has been involved in a prolonged occupation of the West Bank, Gaza, and the Golan Heights for more than thirty years. Although a number of scholars dealt with the relationships between occupation and human rights (e.g. Walsh and Peleg 1998), the effect of prolonged occupation on the human rights situation in the occupying power has not been extensively studied. Ironically, such occupation could push a country in the direction of greater attention to human rights within its own borders.

Second, the Israeli case is potentially important also in terms of the combined impact of internal and external factors. While the occupation introduced the human rights agenda to the Israeli public via international criticism of Israeli behavior in the Occupied Territories, internal factors also affected the human rights equation. Thus, the 1980s and the 1990s saw the expansion of the Israeli middle class, increasing wealth within the society, and increasing contacts with the democratic West. It is likely that these factors contributed to the greater awareness of human rights within the Israeli society (see below).

Third, the Israeli case is a "classic" example of the continuous, unrelenting tensions between the foundations of a "*communal* democracy" and the principles of *liberal* democracy. Such tensions are not limited to the relationships between the majority and the minority; they are as intense within the majority, where large numbers of people and social groups reject the ethnic character of the state or its implications. The Israeli case could teach us about the management of the ethnic drive in a world which is dominated by the ethnic revival (Smith 1981, 1986).

Fourth, the Israeli case is interesting insofar as it demonstrates the quite typical division between those individuals and groups within society who struggle on behalf of the expansion of civil and human rights (the human rights community) and those who are indifferent or even opposed to the enhancement of such rights. The intensity of the political debate in Israel, particularly in relations to the territorial issue, brings the division over human rights into sharper focus than in most countries. Thus, it teaches us about the general pattern.

Finally, the Israeli case is fascinating insofar as it demonstrates the ability and inclination of governments in ethnic democracies to use differentially consociational (or consensus) techniques and control methods in order to maintain the political stability in which they are interested. Thus, the relations between Jewish groups in Israel have always been managed consociationally, while the Jewish-Arabs ones have traditionally been governed by what Lustick calls "control" (1980). It is interesting to note that it is only recently that some measure of consociationalism has been "creeping" into Jewish-Arab relations, a pattern which probably has a promising future.

The occupation of the West Bank/Gaza, an event for which the Israeli leadership was unprepared, presented the young Israeli ethnic democracy with serious challenges. The Israeli notion of democracy has always been that of a majority rule rather than minority rights (Shamir and Sullivan 1983:322). Yet, this notion was easier to defend with an Arab population of about 15 percent within Israel proper than in face of massive human rights violations of a Palestinian population under prolonged occupation. The expansion into the West Bank/Gaza raised a series of uneasy questions over the fundamentals of the Israeli notion of democracy.

The tension within the Israeli polity did not become evident immediately following the smashing, intoxicating victory of 1967, but the Yom Kippur War of 1973 made it abundantly evident. This war broke the national consensus over security issues and generated a relentless debate over the occupation and its consequences for the Israeli democracy. Although most of the debate in Israel was not framed within the context of human rights—certainly not human rights within Israel—the "linkage" was unmistaken. Thus a few years after David Grossman, one of Israel's best known novelists, wrote about human rights violations in the Occupied Territories, he wrote a book on the conditions of Israeli Arabs (Grossman 1988, 1993).

In what areas did the occupation have a possible impact on the Israeli polity? As stated before, the "linkage" has not been studied to date in detail and, therefore, the list which follows ought to be seen as preliminary. Yet, it is possible to hypothesize that in a number of major areas, Israel has indeed witnessed positive human rights developments over the last twenty-five years or so.

Arab-Jewish Relations

Only in the 1970s the Arabs in Israel opened an organized struggle for civil equality. For the first time, they have done so under the leadership of a national body, the National Committee of the Heads of Arab Local Municipalities (Al-Peleg 1988; Genem 1993; Landau 1993). Yiftachel believes that this activity led to "certain moderation of governmental control" over the lives of the Arabs, such as decrease in land expropriation and house demolition (1997:49). Moreover, additional lands were given to Arab villages (ibid:78), and a number of Arab areas were defined as "national priority zones" (with financial incentives granted to investors and inhabitants). Also Smooha believes that Israeli Arabs had a few achievements, especially in the 1990s (1993).

The causes for this positive development vary, although they all point out to an improvement in the civil and human rights condition of the Israeli Arabs:

A increasing assertiveness of the Israeli Arabs and stronger demand on their part for equal treatment;

B growing dependence of Israeli politicians and parties on the support of the Arabs, and, as a result, increasing Arab political leverage (Lustick 1989);

C recognition by some Israeli leaders that, as part of the Oslo process, there should be an equivalent process of rethinking of Arab-Jewish relations inside Israel.

This last factor explains why so many of the positive developments occurred during the Labor government's 1992–96 administration (Ozacky-Lazar and Genem 1995). In its platform (presented to the Knesset) the Rabin government emphasized "full equality to all citizens." It specified a series of areas that required equalization. Rabin himself said he is "ashamed that there is discrimination against Arabs" (Ozacky-Lazar and Genem:6), and he emphasized that the State of Israel is the state of all its citizens (note 8 in Ozacky-Lazar and Genem:21). Also the State Ombudsman warned against the discrimination of the Arabs and called for full equality. She even stated: "when there is no integration, there is polarization" (*Maariv*, December 16, 1994). Yet, in terms of actual *implementation* of the equalization, the picture has been *mixed*. Among the main areas of progress have been the following: dramatic increase in budgets to Arab local governments, more educational facilities and hiring of teachers, working toward equalization of child support, more investment in infrastructure, and more Arab officials in government offices.

Beyond these practical areas of Jewish-Arab relations, where all observers believe that some progress has been made toward equalization, the "macro"-

issues of Israel's ethnic democracy remain unresolved. There are two fundamental, linked issues: (a) the character of the state and its definition as a Jewish state, and (b) the official status of the Arab minority.

While Israel declared itself on a number of occasions "a Jewish state," the full implications of that definition remain somewhat unclear. Over the last few years, Arabs and liberal Jews proposed that Israel declare itself "the state of all its citizens" or possibly "the state of the Jewish people and all its citizens." Such proposals are unlikely to be adopted in the foreseeable future.

Despite the absence of movement toward constitutional equalization, in several areas a "quiet revolution" in the status of Arabs had begun in the late 1990s, with the installment of the Barak government (Sontag 2000). Thus, the Supreme Court ruled (in a landmark decision in March 2000) that Arabs should not be discriminated against in land allocated by the state, land expropriated from an Arab town in central Israel was recently returned to it, the "silent deportation" of Palestinians from East Jerusalem has stopped, and so forth.

Constitutional Developments

Also in the area of constitutionalism, a change toward greater attention to civil rights is evident. Israel is a democracy without a constitution. Efforts to adopt a constitution or a bill of rights failed because of a number of barriers: (a) the *Law of Return*, which favors Jews in matters of immigration; (b) the special *State-Religion relations*, which violate some human rights such as the right of equality; and (c) the Emergency Regulations.

The first two barriers to a liberal constitution are clearly linked to the ethnic character of the state and the third to the precarious Arab-Jewish relations. These three barriers negatively affect both Arabs and Jews (especially those who are liberal and secular).

Despite this fundamental and seemingly irreversible reality, Israel witnessed a few significant constitutional developments over the last few years, most of them highly positive from the perspective of civil and human rights. First, the High Court of Justice has issued a great number of decisions expanding the civil and human rights of all Israelis. Thus, the Court determined that women have equal rights to serve in public institutions (such as religious councils) dealing with religious matters, it allowed the (Arab Party) Progressive List for Peace to run in elections, it recognized the rights of homosexuals, and in September 2000 it outlawed brutal methods used by security agents in interrogating Palestinians (Sontag 2000). Second, the Knesset enacted in April 1992 two new Basic Laws of great significance: (1) *Freedom of Occupation* (a law which can be changed only through special majority), and (2) *Human Dignity and Freedom*, which deals with protection against detention and restraint on movement, the right to dignity, etc.

Says Gavison (ibid:8): "These laws constitute, structurally, the beginning of a Bill of Rights in Israel." While she agrees that there are important human rights areas that are still uncovered, she believes that "the principle of enacting Basic Laws on human rights matters has now been accepted" (8). Kretzmer goes even further: he calls the adoption of the two 1992 Basic Laws a "mini revolution," and Goldstein takes a similar position (606). Third, while Israel signed the Convention on Civil and Political Rights in 1966, it failed to ratify the convention until August 1991. It is, however belated, a move toward greater commitment to civil and human rights.

These developments must be assessed against two realities: (a) The existence of a strong communal democracy and hegemonic state is probably more important to most Israelis than civil and human rights; (b) In the Israeli tradition, in general, individual and minority rights are peripheral (Shamir in Swersky 85). This general attitude is rooted both in the Socialist political culture brought from Eastern Europe (where majority rule was more important than liberal principles) and in the Jewish religious tradition (emphasizing duties, not rights).

Institutional Developments

In terms of the overall balance of power between various Israeli governmental branches, there has clearly been an increase in the relative power of institutions sensitive to individual rights. The courts have always been among Israel's most liberal components (along with the academe and the artistic community). This is particularly the case in regard to the High Court of Justice. The power of the High Court has been on the ascendance over the last two decades, and this is a positive sign for human and civil rights. In the absence of a constitution, the Court has, historically, played a major role in guaranteeing, and more importantly expanding, the civil and human rights of Israelis. It gained a reputation as the 'guardian' of human rights (Briskman 1988:5; Bracha 1982).

Goldstein maintains that Israeli judges created an extensive system of human rights despite the absence of a constitution and constitutional tradition. In fact, he argues, in Israeli law, "human rights have been protected almost exclusively by judge-made law" (605). He points out the special role of the High Court of Justice, established by the British as a powerful institution in order not to grant lower courts, staffed by Jewish and Arab judges, too much power(!).

Over the last few years, the High Court of Justice has been very active in protecting human rights, and especially freedom of speech, press, and association. Thus, in the late 1980s it decided against censorship of plays ("Efraim Returns to the Army" case). The Court has shown increasing willingness to challenge governmental assertion of "security interest" as grounds for restricting human rights, and did not shy away from intervening in other branches' activities (Goldstein:613). Lower courts followed the liberal line of the High Court. Thus, a Jerusalem Justice of the Peace allowed in the 1980s the showing of films on the Sabbath.

The institutional changes, as well as the constitutional ones, indicate that the system has not only the capacity but also the inclination to adopt liberal solutions to many, if not all, long-term problems.

Conscientious Objection

Fundamental changes are conditioned on the emergence of new political culture, and changes in attitudes toward conscientious objection are indicative of interesting developments in this regard. The Israel Defense Forces, Tzhal in Hebrew, have always been a symbol of Israeli, Jewish nationalism. The vast majority of Israeli Jews have, therefore, viewed the service in the IDF not only as a duty but as a privilege. The level of volunteerism has always been extremely high.

One of the effects of the occupation, and the human rights violations which it entailed, was the appearance of conscientious objection on the Israeli political scene, resulting especially from the War in Lebanon (1982) and the Intifada (1987), a phenomenon analyzed by Ruth Linn (1996).

How is conscientious objection related to human rights? First, it is an indication of the decline of the communal spirit and increase in the assertion

of individual prerogative in a society that originally has been strongly communal and decidedly nonindividualistic. Second, many believe that conscientious objection is a fundamental human right and the pursuit of that
option by growing number of Israelis is, in itself, a measure of increasing
awareness of human rights. Although the Israeli authorities never accepted
conscientious objection as legitimate, they have dealt with it quite liberally,
sending people to prison for relatively brief periods or releasing them from
military duty altogether.

Security

The Israeli society has always been strongly committed to, focused on,
and some would say obsessed with issues of security. The long struggle with
the Arabs and the British, the historical experience with anti-Semitism and
the Holocaust, could possibly explain this condition.

A strong commitment to state security, in any country, is usually correlated negatively with adherence to civil and human rights, particularly when
there is a large minority within the country and when that minority is assumed to be hostile to the majority. In that kind of situation, civil and human
rights violations are built-in, structural, and inevitable.

And, indeed, the State of Israel has violated for years the civil and human
rights of its Arab citizens and established, in general, an unfriendly human
rights environment for all of its citizens. Thus, while the Arabs lived under
Military Government until 1966, all Israelis had to endure censorship.

Nevertheless, the last thirty years have witnessed a relative strengthening
of human rights. Says Gavison: "on balance, between state security and
human rights, we see in Israel consistent improvement of human rights"
(144). Yet, Gavison recognizes that "the situation is still far from satisfactory."
Briskman, who studied the Supreme Court's attitude toward national security by comparing Israel's formative era with its more recent past, noted "a
shift in the Court's approach to the issue of national security. The Court
became more active both in its interpretive and its reviewal role. The notion
of security became more specific as a result, narrower than the notion of
security accepted by the Court in the first period" (123). Yet, the Court is
still (1988!) reluctant to adopt a decisive pro-human rights approach when
security is involved: "In the arena of national security, human rights were
less protected than in other fields" (123).

The duality of Israel's ethnic democracy is most clearly demonstrated, then, in the area of national security.

The Emergence of New Human Rights Organizations

Over the last thirty years, Israel has experienced the mushrooming of human rights activity on an unprecedented level. Although it is difficult to establish direct cause-and-effect relationships between this phenomenon and the occupation, some link is self-evident and a serious link is almost surely in existence.

Thus, there are a great number of organizations that came into being specifically in response to the occupation. Some deal with human rights violations in the Occupied Territories (e.g. B'Tselem), and others with the involvement of the Israeli society in the occupation or other military activity (e.g. Dai Lakibush, the 21st year, Women in Black, Physicians for Human Rights, and Yesh Gvul are but a few of these).

Moreover, a very large number of organizations dedicate themselves to the fostering of understanding and tolerance between Arabs and Jews (Van Leer Institute and Givat Haviva are among the largest organizations of that type; others are Interns for Peace, Sikkuy, Beit Hagefen, the Open House, etc.). But beyond the activity of organizations dealing with various aspects of the Arab-Israeli conflict, Israel has witnessed the development of a large number of organizations dealing with women's issues, the rights of the handicapped, gay and lesbian concerns, etc. (see Directory of Abraham Fund). Existing civil rights organizations (such as the Association for Civil Rights in Israel—ACRI) intensified their activity in a rather significant way.

The Politicization of the Human Rights Agenda

Traditional Israeli politics was not about "rights"; it was about "nation-building" and "survival." Thus, the very first national survey of public attitudes toward civil liberties in Israel was not conducted (by the Institute for Applied Social Research in Jerusalem) until 1975 (Simon and Landis 1990). Yet, over the last two decades, or even less, human rights had become a "leadership resource base," a pad for the launching of a national political career. Thus, several political figures in Israel "made it" through activities focusing on civil and human rights (e.g. M. K. Dedi Zucker and before him M. K. Shulamit Aloni).

Moreover, some parties have become identified with the "Rights Agenda." While in the past only Arab parties focused on civil and human rights, and almost exclusively on the concerns of the Arab minority (with the exception of the Zionist-Socialist Mapam), in the 1970s and 1980s more "Jewish" parties became involved (notably Dash, Ratz, Shinui, and eventually Meretz). Today, more and more parties use "rights terminology" in their political platforms.

In general, a human rights focus in the political arena has become legitimate and even respectable. Large numbers of Israelis, especially members of the middle and upper-middle class, professionals and intellectuals, are strongly committed to civil and human rights. Most importantly, the activity in one area of human rights (e.g., human rights violations in the Occupied Territories) is likely to spill over into other areas of human rights (e.g. women's issues, state-religion relations, etc.).

Political Tolerance

The overall situation in Israel does not promise a high degree of political tolerance. There are a number of factors weighing against tolerance: (1) an intense interethnic conflict inside the country, and between the state and all of its neighbors; (2) a rather weak liberal tradition, attitudinally, behaviorally, and legalistically; (3) a strong commitment to the national collective *against* adherence to individual rights and private concerns, as well as loyalty to group, sectarian interest.

It is interesting to note that *despite* these "negatives," a measure of what might be defined as *"guarded liberalism"* has evolved in Israel, particularly over the last three decades. The mechanisms through which this phenomenon occurred are not yet fully clear, but the emergence of "political tolerance" is promising.

Michal Shamir compared Israeli public opinion to that of the U.S. and New Zealand. Not surprisingly, she found out that Israelis are less tolerant than Americans and even less than New Zealanders. On the other hand, Shamir found out that Israeli political elites are more tolerant than the general public, although not by much. This relative elite's tolerance operates particularly vis-à-vis the Arabs. Thus, while 75 percent of the Knesset members interviewed support equal rights to Israeli Arabs, among the public the range is 40–55 percent. On the other hand, the elites were intolerant toward extreme rightwing groups, whom they apparently saw as a danger to democracy.

Even more interesting, in terms of this study, are findings regarding *nonpolitical elites* (academics, intellectuals, journalists, etc.). These findings indicate that such elites are even more tolerant than political elites. Shamir states about these elites: "These groups have influence in society. They can effect tolerance (since they have financial, political and social resources) by adopting the role of *activist groups on behalf of civil and human rights* and political tolerance, within educational, legal and judicial frameworks" (91).

There is no doubt that this is exactly what has occurred in Israel, particularly since 1977. Much of the energy of the growingly affluent, educated civil society has gone toward the liberalization of the society and the political system.

The Duality of Human Rights

The progress of civil and human rights in Israel has not been linear, consistent, or unambiguous, because civil and human rights are part of the much larger, murky, and conflictual political picture of the country. Only within a vacuum could one have a sudden, full-blown appearance of rights on a political scene. Such a vacuum occurred, for example, in Germany and Japan following World War II, or in France and the U.S. following their revolutions. When civil and human rights are the subject of a larger political game, their development is likely to be "messy," as indeed has been the case of Israel.

Thus, Simon and Landis (97–99) report sharp decline between 1975 and 1986–87 in the overall tolerance in Israel toward persons supporting direct talks with the PLO, the establishment of a Palestinian state, etc. I would venture that this seemingly anti-human rights attitude is reflective of the reign of Likud and this party's position toward these substantive issues.

Like Shamir, Simon and Landis report that "persons with higher education and higher incomes were more likely than less educated and poorer respondents to be tolerant of unpopular political sentiments" (98). Moreover, secular Jews were more tolerant than religious ones.

These findings are indicative (along with many other phenomena) of the evolving of two camps, two publics, and two agendas, competing with each other for dominance within the Israeli polity:

A the communal, ethnic, nationalist camp of the Likud and the religious parties, which speaks the language of primordial tribalism, a language which rejects civil and human rights as nonexistent, unimportant, peripheral, or, at best, secondary;

B the liberal, open, secular, Westernized public of Labor and Meretz, which increasingly uses the language of civil and human rights, not only or even mainly in regard to the Arab issue. For this camp, civil and human rights have become the litmus test for the quality of Israel's democracy.

The split in the Israeli society is reflected institutionally, where certain groups (artists, academics, jurists, journalists) are in the forefront of the movement toward greater civil and human rights. To state that "the Israeli public is not homogeneous in its support" of civil and human rights (Simon and Landis 102) is to *understate* the case: the division is extremely deep.

In terms of the larger historical picture, it seems that the traditional Israeli policy of total domination over the Arabs—inside and outside Israel—has backfired insofar as civil and human rights are concerned. It has not only galvanized Arab resistance inside Israel, but has also led to practically worldwide condemnation of Israeli human rights policy in the Occupied Territories.

The debate over civil and human rights has now "spread" into a much more fundamental question regarding the Israeli polity. The single most important question has now become the following: Can Israel be both Jewish and Democratic, or, in the language of this essay, is the notion of "communal democracy" oxymoronic? While there is a consensus today that the relations between Judaism and democracy in Israel is *the key* for the country's civil and human rights status (a consensus reflected in a 1996 volume edited by Dafna Barak-Erez), there is a serious debate over the solution to that dilemma.

Summary

The Israeli case should be regarded as a "classic" for the dilemma of communality vs. rights. While Israel is a Jewish state by both self-definition and even international status, a precise definition of that "Jewishness" and its implications remains unclear and hotly debated. Interestingly, the "Jewishness" of Israel is a bone of contention not only (and quite naturally) between Jewish and Arab citizens of Israel but also inside Israel's Jewish community.

The establishment of a Palestinian state in the West Bank and the Gaza Strip could, possibly, ease some of the Arab frustrations vis-à-vis the Jewish state. Thus, if the Palestinian state would enact its own Law of Return (which it almost surely will) and limit it to Palestinians, a certain equality between that Arab state and its Israeli neighbor would emerge. On the other hand, a peace settlement between Israel and the Palestinians is likely to lead to the intensification of Arab demands, within Israel, for full equality as individuals and, possibly, national (or minority) rights. While the equalization of individual rights is likely, the recognition of the Palestinians as a political minority within Israel is unlikely in the foreseeable future. In this sense, the struggle between the communal agenda and the right agenda is likely to continue for some time to come.

The Israeli case is by no means unique. The struggle between communal and individual rights is extremely widespread and is likely to become even more prevalent in view of growing democratization *and* ethnic conscience all over the world. India, for example, has recently installed a nationalist Hindu government, clearly negating the universalistic principles of its founders. Sri Lanka went the same way decades ago.

In numerous ethnically divided societies, the state is conceived as the state of and for the "core nation," not as belonging to the entire citizenry. Many democracies are, in fact, what the historian Rogers Brubaker called "nationalizing states, ethnically heterogenous yet conceived as nation-states" (1996:57). In the past, a number of states were clearly identified with one "core nation:" Canada between 1867 and the 1960s, Northern Ireland between 1921 and 1972, and Poland between the wars are good examples of national or even nationalizing states.

In the more recent past, in addition to Israel, communal democracies have emerged in Malaysia, Sri Lanka, and in some of the former Yugoslav (e.g. Croatia) and Soviet (e.g. Georgia) Republics. Even in Germany (and previously West Germany), persons of German descent, however remote, have been able to obtain citizenship, while persons of non-German parentage could not, even if born in Germany.

In examining different regime types, it is important to remember that their implication for the human rights of their population is enormous. This is the case especially for minorities. It is also important to realize that no regime is beyond changing, as clearly demonstrated over the last decade in world politics.

Bibliography

Al-Peleg, Zvi. 1988. "Arabs' Rights." In Ann Swersky, ed. ACRI: Tel Aviv, 94–108 (in Hebrew).

Aranoff, Myron. 1989. *Israeli Visions and Divisions: Cultural Change and Political Conflict*. New Brunswick, NJ: Transaction Press.

Barak-Erez, Dafna, ed. 1996. *A Jewish and Democratic State*. Tel-Aviv: Tel-Aviv University School of Law (in Hebrew).

Barzilai, Gad. 1998. "Political Institutions and Conflict Resolution: The Israeli Supreme Court and the Peace Process." In Ilan Peleg, ed. *The Middle East Peace Process*. Albany: SUNY Press.

Bracha, Baruch. 1982. "The Protection of Human Rights in Israel." *Israel Yearbook of Human Rights*. Vol. 12, No. 2, Tel Aviv University.

Briskman, Dana. 1988. "National Security vs. Human Rights: An Analysis of the Approach of the Israeli Supreme Court to the Conflict between National Security and Civil Liberties." Harvard Law School, unpublished thesis.

Brubaker, Rogers. 1996. *Nationalism Reframed: Nationhood and the National Question in New Europe*. Cambridge: Cambridge University Press.

Esman, Milton J. 1973. "The Management of Communal Conflict." *Public Policy* 21:49–78.

Evans, Peter B., Dietrich Rueschemeyer, and Theda Skocpol, eds. 1985. *Bringing the State Back In*. Cambridge: Cambridge University Press.

Gavison, Ruth. 1994. Human Rights in Israel. Tel Aviv: Ministry of Defense (in Hebrew).

Genem, Asad. 1993. *Israeli Arabs Toward the 21st Century: A Review*. The Institute for the Study of Peace, Givat Haviva (in Hebrew).

Goldstein, Stephen. 1994. "Protection of Human Rights by Judges: The Israeli Experience." *St. Louis University Law Review* 38 (Spring):605–618.

Grossman, David. 1988. *The Yellow Wind*. New York: Farrar, Straus, Giroux.

Grossman, David. 1993. *Sleeping On a Wire: Conversations With Palestinians in Israel*. New York: Farrar, Straus, Giroux.

Gurr, Ted Robert. 1993. *Minorities at Risk: An Ethnopolitical Conflict* Washington D.C.: Institute of Peace Press.

Inoue, Tatsuo. 1999. "Human Rights and Asian Values." In Joanne R. Bauer and Daniel A. Bell, eds. *The East Asian Challenge for Human Rights* Cambridge: Cambridge University Press.

Kretzmer, David. 1990. *The Legal Status of the Arabs in Israel*. Boulder, CO: West-view Press.

Kretzmer, David. 1992. "The New Basic Laws on Human Rights: A Mini-Revolution in Israeli Constitutional Law?" *Israel Law Review*, Vol. 26.

Kymlicka, Will. 1995. *Multicultural Citizenship: A Liberal Theory of Minority Rights*. Oxford: Clarendon Press.

Laczko, Leslie. 1994. "Canada's Pluralism in Comparative Perspective." *Ethnic and Racial Studies* 17 (1):20–41.

Landau, Jacob. 1993. *The Arab Minority in Israel 1967–1991: Political Perspectives*. Tel-Aviv: Am Oved (in Hebrew).

Lijphart, Arend. 1977. *Democracy in Plural Societies: A Comparative Exploration*. New Haven: Yale University Press.

Lijphart, Arend. 1984. *Democracies: Patterns of Majoritarican and Consensual Government in Twenty-One Countries*. New Haven: Yale University Press.

Linn, Ruth. 1996. *Conscience At War: The Israeli Soldier As A Moral Critic*. Albany: SUNY Press.

Lustick, Ian. 1979. "Stability in Deeply Divided Societies: Consociationalisation vs. Control." *World Politics* 31 (3) (April):325–344.

Lustick, Ian. 1989. "The Political Road to Binationalism: Arabs in Jewish Politics." In Ilan Peleg and Ofira Seliktar, eds. *The Emergence of a Binational Israel: The Second Republic in the Making*. Boulder: Westview Press, 97–123.

Lustick, Ian. 1980. *Arabs In the Jewish State: Israel's Control Over a National Minority*. Austin: University of Texas Press.

Nielsson, Gunnar. 1985. "States and "Nation-Groups": A Global Taxonomy." In Edward Tiryakian and Ronald Rogowski, eds. *New Nationalisms in the Developed West*. London: Allen and Unwin, 27–56.

Ozacky-Lazar, Sarah and Asad Genem. 1995. "Between Peace and Equality: The Arabs in Israel in the Midterm of Labor-Meretz Government." Institute for the Study of Peace, Givat Haviva, January, 23 pp (in Hebrew).

Peled, Yoav. 1992 "Ethnic Democracy and the Legal Construction of Citizenship: Arab Citizens of the Jewish State." *American Political Science Review* 86 (June):432–443.

Peleg, Ilan. 1987. *Begin's Foreign Policy*. Westport, CT: Greenwood Press.

Peleg, Ilan and Ofira Seliktar, eds. 1989. *The Emergence of a Binational Israel: The Second Republic in the Making*. Boulder: Westview Press.

Peleg, Ilan, ed. 1993. *Patterns of Censorship Around the World*. Boulder: Westview Press.

Peleg, Ilan. 1994. "Begin-Sharon's War in Lebanon." In Michael Stohl, ed. *Terrorism*. Boulder: Westview Press.

Peleg, Ilan. 1995. *Human Rights in the West Bank Gaza: Legacy and Politics*. Syracuse: Syracuse University Press.

Peleg, Ilan. 1998. *The Middle East Peace Process: Interdisciplinary Perspectives*. Albany: SUNY Press.

Senelle, Robert. 1978. *The Reform of the Belgian State*. Brussels, Ministry of Foreign Affairs.

Shafir, Gershon L. and Yoav Peled. 1998. "Citizenship and Stratification in an Ethinic Democracy." *Ethnic and Racial Studies* 21(3) (May):408–27.

Shamir, Michal. "Political Tolerance and Leadership in the Israeli Society." In Swersky (1988), 81–93 (in Hebrew).

Shamir, Michal and John Sullivan. 1983. "The Political Context of Tolerance: The U.S. and Israel." *American Political Science Review* 73:92–106.

Simon, Rita J. and Jean M. Landis. 1990. "Trends in Public Support for Civil Liberties and Due Process in Israeli Society." *Social Science Quarterly* 71 (1) (Spring):93–104.

Smith, Anthony. 1981. *The Ethnic Revival*. New York and Cambridge: Cambridge University Press.

Smith, Anthony. 1986. *The Ethnic Origins of a Nation*. Oxford: Basil Blackwell.

Smooha, Sammy. 1990. "Minority Status in an Ethnic Democracy: The Status of the Arab Minority in Israel." *Ethnic and Racial Studies* 13 (3):389–413.

Smooha, Sammy. 1993. "National, Ethnic and Class Cleavages, and Israel's Democracy." In Uri Ram, ed. *The Israeli Society: Critical Perspectives*. Tel-Aviv: Breirot (in Hebrew).

Sontag, Deborah. 2000. "Israel Is Slowly Shedding Harsh Treatment of Arabs." *New York Times* (April 7):A1, A12.

Swersky, Ann, ed. 1988. Human Rights in Israel: Articles in Memory of Judge Hamm Shelah Edanim Publishers/Yediot Ahrouot, Tel-Aviv (in Hebrew).

Walsh, Brian and Ilan Peleg. 1998. "Human Rights Under Military Occupation: The Need for Expansion." *International Journal of Human Rights* 2(1):62–78.

Xin, Chunying. 1995. "A Brief History of the Modern Human Rights Discourse in China." *Human Rights Dialogue* 3 (December):4–5.

Yiftachel, Oren. 1997. *Watching Over the Vineyard: The Example of Majd Al-Korum*. The Institute for Israeli Arab Studies, Ra'anana, (in Hebrew).

Yiftachel, Oren. 1998. "Democracy of Ethnocracy? Territory and Settler Politics in Israel/Palestine." *Middle East Report* (Summer):8–13.

Zakaria, Fareed. 1997. "The Rise of Illiberal Democracy." *Foreign Affairs* 76 (2) (November–December):22–43.

Zerubavel, Yael. 1995. *Recovered Roots: Collective Memory and the Making of Israeli National Tradition*. Chicago: University of Chicago Press.

12 Walking Two Roads

Reading Human Rights in Contemporary Chinese Fiction

Tomas N. Santos

Literary realism bears a tenuous relationship to life. As literature, it is mere representation, a facsimile of life; yet, in its capacity to share experience, it seeks to *be* life. In the People's Republic of China (PRC), where literary practice is entangled with the party bureaucracy, writers have had little freedom and, at best, few guidelines. No one can tell you the difference between socialist realism and rightist literature. Ever since the establishment of the PRC in 1949, its writers have had to practice—consciously or unconsciously—the Taoist dictum of "walking two roads." Faced with censorship on the one hand, and the need to tell the truth on the other, Chinese writers have had to constantly test the limits of artistic freedom.

In his by now infamous "Talks at the Yan'an Forum on Literature and Art" (1942), Mao Zedong declared that writers and artists need adhere to only two criteria: the political and the artistic, with the political criterion the more important of the two. The political criterion, never clearly defined from its promulgation, remains vague to allow for changing social needs. This vagueness allows policy to be made up on a whim, and creates an unstable field for writers. Thus, writers have had to simultaneously walk the two roads of political imperative and artistic freedom in their effort to turn life to writing, writing to life. Says Feng Jicai (b. 1942) of his writing during the Cultural Revolution: "If anyone knocked on the door, I would immediately put down my pen and hide anything I'd written. Had someone discovered even a line or two of it, not only would I have been a goner, my family would have been wiped out as well"(Martin and Kinkley 1992).

Why write at all? Why even tell one's story? As a creative writer myself, I am sensitive to the conflict between art and politics. In the early seventies, my late father, Filipino writer Bienvenido Santos, was advised by friends not go back to Manila because writers were being jailed "for their protection" by the Marcos dictatorship. One of the things he kept repeating both to me and to other Asian writers was this: "You have to tell your own story. If you don't, no one else will tell it for you—or worse, someone else will tell it for you." Witnessing my father's exile has made me more appreciative of Chinese writers for whom even exile may be a luxury.

I wish to explore how writers in the PRC deal with human rights issues, and, if possible, seek a literature of testimony in the short story. Stories turn private issues into public ones; inevitably, one senses recurring themes of protest. My assumption is that, even in translation, a close reading of stories presents us with a way to view human rights in China. The discipline of literature works within the tension of the universal and the relative. It is universal because it deals with thought and emotion across cultures. It is relative because our understanding of culture is guided by particular notions of self and language. Driving the works I have chosen is something I can only describe as an unspeakable core. Elaine Scarry says that the aspects of pain are negation, the destruction of language, the conflation of private and public, and the obliteration of the contents of consciousness. The possibility is that one can read a literature of testimony by peeling away layers of narrative and getting to the core of suffering in a story. Buddhists would say that the narrative of life is driven by desire and its concomitant suffering. In a general sense then, all narratives have this core. However, in very specific ways, these stories bear witness to social injustice. In the first story, Liu Binyan's "The Fifth Man in the Overcoat" (1979), the center of pain is the unspoken anguish of Jin Daqing's wife; in the second story, Zhang Jie's "Love Must Not Be Forgotten" (1983), it is the silence of Zhong Yu's lover; in the third, Can Xue's "The Summons" (1993), it is Old Mu Xi's inability to speak his guilt. I would like to show how contemporary Chinese fiction teaches us ways to read views from inside, to perceive contexts of suffering, and to demonstrate how in stories truth is adumbrated in silence.

Andrew J. Nathan (1997) has argued that the PRC should guarantee freedom of speech as part of a long-term strategy for political stability. The party leadership seems to recognize this, but their strategy has nevertheless been to "allow the wind to blow alternately warm and cold." The current publishing situation in the PRC reflects a complex economy of power and privilege (Link 1984:1–13). Publication is a privilege that operates within this complex economy. Privileges can be bartered. An editor may gain favor by publishing the work of a top official's close relative, and be favored in return by being given the freedom to publish a controversial article (within limits, of course). In the domain of writers, critics, editors, censors, and officials, this complex economy can have periods of *shou* (restriction) and *fang* (latitude). When *shou* is in the air, the literary-political climate is described as beset by a cold wind; when *fang* is in the air, the wind blows warm. The leadership tries to manipulate cold and warm to suit their political ends—to gain support for new projects, warm wind; to crack down on permissiveness, cold wind.

Writers and editors are constantly reading the winds, seeking chances to speak freely. In a climate where one doesn't know which way the wind will blow, it is surprising that anyone would write at all. The fact that writers do speak out and take chances suggests that social criticism is a moral imperative. The history of Chinese literature demonstrates that literature and social criticism go hand in hand. The Confucian scholar, for instance, made no distinction between literature, politics, and morality. You were what you wrote (you were even *how* you wrote, as calligraphy was said to express your true character), and who you were was inseparable from the social good.

Baogao Wenxue

Liu Binyan, now living in the U.S., was a journalist in the PRC who in the late 1970s made popular a type of literature called journalistic fiction or reportage writing (*baogao wenxue*), where little distinction was made or claimed between "reporting" and "telling a story." Here, literary realism acquires a kind of "actualism"; one could go to Y city in X province to verify the content of the story. Only the names are changed to protect the innocent, or, in this case, the guilty. His story entitled "The Fifth Man in the Overcoat" (1983) is a thinly disguised attack on a party leader who sent people into labor camps during the Cultural Revolution. The names clearly separate good and bad: the journalist's name is Jin Daqing (Gold Great Clarity), the treacherous cadre's name is Ho Qixiong (Where's His Heroism?).

Jin Daqing has been returned to his old job in a newspaper office after twenty years in forced exile. Jin is "the fifth man in the overcoat," meaning that the old army trenchcoat he owns has been "bequeathed" four times during his imprisonment, the last owner being his friend Gu Tiancheng. At the newspaper office, Jin meets deputy secretary Ho Qixiong. Ho is now on the editorial staff of the newspaper. In a routine investigation, Jin discovers that Ho had unjustly labeled Gu Tiancheng a rightist. Ho had sent his own wife into exile, divorced her, and had set his sights on Jiang Zhenfang, Gu Tiancheng's wife. When refused by Jiang Zhenfang, Ho started a rumor that Jiang was an adulteress.

The result of Jin's investigations is to restore Jiang Zhenfang's good name. The scene where Jiang's exoneration takes place is the newspaper office, at a meeting of the editorial board. The meeting acquires the semblance of a court of law. Jin interrogates Comrade Dong:

> Comrade Dong, you say you had illicit sexual relations with Jiang Zhenfang and cite two pieces of evidence to substantiate your claim. I want to ask you, since you say you have seen a black mole on her breast: just how big was that black mole? And was there one, or more than one? (87)

In the mock trial, where the issue of whether Jiang's putative lover has really seen her body, private truth crosses over into the public realm — exactly the opposite of how rumor works, where public judgment is exercised over private rights — and eventually we see that Comrade Dong had lied about the affair. In exonerating Jiang Zhenfang, Jin Daqing exonerates other women like her who are victims of false accusation. Jin tells Jiang's sister, "This isn't just for your sister. There are so many others like her!"(89). Jin's victory is for Ho's exiled wife. It is for Jin Daqing's wife, who died just a few days before his release. It is a victory for those who have been sent away and silenced.

In a story that is supposed to be closer to documentary than fiction, Liu Binyan moves more and more toward a sense of the general (many women) as opposed to the particular (Jiang Zhenfang); in saying that Jin is the fifth man in the overcoat, he alludes to all the others who died in the labor camps; in conflating public and private in the "courtroom scene," he allows the audience (the implied newsroom audience as well as the reader) to participate in the investigation and to see the need for justice; and in turning newsroom to courtroom, he is saying that journalists have a moral obligation to tell the truth. Beyond the exposure of Ho Qixiong's treachery, Liu's story speaks strongly for all who were silenced during the Cultural Revolution.

Jin's investigation is not a simple inquiry into facts, it is a means to restore a proper relationship between the individual and society. Just as the reporter in the story was compelled to denounce the injustices perpetrated against women, so also the author make a statement about how stories can be used to criticize heinous practices that were condoned in the past. The reasoning is this: if these practices were permissible before, do they not still exist? The suggestion is that they do exist. Of course, all that Liu Binyan could do was to suggest that they did, because to say that they in fact do *in the present* would have placed him in grave danger.

From a Western perspective, all people are entitled to basic rights; just because one person has behaved badly doesn't mean he isn't deserving of his rights as a human being. From a Chinese perspective, a person who behaves like Ho Qixiong needs to be punished. He should not have used his office to gain selfish ends. His duty was first to the people. There's a clash between the Chinese perception of duty and the Western perception of rights. From the outside, looking in, we can say that rights apply equally to all; from the inside, looking out, the Chinese can say, Ho didn't do his duty, and the question of rights need not even be raised. The moral dilemma this presents impacts on our idea of universal rights. When an injustice has been done, rights have been violated. Theoretically, the perpetrator of the injustice doesn't lose his/her rights as a human being and is still entitled to due process. In the case of Ho, the story's bias against him predisposes the reader to say that he has already given up his human rights by acting inhumanely. From the inside, the question of rights is elided, subsumed by the Chinese concept of duty. From the outside, we are invited to forge a compromise between duty and rights. *Baogao wenxue* emerged in the late 1970s. At about the same time, a new type of socialist realism emerged as well. It was intended to engage private truth, a departure from the public truth of journalistic fiction. Writers of journalistic fiction used reportage as forums for social criticism. Writers such as Zhang Jie use the mask of the personal to explore the realm of the private.

Socialist Realism as Private Utterance

The title story of Zhang Jie's collection *Love Must Not Be Forgotten* (*Ai, shi bu neng wangji de*) was a cause célèbre and widely read due to its topic: extramarital love. The story could have been censored, but at the time of its writing, the winds were blowing warm, and the new policy being put forth in the Deng Xiaoping era was that the state should withdraw from interference in the private sphere. The narrator, Shanshan, has chosen not to marry. She says, "To live single is not such a fearful disaster. I believe it may be a sign of a step forward in culture, education and the quality of life" (13). Individual desire does not seem to be as important as the three greater goods of culture, education and the quality of life. A closer look at the story, however, discloses a truer intent: it *is* about individual desire, the persistence of love, and the tragic sublimation of desire for social and political reasons. It is not about Shanshan; it is about her mother Zhong Yu; ultimately, it is about Zhong Yu's lover. After her mother dies, Shanshan discovers her mother's diary "Love Must Not Be Forgotten" (thus nesting one text within another, and yet another, considering that the collection of stories bears the same title) and reads it. She says, "They read neither like stories, essays, a diary or letters. But after reading the whole I formed a hazy impression, helped out by my imperfect memory. Thinking it over, I finally realized that this was not a lifeless manuscript I was holding, but an anguished, loving heart" (5). Her mother had never loved her husband. She had been for twenty years in love with another, a former colleague who in the 1930s had married the daughter of a man who saved his life ("Out of a sense of duty, of gratitude to the dead and deep class feeling, he had unhesitatingly married the daughter"[6]). The man becomes a high-ranking party member, but is denounced and killed during the Cultural Revolution. To the day she dies, her mother can love no one else.

By nesting one "incoherent" narrative within a larger, more coherent account, the narrator shelters her mother's story and writes around the atrocities that took place during the Cultural Revolution. Mother's story can be regarded as pure romantic idealism, and therefore harmless. She never even once clasped hands with the man she loved. The core of the diary—and by extension—the story, is the man's presence. Even when he is not there, her mother feels his presence. From mother's diary notes:

> I often stay far away from Beijing, hoping time and distance will help me to forget you. But when I return, as the train pulls into the station, my head reels. I stand on the platform looking round intently, as if someone were waiting for me. (9)

This is corroborated in the main narrative when Shanshan says,

Yes, mother never let me go to the station to meet her when she came back from a trip, preferring to stand alone on the platform and imagine that he had met her. Poor mother with her greying hair was as infatuated as a girl. (9)

The part of the story where the daughter's account coincides less perfectly with the mother's diary is when each recounts what happened to the old cadre. The daughter's account:

He must have been killed in the Cultural Revolution. Perhaps because of the conditions then, that section of the diary is ambiguous and obscure. Mother had been so fiercely attacked for her writing; it amazed me that she went on keeping a diary. (10)

Mother's diary entry, as she speaks in it to the man she loves:

If only I could have borne that inhuman treatment for you, so that you could have lived on! You should have lived to see your name cleared and take up your work again, for the sake of those who loved you. I knew you could not be a counter-revolutionary. You were one of the finest men killed. That's why I love you—I am not afraid now to avow it. (11)

The mother and daughter hold widely dissimilar views on the death of the lover. Mother mentions the "inhuman treatment" and wishes she could have borne his suffering for him; she says that he was killed for being a counter-revolutionary. The mother says very definite things about what happened to the man. On the other hand, Shanshan's account is almost conjectural ("He must have been killed in the Cultural Revolution"), and she is disinclined to investigate further, saying that "that section of the diary is *ambiguous* and *obscure*." (Italics mine; there is nothing ambiguous or obscure about it.) She even changes the subject, saying it amazed her that mother kept a diary even after being attacked for her writing.

The gap between the daughter's account and the mother's is generational, rhetorical, and tactical. It is a generational difference insofar as mother is a throwback to the bourgeois romantic idealism of the 1930s; Shanshan is a child of the republic, she is pragmatic, optimistic. It is rhetorical insofar as each addresses a different audience: mother addresses her lover, the daughter addresses an amorphous group. Shanshan creates an audience of casual onlookers when she says it amazed her that mother kept a diary in spite of the political situation. It almost sounds like a disavowal of her mother's actions. There may be a reason for this rhetorical stance because ultimately, the space between mother and daughter may be a tactic by the author to encase the unspoken suffering of the old cadre. Stories open paths. The old cadre's suffering is accessible only through Zhong Yu, and Zhong Yu's suffering is accessible only through her daughter, and finally, the daughter's perplexity is masked by the platitudinous moral: "To live single is not such a fearful disaster. I believe it may be a sign of a step forward in culture, education and the quality of life." The author Zhang Jie moves us through various encrustations of a political life, and before we know it, has allowed us to witness the unspoken center of pain.

Zhang Jie uses the mother-daughter relationship to negotiate a tricky terrain in modern Chinese life. Shanshan is very patriotic, and to her, the betterment of society takes priority over private joy. However, she is not much different from her mother because both of them are trapped by their ideals—mother by romantic love, daughter by revolutionary idealism. By showing how both women are trapped by their ideals, the author dramatizes the dilemma most women face in the PRC: the traditional idea of family is subsumed by the state, and one's private life is controlled by the state; love is shunned in favor of work. The story could just as easily be titled "Love Must Be Forgotten."

To add further complexity to the comparison of Shanshan and Zhong Yu, the author finesses mother's romance by the device of a collection of Chekhov's works. The collected works of Anton Chekhov was a gift from Zhong Yu's proletarian "lover," and she would rather purchase a duplicate set for her daughter than give up her own carefully annotated volumes. Russian writers have been popular in China because of their ability to provide social criticism. In this case, where Shanshan would read Chekhov for social criticism, her mother read him for the deepest romantic experience. Zhong Yu feels that whatever reverberates within her from those texts must come from her silent lover. For Shanshan, whose boyfriend is a stunning replica of Myron's Discobulus, a relationship seems out of the question. He has the body, but he may not be very bright. Her friends tell her to take him seriously, but she would rather not. Her mother's diary keeps pressing into her thoughts. Perhaps she has learned from her mother that love isn't a matter of availability. This is the daughter's personal struggle.

Zhang Jie strikes a chord for a woman's right to freedom. By showing both mother and daughter as equally unfulfilled, she writes a story for women who, like the mother, could not speak but in a diary and, like the daughter, could not realize the depth of her own unhappiness.

What ultimately becomes of the old cadre's suffering and death? The more noble his portrayal, the stronger the protest over the injustices that took place during the Cultural Revolution. This is the most disturbing part of the text, and it is not fully articulated. The matter of his death is third-hand speculation. But mother's diary suggests the truth: like many other loyal party members, he was betrayed and killed by his own people.

If Liu Binyan's actualism found further refinement in the private masks of Zhang Jie's work, by the time we get to Can Xue, the writing seems so far removed from the real that her critics will label her "insane" and "paranoid." Such criticism may well remove her from censure and allow her to write the more innovative pieces in contemporary Chinese literature. Says critic Lu Tonglin, "Can Xue in her fiction captures the absurd essence of the world of post-Mao China, where any well-defined value system has been dismantled, discredited, and dissimulated" (68).

Walking Two Roads

"The Summons" has many unrealistic elements: a dreamlike ending, a vague location, an unspecified time. Old Mu Xi awakens in a boat on a river so dirty and so wide that he cannot see its banks. He is in the river he has sought after all his life, the river that erases memory. But now he cannot remember why he sought this river in the first place. So much time has passed between now and the time he ran away from his village that he can no longer be sure if the events that prompted his escape ever really happened. He may have killed a man in a dispute over property. The dispute concerned "a distribution plan" in which Mu Xi lost all of his land to his friend. The plan had been approved by the villagers. Later, Mu Xi kills his friend with a sickle and begins "his prolonged life as a fugitive" (207). He lives in the forest. He is plagued by nightmares. He loses his voice, his understanding of language; he eats leaves, goes about naked, and slowly begins to mummify. Children are heard calling out "Old Mu Xi! Old Mu Xi!" but they are not really calling out to him because he has become the stuff of folklore. As he expires, he enters a dreamland. The last line of the story reads: "And that dreamland led to all that was written afterward."

The "distribution plan" backed by the villagers alludes to the era of Mao with its land reform, purges, and the excoriation of landowners. We do not know if the action his friend took against him was justified; nor can we determine whether the villagers had good reason to support his friend.

"The Summons" reverses some of the elements we saw in "The Fifth Man in the Overcoat." 1) There is no sense of history. We cannot say whether any of this happened during the Cultural Revolution. The dispute over property could have taken place at any period. 2) The point of view character Mu Xi is the villain; he goes against the will of the collective. He should not have killed his friend. It's ironic, too, that he uses a sickle—the symbol of Communism—to commit murder. 3) The villain is never brought to justice. At the end of the story, the "summons" isn't a summons to appear in a court of law. It is a call to be integrated into a larger whole, the whole of nature, perhaps. 4) The moral stance of the writer isn't clear. At times, Mu Xi imagines his victim before him again, and kills him again. At other times, he wonders if all of it had been an illusion. The only thing he is certain of is that something had forced his departure.

How can this be a literature of witness? The key, I believe, is that Can Xue takes a larger view of testimony. She witnesses the effects of violence, the persistent nightmare of living under one-party rule, and the consequences of a life that is cut off from its past. The most terrifying passage in "The Summons" occurs where Mu Xi imagines himself floating in space:

Whenever he fell asleep, he felt clearly that he was suspended in midair. Beneath him, the villagers were busy working their fields, barefoot children ambled along the bank between the plots, chimneys gave out a light-gray smoke; yet all of that had nothing to do with him. Hanging in midair, he felt dizzy; it seemed as if his innards were flying out of his body. (209)

The horror in this passage comes from Mu Xi's disembodiment/disembowelment overlaid onto a peaceful rural scene. It is as though Can Xue is asking us to see something beyond the ordinary. In her Foreword to *Dialogues in Paradise* she says, "All of a sudden, I was thirty. Ten years of youth had slipped by in a struggle. What I have to say is something beyond ordinary consciousness, beyond ordinary talk. I want to say it in the form of literature and imagination. Something abstract, something emotional condenses itself in me." Can Xue was born in 1952. The "ten years of youth (that) had slipped by in a struggle" correspond historically with the last years of the Cultural Revolution and the first years of the post-Mao era. It is very likely that the abstract, emotional "something" that we are invited to experience in "The Summons," is the grotesque fear that prevents people from leading ordinary lives, the ever-present threat of violence and reprisal. In both an intangible and a real way, there will always be that unspoken guilt about lives taken, friendships sacrificed, loyalties betrayed—the sum of guilt and fear: the "summons" that may arrive at any moment.

Abstract though her stories might be, Can Xue is probably better connected to the tradition of Chinese literature than her contemporaries. One example is her other dreamlike piece "Yellow Mud Street," a novella. She uses traditional imagery: the stagnant water in Yellow Mud Street reminds us of "Dead Water" (1927), the protest poem by Wen Yiduo; the sleepy almost drugged out existence of the people on Yellow Mud Street recalls the eaters of reverie-leaves in the satirical Cat Country by Lao She, and the dreamlike quality of most of her fiction has antecedents in such classics as Dream of the Red Chamber. She puzzles over the question of individual identity (Old Floating Cloud, 47)—and to such an extent that the novella is reminiscent of Lu Xun's "The True Story of Ah Q" (1918), where Lu Xun uses the "nobody" Ah Q as a figure for China. The character Ah Q is simultaneously an individual and a type. He is individual for his peculiar arrogance and for his ringworms. He is a type because Lu Xun gives him allegorical status: Ah Q is to his tormentors as China is in the face of Western powers. The "truth" of Lu Xun's short story goes beyond the facts of ordinary life toward a critique of Chinese society. To the outsider, this story about a stupid peasant who gets himself killed is a satire, a critique of China's complacency in the midst of imminent partition by Western powers. What may not be so evident to the outsider, but obvious to the insider, is the intense bitterness of Lu Xun's critique. In sum, Can Xue links many literary practices that have been utilized throughout the history of Chinese imaginative literature.

The last line of "The Summons" tells us that Mu Xi has entered a dreamland that "led to all that was written afterward." The ending signals the transformation of Mu Xi, not the end of Mu Xi. Mu Xi is like the self/nation that has to be transformed, and the new China is the new text that has yet to be written—and in a context that allows for transcendence of previous conflicts. The figure of Mu Xi, especially in the later stages of his transformation, acquires the quality of a Taoist sage: incomprehensible, incongruous, mystical. Animals do not harm him. His blood turns green, indicating that he has become more vegetable than human, and in the end he completes the cycle by being one with nature.

Conclusion

How then does one read these stories? Knowing what the constraints are on writers in the PRC, we read these stories as testimonies of survival, witnesses to private grief. Each story discloses a common core of silence and of suffering. Liu Binyan, through journalistic fiction, has faced up to the evils of one-party rule. Zhang Jie, by concealing the "heart" of the story in a socialist narrative, has exposed the lack of heart in socialist thinking. Can Xue, through experimental fiction, has touched the soul of fear in contemporary life. Each of these stories has explored the realm of the private, and with different results: the first deals with the "factual" aspects of privacy in order to publicly vindicate Jiang Zhenfang; the second treats of an extramarital love that criticizes rightist hypocrisy, a love that, in spite of its "wrong" character, nevertheless remains within the boundaries of what is publicly permissible; the last, an exploration of Mu Xi's tortured mind, brings us face-to-face with a self yearning for renewal. Paradoxically, the farther we get from the factual, the closer we get to the unspeakable fear, which I think is this: the loss of identity, the loss of one's individuality. For the many who have lived through the Cultural Revolution, and who have survived various rectification campaigns, this fear stems from the realization that the PRC is in danger of losing its national identity. Can Xue's experiments, far from being irrelevant to our struggle with rights, point to another path. Questions of duty, virtue, and justice have to be asked again and again.

The hope is that we can address these questions in a new light. In spite of the curtailment of freedom of expression, writers have come this far by measuring what is possible for them to say within their limits; they have learned to negotiate the political terrain, to read the winds, to walk two roads.

On November 2, 1997, during his visit to the U.S., President Jiang Zemin replied to a question about why the Chinese government had chosen confrontation over dialogue at Tiananmen. He said, "naturally, we may have shortcomings and even make mistakes in our work. However, we have been working on a constant basis to further improve our work." Jiang Zemin has never offered an apology for the Communist government's ordering tanks in Tiananmen to quell the student riot, nor did he in his reply directly refer to the crackdown as a mistake. The suppression of the protest at Tiananmen Square left hundreds dead and hundreds more either jailed or exiled. The reality is that traumatizing events persist even after the Cultural Revolution, and—thinking back to June 4, 1989—we are constantly reminded of their ferocity.

Bibliography

Barmé, Geremie and John Minford. 1988. *Seeds of Fire: Chinese Voices of Conscience*. New York: Hill and Wang.

Bei, Ai. 1990. *Red Ivy: Green Earth Mother*. Translated by Howard Goldblatt. Salt Lake City: Gibbs-Smith.

Can Xue. 1989. *Dialogues in Paradise*. Translated by Ronald R. Janssen and Jian Zhang. Evanston: Northwestern University Press.

————. 1991. *Old Floating Cloud: Two Novellas*. Translated by Ronald R. Janssen and Jian Zhang. Evanston: Northwestern University Press.

————. 1995. "The Summons." *Chairman Mao Would Not Be Amused: Fiction for Today's China*. Edited by Howard Goldblatt. New York: Grove Press, 207–11.

Link, Perry. 1983. *Stubborn Weeds: Popular and Controversial Chinese Literature After the Cultural Revolution*. Bloomington: Indiana University Press.

————, ed. 1984. *Roses and Thorns: The Second Coming of the Hundred Flowers in Chinese Fiction 1979–1980*. Berkeley: University of California Press.

Liu Binyan. 1983. *People or Monsters? And Other Stories and Reportage from China After Mao*. Edited by Perry Link. Bloomington: Indiana University Press.

Lu Tonglin. 1995. *Misogyny, Cultural Nihilism, and Oppositional Politics: Contemporary Chinese Experimental Fiction*. Stanford: Stanford University Press.

Martin, Helmut and Jeffrey Kinkley, eds. 1992. *Modern Chinese Writers: Self Portrayals*. Armonk: M.E. Sharpe.

Nathan, Andrew J. "China: Getting Human Rights Right." *The Washington Quarterly* (Spring 1997):135–51.

O'Neill, Patrick. 1994. *Fictions of Discourse: Reading Narrative*. Toronto: University of Toronto Press.

Scarry, Elaine. 1985. *The Body in Pain: The Making and the Unmaking of the World*. New York: Oxford University Press.

Zhang Jie. 1986. *Love Must Not Be Forgotten*. San Francisco: China Books and Periodicals.

Part 5

Beyond Universalism and Relativism

13 Universalism

A Particularistic Account

Andrew J. Nathan

The concept of universalism underlies many of the essays in this book as it does the "Asian Values Debate" as a whole. The core question in the debate is whether human rights are in some sense universal. As suggested in Part I of this book, one philosophical issue implied by that question is whether moral reasoning is autonomous and hence universal, or culturally rooted and thus different from place to place. But the issue of universalism versus relativism implies another philosophical question as well, concerning the universality not of values but of concepts. Are there universal categories that allow us to gain knowledge of people and their beliefs across the boundaries of cultural difference? We can call this issue—how much of what we know about our own and other cultures is part of a body of universally valid knowledge and how much of it is particular knowledge—the question of epistemological or cognitive universalism, as opposed to the question of value universalism.

The two questions—of values and conceptual categories—are linked, because we need cognitive categories before we can begin to describe the value differences across cultures. In order to decide whether cultural values differ or concur, we need concepts to describe the bearers of values, the content of values, and the value preferences of the bearers. Indeed, an answer to the conceptual question is necessary to make possible the whole enterprise of cross-cultural studies, within whose ambit is generated the more specific issue of value universalism.

In both its aspects, the universalism-relativism controversy is based on a peculiar opposition between the idea of the universal and that of culture.

What is universal is considered to be beyond culture, and what is culturally valued is thought to be nonuniversal.[1] Where does this opposition come from? I will suggest that the answer lies in the particular division of labor our contemporary intellectual arrangements enforce between area studies and the social-science disciplines, in which the former is understood as the study of culture and the latter as the study of general rules of behavior.

Universalism, I hope to show through this example, is itself not a universal idea, but one which, today as in the past, takes on particular forms depending on the organization of knowledge at particular times and places. If we make ourselves more aware of the particularity of our contemporary conception of the universal as it applies to the study of societies, we may alleviate some of the problems it imposes not only for the issues involved in the Asian Values Debate but for cross-cultural studies in general.

Area Studies and the Social Science Disciplines

Area studies and the social science disciplines constitute two major parts of the academic enterprise in American colleges and universities. And because of the widespread influence of American academia since World War II, the area studies/social sciences division marks academic life in much of the rest of the world as well.

Area studies in the American academy grew out of the World War II and postwar need to understand other countries' behavior as America became a global power. The concept of area studies was built on the basis of nineteenth-century social anthropology, which used the theory of functionalism to argue that each society's cultural and social system serves its functional needs. According to this view, all societies have the same functional requirements, but each fulfills them through its own, integrated set of institutions and norms, practices, and values. The founding idea of area studies was that otherwise puzzling political, economic, and other practices overseas could be understood by a holistic, interdisciplinary knowledge of something called their "cultures," understood as encompassing history, thought, social practices, the arts and literature, as well as a society's specific ways of conducting politics, economics, warfare, and so on (Wood 1968). Area studies so defined exist in the American academy alongside and in contradistinction to the social-science disciplines.[2] These are understood as conducting research into general (or nomothetic) principles of human behavior in various spheres of activity (the economy, the political system, society, etc.).[3]

The division of labor and complementarity between these two forms of social studies reflects a distinction deeply rooted in Western thought, between what is of universal significance in human life and what is only accidental or contingent. Plato posited an eternal world of forms that contained whatever was universal in the world and that existed separately from the world of material phenomena which were imperfect and transitory because of their embodiment in the particular. St. Augustine wrote of a universal history of the world, which was the story of the salvation of those belonging to the City of God, while he considered devoid of meaning the damnation of those who did not receive God's grace. For Hegel, history was the progress to self-realization of the Idea of Freedom, and the parts of the world not involved in this story were outside history. For all of these authors and others under their influence, what made sense according to general philosophical principles was defined as the universal, and what did not was defined as the particular.

Area studies and the disciplines have inherited this distinction. They both "explain" behavior, but their distinctive roles are to do so differently. Area studies asks what makes people in particular sociopolitical systems behave differently from the ways in which people would be expected to behave according to the rational principles that have been discovered by the social-science disciplines.[4] The job of area studies is to find an explanation in terms of culture.

Culture, as defined by area studies, encompasses the whole congeries of mental and social factors that makes people in another country behave differently from the expectations of the disciplines. It consists of history, traditions, practices, institutions, networks, ideas, beliefs, values, attitudes, and emotions that are handed down, inculcated, and maintained by social interactions and group identity. Culture functions as an explanation for area studies when it is shown to infuse patterns of action with reasons or motives which are in some sense beyond other explanation or appeal, because they are the given or prior—probably inherited—preferences or choices of the people in those societies.

Culture in this construct is counterposed to, and defines by opposition, whatever in the causation of human behavior is universal. The explanations offered by the disciplines in terms of nomothetic (rule-like) principles are by definition universalistic, and those offered by area studies in terms of culture are by definition particularistic. The expertise of area studies is thus the complement of that of the disciplines, invoked just in the sense and to the degree that the disciplines fail to explain certain behaviors.

The concept of culture is sometimes used in explanations in the disciplines as well, but in a different sense from the way it is used in area studies. For example, Inglehart (1997) speaks of postmodern culture, meaning a set of attitudes which can be identified and measured across cultures. Inglehart's postmodern culture comes into existence and spreads across time and space in ways he can explain on the basis of the universal social processes by which economic growth affects individual and group psychology; and in turn he finds its impact on politics and government to be equally lawlike and predictable. Culture in this sense—as an operationally measured set of independent or dependent variables in a generalizable pattern of causation—is not the same as culture in the area specialist's sense, as a complex configuration of attributes unique to a particular society. In the disciplines culture works as a set of variables in nomothetic explanations; in area studies, it supports idiographic (case-specific and descriptive) forms of explanation.

To the extent that a phenomenon becomes subject to nomothetic explanation, it moves from the realm of area studies into the realm of the disciplines. If peasants rebel out of rational self-interest, their behavior is comprehensible to the social scientist and is no longer the expression of a particular peasant culture (Popkin 1979);[5] if non-market behavior can be shown to be a self-interested response to institutional incentives, it moves from the realm of traditional or neotraditional cultural practice into the purview of neoinstitutional economics (Bates 1981); if self-defeating political behavior has a longer-term payoff in terms of an actor's preferences, it becomes part of game theory (Tsebelis 1990:ch. 5). The disciplines "advance" when behavior previously considered "anomalous" (inexplicable within the nomothetic structures of the disciplines) can be shown to be a case of universal principles in action. Whatever social knowledge remains understandable only idiographically and not nomothetically remains residual to the disciplines and within the domain of area studies.

Through the influence especially of Max Weber, the modern social-science disciplines count as universal those patterns of causation and motivation that are held to be characteristic of science, modernity, technology, and, in general, rationality—understood as the pursuit of self-interest through the manipulation of objectively existing means-ends relationships in the world around us. Some of the main forms of what counts as explanation in the disciplines are as follows (*inter alia*, King, Keohane, and Verba 1994; Little 1991; Stinchcombe 1968). A social phenomenon is explained:

- when it is shown to be rational given a certain goal structure on the part of the actor and certain specified conditions in his environment that affect his ability to attain that goal (as in, for example, economics and game theoretic political science);
- when it can be interpreted as a functional requirement of, or functionally beneficial to, a social system (as in anthropology and sociology);
- when it can be treated as an evolutionary outcome, in the sense that it is explained by functional fitness emerging over time (as in history and historical economics and sociology);
- when it can be treated as a dependent variable that varies regularly with certain independent variables for a theoretically intelligible reason (as in social psychology and political science).

Such explanations in terms of goal-seeking, functionality, or evolution are accepted as explanations because they satisfy certain assumptions about what makes an action or outcome make sense.

It is often acknowledged that rationality itself is a culture, and similarly that modernity and science are cultures. Scholars write the history of these cultures and investigate the sociology of their transfer and inculcation. But when they are invoked by the social science disciplines as causal forces or explanatory factors they are not thought of as "culture" in the area-studies sense. The distinction lies in the fact that these universal cultures, to coin a term, are conceived to exist because they are ontologically correct (rationality, science) or functionally or evolutionarily superior (technology, modernization)—because they are, in general, consistent with some kind of rationality.[6] Even though they generate institutional complexes that are acculturated, these cultures are seen as self-explaining and as not requiring reference to concrete histories or traditions to make sense.

When the parametric conditions that bring rationality into play are taken for granted, not noticed, do not matter, or have already been assumed and taken into account as part of the "other things equal" clause of the nomothetic generalization being applied, then the causes of events or phenomena become transparent to the analyst and they are conceived as instances of universals. In contrast, patterns of action are construed as particular when their underlying consistency with rational means-ends behavior has not been perceived, so that they appear to depart from rationality and to hew to cultural, traditional, or religious ways of thought. In other words, particularity (the failure of an episode to be seen as an instance of a universal) is perceived when the parametric conditions that apply are other than those assumed in the generalization that would have been put to use, and hence the motives that operate are or seem to be different from those that operate under conditions productive of transparently "rational "behavior. In short, when we do not understand how an actor's behavior is rational, we attribute it to culture. Once a rational explanation is adduced, culture bows out of the argument.

In the natural sciences, whatever is not explained nomothetically is regarded as yet to be explained. (An exception might be the views of those scientists who argue that certain ultimate facts in nature can never be explained scientifically and must be explained by recourse to religious faith; in such arguments, religious faith serves as the functional equivalent of culture in social studies.) In social studies, what is cultural is not expected to yield to explanation, but in fact to disappear. Area studies and the disciplines tend to share the view that the particularities of culture are being swept away by the homogenizing forces of modernization. They may celebrate or regret this, but both forms of study are filled with theories of convergence based on ideas of functional necessity, modernization, and diffusion. Many scholars of both the disciplines and area studies consider inevitable the long-term spread of the market, democracy, the world system, and human rights, and assume that this spread entails a steadily reduced role for "culture" in the area-studies sense.

In taking this position, the area studies/disciplines complex endows instances of convergence with an ontological status superior to those of episodes where convergence does not occur. The spread of industry, the market, and democracy are treated as having a higher reality than the non-spread or retreat of these forces. One is the secular trend, the other is resistance, lag, backsliding, or "resurgence." Culture is disappearing because it is not rational.

In conclusion, neither universality nor particularity is an objective attribute of social facts. Rather, through the division of labor between the disciplines and the social sciences, they are mutually constituted, the one as the residuum of the other. Universality is the result of, rather than the precondition for, inclusion in the disciplines and particularity the result of, rather than the precondition for, exclusion from the disciplines. Particularity happens when social science fails in its project of universalization. The culturally particular is a name for the unexplained. In this perspective, both universality and particularity lose their universality.

Beyond Universalism and Relativism in the Asian Values Debate

The Asian Values Debate takes root in this distinction between culture and the universal. It accepts that some values are or might be universal and that others differ from culture to culture because of the particularity of cultures. In this book we have used human rights as an example of important values whose universality becomes an issue in the context of the idea of culture created by the area studies/disciplines construct.

"The pioneers of area studies," I have argued elsewhere, "believed that Americans must reconcile themselves to the fact that their way of life was not going to sweep the world. Other cultures must be understood on their own terms in order to avoid confrontations that no one would profit from" (Nathan 1997:201). Relativism emerged as the commonest position among practitioners of area studies. If values differ across cultures, and each culture's values are a priori as valid as any other culture's values, it follows—or seems to—that universalistic value claims are invalid.

According to this view, the only human rights that are universally valid are those on which all cultures agree. In an influential article cited in several of our papers, for example, Ambassador Bilahari Kausikan states that "genocide, murder, torture, [and] slavery" are universally regarded as violations of international law but that at some times and places "good government may require, among other things, detention without trial . . . ; curbs on press freedoms . . . ; and draconian laws to break the power of entrenched interests. . . . " Westerners cannot enforce a consensus against such policies where none exists (Kausikan 1993:38–40).[7]

Most participants in our NEH Summer Seminar, trained as practitioners of area studies, started the seminar sympathetic to the relativist position. But as the summer went by we discovered a number of weaknesses in the relativist position and by extension, in the area studies concept of culture in which it is rooted. These difficulties emerged most clearly in the consideration of women's rights. Perhaps this should not be surprising. Women's rights have often seemed peripheral to the international human rights regime because the regime has done little to disturb the status of women in most societies. The main international human rights documents—the Universal Declaration of Human Rights (1948) and the two international covenants on civil and political, and economic, social, and cultural rights (1966)—refer seldom to gender and speak rather of rights to be granted to "everyone" or denied to "no one," usually referring to rights that in practice are almost everywhere exercised chiefly by men. Such rights are universal both in the form in which they are expressed and in their ready applicability in principle (despite their frequent denial in practice) to males in a wide variety of cultural settings.

Rights that change the relations of women and men, however, are much less readily applicable across cultures, because the roles of women are central to the self-definitions of all cultures and hence to all cultures' sense of the differences among cultures. Women are the bearers of culture not just in the cliched senses that they socialize children or (some believe) embody the gentler aspirations of each civilization, but in the more fundamental sense that groups of people define their identities—what makes them different—in large part through the statuses and roles that they ascribe to women (cf. Cook 1994; Coomaraswamy 1996; Peters and Wolper 1995).

The attempt to homogenize the status of women has thus encountered deeper resistance than the attempt to universalize gender-free rights. Even cultural relativists do not wish to deny rights to free speech and association outright or in principle, but merely to postpone them in favor of other priorities deemed more pressing. By contrast, consider the rights that are claimed for women by what is perhaps the most culturally radical human rights document in international law, the Convention on the Elimination of All Forms of Discrimination Against Women (CEDAW), adopted by the UN General Assembly in 1979.

This document calls on governments to do their best "to modify the social and cultural patterns of conduct of men and women, with a view to achieving the elimination of prejudices and customary and all other practices which are based on the idea of the inferiority or the superiority of either of the sexes or on stereotyped roles for men and women" (Article 5). There is no culture including our own for which this is not a revolutionary prescription. The CEDAW goes on to call for certain changes that nearly all governments accept in principle, for example an end to trafficking in women. But it also demands a number of measures which go beyond what the majority of the population probably accepts in almost any country in the world.

These include equal access for women to all types of vocational training and other education, the same opportunities for women as for men in sports, equal access to all forms of work, provision of maternity leave with pay, equal rights as parents irrespective of marital status, and the same rights as men to chose a family name.

In some societies, including our own, these principles are accepted as rhetoric; in few if any are they accepted at the level of widespread popular beliefs. Lucinda Joy Peach tells about beliefs prevalent in Thai Buddhist culture, where women are not considered equal to men, and where the culture does not disapprove of a parent under certain circumstances selling a daughter into sexual slavery. Another common example of a culture that stands in opposition to CEDAW's conception of women's rights is Islam, at least in its fundamentalist form. According to Ann Elizabeth Mayer, conservative Islamic jurists reject the idea of equality of the sexes before the law and sanction the denial to women of virtually all the rights listed in CEDAW (Mayer 1995:chs. 5–6). To be sure, Islam in its original historical context was progressive on the question of women's rights—providing females with hitherto unavailable access to inheritance rights, new procedural protections in divorce, and enhanced dignity before the law—and today many countries are dominated by liberal forms of Islam that treat women as juridically equal to men. As Farhat Haq points out, even some renewalist forms of Islam consider themselves as vindicating women's rights. Yet Islamic movements fully as repressive as those that Mayer refers to govern in several states and territories today, and even the most liberal Islamic-influenced regimes are far from implementing the full range of rights that CEDAW demands.

The example of women's rights focused the minds of the seminar participants on the hard question at the core of the Asian Values Debate. If widely held value systems deny as a matter of principle the validity of certain rights that are dear to me, am I thereby deprived of the ability logically to claim that they are universally valid? Confronting the issue in this way, many of the seminar participants began to shift their views toward the tempered universalism displayed in several chapters in this book. While hesitant to impose our values on others, neither were most of us willing to accept that any pretext could justify a cultural or religious community in denying rights we considered fundamental to women—and hence, by extension, to other categories of persons or to people as a whole.

As we scrutinized our reasons for taking this position, they related less to the merits of the values themselves than to weaknesses in the conception of culture that underlies the logic of cultural relativism. First, cultures are not unified. As Bell and Haq ask, who speaks for Asia or for Islam? To say that "a culture" does not "agree" with us on a position apparently means that those who hold the microphones do not agree, but experience tells us there are always some, often many, dissidents within the culture who do believe in those rights. While Michael Dowdle in his essay calls upon the government-backed Bangkok Declaration to represent the views of Asian cultures, seminar participants were also aware that Asian NGOs meeting on the periphery of the Bangkok conference generated their own declaration, which defended the universality of human rights in opposition to the line of their governments. And as Charles Taylor has argued, it is open to question whether Buddhism as such is unprotective of the rights of women even if certain poverty-stricken Thai families behave as if their daughters' rights were of little value (Taylor 1999).

In treating cultures as unities, moreover, cultural relativism—this is the second problem—ignores the power relationships within cultures. Those who deny a right to others are usually the beneficiaries of such a denial, and those whose rights are denied are usually the worse off for losing them. Even if the victims accept the denial of the right—as Lucinda Joy Peach's essay shows they sometimes do—we as outsiders are not inclined to endorse their self-abnegation.

To be sure, there is also a power relationship between cultures, in which we participate when we try to use international influence to combat rights violations in other societies. But noticing this fact does not provide a ready key to its implications. Rather, it uncovers a third weakness in the cultural relativist position. While the history of colonialism and racism cautions us against the misuse of power across cultures, other examples, such as the failure to stop various genocides in recent times, remind us that power also brings a responsibility to engage. The correct response to a power relationship is not necessarily to stand back. To refrain from intervening is to side with those on top. Given the ubiquity of power, between and within cultures, there is no option of a power-free discourse over values. One way or another, moral choice is unavoidable.

Fourth, as Michael Barnhart argues, it does not follow from the empirical nonuniversality of a value that the contested value is not universally valid. He distinguishes between two different kinds of claims about the universality of a value, the universality of its validity, and the universality of belief in it. The first claim, Barnhart argues, does not entail the other. Value issues are

not matters to be decided by popularity polls or ç
Value reasoning has its own sovereignty. Matter:
to resolve, or may remain eternally unresolved, '
be discussed through value-based reasoning. '
merely to the opinions of the numerous or the ʿ
power over moral considerations. Only throug
one get beneath posturing to find out what ıs ⌐
disagreement is real.

In the end, most of our essays suggest that it is contradictory to argue for a value as being valid in any other way than universally. A state of affairs alleged to be relativistically right is only a preference, not a value. One is reminded of Kant's warning that moral philosophy is not anthropology. If human rights are matters of value, then the issue to debate is whether they are right or wrong, not how widely they are held.

As we worked our way through these considerations, we were reminded that the culturally relativist position is itself an unusual one in the history of world cultures. None of the great religions—Judaism, Christianity, Islam, Buddhism—has had any trouble advocating its own values as valid for everyone, even though its adherents are seldom unaware that rival religions exist. Adherents of political ideologies like Marxism, Maoism, and even Kim Ilsungism have had no difficulty seeing themselves as embattled minorities possessing values that ought to be accepted by everybody even though they are not. The same is true, as Haq suggests, of fundamentalist Islam. Confucianism, whether deemed a religion or a political belief, is universalist in its conviction that it is a superior way even though it is a way not available to everyone. In the United States, relativism is popular only among academics.

In fact, the kind of cultural relativism we wrestle with in this book may be unique to the Westernized international intelligentsia of our time, a group whose conception of cultural difference has been formed by the doctrine of area studies. Cultural relativism is itself, in other words—like the distinction that underlies it between universality and culture—a culturally situated rather than universally valid idea. It is paradoxical that it should make universalistic claims, suggesting itself as a general principle even thought most people do not believe in it.

For most contributors to this volume, however, these considerations did not justify a full-blown universalism, but rather, one tempered by the realization that human rights and other important values do remain contested—

ong essentialized "cultures," then among movements, groups, and
vities as well as among individuals around the globe including the
n-plus participants in our seminar. Most of us came away prepared to
gue for the universal validity of the rights we believe in, but undeluded
that others would accept our arguments easily or soon.

Toward a New Area Studies/Disciplines Construct

But if tempered universalism is a solution to the Asian Values Debate, it
is not yet a thorough-going one because it does not confront the need to
reconstruct the area studies/disciplines conceptual structure out of which
the Asian Studies Debate grows and out of which similar confusions will
continue to grow. Is there a parallel revision to be suggested for the way in
which we organize cross-cultural knowledge that might offer an escape from
the essentializing of cultures and cultural differences?

The symbiosis of area studies and the disciplines has become troubled in
recent years in any case. A long-standing struggle over resources in cash-
tight universities has been exacerbated by the end of the Cold War and the
decline in the national security rationale for the government and foundations to support area studies (Cumings 1997). The opening of former communist societies and most remaining communist societies has allowed foundations like Ford and the Open Society Institute to channel resources to
projects on the ground overseas rather than to Western university centers
that study them. The American Council of Learned Societies and Social
Science Research Council have closed down most of their area-studies com-
mittees for lack of funding and created a "new architecture" that tries to
involve scholars of (and from) various regions in projects focused on disciplinary or interdisciplinary issues.

The disciplines tend to dominate in struggle for funding because they
are more deeply embedded in the structure of universities. They are older,
more directly represented in faculty governance, and make academic appointments while area centers usually do not. Funding, appointments, and
prestige have declined for work construed as area studies, and promising
young social-science scholars try to locate themselves closer to the perceived
mainstreams of their disciplines (e.g., Bates 1997).

Students of area studies have identified two ways out of this dilemma.
One is to serve as the data-supplying handmaiden of the nomothetic disci-

plines. The other is to embrace relativism to an extent that undermines the possibility of cross-cultural generalization, understanding, ethical engagement, and action. Both approaches are flawed. The data-handmaiden approach wrongly assumes that data are culturally neutral, and that culturally informed interpretation is not needed to use them correctly. The relativism approach wrongly accepts that cultures are mutually unintelligible. The resolution to the problems of area studies lies not in area studies itself but in its relation to the disciplines and indeed chiefly within the disciplines.

Part of the dynamic behind the decline of area studies grows from its very successes in serving the needs of the disciplines, and the road to the revaluation of area studies lies in appreciating the new relationship that is emerging between them. In half a century the academic understanding of foreign cultures and of culture as an analytic construct has advanced markedly. Work on historical and contemporary Chinese culture, for example, is unimaginably more sophisticated than it was when I studied the subject in graduate school in the 1960s. Researchers have better language skills than in the past, more access to field sites and archives, and regular interaction with Chinese colleagues. We now have studies of popular culture as well as elite culture, of material culture as well as of symbolic culture, of historical and contemporary economic practice as well as of economic policy and doctrine, of empirically distributed mass attitudes as well as of official ideology, of variation in as well as norms of kinship behavior and family structure, of regional diversity as well as of national patterns.

At the same time, approaches like "cultural studies" and cultural anthropology, through their emphasis on reflexivity (self-awareness), have encouraged acknowledgement of the complexity of cultures, their multidimensionality and ambiguity, and of the fact that the observer as well as the subject approaches the study of culture from an acculturated position. Many of these insights have been employed in the essays in this book. This approach counters the essentialization of cultural differences and insists on a more complex interpretation both of the culture being studied and of the process of studying it.

The disciplines have benefited in large part just as they were supposed to do from this two-sided maturation of area studies. With access to a larger, more diverse body of data and a more nuanced understanding of what those data mean, the disciplines have gradually expanded their reach and have incorporated more and better-understood information from more different places. Scholars working on Latin America, the former Soviet Union, East

Europe, China, Japan, and elsewhere have joined those who work on the United States and Europe in making theoretical contributions to their disciplines.

But the disciplines have not taken advantage of the maturation of area studies in quite the way that the original designers of the area studies/disciplines complex envisioned. Instead of homogenizing data from the rest of the world to fit universalistic theoretical categories, they have expanded their reach by becoming more idiographic or configurative—in effect, more particularistic. They have deepened their understandings of the ways in which institutional settings and other boundary conditions affect the operations in diverse settings of the various kinds of rationalities that remain their central concern.

Neo-institutionalism in economics, sociology, and political science is a prime example of this approach. In neo-institutional analysis in the disciplines, what used to be seen as cultural differences are treated as institutional differences, that is, as historically constructed parameters or settings which cause actors—still motivated by a Weberian means-ends rationality—to behave in ways that would not be expected based on Western examples but that become understandable as instantiations of universal behavioral principles under particular, historically created institutional conditions. Robert Bates, for example, suggests that the convergent interests of particular domestic political coalitions mediated through particular institutional configurations in a variety of countries explained the rise and twenty-year reign of an international agency to regulate the coffee trade (1997). Tianjian Shi argues that patterns of political participation in Beijing emerge from the adaptation of citizens to the opportunities and costs offered by specific Chinese political institutions (1997). The institutions and the participatory patterns are unique, but the processes by which one adapts to the other are not.

Comparative history is another approach within economics, sociology, and political science which marries the configurative procedures of area studies to the generalizing goals of the disciplines.[8] Thus, Sidney Tarrow (1994) studies numerous particular social movements, Linz and Stepan (1996) numerous particular instances of democratic transition and consolidation, and Rueschemeyer, Stephens and Stephens (1992) numerous particular instances of the expansion of mass participation, in each case to see how certain complex yet generalizable constellations of actors and interests produced distinctive outcomes through universalistically intelligible processes.

In such ways, the universalism of the disciplines has been tempered by the recognition of the embeddedness of social facts. This does not mean the acceptance by the nomothetic disciplines of Clifford Geertz's claim that social facts are understandable only through the use of native concepts, a claim which threatens area studies' ability to make cross-cultural sense out of culturally situated facts (1983; cf. Nathan 1997:chap. 10). Such questioning of the mutual intelligibility of cultures and the consequent privileging of "local knowledge" would in the long run undermine area studies' justification for existence in the academy as today constructed.

Rather, the tempered universalism emerging in the disciplines today is an appreciation of the fact that all social events are contextualized and hence all social-science generalizations are radically bounded in their applicability. In effect, it is an acknowledgment at the theoretical level of the reasons for the well-known puzzle that the strongest variables in social science rarely produce statistical results that can explain more than about 30 percent of the variance in outcomes (Blalock 1984:88–89). This is the case because social action is the product of many causes, only a relative few of which can be measured in any comparative research design.

However, the new research in the social sciences has a distressingly ad hoc quality when seen from the viewpoint of classic social-science aspirations for nomothetic explanation. Culturally situated analysis of means-ends behavior leads to unique explanations for unique patterns of behavior in unique settings. What is nomothetic about such research is not the discovery of general (or "covering") laws that say that certain consequences always follow from certain conditions (Hempel 1942), but rather the heuristic application of a broad concept of rationality to an endless line of particular circumstances. Reflecting on this situation, the psychologist and theorist of social science Lawrence B. Mohr concluded that the nomothetic aspirations of classic postwar behavioral social science have failed. "Unfortunately, our experience with discovering good, strong, important, and broadly applicable causes-and-effect relations is negative—we have not made any such discoveries," he says (Mohr 1996:112). What the disciplines have proven good at doing, instead, he argues, is producing "singular explanations," which are valid not for a whole class of events but for one or a limited number of members of such a class (Mohr 1996:143).

The disciplines, in short, have themselves changed as area studies has evolved. But they have not entirely come to terms with the implications of these changes for their theories of what they do. Strong voices in each discipline continue to push for the classic nomothetic model of social science and for the ultimate supercession of area studies. They attack the value of the information produced by area studies because it remains situationally confined, and they decry the failure of area studies to produce data in forms that can help the disciplines perform broad positivist tasks.

The underappreciated danger is that if area studies cease to perform their functions, the disciplines will also cease to perform theirs. Without area studies to take up what is residual to the disciplines, the disciplines will transparently become an area studies of their own, an area studies predominantly of the modern, marketized, democratic West and the times and places where modern and Western values have exerted influence. The disciplines need to get rid not of area studies, but of the idea of situationally uncontaminated or area-neutral data, data from nowhere, just as they have begun to question the idea of the observer from nowhere.

The long frustration of the disciplines in failing to produce scientific, lawlike generalizations about human behavior stemmed from a willing-out-of-existence of context. The "all other things equal" phrase so common in the disciplines has been a thin cover for the nonuniversality of social science findings. The way out of this problem is to specify context, to say where and when a generalization holds and to recognize that at most of the levels of abstraction at which we are interested in working, context (or what area studies calls culture) does matter. Culture in this meaning of the term should be recognized for what it has long been, a code-word for the "everything else" that social sciences have fallaciously aspired to "hold constant."[9]

The disciplines thus should qualify their conception of universality. No social phenomenon is intrinsically any more particular than any other. Everything happens someplace, sometime, under specific concrete conditions. Every social phenomenon is in this sense intrinsically particular. The universality that we attribute to social phenomena is conceptual, imposed and posited, not intrinsic to them as phenomena. The validity of universals lies in the validity of their construction rather than in anything intrinsically universal in the facts.

For its part, area studies must retain its epistemological commitment to cross-cultural intelligibility. It should use the methods of anthropology to gather data; of sociology and economics to locate respondents; and of cultural studies and feminist discourse analysis to uncover layers of meaning in symbols and actions. Combining interpretivism and positivism, area studies should uncover the local embodiments of universal phenomena, knowing that there are no nonlocal embodiments.[10]

Such a relationship between area studies and the disciplines would do away with the old division between universal forms of rationality and culturally particular values, which has made it so difficult to conduct a debate about values across cultures. Our present notions do us a disservice when they set culture against the universal, as if anything that is culturally valued cannot be conceived of as universal. We will dissolve this dilemma when we acknowledge that all social facts and all values are culturally situated and are for all that nonetheless facts and values. Such an acknowledgment might open new prospects not only for the human rights debate but for the study of culture more generally.

Acknowledgments

The members of the 1997 NEH Summer Seminar taught me a lot about the subjects discussed here. I benefited especially from Michael Barnhart's essay and his comments and from generous editorial help from Lynda S. Bell. I am also grateful for comments from Mark Kesselman.

Endnotes

1. Alasdair MacIntyre (1978) and Peter Winch (1958, 1964) conducted an influential debate over the issue of whether cross-cultural universals exist for the social sciences. I start from the same issue but take it in a different direction.
2. I have in mind mainstream economics, political science, and sociology, and the positivist branches of anthropology, history, and other academic departments. Of course each of the more positivist disciplines has its post-positivist and interpretivist practitioners, and each of the humanistic disciplines has its positivists.
3. If area studies itself makes occasional claims to be a discipline, it is a discipline which applies theories eclectically and contextually and abjures what it sees as the scientistic pretensions of the mainstream disciplines (Schwartz 1980).
4. This is not the same as asking why foreigners behave differently from Americans and Europeans. To be sure, the knowledge of the nomothetic disciplines depends heavily on information drawn from the American and European cases. But on the other hand, the disciplines acknowledge that Americans and Europeans also sometimes behave irrationally. When people at home or abroad behave as the disciplines predict (or can retrospectively explain), their behavior is studied as evidence for the universal applicability of the laws of that discipline. When they don't, the "area studies" of the West—French studies, American studies—come into play.

5. It is still social science, and not area studies, if peasant rebellion can be explained not in directly economistic terms but as part of a "moral economy" that in turn has rational roots as part of a long-term strategy of survival (Scott 1976).

6. I am using the term rationality in both a narrow and a broad sense. Narrowly, rationality refers to economistic and game-theoretic models of human behavior. Broadly, it is the general name for the kind of thinking that Weber identified as underlying science, technology, market behavior, secularized politics, legal-rational legitimacy, and so on. Even more broadly, rationality can refer to any intelligible means-end relationship, so that, for example, "irrational" neurotic behavior is "explained" in the Freudian tradition, and hence made comprehensible to the rational mind, when we can point to the emotional wish that it expresses and to the forces by which and pathways through which this emotional wish is displaced or distorted.

7. Cultural relativists like Ambassador Kausikan assume that the limits they regard as culturally mandated are also acceptable under the derogation principles of international law. I think these are two separate questions. As I argue below in discussing CEDAW, international law may require certain things that few cultures accept. These requirements are nonetheless legally obligating.

8. Some scholars consider comparative history a sub-form of neo-institutionalism.

9. My advice here is not necessarily the opposite of the influential suggestion by Adam Przeworski and Henry Teune (1970:8): "The goal of comparative research is to substitute names of variables for the names of social systems." My point is that this worthy goal cannot be achieved by willing out of existence most of the numerous variables that make systems different.

10. This advice is similar to that which animates the new direction of area studies at the Social Science Research Council. See for example Prewitt 1996.

Bibliography

Bates, Robert H. 1981. *Markets and States in Tropical Africa: The Political Basis of Agricultural Policies.* Berkeley: University of California Press.

Bates, Robert H. 1997. "Area Studies and the Disciplines: A Useful Controversy?" *PS: Political Science and Politics* 30 (2) (June):166–169.

Blalock, Hubert M., Jr. 1984. *Basic Dilemmas in the Social Sciences.* Beverly Hills: Sage.

Cook, Rebecca J., ed. 1994. *Human Rights of Women: National and International Perspectives.* Philadelphia: University of Pennsylvania Press.

Coomaraswamy, Radhika. 1996. "Reinventing International Law: Women's Rights as Human Rights in the International Community." *Bulletin of Concerned Asian Scholars* (April-June), 28 (2):16–26.

Cumings, Bruce. 1997. "Boundary Displacement: Area Studies and International Studies during and after the Cold War." *Bulletin of Concerned Asian Scholars* 29 (1):6–26.

Geertz, Clifford. 1983. *Local Knowledge: Further Essays in Interpretative Anthropology.* New York: Basic Books.

Inglehart, Ronald. 1997. *Modernization and Postmodernization: Cultural, Economic, and Political Change in 43 Societies.* Princeton: Princeton University Press.

Hempel, Carl G. 1942. "The Function of General Laws in History." *The Journal of Philosophy* 45 (2) (January 15):29–48.

Kausikan, Bilahari. 1993. "Asia's Different Standard." *Foreign Policy* (Fall):24–41.

King, Gary, Robert O. Keohane, and Sidney Verba. 1994. *Designing Social Inquiry: Scientific Inference in Qualitative Research.* Princeton: Princeton University Press.

Little, Daniel. 1991. *Varieties of Social Explanation: An Introduction to the Philosophy of Social Science.* Boulder: Westview Press.

Linz, Juan J. and Alfred Stepan. 1996. *Problems of Democratic Transition and Consolidation: Southern Europe, South America, and Post-Communist Europe.* Baltimore: The John Hopkins University Press.

MacIntyre, Alasdair. 1978. *Against the Self-Images of the Age: Essays on Ideology and Philosophy.* Notre Dame: University of Notre Dame Press.

Mayer, Ann Elizabeth. 1995. *Islam and Human Rights: Tradition and Politics.* Boulder: Westview.

Mohr, Lawrence B. 1996. *The Causes of Human Behavior: Implications for Theory and Method in the Social Sciences.* Ann Arbor: University of Michigan Press.

Nathan, Andrew J. 1997. *China's Transition.* New York: Columbia University Press.

Peters, Julie Stone and Andrea Wolper, eds. 1995. *Women's Rights, Human Rights: International Feminist Perspectives.* New York: Routledge.

Popkin, Samuel L. 1979. *The Rational Peasant; The Political Economy of Rural Society in Vietnam.* Berkeley: University of California Press.

Prewitt, Kenneth. 1996. "Presidential Items," in *Items,* Social Science Research Council, 50 (2–3) (June–September):31–40.

Przeworski, Adam and Henry Teune. 1970. *The Logic of Social Inquiry.* Repriint ed. 1982. Malabar: Krieger Publishing Company.

Rueschemeyer, Dietrich, Evelyne Huber Stephens, and John D. Stephens. 1992. *Capitalist Development and Democracy.* Chicago: University of Chicago Press.

Schwartz, Benjamin I. 1980. "Presidential Address: Area Studies as a Critical Discipline." *Journal of Asian Studies* 40 (1) (November):15–25.

Scott, James E. 1976. *Moral Economy of the Peasant: Rebellion and Subsistence in Southeast Asia.* New Haven: Yale University Press.

Shi, Tianjian. 1997. *Political Participation in Beijing.* Cambridge: Harvard University Press.

Stinchcombe, Arthur L. 1968. *Constructing Social Inquiry*. New York: Harcourt, Brace and World.

Tarrow, Sidney. 1994. *Power in Movement: Social Movements, Collective Action and Politics*. New York: Cambridge University Press.

Taylor, Charles. 1999. "Conditions of an Unforced Consensus on Human Rights." In Joanne R. Bauer and Daniel A. Bell, eds. *The East Asian Challenge for Human Rights*. Cambridge: Cambridge University Press:124–144.

Tsebelis, George. 1990. *Nested Games: Rational Choice in Comparative Politics*. Berkeley: University of California Press.

Universal Declaration of Human Rights, International Covenant on Economic, Social and Cultural Rights, International Covenant on Civil and Political Rights, Convention on Elimination of All Forms of Discrimination Against Women, Declaration on the Elimination of All Forms of Intolerance and of Discrimination Based on Religion or Belief, Convention on the Rights of the Child, In Winston E. Langley, ed. *Human Rights: Sixty Major Global Instruments*. 1992. Jefferson: McFarland and Co.

Winch, Peter. 1958. *The Idea of a Social Science and Its Relation to Philosophy*. New York: Humanities Press.

Winch, Peter. 1964. "Understanding a Primitive Society," *American Philosophical Quarterly* 1:307–324.

Wood, Bryce. 1968. "Area Studies." In David L. Sills, ed. *International Encyclopedia of the Social Sciences*, 401–407. New York: The Macmillan Company and The Free Press.

14   Dedichotomizing Discourse

Three Gorges, Two Cultures, One Nature

Jennifer R. Goodman

East is East and West is West.
Rudyard Kipling

Nothing annoys me more than the use of the words 'Eastern'
and 'Western,' still worse 'Oriental,' because the Arabs, and the Indians and
the Chinese, differed from each other really even more profoundly than the
Europeans differed from some of them.
Joseph Needham (1981:107)

It might seem a long way from fourteenth-century English
poetry to the current debate over universal standards of human rights and
their applicability to Asia. Yet they do connect. And through these unex-
pected connections between medieval European and traditional Asian
thought some sort of mutual understanding may be found.

To put the problem in a nutshell: as of the summer of 1997, the conversation between Eastern and Western governments over human rights seemed
to have arrived at an impasse. Certain Asian statesmen objected that Western
declarations of universal human rights were at odds with Eastern tradition.
Western declarations of human rights stress such individual rights as the
freedom of speech, freedom of religion, and self-determination. The East
Asian governments argued that while Eastern societies support many of these
principles, they differ from the West primarily in that they prefer cooperation, political stability, and respect for authority. These values, they suggested, are embodied in Asian social and political systems that promote the
good of the society as a whole, not just the welfare of individuals. While

authoritarian regimes appear less free to Western eyes, their rulers insisted that the peoples under their jurisdiction find them eminently satisfactory for the deepest historical and cultural reasons. In the view of these East Asian politicians, no universal principles of human rights can or should be established. Instead, each culture should maintain its own values and mind its own business, rather than trying to reshape the world to fit a single mold.

The Asian financial crisis of 1997–98 represented, for many Western observers, the failure of this argument, and the complete victory of the forces of globalization and democracy. With the economies of Japan, Thailand, South Korea, Malaysia, and Indonesia in disarray, their Western analysts looked forward to the breakdown of entrenched elite power structures, to be replaced by something much more like Western representative democracies. This they see as a victory promising greater freedom for the peoples of many Asian countries, a historic shift paralleling the revolutions that swept aside the aristocracies of Europe (Kristof 1998). On closer examination, though, both the "Asian model" and the apparent victory of the Western system turn out to be questionable.

In some respects the Asian argument was attractive. It seemed to support cultural diversity, historical tradition, social cooperation, sovereignty, stability, and prosperity, all good things. It reflected a healthy sense of regional self-respect. Such factors are becoming more and more desirable in an increasingly homogenized and monopolistic world.

A faint whiff of something disquieting certainly did seep from the discussion. Perhaps it stemmed from the fact that the words and the accompanying deeds of the speakers were nothing like one another. At the same time they were appealing to Asian traditions, the leaders of China, to take one example, had immersed themselves in enterprises that were neither traditional nor particularly Asian. Actions speak louder than words. The seeming contradictions cast doubt on both deeds and words.

For an instance of a representative deed to set beside the words of the Chinese leadership, it is not necessary to look far. The Three Gorges Dam might be the project that the Chinese government would choose, itself, to stand as an example of its most recent policies. Hydroelectric power for the modernization of China is to be bought at the cost of displacing millions of people from their homes and flooding a countryside whose beauty, historic significance, and ecological importance cannot be overestimated.

Can such a project be justified in terms of traditional Chinese values? Of course. All one has to say is that it stands for the Chinese respect for authority, and for the great bureaucratic heritage of ancient China at its best. Centralized planning, the pragmatic application of technical innovations, and energetic activity on the part of the authorities, with the compliance of the people mandated from on high—how could Confucius and the emperors not approve? After all, Chinese tradition teaches that "the first legendary ruler is believed to have spent a good part of his life digging watercourses for the rivers in order to stop floods" (Nakamura 1964:248). Joseph Needham, the great English historian of Chinese science, recalls fondly having visited Kuan Hsien, the temple dedicated to Li Ping,

> the great hydraulic engineer of Szechuan, of the 3rd century. . . . which stands and has for centuries stood beside the great cutting made under his leadership through the shoulder of a whole mountain. This venerable public work divided the river into two parts, and still irrigates today an area fifty miles square supporting some five million people (Needham 1981:111).

Needham also cites the Yüeh Chüeh Shu (Lost Records of the State of Yüeh), a historical classic attributed to Yüan K'ang, completed by the year A.D. 52, on ancient Chinese waterworks:

> Then when Yü the Great was digging dykes and managing the waters, weapons were made of bronze; with tools of bronze the I Ch'üeh defile was cut open and the Lung-mIn gate pierced through. The Yangtze was led and the Yellow River guided, until they poured into the Eastern Sea. Thus there was a communication everywhere and the whole empire was at peace (1981:114).

These are venerable native traditions of the application of technology in the public interest, with specific reference to hydraulic engineering. Needham points out that the ancient Chinese scientists were also like their modern counterparts in preferring empiricism to traditional lore. He writes: "I love that passage in the Shên Tzu book which says, 'those who can manage the dykes and the rivers are the same in all the ages; they did not learn their business from Yü the Great, they learned it from the waters' " (1981:119).

Yet for all that, a project such as Three Gorges remains profoundly un-Asian. It belongs much more properly to the era of hydroelectric megaprojects like the Tennessee Valley Authority or the Aswan High Dam—big technology for its own sake. Scientists are now recognizing that such alterations of natural river systems and regional drainage patterns create more problems than they solve. Adjusting settlement to the local geography makes better sense than struggling to tame the waters by force. At a time when such massive, centrally mandated dam projects are being rejected in the United States and Europe in favor of traditional irrigation projects, managed communally, China is forging ahead with this prime example of the unidirectional model of development as the only modern thing to do. The Three Gorges Dam, considered as a representative example of Chinese governmental thinking, goes to the heart of what is wrong with the Asian Values Debate.

The inescapable fact about Three Gorges is that the Chinese government, and many present-day Asian governments, have been emulating a concept of development laid down by twentieth-century international agencies and Western governments, and receive critical support in these enterprises from Western investors, corporations, governments, and technicians (Sachs 1992). A modern totalitarian state on the Communist model, the present-day government of China represents an abrupt break with Chinese tradition—a fact they themselves were very explicit about, and that was perfectly obvious until the recent trade expansion. Indeed, the current leadership represents a break with the ideals of Mao and toward Western capitalism in its stress on financial success as the basis of its rule. Like proselytes to a new religion everywhere, the current generation of East Asian leaders is in many ways more Western than the Westerners. Thus their appeal to ancient Asia for justification was at least ironic, if not hypocritical.

One way to make sense of this disjunction between Eastern cultural values and Western conduct is to recognize that the leaders do not seem to be talking about themselves when they praise the social principles of Asian tradition. It was the Chinese people, rather than the ruling elite, who were being characterized as traditional. The people, according to the leaders, do not need intrusive external principles of human rights because they are happy with the age-old Chinese heritage of cooperation and respect for authority. The leaders said nothing about their own principles of conduct or adherence to tradition: they would much prefer to be accepted by their contemporaries as up-to-date, post-Newtonian premiers (New York Times, October 30, 1997:A20). Such a disjunction between the traditionalism of the lower classes in many Asian countries and the anti-traditional modernism of those in power was already being commented on much earlier in this century (e.g., by William Massey in his translator's preface to Guénon's East and West [1941:2–5]). Perhaps only in the Chinese traditions of pragmatic empiricism and adaptation to the times should contemporary statesmen be seen as grounded in the China of the ancients (Needham 1981:119–121).

Why did the West so readily accept this line of argument? On the one hand, it targeted Western liberals at their weakest point, aiming at their sense of post-colonial guilt. Universal declarations of human rights can be seen as imperialist aggression in a new form. Our belief in the desirability of multiculturalism, and in the equal validity and value of all global cultures, also led Westerners to admit the notion of "Asian values for the Asians," however reluctantly. Tolerance and relativism have become recognized as the hallmarks of the civilized twentieth-century thinker, while absolute moral principles seem somehow intellectually backward. It is not particularly "modern" to express ethical condemnations of anyone else's conduct, and may indeed be viewed as ethnocentric. These internal factors blind us to the shortcomings of the argument, and the extent to which it represented a gross oversimplification of the situation at hand.

The Western mind seems to think in binary oppositions for ancient cultural reasons. The book of Genesis recounts how the universe was formed of contrasting elements: night, day, earth, sky, sea, land, male, female, making it clear how ancient a way of understanding our surroundings this is. Zoroaster of Persia encouraged the West to envision the world as a battleground of light and dark, good and evil. The Gnostics and later sects like the Manichees and Cathars continued this way of thinking, which also contributes to mainstream Jewish, Islamic, and especially Christian theology (Runciman). The classical and medieval tradition of legal and academic disputation, pitting a pair of opponents against one another in a duel concluding with the victory of one side over the other, fits into this same pattern (Tannen). Post-Cartesian science and mathematics have only intensified this tendency to think in dichotomies. The idea of a debate between East and West over universal and culturally relative values pealed to the innately dualistic Western mind on a profound level. We saw it so clearly that it remains difficult for us to realize that it is in fact a mirage.

The reason it was a mirage is that neither the Western nor the Asian position rested on solid ground. The Asian position was unstable, as I suggested earlier, because it was a smoke screen. It asserted the need to maintain distinctive Asian traditions for the Asians, yet only selected aspects of traditional culture, those that supported the political status quo, seemed to be recognized as authentically Asian. The term "Asian Tradition" after all covers a vast, ancient body of culture. Many inconvenient aspects of the great Asian cultural legacy that defied or criticized current practices were cheerfully ignored except by figures of the opposition, who were just as traditionally Asian, it turns out, as their adversaries. (In this context I could cite Mencius on the "mandate of heaven" to overthrow oppressive rulers, or the tradition of heroic acts of sabotage against evil rulers represented in the classic romance *The Water Margin*, to mention two of the best-known precedents for resistance to authority in the history of Chinese literature.) Besides, this ideal of Asian distinctiveness was being asserted, too often, by Asians whose own conduct clearly belonged to the tradition of Western capitalism of the most unbridled type.

The West's position began with the idea that universal values exist. This turns out to be a variant of the classic debate, running all through the history of Western philosophy, on the question of universals. Plato and his followers had maintained that abstract ideas, "universals," like human rights, existed in reality on some level; they were not just useful terms coined by philosophers, like all words subject to constant reinterpretation (Knowles 1962:107–115, 321–22). There are, many Western idealists believe, certain rights with which every human being is endowed at birth, rights that cannot be denied by any human authority. This concept of human rights seems to be founded in the idea of a standard of human dignity that transcends culture, springing from a sense of shared human nature. At this point the Western thinker holds with the Realists, that there are abstract values, "universals," that really exist, and that human rights are entities of this kind. This way of thinking leads to a concept of international law as based in natural law, and to the idea that human rights exist in nature, something accepted by Western legal thinkers as late as Hugo Grotius in the seventeenth century, and by a number still today (Edwards 1981; Gordley 1991:121–25).

This view of nature as the foundation of international law presupposes a sense that nature is just and benign on some level. Such a positive concept of nature was in harmony with both Aristotle and the first book of Genesis. It did not by any means go unchallenged through the Middle Ages and Renaissance, but nevertheless became established as the belief underlying the support for natural law. In the seventeenth century Hobbes would change the meaning of "natural" law, with his celebrated "bellum omnium contra omnes," the "war of all against all," and his depiction of natural human life as "nasty, brutish, and short." This is the "nature red in tooth and claw" that repelled Tennyson and his fellow Victorians, and that still repels many twentieth-century thinkers. No one with this jaundiced view of nature as profoundly lawless can contemplate the idea of basing international laws on it with any degree of comfort. It is perhaps only with the twentieth century and the Nuremburg war trials for "crimes against humanity" that Western legal theorists have begun to move back toward a positive sense of humanity, human nature, and nature itself.

Perhaps because of a loss of confidence in natural justice, as the Western argument was reformulated in the nineteenth and twentieth centuries, statements of absolute principle seem to dissolve into less confident proposals. The Westerner now announces that "universal values exist which you must agree to if we are to do business with you." This approach is essentially Nominalist, like much of modern thought. It denies that universals are real. They become universal only because we agree to them. Making any universal principle the subject of negotiation rather undermines it as an ideal. It loses the force that comes from the recognition of its transcendent reality as a law of nature or inalienable birthright. The principle becomes, instead, a convention on which the parties to a contract agree. Presumably contracts are subject to adjustment to suit the parties involved. They can be revised, revoked, altered, and emended at will, because they are only words on paper. This step away from the recognition of values as universal suggests that the West no longer believes quite so strongly in its own beliefs. They can be compromised, at a price.

In fact, this second position also proves to be nebulous, since business takes place without any form of agreement on human rights. It would seem that the West is not especially interested in doing anything to support its ideals of human rights, other than talk about them as possible bargaining points. With respect to China, it is difficult to condemn activities that the United States has itself engaged in, and still engages in, or supported in many other countries, let alone activities from which American companies and consumers profit.

International contracts used to be treaties. Now they are trade agreements, loans, and bailouts. The "Asian meltdown" shows that the only morality of the contract is just to honor the terms of the contract, in which investors are compensated and everyone else is flung on the scrap-heap.

The shift from Realism to Nominalism in Western thought beginning in the fourteenth century and taking hold with Descartes, Hobbes, and Locke from the seventeenth century onward, parallels the post-Enlightenment shift in the basis of international law from natural law to law as a convention, the law of contracts. From Aquinas in the thirteenth century (or even Aristotle) to Grotius in the seventeenth century, Western legal scholars saw the underlying laws of the divinely created universe as the source of the principles of the laws of nations. (E. O. Wilson may be returning to this way of thinking in his recent essays on the biological roots of morality, but with a quite different perspective, that of the twentieth-century scientist [Wilson 1998].) This belief in universally recognized truths of nature leading to universally applicable laws has gradually been abandoned by most lawyers. In its place they have brought in the law of contracts, which, today, more and more, means the law of the marketplace. Every legal event becomes a transaction, self-contained, and limited in its force to the parties and the matter at hand. Every event becomes a self-contained unit, and every human being a free agent. Any action can be justified as an agreement between the parties involved. Where international laws of human rights are concerned this change subverts any form of international moral authority. There is no sense of transcendent unity, biological, philosophical, or supernatural, to support any universal moral code. In this relatively recent, economically based system, every culture, religion, and individual is theoretically equal, free to negotiate its own moral decisions in response to its own social context. Without any universal ideal, there is no vantage point from which these decisions can be weighed.

Meanwhile, the Asian governments were prone to retort that, yes, they agree that there are human rights, but that they take different forms in different parts of the world because of the natural diversity of cultures. They asserted that Eastern forms of government, with their emphasis on community and veneration for authority, in fact eliminate many problems now plaguing the West. What to the West might appear as a gross violation of human rights was, in Eastern terms, merely an expression of the values of the traditional community by its leaders. Clearly this approach is compatible with the modern Western idea of law as infinitely mutable social convention, though perhaps not altogether with the older idea of universal values based in nature.

The "Asian Values Debate" should be recognized not only as a mirage, but also as a gross oversimplification. The terms "Asian values" and "Western human rights" lump together what are in fact complex and often contradictory cultures with long histories of their own. The many philosophical schools that have throughout history developed in China have their counterparts in the clashing views of contemporary Chinese thinkers, all grounded in some aspect of Chinese tradition. The many different peoples that make up China today also have their own cultural viewpoints. Outside of China, Asia can hardly be said to be unanimous in its philosophy of life. The West is by no means a monolith, either. Both the East-West split and the unity of either East or West ought to be questioned.

There are other ways of looking at the world. For instance, an example of an authentically Chinese tradition of thought, as yet undiscussed in this context, is Daoism, a long and complex philosophical tradition of great antiquity. What would be a Daoist view of all this, put as simply as possible? In the first place, the attitude to dichotomies differs. Instead of battling for mastery to the death, paired elements (yin/yang, male/female) in dynamic equilibrium seek to balance one another. The ideal is not victory but harmony. The *Tao Te Ching* favors a sense of unity, a focus on the whole as the sum of its contrasting component parts. Daoism looks beyond the limited world of human beings—the Western Renaissance notion that "man is the measure of all things"—to a larger universal order, the Dao. It values "actionless activity" over force, taking what might be described as a feminine approach to government and to life itself. While Daoism gave rise to much of Chinese science, by encouraging the observation of natural phenomena, it never encouraged the idea that man should conquer the universe. The Daoist sage gains wisdom and power by aligning himself with the Dao, not by overcoming it. Much more could be said by the specialist, which I am far from being, but this rough summary may begin to suggest the possibilities of such an alternative approach.

The Daoist view of Three Gorges would certainly be critical. A Daoist sage would suggest that rulers who perpetrate such enterprises are destroying themselves and their countries through excessive activity, unquestionably out of alignment with the Dao. The Daoists might also express a sense of the utter futility and destructiveness of a project, tampering with cosmic forces—people, culture, history, and rivers—far beyond human control. Such activities might in the Daoist view unleash forms of power of a different kind than the central authorities in Beijing imagine. The teachings of the *Tao Te Ching* suggest that such strenuous acts call forth a balancing reaction on the part of the disturbed forces of nature, an equal and opposite reaction to restore equilibrium to the system. The limitations of technology as a form of human action, and its costs, are becoming abundantly clear all across the globe. So is the wisdom of the ancients.

The Daoist philosophy of Lao Tzu supports the idea of universal human rights because it is based on a belief that there are underlying universal principles that form and control the natural world. By recognizing a natural order of things the Daoist sage also recognizes the existence of innate human nature, underlying the many variations created by human cultural practices. This the Daoist contrasts against the artificial qualities imposed by higher forms of civilization, which tend to detract from the original natural order of society. The Daoist believes in the desirability of bringing first himself, followed by the household, village, and entire country, into harmony with nature. Living in balance with nature (the Dao) and freely exercising one's natural rights may only be different ways of expressing a similar idea.

The Chinese authorities, it would seem, know less than they should of their own culture. This is equally true of us in the West. For all our declarations of respect for "multiculturalism," all moderns, both Eastern and Western, are culturally uprooted. This is why too many of us are profoundly ill-prepared to say anything about any culture at all, because we have no experience of any traditional culture in depth, our own or anyone else's. All we have, at most, is a veneer. This is in part because modernity is profoundly disrespectful of cultural tradition, geography, religion, or history. Enrique Dussel criticizes the myth of modernity, which he sees as beginning in 1492: "Modernity elaborated a myth of its own goodness, rationalized its violence as civilizing, and finally declared itself innocent of the assassination of the Other" (Dussel 1995:50). His critique applies, without question, to overenthusiastic human rights advocates whose prescription for the improvement of the world requires all peoples to embrace a twentieth-century Western way of life as without question the most beneficial and desirable. In this case they are the moderns, and the Other their work threatens is the member of a traditional non-Western culture. Dussel's words also refer to any government that imposes forcible modernization on its own people "for their own good" and that of the state. Both of these authorities see themselves as bringing new and better ways of life. The destructive side of their approach, its insensitivity to the value of traditional lifestyles, is too often ignored. What is needed, a Daoist might argue, is greater balance, recognizing the desirability of many aspects of modern Western culture but also its defects and its terrible capacity to erase much of proven value. The Daoist would prefer that traditional and modern arrive at a balance naturally, as seems to be happening in many places where modernized Westerners are trying painfully to get back in touch with their own lost cultural legacies, and with simpler ways of living that are easier on the earth.

Nor is the Daoist mode of thought exclusively eastern. We in the West have our own form of "Daoism"—an approach to life most characteristic of the medieval period (Holbrook 1981:199–216). The notion of the autonomy of the individual and his or her property at the expense of family or community, the loss of respect for nature or life forces larger than ourselves (which has been replaced in the modern psyche by fear and hostility), the primary emphasis on trade above all other considerations—all this is post-Renaissance. It belongs to the heritage of Newton, Descartes, Locke, and the Enlightenment. This is also a veneer. When we look behind it in earlier Western thought we find a much more balanced view of the world. Against the teachings of Lao Tzu might be set, for comparison, those of Hillel, Boethius, Aquinas, Maimonides, or even the English poet Geoffrey Chaucer, who takes much of his philosophy from Boethius. Chaucer in particular offers a sense of balance that could well benefit the twentieth century. "Women, by nature, desire freedom, and not to be constrained like a slave, and so do men, to tell the truth." ("Women, of kynde, desiren libertee, / And nat to ben constreyned as a thral; / And so don men, if I sooth seyen shall" (Chaucer 1987: Franklin's Tale, lines 768–70). No one, male or female, likes to be controlled from the outside. The only answer, if any human relationship is to last, is to obey and respect one another. The good of the individual and the common good are both part of the system, though the pursuit of the common good is rewarded, and unbridled self-interest proves to be self-defeating and unsatisfying, as Chaucer's Pardoner testifies. Chaucer's writings betray a fascination with the possibilities of technology, as in his description of a magical flying horse, to all appearances just like a real horse, but made of brass (Chaucer 1987: Squire's Tale, lines 189–200). He also details the destructive power of science—its seduction, its expense, its uncertainty, potential fraudulence, and its ultimate frustration when everything collapses in the face of the alchemist (Chaucer 1987: Canon's Yeoman's Tale). When in "Trouthe," his poem of good advice, Chaucer advises his activist friend to amend his own life rather than trying to fix the whole world—"Don't try to straighten everything crooked, trusting in a world where fortune turns like a ball; great peace is based in minimizing activity." "Reprove yourself, you who reprove others' actions, and truth will set you free, don't be afraid." ("Tempest thee nought al croked to redresse / In trust of hir that turneth as a a bal; / Gret reste stant in litel besinesse." "Daunte thyself, that dauntest otheres dede, / And trouthe thee shal delivere, it is no drede,") he might be echoing the ancient Daoist approach to life (Chaucer 1987:653, lines 8–10, 13–14). In Chaucer as in Lao Tzu, universal harmony begins with the individual, and then by extension affects the household, the village, and the kingdom.

The attitude to life that makes Chaucer so compatible with ancient Daoism comes from the main stream of Western philosophy. The primary source of the vision of cosmic harmony, and the need for patient acceptance of this unstable world may be Boethius's Consolation of Philosophy, where that author attempted to integrate Aristotle, Plato, the Stoics, and Christian teachings into a single vision of the universe.

There are clear differences. The Daoist sees the understanding of the ways of the Dao, the universe, as a way to deceptive power and personal immortality, while the Boethian philosopher seeks to free himself from worldly illusions and find a way out of here, though he too has a vision of immortality as a reward for those who work for the common good. Both view primitive simplicity of life as preferable to the decadent luxury, greed, and violence of the present, but where Boethius and Chaucer look back to this peaceful 'former age' as the distant past, Lao Tzu also proposes returning to it to create a utopian Daoist state (Chaucer 1987: "The Former Age"). "There might still be boats and carriages, but no one would go in them; there might still be weapons of war but no one would drill with them. He could bring it about that 'the people should have no use for any form of writing save knotted ropes, should be contented with their food, pleased with their clothing, satisfied with their homes, should take pleasure in their rustic tasks' " (Lao Tzu: chapter 80). Being rather more linear thinkers and imbued with the Christian doctrine of original sin as tainting nature, Boethius and Chaucer are clearly more pessimistic. They do not believe that it is possible to turn back the clock, though Chaucer at least thinks the virtuous ruler and citizen can improve their own conduct and by this means help to restore the rights of those around them (Chaucer 1987: "Trouthe," and "Lak of Stedfastnesse").

As modernity wears thin, the West is rediscovering the depth and power of its own underlying cultural traditions. Western middle-class parents are confronted by the curious prospect of children who want to learn the languages, religious and cultural traditions of their grandparents, go back to the land, live more simply, escape the pressure of twenty-first century corporate life. Scottish, Welsh, Catalan, Basque, and French-Canadian nationalisms, the reassertion of the sovereignty of indigenous nations and the peoples of the former Soviet bloc all point in this direction. So, too, throughout Asia, the value of native forms of wisdom may be reasserting itself. (This may take its most aggressive form in Islamic and Hindu fundamentalisms.) At first sight this resurgence of traditional cultures would seem to be promoting violent conflict almost everywhere it emerges, while the movement toward international nonsectarian modernism across the board, global homogenization, would seem to promote world peace. (This is the Western ideal of the one true faith, that we can find salvation only by accepting a single identity.) Yet I believe the return of tradition is an essential attempt to arrive at a balance, and to rescue much of value that the modern world has thoughtlessly scrapped.

A more Daoist—or more Chaucerian—approach to human rights would return from thinking in terms of contracts to thinking in terms of nature. What it offers is a more natural and dynamic view of rights, not as a list of criteria, demands, conditions of trade, or legal requirements to be enforced from outside, but as springing from a sense of the shared nature of human beings. Rights from this viewpoint are natural; they come from innate human needs, and are necessary to preserve and nurture life. Daoism would encourage us to look beyond the "social construction of identity," the postmodern version of the "social contract," to the fundamental needs of the physical—and spiritual—human being. This shift of emphasis from law to everyday life could have a helpful psychological effect simply by lowering the sense of conflict that is in itself a great impediment to progress. This neo-Daoist-medieval approach also shifts attention from the global to the personal. It offers a much greater sense of the capacity of the individual, through the adjustment of his or her own conduct and attitude, to affect the universe. (It also suggests why large-scale international programs are not getting the desired results.) Such a change in approach has the potential to bring the peoples of the world into accord, not by imposing standards from the outside, but by encouraging complementary local traditions to emerge. That traditions are re-emerging on their own, in spite of the struggles of modernity to dam them and divert their power to suit its own purposes, is an excellent sign.

Acknowledgments

My thanks to my fellow members of the Summer Seminar, and to Andy Nathan and Jeffrey Wollock of the Solidarity Foundation of New York City for much wise counsel and editorial assistance.

Bibliography

Chaucer, Geoffrey. 1987. *The Riverside Chaucer*. Edited by Larry D. Benson. Boston: Houghton Mifflin.

Culbertson, John M. 1984. *International Trade and the Future of the West*. Madison: 21st Century Press.

Dussel, Enrique. 1992. *The Invention of the Americas: Eclipse of "the Other" and the Myth of Modernity*. Translated by Michael D. Barber. New York: Continuum.

Edwards, Charles S. 1981. *Hugo Grotius: The Miracle of Holland: A Study of Political and Legal Thought*. Chicago: Nelson Hall.

Gordley, James. 1991. *The Philosophical Origins of Modern Contract Doctrine*. Oxford: Clarendon Press.

Guénon, René. 1941. *East and West*. Trans. William Massey. London: Luzac & Co.

Holbrook, Bruce. 1981. *The Stone Monkey: An Alternative, Chinese-Scientific Reality*. New York: William Morrow.

Knowles, David. 1962. *The Evolution of Medieval Thought*. New York: Vintage.

Kristof, Nicholas. "Suharto's Stealthy Foe: Globalizing Capitalism." *New York Times*. May 20, 1998:A10.

Lao Tzu. 1997. *Tao te Ching*. Translated by Arthur Waley. Ware, Hertfordshire: Wordsworth.

Nakamura, Hajime. 1964. *Ways of Thinking of Eastern Peoples; India-China-Tibet-Japan*. Revised English translation. Edited by Philip P. Wiener. Honolulu: East-West Center Press.

Needham, Joseph. 1981. *Science in Traditional China*. Hong Kong and Cambridge, MA: The Chinese University of Hong Kong and Harvard University Press.

Runciman, Stephen. 1947. *The Medieval Manichee: A Study of the Christian Dualist Heresy*. Cambridge: Cambridge University Press.

Sachs, Wolfgang. 1992. *The Development Dictionary: A Guide to Knowledge and Power*. London and New Jersey: Zed Books.

Tannen, Deborah. 1998. *The Argument Culture: Moving from Debate to Dialogue*. New York: Random House.

Wilson, Edward O. "The Biological Basis of Morality." *Atlantic Monthly* 281 (4) (April 1998):53–70.

Appendix A

Universal Declaration of Human Rights (Excerpts) Adopted and Proclaimed by General Assembly (Resolution 217) 10 December 1948

Preamble

Whereas recognition of the inherent dignity and of the equal and inalienable rights of all members of the human family is the foundation of freedom, justice and peace in the world.

Whereas disregard and contempt for human rights have resulted in barbarous acts which have outraged the conscience of mankind, and the advent of a world in which human beings shall enjoy freedom of speech and belief and freedom from fear and want has been proclaimed as the highest aspiration of the common people,

Whereas it is essential, if man is not to be compelled to have recourse, as a last resort, to rebellion against tyranny and oppression. that human rights should be protected by the rule of law,

Whereas it is essential to promote the development of friendly relations between nations,

Whereas the peoples of the United Nations have in the Charter reaffirmed their faith in fundamental human rights, in the dignity and worth of the human person and in the equal rights of men and women and have determined to promote social progress and better standards of life in larger freedom,

Whereas Member States have pledged themselves to achieve, in cooperation with the United Nations, the promotion of universal respect for and observance of human rights and fundamental freedoms,

Whereas a common understanding of these rights and freedoms is of the greatest importance for the full realization of this pledge,

Now, Therefore,

The General Assembly

Proclaims this Universal Declaration of Human Rights as a common standard of achievement for all peoples and all nations, to the end that every individual and every organ of society, keeping this Declaration constantly in mind, shall strive by teaching and education to promote respect for these rights and freedoms and by progressive measures, national and international to secure their universal and effective recognition and observance, both among the peoples of Member States themselves and among the peoples of territories under their jurisdiction.

Article 1

All human beings are born free and equal in dignity and rights. They are endowed with reason and conscience and should act towards one another in a spirit of brotherhood.

Article 2

Everyone is entitled to all the rights and freedoms set forth in this Declaration, without distinction of any kind, such as race, color, sex, language, religion, political or other opinion, national or social origin, property, birth or other status.

Furthermore, no distinction shall be made on the basis of the political, jurisdictional or international status of the country or territory to which a person belongs, whether it be independent, trust, non-self-governing or under any other limitation of sovereignty.

Article 3

Everyone has the right to life, liberty and the security of person.

Article 4

No one shall be held in slavery or servitude; slavery and the slave trade shall be prohibited in all their forms.

Article 5

No one shall be subjected to torture or to cruel, inhuman or degrading treatment or punishment.

Article 6

Everyone has the right to recognition everywhere as a person before the law.

Article 7

All are equal before the law are entitled without any discrimination to equal protection of the law. All are entitled to equal protection against any discrimination in violation of this Declaration and against any incitement to such discrimination.

Article 8

Everyone has the right to an effective remedy by the competent national tribunals for acts violating the fundamental rights granted him by the constitution or by law.

Article 9

No one shall be subjected to arbitrary arrest, detention or exile.

Article 10

Everyone is entitled in full equality to a fair and public hearing by an independent and impartial tribunal, in the determination of his rights and obligations and of any criminal charge against him.

Article 11

1. Everyone charged with a penal offence has the right to be presumed innocent until proved guilty according to law in a public trial at which he has had all the guarantees necessary for his defence.
2. No one shall be held guilty of any penal offence on account of any act or omission which did not constitute a penal offence, under national or international law, at the time when it was committed. Nor shall a heavier penalty be imposed than the one that was applicable at the time the penal offence was committed.

Article 12

No one shall be subjected to arbitrary interference with his privacy, family, home or correspondence, nor to attacks upon his honor and reputation. Everyone has the right to the protection of the law against such interference or attacks.

Article 13

1. Everyone has the right to freedom of movement and residence within the borders of each State.
2. Everyone has the right to leave any country, including his own, and to return to his country.

Article 14

1. Everyone has the right to seek and to enjoy in other countries asylum from persecution.
2. This right may not be invoked in the case of prosecutions genuinely arising from non-political crimes or from acts contrary to the purposes and principles of the United Nations.

Article 15

1. Everyone has the right to a nationality.
2. No one shall be arbitrarily deprived of his nationality nor denied the right to change his nationality.

Article 16

1. Men and women of full age, without any limitation due to race, nationality or religion, have the right to marry and to found a family. They are entitled to equal rights as to marriage, during marriage and at its dissolution.
2. Marriage shall be entered into only with the free and full consent of the intending spouses.
3. The family is the natural and fundamental group unit of society and is entitled to protection by society and the State.

Article 17

1. Everyone has the right to own property alone as well as in association with others.
2. No one shall be arbitrarily deprived of his property.

Article 18

Everyone has the right to freedom of thought, conscience and religion; this right includes freedom to change his religion or belief, and freedom, either alone or in community with others and in public or private, to manifest his religion or belief in teaching, practice, worship and observance.

Article 19

Everyone has the right to freedom of opinion and expression; this right includes freedom to hold opinions without interference and to seek, receive and impart information and ideas through any media and regardless of frontiers.

Article 20

1. Everyone has the right to freedom of peaceful assembly and association.
2. No one may be compelled to belong to an association.

Article 21

1. Everyone has the right to take part in the government of his country, directly or through freely chosen representatives.
2. Everyone has the right of equal access to public service in his country.
3. The will of the people shall be the basis of the authority of government; this will shall be expressed in periodic and genuine elections which shall be by universal and equal suffrage and shall be held by secret vote or by equivalent free voting procedures.

Article 22

Everyone, as a member of society, has the right to social security and is entitled to realization, through national effort and international cooperation and in accordance with the organization and resources of each State, of the economic, social and cultural rights indispensable for his dignity and the free development of his personality.

Article 23

1. Everyone has the right to work, to free choice of employment, to just and favourable conditions of work and to protection against unemployment.
2. Everyone, without any discrimination, has the right to equal pay for equal work.
3. Everyone who works has the right to just and favourable remuneration ensuring for himself and his family an existence worthy of human dignity, and supplemented, if necessary, by other means of social protection.

4. Everyone has the right to form and to join trade unions for the protection of his interests.

Article 24
Everyone has the right to rest and leisure, including reasonable limitation of working hours and periodic holidays with pay.

Article 25
1. Everyone has the right to a standard of living adequate for the health and well-being of himself and of his family, including food, clothing, housing and medical care and necessary social services, and the right to security in the event of unemployment, sickness, disability, widowhood, old age or other lack of livelihood in circumstances beyond his control.
2. Motherhood and childhood are entitled to special care and assistance. All children, whether born in or out of wedlock, shall enjoy the same social protection.

Article 26
1. Everyone has the right to education. Education shall be free, at least in the elementary and fundamental stages. Elementary education shall be compulsory. Technical and professional education shall be made generally available and higher education shall be equally accessible to all on the basis of merit.
2. Education shall be directed to the full development of the human personality and to the strengthening of respect for human rights and fundamental freedoms. It shall promote understanding, tolerance and friendship among all nations, racial or religious groups, and shall further the activities of the United Nations for the maintenance of peace.
3. Parents have a prior right to choose the kind of education that shall be given to their children.

Article 27
1. Everyone has the right freely to participate in the cultural life of the community, to enjoy the arts and to share in scientific advancement and its benefits.

2. Everyone has the right to the protection of the moral and material interests resulting from any scientific, literary or artistic production of which he is the author.

Article 28
Everyone is entitled to a social and international order in which the rights and freedoms set forth in this Declaration can be fully realized.

Article 29
1. Everyone has duties to the community in which alone the free and full development of his personality is possible.
2. In the exercise of his rights and freedoms, everyone shall be subject only to such limitations as are determined by law solely for the purpose of securing due recognition and respect for the rights and freedoms of others and of meeting the just requirements of morality, public order and the general welfare in a democratic society.
3. These rights and freedoms may in no case be exercised contrary to the purposes and principles of the United Nations.

Article 30
Nothing in this Declaration may be interpreted as implying for any State, group or person any right to engage in any activity or to perform any act aimed at the destruction of any of the rights and freedoms set forth herein.

Appendix B

Bangkok Declaration on Human Rights
(Excerpts)

The Declaration adopted by the Ministers and Representatives of Asian States, who met in Bangkok from 29 March to 2 April 1993, pursuant to General Assembly Resolution 46/116 of 17 December 1991 in the context of preparations for the World Conference on Human Rights:

Emphasizing the significance of the World Conference on Human Rights, which provides an invaluable opportunity to review all aspects of human rights and ensure a just and balanced approach thereto,

Recognizing the contribution that can be made to the World Conference by Asian countries with their diverse and rich cultures and traditions,

Welcoming the increased attention being paid to human rights in the international community,

Reaffirming their commitment to principles contained in the Charter of the United Nations and the Universal Declaration on Human Rights,

Recalling that in the Charter of the United Nations the question of universal observance and promotion of human rights and fundamental freedoms has been rightly placed within the context of international cooperation,

Noting the progress made in the codification of human rights instruments, and in the establishment of international human rights mechanisms, while expressing concern that these mechanisms relate mainly to one category of rights,

Emphasizing that ratification of international human rights instruments, particularly the International Covenant on Civil and Political Rights and the International Covenant an Economic, Social and Cultural Rights, by all States should be further encouraged,

Reaffirming the principles of respect for national sovereignty, territorial integrity and non-interference in the internal affairs of States,

Stressing the universality, objectivity and non-selectivity of all human rights and the need to avoid the application of double standards in the implementation of human rights and its politicization,

Recognizing that the promotion of human rights should be encouraged by cooperation and consensus, and not through confrontation and the imposition of incompatible values,

Reiterating the interdependence and indivisibility of economic, social, cultural, civil and political rights, and the inherent interrelationship between development, democracy, universal enjoyment of all human rights, and social justice which must be addressed in an integrated and balanced manner,

Recalling that the Declaration on the Right to Development has recognized the right to development as a universal and inalienable right and an integral part of fundamental human rights,

Emphasizing that endeavors to move towards the creation of uniform international human rights norms must go hand in hand with endeavors to work towards a just and fair world economic order,

Convinced that economic and social progress facilitates the growing trend towards democracy and the promotion and protection of human rights,

Stressing the importance of education and training in human rights at the national, regional and international levels and the need for international cooperation aimed at overcoming the lack of public awareness of human rights,

1. *Reaffirm* their commitment to the principles contained in the Charter of the United Nations and the Universal Declaration on Human Rights as well as the full realization of all human rights throughout the world;

2. *Underline* the essential need to create favorable conditions for effective enjoyment of human rights at both the national and international levels;

3. *Stress* the urgent need to democratize the United Nations system, eliminate selectivity and improve procedures and mechanisms in order to strengthen international cooperation, based on principles of equality and mutual respect, and ensure a positive, balanced and non-confrontational approach in addressing and realizing all aspects of human rights;

4. *Discourage* any attempt to use human rights as a conditionality for extending development assistance;

5. *Emphasize* the principles of respect for national sovereignty and territorial integrity as well as non-interference in the internal affairs of States, and the non-use of human rights as an instrument of political pressure;

6. *Reiterate* that all countries, large and small, have the right to determine their political systems, control and freely *utilize* their resources, and freely pursue their economic, social and cultural development;

7. *Stress* the universality, objectivity and non-selectivity of all human rights and the need to avoid the application of double standards in the implementation of human rights and its politicization, and that no violation of human rights can be justified;

8. *Recognize* that while human rights are universal in nature, they must be considered in the context of a dynamic and evolving process of international norm-setting, bearing in mind the significance of national and regional particularities and various historical, cultural and religious backgrounds;

9. *Recognize further* that States have the primary responsibility for the promotion and protection of human rights through appropriate infrastructure and mechanisms, and also recognize that remedies must be sought and provided primarily through such mechanisms and procedures;

10. *Reaffirm* the interdependence and indivisibility of economic, social, cultural, civil and political rights, and the need to give equal emphasis to all categories of human rights;

11. *Emphasize* the importance of guaranteeing the human rights and fundamental freedoms of vulnerable groups such as ethnic, national, racial, religious and linguistic minorities, migrant workers, disabled persons, indigenous peoples, refugees and displaced persons;

12. *Reiterate* that self-determination is a principle of international law and a universal right recognized by the United Nations for peoples under alien or colonial domination or foreign occupation, by virtue of which they can freely determine their political status and freely pursue their economic, social and cultural development, and that its denial constitutes a grave violation of human rights;

13. *Stress* that the right to self-determination is applicable to peoples under alien or colonial domination or foreign occupation, and should not be used to undermine the territorial integrity, national sovereignty and political independence of States;

14. *Express concern* over all forms of violation of human rights, including manifestations of racial discrimination, racism, apartheid, colonialism, for-

eign aggression and occupation, and the establishment of illegal settlements in occupied territories, as well as the recent resurgence of neo-nazism, xenophobia and ethnic cleansing;

15. *Underline* the need for taking effective international measures in order to guarantee and monitor the implementation of human rights standards and effective and legal protection of people under foreign occupation;

16. *Strongly affirm* their support for the legitimate struggle of the Palestinian people to restore their national and inalienable rights to self-determination and independence, and demand an immediate end to the grave violations of human rights in the Palestinian, Syrian Golan and other occupied Arab territories including Jerusalem;

17. *Reaffirm* the right to development, as established in the Declaration on the Right to Development, as a universal and inalienable right and an integral part of fundamental human rights, which must be realized through international cooperation, respect for fundamental human rights, the establishment of a monitoring mechanism and the creation of essential international conditions for the realization of such right;

18. *Recognize* that the main obstacle to the realization of the right to development lies at the international macroeconomic level, as reflected in the widening gap between the North and the South, the rich and the poor;

19. *Affirm* that poverty is one of the major obstacles hindering the full enjoyment of human rights;

20. *Affirm also* the need to develop the right of humankind regarding a clean, safe and healthy environment;

21. *Note* that terrorism, in all its forms and manifestations, as distinguished from the legitimate struggle of peoples under colonial or alien domination or foreign occupation, has emerged as one of the most dangerous threes to the enjoyment of human rights and democracy, threatening the territorial integrity and security of States and destabilizing legitimately constituted governments, and that it must be unequivocally condemned by the international community;

22. *Reaffirm* their strong commitment to the promotion and protection of the rights of women through the guarantee of equal participation in the political, social, economic and cultural concerns of society, and the eradication of all forms of discrimination and of gender-based violence against women;

23. *Recognize* the rights of the child to enjoy special protection and to be afforded the opportunities and facilities to develop physically, mentally,

morally, spiritually and socially in a healthy and normal manner and in conditions of freedom and dignity;

24. *Welcome* the important role played by national institutions in the genuine and constructive promotion of human rights, and believe that the conceptualization and eventual establishment of such institutions are best left for the States to decide;

25. *Acknowledge* the importance of cooperation and dialogue between governments and non-governmental organizations on the basis of shared values as well as mutual respect and understanding in the promotion of human rights, and encourage the non-governmental organizations in consultative status with the Economic and Social Council to contribute positively to this process in accordance with Council Resolution 1296 (XLIV);

26. *Reiterate* the need to explore the possibilities of establishing regional arrangements for the promotion and protection of human rights in Asia;

27. *Reiterate further* the need to explore ways to generate international cooperation and financial support for education and training in the field of human rights at the national level and for the establishment of national infrastructures to promote and protect human rights if requested by States;

28. *Emphasize* the necessity to rationalize the United Nations human rights mechanism in order to enhance its effectiveness and efficiency and the need to ensure avoidance of the duplication of work that exists between the treaty bodies, the Sub-Commission on Prevention of Discrimination and Protection of Minorities and the Commission on Human Rights, as well as the need to avoid the multiplicity of parallel mechanisms;

29. *Stress* the importance of strengthening the United Nations Center for Human Rights with the necessary resources to enable it to provide a wide range of advisory services and technical assistance programs in the promotion of human rights to requesting States in a timely and effective manner, as well as to enable it to finance adequately other activities in the field of human rights authorized by competent bodies;

30. *Call for* increased representation of the developing countries in the Center for Human Rights.

Appendix C

Bangkok NGO Declaration on Human Rights (Excerpts) 27 March 1993

Introduction

Some 240 participants from 110 non-governmental organisations (NGOs) concerned with issues of human rights and democratic development from the Asia-Pacific region representing women, children, indigenous peoples, workers, community development and other concerns met in Bangkok from 24–28 March 1993 to review the current human rights situation in the region and to formulate strategies for the future promotion and protection of human rights.

This gathering was motivated by the need to offer, in a spirit of international solidarity, ideas and suggestions in the lead-up to the Asian intergovernmental conference on human rights (Bangkok, 29 March–2 April 1993), the World Conference on Human Rights (Vienna, June 1993), and beyond.

Challenges

The participants identified the following essential challenges:

1. *Universality.* We can learn from different cultures in a pluralistic perspective and draw lessons from the humanity of these cultures to deepen respect for human rights. There is emerging a new understanding of universalism encompassing the richness and wisdom of Asia-Pacific cultures.

Universal human rights standards are rooted in many cultures. We affirm the basis of universality of human rights which afford protection to all of humanity, including special groups such as women, children, minorities and indigenous peoples, workers, refugees and displaced persons, the disabled and the elderly. While advocating cultural pluralism, those cultural practices which derogate from universally accepted human rights, including women's rights, must not be tolerated.

As human rights are of universal concern and are universal in value, the advocacy of human rights cannot be considered to be an encroachment upon national sovereignty.

2. *Indivisibility.* We affirm our commitment to the principle of indivisibility and interdependence of human rights, be they civil, political, economic, social or cultural rights. The protection of human rights concerns both individuals and collectivities. The enjoyment of human rights implies a degree of social responsibility to the community.

Violations of civil and political rights are perpetrated every day. These include the stifling of self-determination, military occupation, killings, torture, political repression, and suppression of freedom of expression and other freedoms. By contrast, poverty and the lack of basic necessities constitute key violations of economic, social and cultural rights.

Violations of civil, political and economic rights frequently result from the emphasis on economic development at the expense of human rights. Violations of social and cultural rights are often the result of political systems which treat human rights as being of secondary importance.

Economic rights involve a fair distribution of resources and income, the right to freedom from hunger and poverty. These can only be protected where people are able to exercise their civil and political rights, for example, the right of workers to organise and form unions to protect their economic rights. Poverty arises from maldevelopment in the face of systemic denial of human rights.

There must be a holistic and integrated approach to human rights. One set of rights cannot be used to bargain for another.

3. *Women's Rights as Human Rights.* The issue of women's rights has not been sufficiently visible the human rights discourse, in human rights institutions and practices. Patriarchy which operates through gender, class, caste and ethnicity, is integral to the problems facing women. Patriarchy is a form

of slavery and must be eradicated. Women's rights must be addressed in both the public and private spheres of society, in particular in the family.

To provide women a life with dignity and self-determination, it is important that women have inalienable, equal economic rights (e.g. right to agricultural land, housing and other resources, and property). It is imperative for governments and the United Nations (UN) to guarantee these rights.

Crimes against women, including rape, sexual slavery and trafficking, and domestic violence are rampant. *Crimes against women are crimes against humanity, and the failure of governments to prosecute those responsible for such crimes implies complicity.*

In the Asia-Pacific region, women's rights are violated by increasingly militant assertions of religious and ethnic identity; the fact that these violations often take place through private actors is used by states as a pretext for failing to counter them as transgressions of human rights. In crisis situations—ethnic violence, communal riots, armed conflicts, military occupation and displacement—women's rights are specifically violated.

In the case where countries have acceded to the relevant international instruments on women's rights, many countries have entered too many reservations to exempt themselves from responsibility. This illustrates the lack of political and social will to protect women's rights.

4. *Solidarity.* We are entitled to join hands to protect human rights worldwide. We commit ourselves to international solidarity and to voice the concerns of our brothers and sisters without boundaries and barriers. Discrimination based upon race, gender, political, economic, social, religious or ethnic origin must not be tolerated. *International solidarity transcends the national order to refute claims of state sovereignty and non-interference in the internal affairs of a state.*

5. *Sustainable Development.* No country can attain genuine development if it is not truly free, if it has not been able to successfully liberate itself from foreign domination and control. A major cause of maldevelopment and gross violations of human rights is the dominance and consequence of imperialism in the Asia-Pacific region. A pre-condition to genuine development is the attainment of national liberation and self-determination of the peoples in the region.

We re-emphasis the need for balanced development, bearing in mind maximisation of people's development; integrated approaches on civil, political, economic, social and cultural rights; equity and social justice; income distribution and fair resource allocation. Particular attention must be paid to the needs of different groups including women, children, rural people, the urban poor, minorities and indigenous peoples, refugees and displaced persons, workers, and others in disadvantaged positions. The natural environment must be protected as part and parcel of human rights.

Various top-down development models have led to maldevelopment. Action against national liberation and the people's right of self-determination against political/military repression are key constraints for the realisation of development. These are compounded by regional peculiarities whereby state boundaries are at times artificial when viewed from the commonalities between peoples across frontiers.

On the one hand, we must restructure the international development framework to respond more directly to the needs of people in our societies and communities—both men and women, including debt relief, reform of the international financial, economic and commercial systems, and greater democratisation of the decision-making process. The role of international aid agencies—multilateral and bilateral—and financial institutions has given rise to a number of human rights violations; they must be held accountable for the human rights violations caused by their polices and deeds.

International economic forces have great impact on human rights. The divide between North and South in terms of global equity and resource base, compounded by elitism, perpetuates social and economic disparities. The shift to a market economy has led to various human rights violations linked with development. Market rights do not mean human rights. "One dollar, one vote" does not mean democracy. Freedom to exploit does not deliver economic rights to the poor.

On the other hand, reform is also required at the national level. Maldevelopment leads to increasing poverty, income disparities, dispossession and deprivation, including land and resource holdings, environmental degradation, and over- emphasis on macro-economic development without sufficient enhancement of human development, freedoms and dignity, including dignity of men and women.

There is an urgent call to democratise the development process at both the national and international levels so as to ensure a harmonious relationship between humanity and the natural environment and to create processes to enhance the empowerment of women and gender equality. The thrust is to promote human and humane development.

6. *Democracy.* Democracy is more than a legalistic or formal process. Democracy is more than the ritual casting of a ballot at one party or multi-

party elections. True democracy involves participatory democracy by the people at all levels so that the people have a voice in the discussions by which they are governed.

It must be realised in the form of people's empowerment and participation at the grassroots and other levels with responsive and accountable processes and institutions at both the local and national levels. It demands good governance, freedom from corruption, and accountability of state and other authorities to the people. It involves the protection and participation of those groups which are not in the majority, namely minorities and disempowered groups. It is intertwined with the issue of land and social justice for rural people and other disadvantaged groups.

Democracy is a way of life; it pervades all aspects of human life—in the home, in the local community, and beyond. It must be fostered and guaranteed in all countries.

7. *Militarisation.* We express deep concern over the increasing militarisation throughout the region and the diversion of resources for this purpose. Militarisation has led to the destruction of civil society, undermined the right of self-determination, and denied the people the right to liberate themselves and their freedom from fear. At times, militarisation has taken the guise of civilian groups, such as vigilantes.

It has particularly harmed indigenous peoples and has resulted in forced migration. It is interrelated with violence against women, such as sexual slavery, rape and other crimes committed in armed conflicts. It has particularly harmed the children. They suffer from physical arrest and torture, evacuation, massacre, disappearance, and other forms of human rights violations.

Militarisation of smaller, less militaristic states is often abetted by superpowers and regional powers. Profiteering from the sale of weapons of mass destruction has been a prime cause of economic growth in developed countries and maldevelopment in developing countries. It is aggravated by the proliferation of nuclear weapons and energy, and environmental damage due to toxic wastes.

The quest for peace and human rights is intertwined with the need to demilitarise.

8. *Self-determination.* The right of self-determination of peoples is well-established in international human rights instruments and international law. The root cause of most internal conflicts can be traced back to this fundamental human right.

We affirm that all peoples have the right to self-determination. By virtue of that right they freely determine their political status, and freely pursue their economic, social and cultural development. The right of peoples to self-determination must, therefore, be observed by all governments.

It is understood also that self-determination does not necessarily imply secession or independence. Self-determination can mean independence, free association, integration with an independent state or other constitutional arrangement arrived at through popular consultation and consent.

9. *Torture.* The existence of torture and inhuman and degrading treatment in the Asia-Pacific region gives rise to increasing concern. *These practices must be eradicated.*

In many countries, suspects are tortured by law enforcement personnel for extracting "confessions." This inhuman practice is officially encouraged by some authorities as a cheap and convenient method of crime control. These so-called "confessions" are used as "evidence" in court cases.

The action needed to counter such practices needs to be both preventive and curative. The latter implies prosecution of those responsible, as well as rehabilitation assistance for torture victims.

10. *Freedom of Expression.* This freedom is constrained In many Asia-Pacific countries, It is necessarily interrelated with the call for civil and political rights, and democracy.

In several countries, there are no independent media. People cannot express themselves without fear. Many people are persecuted, jailed, and even killed because they speak out their thoughts. *The pretext for constraining these channels of expression is often national security and law and order; this is a facade for authoritarianism and for the suppression of democratic aspirations.*

11. *Human Rights Education and Training.* Human rights education and training have so far not been incorporated sufficiently into both formal and non-formal education. Illiteracy remains widespread.

School curriculum tends to favour the ruling elites. Not only are millions of people unaware of their rights, but also receive no encouragement or assistance in asserting their rights. Human rights education and training have both preventive and curative impact—they can empower people to prevent problems from arising by nurturing respect for other people's rights, and vice versa, as well as to inform people of the possibilities of redress.

If we wish to promote democracy and respect for human rights, we must develop comprehensive human rights education and training in both governmental and non-governmental programmes, in and out-of-school.

12. *Indigenous Peoples.* The Asia-Pacific region is home to many indigenous peoples. *A basic issue among these indigenous peoples is the fact that many are not recognised as indigenous by governments and as such are denied the right to self-determination.*

They are denied their specific cultural identity and entitlement to protection under relevant international human rights instruments. They are victims of ethnocide and genocide perpetrated by certain governments — whether from the North, the South or together, international financial institutions and transnational corporations. International legal instruments presently available are weak in ensuring collective human rights protection.

In many parts of the region, their right to land and other rights are not respected. Among the consequences are the expropriation and despoliation of their lands, armed conflicts and displacement as refugees. This has been accompanied by persecution and suppression by force. On another front, tourism has at times led to the degradation of indigenous lifestyles through commercial exploitation.

13. *Children.* A variety of abuses and exploitation of children arise in the region. These include child labour, children in bondage and sexual slavery, child prostitution, sale and trafficking of children, children in armed conflict situations, children in prison, children in poverty situations and other deprivations, and children abused in families compounded by family break-up and breakdown. Basic needs, such as physical and mental health, nutrition, education, shelter, and participation are often unsatisfied. The advent of AIDS has increased the plight of children; discrimination is increasing both against children with AIDS and orphans of AIDS affected families.

Children's rights are endangered in a wide variety of situations. At a very early age, they are exposed to violence in many forms by governments — poverty, malnutrition, disease, and lack of education which stultify their growth and deprive them of their childhood.

The scenario is much linked with discrimination against the girl child, militarisation, and the distorted development process. Although many countries have now acceded to the International Convention on the Rights of the Child, implementation remains weak, with much lip-service rather effective action to protect children and to assist their families.

Implementation of the rights of children to survival, protection. development and participation as embodied In the International Convention on the Rights of the Child must be a paramount concern of every state regardless of considerations of national capacity and security.

14. *Workers.* Workers of the Asia-Pacific region do not enjoy acceptable standards of human rights. *Too often it is workers and trade union leaders who endure the worst cases of human rights abuses in the region.* The right of freedom of association and the right to organise trade unions are very restricted in several countries.

In this setting, human rights that are taken for granted in the civil society are ignored within the factory and workplace. The human rights of workers such as women, migrants, bonded labourers, children and youths, and those in the informal/unorganised sector are in an even more critical situation.

The economic rights of workers, especially their access to an adequate standard of living, is often neglected in the region. Transnational corporations and agencies such as the International Monetary Fund and the World Bank at times work to undermine this right in the name of economic freedom. Many abuses of worker rights in this region come from the same countries of the North which preach human rights to the South.

15. *Refugees and Displaced Persons.* The problem of refugees and displaced persons is widespread and growing in the region; it is becoming a permanent phenomenon. It is intermingled with political repression, armed conflicts, ethnic discord, and other factors. Economic factors also push people to move in search of a livelihood elsewhere.

Inadequate attention is paid to their plight. Their position is compounded by the lack of effective, national and international machinery to ensure their protection and assistance.

The safety of refugees and displaced persons is often jeopardised by restrictive state policies and discrimination. The basic right of refugees not to be pushed back to the frontiers of dangers is violated on many occasions. The procedures established to determine refugee status are often defective, and voluntary repatriation to the country of origin is not always guaranteed. *The human rights of refugees and displaced persons, including freedom of expression, are violated in the name of restrictive national policies.*

Few countries have acceded to the relevant refugee instruments. This displays a reticence to recognise international human rights standards and to render thee situation more transparent internationally.

16. *Derogations.* Several countries seek to constrain the enjoyment of human rights by means of derogations. In cases of militarisation, military occupation and rule—at times in the guise of civilian governments, the space for civil society is becoming narrowed with negative impact for human rights.

We re-emphasise that states must not derogate from human rights standards for reasons of national security, law and order, or the equivalent. *We reiterate that states are bound to respect human rights in their totality in all circumstances.*

17. *Human Rights Activists/Defenders.* Increasing restrictions are being imposed on the work of human rights activists/defenders—peoples from all walks of life involved with human rights and social movements in the region, including the operations of NGOs. Often they are intimidated, harassed, and even murdered. In some countries, NGOs are not even allowed to exist.

As these groups voice the interests of the people and work for their advancement, it is imperative that they be permitted to work freely; their right to participate in community life and to enjoy the totality of human rights must be respected.

18. *Judicial independence and responsibility.* In many societies, the independence of the judiciary and the administration of justice are being jeopardized by authoritarian elements. This is compounded by various national laws that conflict with human rights standards, particularly discrimination and inequality, and the complicity of certain judges in perpetuating authoritarian regimes.

The legal structure is also distant from many communities. There is a key question concerning access by people to the courts system. This is intertwined with the issue of legal aid, assistance and dissemination of legal knowledge.

We re-affirm the need for judicial independence and call for judicial responsibility to render justice more accessible to the people.

Appendix D

Convention on the Elimination of All Forms of Discrimination Against Women (Excerpts)

[Adopted and opened for signature, ratification and accession by General Assembly resolution 34/180 of 18 December 1979.]

The States Parties to the Present Convention,

Noting that the Charter of the United Nations reaffirms faith in fundamental human rights, in the dignity and worth of the human person and in the equal rights of men and women,

Noting that the Universal Declaration of Human Rights affirms the principle of the inadmissibility of discrimination and proclaims that all human beings are born free and equal in dignity and rights and that everyone is entitled to all the rights and freedoms set forth therein, without distinction of any kind, including distinction based on sex,

Noting that the States Parties to the International Covenants on Human Rights have the obligation to ensure the equal right of men and women to enjoy all economic, social, cultural, civil and political rights,

Considering the international conventions concluded under the auspices of the United Nations and the specialized agencies promoting equality of rights of men and women,

Noting also the resolutions, declarations and recommendations adopted by the United Nations and the specialized agencies promoting equality of rights of men and women,

Concerned, however, that despite these various instruments extensive discrimination against women continues to exist,

Recalling that discrimination against women violates the principles of equality of rights and respect for human dignity, is an obstacle to the participation of women, on equal terms with men, in the political, social, economic and cultural life of their countries, hampers the growth of the prosperity of society and the family and makes more difficult the full development of the potentialities of women in the service of their countries and of humanity,

Concerned that in situations of poverty women have the least access to food, health, education, training and opportunities for employment and other needs,

Convinced that the establishment of the new international economic order based on equity and justice will contribute significantly towards the promotion of equality between men and women;

Emphasizing that the eradication of apartheid, all forms of racism, racial discrimination, colonialism, neocolonialism, aggression, foreign occupation and domination and interference in the internal affairs of States is essential to the full enjoyment of the rights of men and women,

Affirming that the strengthening of international peace and security, the relaxation of international tension, mutual co-operation among all States irrespective of their social and economic systems, general and complete disarmament, in particular nuclear disarmament under strict and effective international control, the affirmation of the principles of justice, equality and mutual benefit in relations among countries and the realization of the right of peoples under alien and colonial domination and foreign occupation to self-determination and independence, as well as respect for national sovereignty and territorial integrity, will promote social progress and development and as a consequence will contribute to the attainment of full equality between men and women,

Convinced that the full and complete development of a country, the welfare of the world and the cause of peace require the maximum participation of women on equal terms with men in all fields,

Bearing in mind the great contribution of women to the welfare of the family and to the development of society, so far not fully recognized, the social significance of maternity and the role of both parents in the family and in the upbringing of children, and aware that the role of women in procreation should not be a basis for discrimination but that the upbringing of children requires a sharing of responsibility between men and women and society as a whole,

Aware that a change in the traditional role of men as well as the role of women in society and in the family is needed to achieve full equality between men and women,

Determined to implement the principles set forth in the Declaration on the Elimination of Discrimination against Women and, for that purpose, to adopt the measures required for the elimination of such discrimination in all its forms and manifestations,

Have agreed on the following:

Part I

Article 1

For the purposes of the present Convention, the term "discrimination against women" shall mean any distinction, exclusion or restriction made on the basis of sex which ha the effect or purpose of impairing or nullifying the recognition, enjoyment or exercise by women, irrespective of their marital status, on a basis of equality of men and women, of human rights and fundamental freedoms in the political, economic, social, cultural, civil or any other field.

Article 2

States Parties condemn discrimination against women in all its forms, agree to pursue by all appropriate means and without delay a policy of eliminating discrimination against women and, to this end, undertake:

(a) To embody the principle of the equality of men and women in their national constitutions or other appropriate legislation if not yet incorporated therein and to ensure, through law and other appropriate means, the practical realization of this principle;

(b) To adopt appropriate legislative and other measures, including sanctions where appropriate, prohibiting all discrimination against women;

(c) To establish legal protection of the rights of women on an equal basis with men and to ensure through competent national tribunals and other public institutions the effective protection of women against any act of discrimination;

(d) To refrain from engaging in any act or practice of discrimination against women and to ensure that public authorities and institutions shall act in conformity with this obligation;

(e) To take all appropriate measures to eliminate discrimination against women by any person, organization or enterprise;

(f) To take all appropriate measures including legislation, to modify or abolish existing laws, regulations, customs and practices which constitute discrimination against women;

(g) To repeal all national penal provisions which constitute discrimination against women.

Article 3

States Parties shall take in all fields in particular in the political social economic and cultural fields, all appropriate measures, including legislation, to ensure the full development and advancement of women for the purpose of guaranteeing them the exercise and enjoyment of human rights and fundamental freedoms on a basis of equality with men.

Article 4

1. Adoption by States Parties of temporary special measures aimed at accelerating *de facto* equality between men and women shall not be considered discrimination as defined in the present Convention, but shall in no way entail as a consequence the maintenance of unequal or separate standards; these measures shall be discontinued when the objectives of equality of opportunity and treatment have been achieved.

2. Adoption by States Parties of special measures including those measures contained in the present Convention, aimed at protecting maternity shall not be considered discriminatory.

Article 5

States Parties shall take all appropriate measures:

(a) To modify the social and cultural patterns of conduct of men and women with a view to achieving the elimination of prejudices and customary and all other practices which are based on the idea of the inferiority or the superiority of either of the sexes or on stereotyped roles for men and women

(b) To ensure that family education includes a proper understanding of maternity as a social function and the recognition of the common responsibility of men and women in the upbringing and development of their children it being understood that the interest of the children, is the primordial consideration in all cases.

Article 6

States Parties shall take all appropriate measures, including legislation to suppress all forms of traffic in women and exploitation of prostitution of women.

Part II

Article 7

States Parties shall take all appropriate measures to eliminate discrimination against women in the political and public life of the country and in particular, shall ensure to women, on equal terms with men, the right:

(a) To vote in all elections and public referenda and to be eligible for election to all publicly elected bodies;

(b) To participate in the formulation of government policy and the implementation thereof and to hold public office and perform all public functions at all levels of government;

(c) To participate in non-governmental organizations and associations concerned with the public and political life of the country.

Article 8

States Parties shall take all appropriate measures to ensure to women, on equal terms with men and without any discrimination, the opportunity to represent their Governments at the international level and to participate in the work of international organizations.

Article 9

1. States Parties shall grant women equal rights with men to acquire, change or retain their nationality. They shall ensure in particular that neither marriage to an alien nor change of nationality by the husband during marriage shall automatically change the nationality of the wife, render her stateless or force upon her the nationality of the husband.

2. States Parties shall grant women equal rights with men with respect to the nationality of their children.

Part III

Article 10

States Parties shall take all appropriate measures to eliminate discrimination against women in order to ensure to them equal rights with men in the field of education and in particular to ensure, on a basis of equality of men and women:

(a) The same conditions for career and vocational guidance, for access to studies and for the achievement of diplomas in educational establishments of all categories in rural as well as in urban areas; this equality shall be ensured in preschool, general, technical, professional and higher technical education, as well as in all types of vocational training;

(b) Access to the same curricula, the same examinations, teaching staff with qualifications of the same standard and school premises and equipment of the same quality;

(c) The elimination of any stereotyped concept of the roles of men and women at all levels and in all forms of education by encouraging coeducation and other types of education which will help to achieve this aim and, in particular, by the revision of textbooks and school. programs and the adaptation of teaching methods;

(d) The same opportunities to benefit from scholarships and other study grants;

(e) The same opportunities for access to programs of continuing education, including adult and functional literacy programs, particularly those aimed at reducing, at the earliest possible time, any gap in education existing between men and women;

(f) The reduction of female student drop-out rates and the organization of programs for girls and women who have left school prematurely;

(g) The same opportunities to participate actively in sports and physical education;

(h) Access to specific educational information to help to ensure the health and well-being of families, including information and advice on family planning.

Article 11

1. States Parties shall take all appropriate measures to eliminate discrimination against women in the field of employment in order to ensure, on a basis of equality of men and women, the same rights, in particular:

(a) The right to work as an inalienable right of all human beings;

(b) The right to the same employment opportunities, including the application of the same criteria for selection in matters of employment;

(c) The right to free choice of profession and employment, the right to promotion, job security and all benefits and conditions of service and the right to receive vocational training and re-training, including apprenticeships, advanced vocational training and recurrent training;

(d) The right to equal remuneration, including benefits, and to equal treatment in respect of work of equal value, as well as equality of treatment in the evaluation of the quality of work;

(e) The right to social security, particularly in cases of retirement, unemployment, sickness, invalidity and old age and other incapacity to work, as well as the right to paid leave;

(f) The right to protection of health and to safety in working conditions, including the safeguarding of the function of reproduction.

2. In order to prevent discrimination against women on the grounds of marriage or maternity and to ensure their effective right to work, States Parties shall take appropriate measures:

(a) To prohibit, subject to the imposition of sanctions, dismissal on the grounds of pregnancy or of maternity leave and discrimination, in dismissals on the basis of marital status;

(b) To introduce maternity leave with pay or with comparable social benefits without loss of former employment, seniority or social allowances;

(c) To encourage the provision of the necessary supporting social services to enable parents to combine family obligations with work responsibilities and participation in public life, in particular through promoting the establishment and development of a network of child-care facilities;

(d) To provide special protection to women during pregnancy in type of work proved to be harmful to them.

3. Protective legislation relating to matters covered in this article shall
   be reviewed periodically in the light of scientific and technological
   knowledge and shall be revised, repealed or extended as necessary.

Article 12

1. States Parties shall take all appropriate measures to eliminate discrimination against women in the field of health care in order to
   ensure, on a basis of equality of men and women, access to health
   care services, including those related to family planning.
2. Notwithstanding the provisions of paragraph I of this article, States
   Parties shall ensure to women appropriate services in connection
   with pregnancy, confinement and the post-natal period, granting
   free services where necessary, as well as adequate nutrition during
   pregnancy and lactation.

Article 13

States Parties shall take all appropriate measures to eliminate discrimination against women in other areas of economic and social life in order to
ensure, on a basis of equality of men and women, the same rights, in particular:

(a) The right to family benefits;
(b) The right to bank loans, mortgages and other forms of financial
    credit;
(c) The right to participate in recreational activities, sports and all
    aspects of cultural life.

Article 14

1. States Parties shall take into account the particular problems faced
   by rural women and the significant roles which rural women play
   in the economic survival of their families, including their work in
   the non-monetized sectors of the economy, and shall take all appropriate measures to ensure the application of the provisions of
   the present Convention to women in rural areas.
2. States Parties shall take all appropriate measures to eliminate discrimination against women in rural areas in order to ensure, on a
   basis of equality of men and women, that they participate in and
   benefit from rural development and, in particular, shall ensure to
   such women the right:

(a) To participate in the elaboration and implementation of development planning at all levels;

(b) To have access to adequate health care facilities, including information, counselling and services in family planning;

(c) To benefit directly from social security programs;

(d) To obtain all types of training and education, formal and non-formal, including that relating to functional literacy, as well as, *inter alia*, the benefit of all community and extension services, in order to increase their technical proficiency;

(e) To organize self-help groups and co-operatives in order to obtain equal access to economic opportunities through employment or self-employment;

(f) To participate in all community activities;

(g) To have access to agricultural credit and loans, marketing facilities, appropriate technology and equal treatment in land and agrarian reform as well as in land resettlement schemes;

(h) To enjoy adequate living conditions, particularly in relation to housing, sanitation, electricity and water supply, transport and communications.

Part IV

Article 15

1. States Parties shall accord to women equality with men before the law.

2. State Parties shall accord to women, in civil matters, a legal capacity identical to that of men and the same opportunities to exercise that capacity. In particular, they shall give women equal rights to conclude contracts and to administer property and shall treat them equally in all stages of procedure in courts and tribunals.

3. States Parties agree that all contracts and all other private instruments of any kind with a legal effect which is directed at restricting the legal capacity of women shall be deemed null and void.

4. States Parties shall accord to men and women the same rights with regard to the law relating to the movement of persons and the freedom to choose their residence and domicile.

Article 16

1. States Parties shall take all appropriate measures to eliminate discrimination against women in all matters relating to marriage and family relations and in particular shall ensure, on a basis of equality of men and women:

   (a) The same right to enter into marriage;
   (b) The same right freely to choose a spouse and to enter into marriage only with their free and full consent;
   (c) The same rights and responsibilities during marriage and at its dissolution;
   (d) The same rights and responsibilities as parents, irrespective of their marital status, in matters relating to their children; in all cases the interests of the children shall be paramount;
   (e) The same rights to decide freely and responsibly on the number and spacing of their children and to have access to the information, education and means to enable them to exercise these rights;
   (f) The same rights and responsibilities with regard to guardianship, wardship, trusteeship and adoption of children, or similar institutions where these concepts exist in national legislation; in all cases the interests of the children shall be paramount;
   (g) The same personal rights as husband and wife, including the right to choose a family name, a profession and an occupation
   (h) The same right for both spouses in respect of the ownership, acquisition, management, administration, enjoyment and disposition of property, whether free of charge or for a valuable consideration.

2. The betrothal and the marriage of a child shall have no legal effect, and all necessary action, including legislation, shall be taken to specify a minimum age for marriage and to make the registration of marriages in an official registry compulsory.

Index

abortion, 306
accommodation approach, 308–309
AIDs: trafficking and, 186; women's rights and, 9
Alfarabi, 114
Alston, Philip, 126
American Constitution: Native Americans in, 142–143; negative rights in, 186; rights-as-principles in, 128–129; on slavery, 133
American Council of Learned Societies, 360
An-Na'im, Abdullahi Ahmed, 52–53, 162, 188
Anti-Christian movement, 219
Anti-Trafficking Convention. *See* Convention on the Suppression of the Traffic in Persons and the Exploitation of Others
Appadurai, Arjun, 28
Aquinas, Thomas, 99, 113–114, 376
area studies, 6–7: decline of, 360–361; new construct for, 360–365; relativism in, 355–360; social sciences and, 350–355; strengths of, 9–10; universalism in, 19

Aristotle, 259
arts, subsidization of, 77
Asian Development Bank, 140
Asian miracle economies, 197–198, 370
Asian Regional Council on Human Rights, 206
Asian values debate, 3: Asian identity in, 21–42; assumptions in, 27; dedichotomizing, 369–382; dissent in, 8–9; diversity in, 46–59, 209–210; dualism in, 19; feminism and, 76; flaws in, 198–203; identities in, 21–42; Kausikan's position in, 7–9; NGOs in, 8, 205–210; oversimplification in, 376–377; Tiananmen Square and, 7
"The Asian Values Debate: Human Rights and the Study of Culture as Problems for Area Studies," 4
Asia Pacific Forum on Women, Law and Development, 206
Augustine, St., 351
authoritarianism: capitalism and, 119; Confucianism on, 106–107; de-